ALSO BY UCADIA

Lex Divina: Maxims of Divine Law
Lex Naturae: Maxims of Natural Law
Lex Cognitum: Maxims of Cognitive Law
Lex Virtus Naturae: Maxims of Bioethics Law
Lex Ecclesiasticum: Maxims of Ecclesiastical Law
Lex Positivum: Maxims of Positive Law
Lex Regia: Maxims of Sovereign Law
Lex Fidei: Maxims of Fiduciary Law
Lex Administratum: Maxims of Administrative Law
Lex Economica: Maxims of Economic Law
Lex Pecuniaria: Maxims of Monetary Law
Lex Civilis: Maxims of Civil Law
Lex Criminalis: Maxims of Criminal Law
Lex Educationis: Maxims of Education Law
Lex Nutrimens Et Medicina: Maxims of Food & Drugs Law
Lex Urbanus: Maxims of Urban Law
Lex Societatis: Maxims of Company Law
Lex Technologiae: Maxims of Technology Law
Lex Commercii: Maxims of Trade & Intellectual Property Law
Lex Securitas: Maxims of Security Law
Lex Militaris: Maxims of Military Law
Lex Gentium: Maxims of International Law

Carta Sacrum De Congregationis Europa

Ucadia Euro Union Constitutional Charter

Complete System for Sustainable Prosperity

OFFICIAL ENGLISH FIRST EDITION

By
UCADIA

Ucadia Books Company

Published by Ucadia Books Company, a Delaware stock corporation (File Number 6779670)
8 The Green, STE B, Dover, Delaware, 19901 United States.
First edition.

ISBN 978-1-64419-049-4

Why Change is the only solution

The EU (European Union) Model - a vision of a common market and union of prosperity that promised so much hope for Europeans at the end of the Twentieth Century has officially failed. In its present form and foundation it cannot be revived and only portents a not too distant future of a dystopian nightmare of an unelected elite controlling every aspect of the lives of a permanent underclass.

Racked with special clauses, special interests, special deals, wasteful subsidies, unaccountable bureaucracy and snail pace of reform, many people throughout Europe now see much of what the present European Union Model represents. Yet the same special interests have little desire for necessary reform or to deliver on the promised ideals. Rather, they believe that people can continue to be suppressed and distracted by a combination of never ending fear events, language manipulation and personal technology.

Of course, such commentary of the true state of the present European Model is at best denied by those in power, or more often dismissed as misguided noise. Anything that distracts from an inarguable truth that even the most ardent elite defenders of the present European Model cannot defend – the founding architecture of the present European Model beings its Constitution is deliberately unworkable, flawed and rotten to the core.

A Constitution to a nation or group of nations represents its blueprint for its existence, its organs and the flow of power through its body, like any living being. When such a document is well designed, each organ has a purpose and clear function and power is able to flow smoothly in balance and check. Yet when poorly or deliberately badly designed, it creates power conflicts and distortions.

This is precisely the consequences of the present European Constitutional Model. It speaks of the highest ideals of rights and peace, yet denies the very organs and bodies it defines the ability to work efficiently and unencumbered. The same flawed present European Constitutional Model speaks of common purpose and shared power, yet makes the flow of power and checks and balances wholly unworkable and distorted, forcing the operational function of the union to rest with a bloated and unelected bureaucracy – precisely the intention of the document.

The continued distortions of impoverished and under employed European nations versus a handful of nations growing ever wealthier is not simply a consequence, in many respects it is an intentional design of the system. If those that designed these documents really wanted the European Union experiment to function as promised, they would not have designed its present Constitution.

What then of the future? If a handful of people do finally come to the realisation that the Constitution has to change, what should it become? This is the purpose and design of this document. To present a cohesive system and model for authentic and sustainable prosperity of Europe.

The Constitutional Charter for the Ucadia Euro Union is not an isolated model. It is part of a larger framework under the Ucadia Model that respects individual human rights and rejects a world of hedonistic nihilism where a few have any natural, genetic or intellectual right to declare themselves effectively "living Gods" over the rest of humanity. Such arrogance and evil has been the hallmark of many failed civilisations and such behaviour will doom this latest generation of self appointed elites.

The Constitutional Charter for the Ucadia Euro Union is a genuine revelation to provide an optimum position between such extremes in the design of effective constitutions, so that all peoples and all societies may thrive and achieve.

This Constitutional Charter focuses on a model and mechanisms necessary for the sustainable prosperity of all people living in Europe, not just a few.

The future of Europe depends upon those people willing to read this blueprint and stand for a better and brighter future.

CONTENTS

Title X: Systems

PRAENUNTIO

In the name and absolute authority and power of the One God, the God of Abraham, the God of Moses, the God of Solomon and David, the God of the Great Prophets, the God of all Christians, Muslims and Jews; and the Absolute Divine Creator of all Existence and all of Heaven, the Earth and our Solar System and Galaxy:

To all Sovereign, Political and Military Leaders, Officers and Agents of all bodies, associations, orders, fraternities, societies, churches and entities within the bounds of Europe:

You are hereby commanded to take notice of the present most sacred Constitutional Charter known as ***Carta Sacrum De Congregationis Europa***, also known as the Sacred Charter of the Euro Union; and answer within the time allocated, as to any exception or legitimate objection why you should not be firmly and decisively bound by the Articles of the aforementioned most sacred Constitutional Charter as the Revelation, Ratification, Sanctification, Testification, Exemplification, Legislation and Consummation of the Divine Will of the one true God and Divine Creator of all Existence and all Heaven and Earth.

A. WHEREAS the foundation of all civilised Rule of Law begins with the acknowledgement that the highest law comes from Heaven and the Divine Creator of all things in the Universe, expressed through Natural Law, then Cognitive Law and then through the reason and spirit of men and women to make Positive Laws; for the very meaning and essence of the idea of "office" is derived from ecclesiastical and ceremony duty to One Heaven and to One God and the Divine Creator of all Existence; and the very meaning and purpose of the word "authority" is derived from the creation of pronouncements in accord with the ecclesiastical and ceremonial duties to One Heaven and to One God and the Divine Creator of all Existence. Therefore, all Ecclesiastical, Sovereign, Political and Military Leaders, Officers and Agents of all bodies, associations, orders, fraternities, societies, churches and entities within the bounds of Europe ultimately owe their validity and legitimacy to One Heaven and to One God and the Divine Creator of all Existence; and

B. WHEREAS the validity and legitimacy of authority and power of all Ecclesiastical, Sovereign, Political and Military Leaders, Officers and Agents of all bodies, associations, orders, fraternities, societies, churches and entities within the bounds of Europe depends upon the acknowledgement and recognition by such persons that the authority and power of each respective office is ultimately derived from the highest authority being One Heaven and One God and the Divine Creator of all Existence, the very existence and idea of the Rule of Law within each and every society within the bounds of Europe is dependent upon such proper acknowledgement and recognition. Furthermore, as the authority and legitimacy of every office within the bounds of Europe is derived from ecclesiastical authority, obedience to One Heaven and One God and the Divine Creator of all Existence is not merely a duty, but a necessity for the moral, lawful and legal effect of any action. For no spiritual force may flow through Natural Law and Positive Law of the present world, if the sacred rules that establish such Law are willingly broken; and

C. WHEREAS the present most sacred Constitutional Charter known as **Carta Sacrum De Congregationis Europa**, also known as the Sacred Charter of the Euro Union, is revealed through the Spirit of unity of all people, all religions and cultures within the most sacred **Covenant Pactum De Singularis Caelum** and personified by the Universal Ecclesia of One Christ, the Holy Society of One Islam and the Sacred Society of One Spirit, all the people of Europe stand united as equals, possessing certain immutable and unalienable rights as expressed herein, including (but not limited to) the right to a home, the right to life and adequate sustenance and the right to dignified and useful work; and

D. WHEREAS if any Ecclesiastical, Sovereign, Political or Military Leader, Officers or Agent of any body, association, order, fraternity, society, church or entity within the bounds of Europe were to deny the irrefutable truth, authority and power of the present Constitutional Charter known as Carta Sacrum De Congregationis Europa, also known as the Sacred Constitutional Charter of the Euro Union, then such a denial would represent a complete disavowal of any legitimacy or authority of office and would be an act of apostasy, declaring oneself "cut off" and willingly acknowledging themselves to be an outcast against the united forces of Heaven and Earth; and

E. WHEREAS God and the Divine Creator of all Existence reveals true Divine Nature to be Divinely Merciful and Perfect Divine Love, no person or religion is to be condemned or cursed or punished for failing to grasp or acknowledge the truth of the present Constitutional Charter. For whether it take one generation or one hundred generations, by the present most sacred Constitutional Charter, the people of Europe exist as one body of equals, empowered and authorised to build, manage and protect a sustainable future of peace, prosperity and dignity for all.

NOW THEREFORE, IT IS HEREBY COMMANDED that all Ecclesiastical, Sovereign, Political and Military Leaders, Officers and Agents of all bodies, associations, orders, fraternities, societies, churches and entities within the bounds of Europe take Notice of the present most sacred Constitutional Charter and Holy Writ and answer and acknowledge as to any exception or legitimate objection why you should not be firmly and decisively bound by the Articles of the present sacred Constitutional Charter as the Revelation, Ratification, Sanctification, Testification, Exemplification, Legislation and Consummation of the Divine Will of the one true Divine Creator of all Existence and all Heaven and Earth. Amen

As it is Written, it is. Amen

TITLE I: ORIGIN, NATURE & PURPOSE OF UNION

Article 1 – Origin and Nature of Ucadia Euro Union

1. The "**Ucadia Euro Union**" is borne from Divine Mandate and Sacred Decree, according to Article 102 (*Ucadia Regional Unions and Colonies*) of the most sacred Covenant *Pactum De Singularis Caelum* on GAIA E8:Y3209:A1:S1:M6:D1, also known as [Monday, 21 Dec 2009]. Origin of Ucadia Euro Union

2. The Union is granted a maximum life of three thousand two hundred and ten (3210) years, being one full Great Age Cycle of the Precession of Ages. Thereafter, members shall have the power to vote and determine the formation, rules and constitution of a new Union for a life of not less than the same (3210 years). Life and existence

3. The Eleven Primary Objects of the Union shall be:- Primary Objects

   (i) To *Design*, *Nurture* and *Implement* Sustainable Systems of improving health, education, well-being, sanitation, industry, clean environment, law and order and prosperity within communities, towns, villages and cities across the Union; and Sustainable Systems of Improved Living Standards

   (ii) To *Secure*, *Protect* and *Defend* the Union; and all its Realms, Domains, Dominions, Dependencies, Rights, Titles, Instruments, Uses and Property; and to seek peaceful, amicable and harmonious relations, treaties and alliances with non-Ucadian bodies that respect the Golden Rule of Law and Justice and Fair Process; and to pursue, prosecute and bring to justice any individual or body that openly seeks to abuse, trespass or injure Ucadia or the Union or its Realms, Domains, Dominions, Dependencies, Rights, Titles, Instruments, Uses or Property; and Protect and Defend the Union

   (iii) To *Protect*, *Prosecute* and *Enforce* the Laws of the Union; and all associated Covenants, Charters, Canons, Codes, ByLaws, Ordinances, Regulations, Policies and Orders; and to seek mutual recognition of such jurisdictional rights with foreign bodies and courts that respect and operate according to the Golden Rule of Law and Justice and Fair Process; and to ensure that in all matters pertaining to Members that the courts of the Union are recognised as the first, primary and original jurisdiction for the resolution of all matters of controversy, arbitration and dispute; and Protect and Defend Laws and Rights of the Union

   (iv) *Support*, *Reward* and *Grow* Innovation, Employment and Intellectual Property, Capacity, Productivity and Profitability among businesses and companies of the Union; and Employment & Productivity, etc.

   (v) *Educate*, *Encourage* and *Support* growing respect and affection in the institutions of the Union; and to ensure that all Campuses, Educate and Encourage Support of

Provinces and Universities within the bounds of the Union are represented by elected and living Ucadia Members; and to ensure the formation of the Permanent Parliament and the conduct of its first elections and sittings as a valid body politic; and to convey and transfer every authority, powers, legal controls, rights, titles, accounts, registers and financial controls to the Permanent Parliament by the first day of such sittings in accord with the present Constitutional Charter; and Union

(vi) *Select*, *Support* and *Honour* the Commission of key Officers, within the bounds of the Union, in ensuring the fiduciary life of all Ministers and Officers of the Union are conducted according to the discipline and spirit of such sacred Commission; and Support and Honour the Commission of trustworthy Officers

(vii) To Educate and Encourage existing networks of people that share the same common values as Ucadia to consider becoming a Society Member or State Member of the Union, including the acknowledgement of all its existing members as Ordinary Members of the Union; and Educate and encourage State Members and Society Members

(viii) To Support and Operate the Government of the Union holding all administrative rights, powers, faculties, capacities, uses, titles and authorities in relation to all valid Ucadia Provinces, Campuses, Universities, Funds, Trusts, Estates and Companies within the political, territorial and demographic bounds of the Union; and Support and Operate the Government of the Union

(ix) To Administer and Facilitate all lawful and legal transactions, conveyances and communications necessary for the proper financial management of the Union; and to promulgate, enforce and collect any and all forms of taxes, duties, imposts, and excises for revenue, necessary to pay the debts and obligations of the Union; and Administer and Facilitate all Ecclesiastical, Lawful and Legal Transactions

(x) To establish, maintain and strengthen amicable, harmonious and respectful relations with all bodies politic, societies and entities within the bounds of the Union that respect the Rule of Law; and to assist, support, aid, nurture, respect, honour and help the people of Europe and the region and all lesser bodies, using the full resources and powers of the Union; and Amicable and Harmonious Relations

(xi) To protect, defend, support and assist in times of need, the people of Europe and all Regional and Local bodies and to ensure the maintenance and strengthening and improvement of the quality of life for all under true dignity, mercy, honesty, harmony and fair justice. Protect, Defend and Support Relations

4. The Thirty Three Ancillary Objects whereby the Union is established Ancillary Objects are:

(i) To Act and execute all key Offices of the Union including (but not limited to) the Offices of Trustee, Executor, Administrator, Curator, Guardian, Converter, Undertaker, Accountant, Comptroller, Banker, Bursar, Treasurer, Attorney, Conservator, Procurator and Receiver, with the highest and most trusted integrity, independence, frugality, prudence, humility, faculty, competence, accountability and capacity; and

Form and Commission of Offices

(ii) To establish key Charitable Funds using the Authorised and Guaranteed Capital Stock and Ucadia Monies of the Union, for the purposes as defined herein of fulfilling the Primary Objects of the Union; and

Charitable and Religious Funds

(iii) To establish and administer the Government Administration within the jurisdiction of the Union, including (but not limited to) the Divisions and Departments as specified by the Articles herein; and

Establish Government Administration

(iv) To establish, regulate and manage the Financial Control and Management Systems of the Union, including but not limited to the Union Moneta Registers & Accounts, Public Money Accounts, Foreign Currency Accounts, Standard Instruments and Forms, Standard Procedures, Oversight Controls and Reporting; and

Financial Control and Oversight Systems

(v) To establish, regulate and oversee commerce with non-Ucadian bodies, states and nations; and to ensure the protection of local industries and markets from unfair trade, dumping, manipulation or damage; and to encourage systems of fair and transparent commerce between parties, with the minimum of duties, tariffs, restrictions and subsidies by all participating parties; and

Commerce and Trade with Non-Ucadian Bodies, States & Nations

(vi) To establish, control and manage the Registers and Rolls of the Union, including but not limited to Member Rolls, Electoral Rolls, Stockholder (of Charitable Funds) Rolls, Official Rolls, Patent Rolls, Market Rolls, Land Registers, Births, Deaths and Matrimony Registers, Asset Registers, Bond Registers, Notes Registers, Property Registers, Sales and Transaction Registers and Market Registers; and

Registers and Rolls Management Systems

(vii) For the Union, or any company, authority or body, whether limited or unlimited, within the jurisdiction and authority of the Union to carry on the lawful activities of acquiring,

Asset and Financial Management

holding, selling, endorsing, discounting, issuing or otherwise dealing with or disposing of, shares, stocks, debentures, debenture stock, scrip, bonds, mortgages, bills, notes, credits, contracts, certificates, coupons, warrants and other documents, funds, obligations, securities, instruments, investments or loans, whether transferable or negotiable or not; and issued or guaranteed by any company, corporation, society or trust constituted or carrying on business in any part of the world, or by any foreign government, foreign state or foreign dominion, public body or authority pursuant to the Primary Objects of the Union; and

(viii) For the Union, or any company, authority or body, whether limited or unlimited, within the jurisdiction and authority of the Union to purchase or by any other means acquire and take options over, any property whatever, and any rights or privileges of any kind over or in respect of any property, real or personal, any lands, easements, rights, privileges, concessions, machinery, plant and stock in trade and any other rights of any kind pursuant to the Primary Objects of the Union; and

Property Acquisition, Building & Development

(ix) For the Union, or any company, authority or body, whether limited or unlimited, within the jurisdiction and authority of the Union to acquire and assume for any estate or interest and to take options over, construct, develop or exploit any property, real or personal, any lands, easements, rights, privileges, concessions, machinery, plant and stock-in-trade and rights of any kind and the whole or any part of the undertaking, assets and liabilities of any person pursuant to the Primary Objects of the Union; and

Real Property Management

(x) For the Union, or any company, authority or body, whether limited or unlimited, within the jurisdiction and authority of the Union to draw, make, accept, endorse, discount, negotiate, execute and issue cheques, bills of exchange, promissory notes, bills of lading, warrants, debentures, and other negotiable or transferable instruments in such Ucadian and other lawful money pursuant to the Primary Objects of the Union; and

Legal and Financial Instruments

(xi) For the Union, or any company, authority or body, whether limited or unlimited, within the jurisdiction and authority of the Union to subscribe for, take, purchase, or otherwise acquire, hold, sell, guarantee, deal with and dispose of, place and underwrite shares, stocks, debentures, debenture stocks,

Transfer and Transaction of Legal and Financial Instruments

bonds, notes, obligations or securities issued or guaranteed by any other company constituted or carrying on business in any foreign jurisdiction, and debentures, debenture stocks, bonds, notes, obligations or securities issued or guaranteed by any foreign government or authority pursuant to the Primary Objects of the Union; and

(xii) To borrow and raise non-Ucadian funds and other lawful money in any manner for the purposes of any foreign registered instance of the Union; and to secure the repayment of any non-Ucadian and other lawful money borrowed, raised or owing by mortgage, charge, standard security, lien or other security upon the whole or any part of the property or assets (whether present or future) of any such foreign registered subsidiary within the Jurisdiction of the Union, including its uncalled capital, and to create, issue, make, draw, accept and negotiate, acquire and hold perpetual or redeemable debentures or debenture stock, bonds or other obligations, whether or not guaranteed by any government, state or dominion, public body or authority, supreme, municipal, local or otherwise and also by a similar mortgage, charge, standard security, lien or security to secure and guarantee the performance by a company, authority or body within the jurisdiction and authority of the Union of any obligation or liability it may undertake that may become binding on it pursuant to the Primary Objects of the Union; and

Capital and Debt Management

(xiii) To promote, protect and reward the progress of science, innovation and useful arts and ensure the proper acknowledgement and protection of such Intellectual Property of the Union; and to purchase, or by other means acquire and protect, prolong and renew any abstract, extract, certificate or instance of any trademarks, patents, copyrights, trade secrets, or other intellectual property rights, licenses, secret processes, designs, protections and concessions validly registered primarily within a Great Register and Public Record of the Union as then acknowledged and protected within foreign and non-Ucadian jurisdictions; and to disclaim, alter, modify, use and turn to account and to manufacture under or grant licenses or privileges in respect of the same and to expend Ucadian and other lawful money in experimenting upon, testing and improving any patents, inventions or rights recognised within the foreign jurisdiction that the Union may acquire or propose to acquire; and

Protect and Acquire Intellectual Property

(xiv) To apply for, promote, and obtain any valid charter, grant, order, privilege, concession or license of any government, state, municipality or other department or authority from a foreign body or enter into arrangement with such body for enabling the Union to carry any of its Objects into effect and to oppose any proceedings or applications that may seem calculated directly or indirectly to prejudice the interests of the Union or the interests of any company whereby the Union is interested; and

Recognition and Grants of Government Licenses, Permits and Authorisations

(xv) To enter into any arrangements with any foreign government or authority (supreme, municipal, local, or otherwise) that may seem conducive to the attainment of the Objects of the Union or any of them, and to obtain from any such foreign government or authority any valid charters, decrees, rights, privileges or concessions that the Union may think desirable and to carry out, exercise, and comply with any such charters, decrees, rights, privileges and concessions; and

Co-operative Agreements with Government, Agencies and Authorities

(xvi) To establish, commence and manage the courts and judicial systems of the Union and to enable all matters of law, jurisdiction, equity, dispute, arbitration, wrong, civil, criminal, international and contract law to be properly conducted within the courts, in accord with these Articles and the associated sacred covenants, canons and codes of Ucadia, pursuant to the Primary Objects of the Union; and

Courts and Legal Services

(xvii) To invest and deal with the Ucadian and other lawful money of the Union not immediately required in such manner as may from time to time be determined and to hold or otherwise deal with any investments made pursuant to the Primary Objects of the Union; and to lend and advance Ucadian and other lawful money or give credit on any terms and with or without security to any person, firm or company, to enter into guarantees, contracts of indemnity and sureties of all kinds, to receive Ucadian and other lawful money on deposit or loan upon any terms, and to secure or guarantee in any manner and upon any terms the payment of any sum of Ucadian and other lawful money or the performance of any obligation by any person, firm or company pursuant to the Primary Objects of the Union; and

Cash and Investment Management Services for Members

(xviii) To carry on lawful activities as financiers, merchants and bankers, including the borrowing, raising or taking-up of Ucadian and other lawful money, lending or advancing Ucadian or other lawful money, securities and property (and

Financial Services for Members

in particular but without limitation to or for any company that the Union is interested); and managing property; and transacting all kinds of indemnity, guarantee, assurances, insurance agency and other agency activities pursuant to the Primary Objects of the Union; and

(xix) To act as agents or brokers and as trustees for any person, firm or company, to undertake and perform sub-contracts, and to enter into such arrangement (whether by way of amalgamation, partnership, profit sharing, union of interests, co-operation, joint venture or otherwise) of the Union to benefit and advance the Objects of the Union through any foreign company or foreign registration where the Union is interested; and to vest any property of the Union in any person or company on behalf of the Union in accord with the fiduciary obligations of Directors and Officers and the Laws of Ucadia; and

Trustee, Agent and Broker Services for Members

(xx) To improve, manage, construct, repair, develop, exchange, let or lease or otherwise, mortgage, charge, sell, dispose of, turn to account, grant licenses, options, rights and privileges in respect of, or otherwise deal with all or any part of the property and rights or privileges of the Union pursuant to the Primary Objects of the Union; and

Management of Rights, Title and Property for Members

(xxi) To establish and support a strong and vibrant base of Ucadian Campuses, Provinces and Universities within the jurisdiction of the Union, willing and accepting to make regular contributions, regardless of their financial status toward the betterment of the community through the programmes and non-profit charitable services provided by the Union; and

Establish, and Support Ucadian Campuses and Provinces

(xxii) To establish and engage in mutual, amicable, respectful, lawful and trusted relations with any and every form of legislature, judiciary, public service, executive, monarchy, government, military, security, or authority, whether they be supreme, international, national, federal, municipal, local or otherwise, anywhere in the world; and

Declare, Open and Defend Mission Posts

(xxiii) To empower and enable Members and the community to be more innovative in encouraging the sharing of certain kinds of useful resources that help promote sustainable employment programmes that lead toward greater financial stability and less reliance on the need for government subsidies and emergency funding; and

Empower Innovation and Sustainable Employment Programmes

(xxiv) To transact any lawful activity and service in aid and support of communities within the jurisdiction of the Union in the promotion of peace, good will, amicability and harmony between peoples of different religions, cultures and nations; and

Aid and Support Peace, Goodwill, Amicability and Harmony between Religions and Cultures

(xxv) To create, hold, manage, open, suspend or close Ucadia and capital money accounts formed from the legitimate capital money funds of the Union in the name of any non-Ucadian State, municipality, body politic or corporation within the bounds of the Union; and to facilitate the lawful exchange of such capital money for the settlement of any obligations or debts between any non-Ucadian State, municipality, body politic or corporation where such a body has agreed to formalise its relation to the Union through treaty and membership; and

Ucadia & Capital Money Accounts

(xxvi) To act as Converters for all forms of collateral, property and security into Capital; and for the prudent, controlled flow and control of all forms of money and securities; and to guarantee, underwrite, or assure any valid and legitimate debt of any municipality, agency, county, state or branch of government of a non-Ucadian body within the realm and bounds of the Union; and to otherwise facilitate the securitisation, monetisation or collateralisation of such debts; and

Converters, Guarantees & Assurances

(xxvii) To take any and every such necessary action, through any and every possible relation, interest, right, power, privilege, concession, agreement or property of the Union, using any and every possible resource, know-how and ability of the Union, to protect the reputation, well-being and interests of the Union; and

Reputation & Interests

(xxviii) To assume custody, responsibility and care on behalf of any agency, or body within the bounds of the Union or its States or Territories, for the safe keeping, mental and physical health and professional custodial care of minors and vulnerable persons by virtue of mental or physical incapacity; and

Minors & Vulnerable Persons

(xxix) To hire, contract, engage, underwrite, assure or otherwise guarantee the debts or expenses of any official or public body within the bounds of the Union or its States or Territories engaged in matters of military, national security and public safety; and for the safety and protection of the Union and all its officers, staff, agents, contractors and interests; and

Security & Public Safety

(xxx) To protect and enforce the rights of any trust, or estate, or company, or body politic and corporate, or person or entity within the lawful custody, interest and control of the Union; and to use every means and employ every resource to prosecute and bring to justice any person culpable of any unlawful or criminal act, or injury, or wrong against the Union, without limitation to the rights of the Union to seek equitable relief and compensation by any and all means necessary; and — Enforcement & Prosecution

(xxxi) To do all things necessary, including the establishment, training and funding of permanent and professional military, security and defence forces; and the conduct of any and all forms of campaigns and actions to defend the Union and its Members against all forms of threat and belligerence, both domestic and foreign; and — Defend against Threats & Belligerence

(xxxii) To do all or any of the things and matters aforesaid in any part of the world; and either as principles, agents, nominees, contractors, trustees, or otherwise; and by or through trustees, agents, subsidiary companies, nominees or otherwise; and either alone or in conjunction with others; and to carry on any business of any nature whatsoever, consistent and in accord with the Primary Objects of the Union; and — Activities & Business

(xxxiii) To do all other things that may from time to time deem to be incidental or conducive to the effecting of any of the Primary Objects of the Union. — Business of any kind

5. The foregoing clauses shall be construed both as Objects and Powers; and it is hereby expressly provided that the foregoing enumeration of specific Powers shall not be held to limit or restrict in any manner the powers of this Union. — Objects & Powers

6. The Objects and Powers of the Union (except only of and so far as otherwise expressly provided in any preceding clause) shall be separate and distinct Objects and Powers of the Union, and shall not be in any way limited by reference to any other clause or the order whereby the clauses occur or by reference to the name of the Union. — Order of Clauses

Article 2 – Rights, Powers & Authority of Ucadia Euro Union

1. All Rights, Powers and Authority of the Ucadia Euro Union shall be sourced and subscribed through the Articles of the present Constitutional Charter. — Rights, Powers & Authority of Ucadia Euro Union

2. A *Right* is recognised as a positively defined *Capacity, Privilege, Liberty, Faculty, Power, Ownership, Possession, Interest* or *Benefit* — Rights

and its associated obligation, remedy or relief held in Trust for the benefit of a particular type of named or unnamed Person, under some proper Rule of Law and System of Justice.

3. In respect of Rights: Types of Rights

(i) As a *Capacity*, a valid Right is recognised as a form of legal authority, or qualification, or legal condition or status that enables a person to exercise his/her own will in acquiring, holding, using or transferring other certain Rights or performing such associated obligations, without restraint or hindrance; and

(ii) As a *Privilege*, a valid Right is recognised as a form of special (real or personal) Grant whereby either a private Person or particular Corporation is freed from the obligations of certain laws; and

(iii) As a *Liberty*, a valid Right is recognised as a form of Privilege whereby a Person enjoys some Favour or Benefit; and

(iv) As a *Faculty*, a valid Right is recognised as a form of Privilege or special Power granted to a Person by Favour, Indulgence or Dispensation (i.e. a License) that enables a person to do, or refrain from doing something that would otherwise not be permitted by law; and

(v) As a *Power* or Authority, a valid Right is recognised as a form of authority, enforced by law, that enables one person to compel one or more other persons to do or abstain from doing a particular act; and

(vi) As an *Ownership*, is recognised as a form of written possession by registration/recording, whereby a person is recognised by law to possess the most extensive or higher claim of possession, use and enjoyment (of certain Property), to the exclusion of all other persons, or of all except one or more specific persons; and

(vii) As a *Possession*, a valid Right is recognised as the visible possibility and ability of exercising physical control over some form of property, coupled with the intention of doing so, to the exclusion of all others, or one or more persons; and

(viii) As an *Interest*, a valid Right recognised as denoting a title, or certificate or other proof of claim or advantage to other certain Rights or Property; and

(ix) As a *Benefit*, a Right recognised as implying a just and legal claim to hold, or use or enjoy certain Property, or convey, or donate or dispose of it, subject to certain obligations of performance.

4. All valid Rights exist and are ultimately sourced and inherited solely in accord with the one hundred and fifty four (154) Divine Rights, the eighty eight (88) Natural Rights and the four hundred and twenty four (424) Superior Rights as defined by the most sacred Covenant *Pactum De Singularis Caelum.*

Sole Source of True Rights

5. In accord with the most sacred Covenant *Pactum De Singularis Caelum,* the Union recognises only four (4) possible Classes of Rights being *Divine, Natural, Superior* and *Inferior*:-

Classes of Rights

(i) *Divine Rights* are the primary and original form of Rights, corresponding to Divine Trusts and Divine Persons. There exists no higher class, or possible type of Rights. All Rights therefore are inherited from the class of valid Divine Rights; and

(ii) *Natural Rights* are the second highest form of valid Rights, corresponding to True Trusts and True Persons; and owe their existence and provenance to the existence of Divine Rights. All Rights of True Persons in either the Office of Man or the Office of Woman are inherited from the class of valid Natural Rights; and

(iii) *Superior Rights* are the third class and third highest possible form of valid Rights; corresponding to Superior Trusts and Superior Persons; and owe their existence and provenance to either valid Divine Rights or valid Natural Rights. All Rights of valid Ucadia Members, Ucadia Societies and associated bodies, aggregates, societies, associations, communities and unions of two or more people are inherited from the class of Superior Rights; and

(iv) *Inferior Rights* are the fourth class and the lowest possible form of valid Rights and owe their existence to non-Ucadian societies, persons, corporations, associations, bodies politic, agencies or aggregates. All Inferior Rights are inferior to Superior Rights. Where an Inferior Right makes claim to being superior, it is automatically invalid upon such falsity.

6. In accord with the most sacred Covenant *Pactum De Singularis Caelum,* the Union recognises there exists only twelve (12) Sub-Classes of Rights being: *Perfect, Imperfect, Absolute, Relative, Personal, Ecclesiastical, Sovereign, Official, Administrative, Member, Primary* and *Secondary*:-

Twelve Sub-Classes of Rights

(i) *Perfect Divine Rights* (*Perfectum Divinum Iurium*), are a sub-class of Divine Rights whereby such valid Rights are created, defined and donated to a Divine Person by the Divine Creator through the most sacred Covenant *Pactum De Singularis Caelum*. Perfect Divine Rights are Peremptory, Permanent, Eternal, Immutable and Indefeasible; and once bestowed are not subject to any form or condition of waiver, abandonment, conveyance, surrender, disqualification, incapacitation, seizure, capture, arrest, resignation, alienation, suspension, suppression, forfeiture or abrogation. Perfect Divine Rights are therefore the highest possible form of Rights and there exists no higher class, or form, or possible type of Rights. Perfect Divine Rights may be further defined as Perfect Fundamental Divine Rights or Perfect Sacramental Divine Rights; and

(ii) *Imperfect Divine Rights* (*Imperfectum Divinnum Iurium*), are a sub-class of Divine Rights whereby such valid Rights are created, defined and delegated to a Divine Person by the Divine Creator through the most sacred Covenant *Pactum De Singularis Caelum* upon acceptance of the associated obligations and duties attached to them. If any such conditions and obligations are breached or repudiated, then the relevant Imperfect Divine Right is instantly waived, surrendered, suspended, forfeited or revoked until such time as the fundamental breach of duty and obligation is repaired or such a Right is duly restored. Imperfect Divine Rights may be further defined as Imperfect Instrumental Divine Rights or Imperfect Intentional Divine Rights; and

(iii) *Absolute Natural Rights* (*Absolutum Naturae Iurium*), are a sub-class of Natural Rights whereby such valid Rights are created, defined and deposited to a Natural (True) Person by the existence of the one true Universe and all Rule and all Matter in accord with the Rule of Law through the most sacred Covenant *Pactum De Singularis Caelum*. Absolute Natural Rights are Peremptory, Permanent, Immutable and Indefeasible and once bestowed are not subject to any form or condition of waiver, abandonment, conveyance, surrender, disqualification, incapacitation, seizure, capture, arrest, resignation, alienation, suspension, suppression, forfeiture or abrogation. Absolute Natural Rights are therefore the highest possible form of Natural Rights. Absolute Natural Rights may be further defined as Absolute Elemental Natural Rights or Absolute Testamental Natural Rights; and

(iv) *Relative Natural Rights* (*Relativum Naturae Iurium*), are a sub-class of Natural Rights whereby such valid Rights are created, defined and granted to a Natural (True) Person by the existence of the one true Universe and all Rule and all Matter in accord with the Rule of Law through the most sacred Covenant *Pactum De Singularis Caelum* upon acceptance of the associated obligations and duties attached to them. If any such conditions and obligations are breached or repudiated, then the relevant Relative Natural Right may be waived, surrendered, suspended, abandoned, resigned, disqualified, seized, captured, arrested, alienated, suppressed, forfeited or annulled until such time as the fundamental breach of duty and obligation is repaired or such a Right is duly restored. A True Person to whom a Relative Natural Right has been bestowed may also lawfully delegate or confer beneficial title of such a Right to another True Person such as a Ucadia association, body politic, society, company or community. However, such an aggregate person can never legitimately claim legal title over a Relative Natural Right and any such claim is automatically false and null and void, having no force or effect. Relative Natural Rights may be further defined as Relative Delegable Natural Rights or Relative Conferrable Natural Rights; and

(v) *Superior Person Rights* (*Superioris Iurium Personae*), are a sub-class of Superior Rights whereby such valid Rights are created, defined and bestowed to a Superior Person by the existence of a valid Superior Person, or aggregate person, or community, or body politic, or association in accord with the Rule of Law through the most sacred Covenant *Pactum De Singularis Caelum*. Universal Superior Rights are Peremptory, Permanent, Immutable and Indefeasible and once bestowed are not subject to any form or condition of waiver, abandonment, surrender, disqualification, incapacitation, seizure, capture, arrest, resignation, alienation, suspension, suppression, forfeiture or abrogation. Superior Personal Rights are therefore the highest possible form of Superior Rights of any society or aggregate person within the temporal realm; and

(vi) *Ecclesiastical Rights* (*Iurium Ecclesiae*), are a sub-class of Superior Rights associated with a valid Ucadia Ecclesia such as One Christ, One Islam, One Spirit and Ucadia itself. Ecclesiastical Rights are the highest possible rights of any aggregate body, society, fraternity, association or company of two (2) or more people. There exists eight (8) categories of one hundred and thirty-two (132) Superior Rights within the sub class of Ecclesiastical Rights, being Authoritative (22),

Instrumental (22), Sacramental (33), Writs (11), Bills (11), Dogma (11), Decrees (11) and Notices (11); and

(vii) *Sovereign Rights* (*Iurium Regnum*), are a sub-class of Superior Rights associated with the embodiment of the sovereign authority of a valid Ucadia society such as a Campus, or Province, or University or Union. All Sovereign Rights are derived from Ecclesiastical Rights and a Sovereign can never claim to be higher than Ecclesiastical Rights. There exists six categories of seventy-seven (77) Superior Rights within the sub class of Sovereign Rights, being Authoritative (11), Instrumental (22), Writs (11), Bills (11), Decrees (11) and Notices (11); and

(viii) *Official Rights* (*Iurium Publicum*), are a sub-class of Superior Rights associated with an Officer empowered to Office within a valid Ucadia society such as a Campus, or Province, or University or Union. All Official Rights are derived from Sovereign Rights and Official Rights can never be claimed to be higher than Sovereign Rights. There exists six categories of eighty-eight (88) Superior Rights within the class of Official Rights, being Authoritative (11), Instrumental (33), Warrants (11), Complaints (11), Orders (11) and Notices (11); and

(ix) *Administrative Rights* (*Iurium Administrationis*), are a sub-class of Superior Rights associated with a legislative body of a valid Ucadia society such as a Campus, or Province, or University or Union. All Administrative Rights are derived from Official Rights and an Administrator and Agent can never claim to be higher than Official Rights. There exists two categories of forty-four (44) Superior Rights within the sub class of Administrative Rights, being Authoritative (11) and Instrumental (33); and

(x) *Member Rights* (*Iurium Membrum*), are a sub-class of Superior Rights associated with a Member of a valid Ucadia society, body or aggregate; and

(xi) *Primary Inferior Rights*, also known as Primary Rights, are a sub-class of Inferior Rights whereby such Rights are created, defined and bestowed to an Inferior (Legal) Person by a non-Ucadian aggregate person, or community, or body politic, or association. Primary Inferior Rights are frequently claimed and created without reference to rights already existing or proving such provenance to Divine Rights. Therefore, Primary Inferior Rights are equivalent to either Claims or false and unsubstantiated Demands. Primary Inferior Rights are therefore the second lowest possible form of rights of any society or aggregate person within the temporal realm. Primary Inferior Rights may be further defined as Primary Personal Inferior Rights or Primary Public Inferior Rights; and

(xii) *Secondary Inferior Rights*, also known as Secondary Rights, are a sub-class of Inferior Rights whereby such valid Rights are created, defined and delegated to an Inferior (Legal) Person by the existence of a non-Ucadian aggregate person, or community, or body politic, or association upon acceptance of the associated obligations and duties attached to them. If any such conditions and obligations are breached or repudiated, then the relevant Secondary Inferior Right may be waived, surrendered, suspended, abandoned, resigned, disqualified, seized, captured, arrested, rescinded, suppressed, forfeited or revoked. Secondary Inferior Rights are therefore the lowest possible form of rights of any society or aggregate person within the temporal realm. Secondary Inferior Rights may be further defined as Secondary Protective Inferior Rights or Secondary Remedial Inferior Rights.

7. By Divine Mandate of the most sacred Covenants *Pactum De Singularis Caelum*, *Pactum De Singularis Christus*, *Pactum De Singularis Islam* and *Pactum De Singularis Spiritus*, all valid Natural Rights and Superior Rights are reserved in trust to the Basilica as the one supreme court of the Union. The Basilica shall have ultimate and final authority to determine and resolve all disputes of Rights among Members of the Union and between the Union and Non-Ucadian persons and bodies. Basilica and Rights of the Union

8. A *Power* is recognised as a *Right* of Authority, or *Claim of Right* of Authority, consistent with the most sacred Covenant *Pactum De Singularis Caelum;* and conveyed unilaterally by a Person as Donor, Delegator, Grantor or Assignor, that enables another to do or act, or refrain from doing or acting in a way that he could not lawfully otherwise do. Powers

9. *Authority* is recognised as an exclusive Right, being a "Right of Control or Use" to do or act in a particular way, derived solely from the acceptance and promise to perform one or more obligations of Office through a proper Oath and Vow, in accord with the present Constitutional Charter. Where there is no proper Oath or Vow, then there shall exist no Authority. Authority is therefore recognised as an "Ecclesiastical Right" delegated by one possessing the Authority to delegate such a Right to another – with the other then having the capacity and character to accept the Right. Authority

10. In accord with the most sacred Covenant *Pactum De Singularis Caelum,* there are only eight (8) possible forms of Authority of Control or Use or Claim of any Right or the Fruits of any Right, (in order of status and standing) being:- Forms of Authority as Control or Use or Claim

(i) Authority of Control of a Right; and

(ii) Authority of Right of Use of a Right; and

(iii) Authority of Right of Control of the Fruits of Use of a Right; and

(iv) Authority of Right of Use of the Fruits of a Right; and

(v) Authority of Claim of Right of Control of a Right; and

(vi) Authority of Claim of Right of Use of a Right; and

(vii) Authority of Claim of Right of Control of the Fruits of Use of a Right; and

(viii) Authority of Claim of Right of Use of the Fruits of a Right.

11. The highest possible Authority recognised by the Union is Absolute Divine Right of Use, also known as "Divinity" from the Divine Creator, under the most sacred Covenant known as *Pactum de Singularis Caelum*:- Highest Authority

(i) Authority is always vested into a sacred Office and not to the man, woman or spirit occupying such Office; and

(ii) Once legitimately vested, an Officer is said to have a mandate within the limits of their Authority; and

(iii) As Authority is by definition Divine Property, an Officer vested into Office can only exercise the Authority granted by such Office if they remain in Honour under Oath. As soon as they are in dishonour or fail to abide by their sacred Oath, their dishonour immediately prevents any Authority being present in their actions; and

(iv) An Officer while in grave dishonour who fails to rectify the same, yet continues to claim full Authority is guilty of a grave offence against the very nature of Authority itself; and such a man is automatically excommunicated from Office whether notice is given or not; and

(v) There is no such thing as secular Authority nor any other claimed form of legitimate Authority except through Divine Right. Therefore all claims of Authority that denounce Ecclesiastical source or the obligation of honour, duty and oath is an absurdity of law and without validity and therefore null and void from the beginning; and

(vi) By definition, all Officials who refuse to produce their oath and be bound by it have no Authority.

12. *Force* is recognised as either valid lawful compulsion by authority to perform or refrain another from certain actions or unlawful violence against a person. When properly authorised, force is also known as "enforcement". Force

13. The following shall be the fundamental requirements for Force to be considered Lawful Compulsion by the Union:- Fundamental Requirements for Force to be Lawful Compulsion

(i) That the decision whether to apply force is made through the proper Courts of the Ucadia Euro Union or a Competent Forum of Law; and

(ii) That a Case and Case Number has been raised upon review of sufficient evidence to commence an Action; and

(iii) All reasonable alternatives to Force have been exhausted; and

(iv) The compelling argument for Lawful Compulsion is in relation to an Enemy Alien, or Dishonest and Delinquent Person, or Mentally Ill Person.

14. The Ucadia Euro Union reserves its absolute and fundamental Right to duly authorise Lawful Compulsion through its Courts or a Competent Forum of Law, against any Enemy Alien of the Ucadia Euro Union, or its Universities, Provinces, Campuses or Allies:- Lawful Compulsion of Enemy Alien

(i) Where the Ucadia Euro Union is able to demonstrate such a Person is properly in its lawful care, possession, jurisdiction, control or custody; or

(ii) Where the perpetrator is culpable of Assault, Battery, Larceny, Robbery, Kidnapping or Oppression against a Person in the care, possession, control or custody of the Ucadia Euro Union.

15. The Ucadia Euro Union reserves its absolute and fundamental Right to duly authorise Lawful Compulsion through its Courts or a Competent Forum of Law, against any Person culpable of Dishonesty or Delinquency in relation to the Ucadia Euro Union, or its Universities, Provinces, Campuses or Allies:- Lawful Compulsion of Dishonest or Delinquent Person

(i) Where the Ucadia Euro Union is able to demonstrate such a Person is properly in its lawful care, possession, jurisdiction, control or custody; or

(ii) Where the perpetrator is culpable of Dishonesty, Perjury, Misconduct, Maladministration, Malfeasance, Embezzlement, Fraud, Concealment, or Delinquency against a Person in the care, possession, control or custody of the Ucadia Euro Union.

16. The Ucadia Euro Union reserves its absolute and fundamental Right to duly authorise Lawful Compulsion through its Courts or a Competent Forum of Law, against any Person found to be suffering significant Mental Illness in relation to the Ucadia Euro Union, or its Universities, Provinces, Campuses or Allies:- Lawful Compulsion of Mentally Ill Person

(i) Where the Ucadia Euro Union is able to demonstrate such a Person is properly in its lawful care, possession, jurisdiction, control or custody; or

(ii) Where the perpetrator is found to be suffering significant Mental Illness in relation to their behaviour against a Person in the care, possession, control or custody of the Ucadia Euro Union.

17. Any and all of the following Claims to the Right to Use Force against the Ucadia Euro Union, or any Person in the care, possession, jurisdiction, control or custody of the Ucadia Euro Union, are invalid, morally repugnant and null and void *ab inito* (from the beginning); and if used, shall be an unreserved confession by the perpetrator of the use of unlawful violence:- Invalid Claims of Right to Force

(i) Any statute, regulation, ruling or law used to treat the Ucadia Euro Union, or any Person in the care, possession, jurisdiction, control or custody of the Ucadia Euro Union, as an Enemy Alien, Enemy of the state or a criminal by any means whatsoever; and

(ii) Any statute, regulation, ruling or law used to treat the Ucadia Euro Union, or any Person in the care, possession, jurisdiction, control or custody of the Ucadia Euro Union, as being dead to Law, without Standing or Capacity, or a bankrupt, or lost at sea, or wrecked, or having surrendered or abandoned any rights, or a captured prize; and

(iii) Any statute, regulation, ruling or law used to treat the Ucadia Euro Union, or any Person in the care, possession, jurisdiction, control or custody of the Ucadia Euro Union, as being mentally ill or intestate or incapable of forming or expressing a clear Will; and

(iv) Any statute, regulation, ruling or law used to treat the Property of the Ucadia Euro Union, or any Property of a Person in the care, possession, jurisdiction, control or custody of the Ucadia Euro Union, as being confiscated, seized, waived, surrendered, abandoned, alienated, forfeited by any means whatsoever.

18. In each and every instance of use of unlawful violence against the Ucadia Euro Union or any Person in the care, possession, jurisdiction, control or custody of the Ucadia Euro Union, a person, or body or entity found culpable by the Courts of the Ucadia Euro Union or a Competent Forum of Law shall be fully liable to maximum damages and compensation:-

Unlimited Liability against Unlawful Violence against Ucadia Euro Union

(i) No claim of immunity within the Articles of a body or entity found to have used such unlawful violence shall be a valid or lawful excuse or defence against the unlimited liability against them; and

(ii) Each and every officer and person who participated in, or co-ordinated or authorised such unlawful violence shall be jointly and severally liable to maximum damages and compensation, without recourse to claim individual immunity or any form of insurance or assurance; and

(iii) The Ucadia Euro Union shall seek immediately in every and any such case of unlawful violence to seize any insurance or assurance bonds as compensation; and to lawfully file any and every possible form of lien and encumbrance against such bodies, entities and individual persons, until compensation and damages is duly paid; and

(iv) The Ucadia Euro Union reserves the right to seek every possible local, national and international form of compensation and sanctions against any body, entity and individuals culpable of such unlawful violence.

Article 3 – Ucadia Euro Union Trust

1. "**Ucadia Euro Union Trust**" is a supreme Global True Trust formed by God and the Divine Creator of all Existence and all Heaven and Earth as Divine Trustor, for the sustenance, prosperity, management, well-being and protection of all life and property within the bounds of the Ucadia Euro Union on Earth.

Ucadia Euro Union Trust

The Global True Trust Number for the Ucadia Euro Union Trust manifested within the temporal realm is:

945000-000000-000000

2. The Ucadia Euro Union Trust exists for the primary purpose to conserve and protect the Trust Corpus for the benefit of all life and communities within the bounds of the Ucadia Euro Union; and to properly delegate the rights and functions of Trustee to the Government of the said Union, when such offices are lawfully occupied

Primary Purpose of Ucadia Euro Union Trust

and unimpeded.

3. The Trust Body of the Ucadia Euro Union Trust shall include any and all rights, uses, land, funds, assets and property, as defined and vested by the present Constitutional Charter as the *Trust Agreement*. Trust Body

4. The Absolute Legal Title to all Trust Property shall be vested at all times in the Ucadia Euro Union Trust as a separate legal entity. No Person shall have legal title to any part of any lawfully conveyed, transferred and settled Trust Property, nor may any third-party have claim over any such Trust Property. Legal Title to Trust Property

5. Insofar as the present Constitutional Charter as the *Trust Agreement* of the Ucadia Euro Union Trust is applied to matters of Arbitration, all such matters shall be governed by and construed in priority order and accord with the Law Provisions of the most sacred Covenant *Pactum De Singularis Caelum* and the present sacred Constitutional Charter. Jurisdiction

   Insofar as the present Constitutional Charter as the *Trust Agreement* of the *Ucadia Euro Union Trust* is applied to matters of Trust Law or Litigation, all such matters shall be governed by and construed in priority order and accord with the Law Provisions of the Present sacred Constitutional Charter first; and then the Procedures and Rules as defined by the sacred covenants *Pactum De Singularis Christus*, *Pactum De Singularis Islam* and *Pactum De Singularis Spiritus*.

6. The Registered Location and Office of the Ucadia Euro Union Trust shall be the Principal Office and Headquarters of Government of the Union. Location of Trust

7. In constituting the Trust, the Trustor has declared that the Trustees shall hold a capital sum of two million, eight hundred and eighty thousand and nine hundred and ten (2,880,910) Supreme Credo (Credit) lawful money and any further monies, investments or other property that may be paid or transferred to the Trustee by way of additional contributions, subject to the present Constitutional Charter as the *Trust Agreement*; and the Trustees hereby declare that the Trustor has irreversibly transferred, delivered and vested to the Trustee, into Account Number OH5100-999999-999999 in the name of the Trust, a capital sum of two million, eight hundred and eighty thousand and nine hundred and ten (2,880,910) Supreme Credo (Credit). Constitution of Trust

8. The Existence and Life of the Trust in its temporal form shall not exceed one thousand and seventy (1,070) years, being one third the span of a Great Era. Thereafter, it shall be up to a vote of valid and legitimate Members of the Society of the Ucadia Euro Union whether to continue in the same form or a different form. Existence of Trust

9. The Trustees declare that they hold custody of the capital sum of two million, eight hundred and eighty thousand and nine hundred and ten (2,880,910) Supreme Credo (Credit) lawful money; and will hold, control and maintain the Trust Fund on trust at all times, subject to the present Constitutional Charter as the *Trust Agreement*, for the benefit of all life and communities within the bounds of the Ucadia Euro Union. — Declaration of Trust

Article 4 – Trustees of Euro Union Trust

1. The Trustees of the Ucadia Euro Union Trust shall be the permanent Basilica, being the one supreme court of the Union: — Trustees of Trust

(i) If the permanent Basilica has not yet convened, or is impeded or obstructed that it cannot properly exercise its supreme trustee responsibilities, then the Trustees shall temporarily be the prerogative court of the Union; and

(ii) If a prerogative court of the Union has not yet convened, or is impeded or obstructed that they cannot exercise temporary judicial responsibility, then the Trustees shall temporarily be a probational court of the Union; and

(iii) If a probational court has not yet convened, or is impeded or obstructed that it cannot exercise its temporary governing responsibility, then the Trustees shall temporarily be union of Ucadia Foundations of the Union; and

(iv) If three or more Ucadia Foundations have not yet been established within the bounds of the Union, the Trustees shall temporarily be the Trustees of the three Great Faiths in accord with the most sacred Covenant *Pactum De Singularis Caelum*.

Article 5 – Ucadia Euro Union Estate

1. The "**Ucadia Euro Union Estate**" shall be the primary record within the Rolls of the Ucadia Euro Union Trust defining a unique legal entity as a body politic and corporate of capacity and personality, engaged in real and substantive relations, holding temporal goods, real and personal property and sufficient funds to discharge any obligations and meet any objectives as would a natural person. — Ucadia Estate

2. The name of the Ucadia Euro Union Estate as a body politic shall be the "**Ucadia Euro Union**" and in reference to internal instruments and documents as simply the "**Union**". — Name of Estate

3. The *Ucadia Euro Union Estate Inventory* shall be an Inventory of Real Property and Personal Property, secured by the Rights, Property, — Ucadia Euro Union Estate Inventory

Uses, Funds, Certificates and Titles held within the Ucadia Euro Union Trust, as appraised by the Trustees, including but not limited to all that is owed by the Estate (*debiti*) and all owed to the Estate (*crediti*) as valued and measured in Units of *Ucadia Moneta* in accord with the most sacred Covenant *Pactum De Singularis Caelum*.

4. In constituting the Ucadia Euro Union, the Trustees hereby declare that the Ucadia Euro Union Treasury of the Ucadia Euro Union shall hold a capital sum of two hundred and eighty eight million, ninety one thousand (288,091,000) Gold Credo (Credit) in lawful money, with the fund underwritten by two million, eight hundred and eighty thousand and nine hundred and ten (2,880,910) Supreme Credo (Credit) lawful money, subject to the present Constitutional Charter as the *Fund Agreement*; and the Fiduciaries of the Ucadia Euro Union Treasury Fund hereby declare that the Trustees have irreversibly transferred, delivered and vested to the Ucadia Euro Union Treasury, into Account Number GU5100-999999-99999 in the name of the Ucadia Euro Union Treasury, a capital sum of two hundred and eighty eight million, ninety one thousand (288,091,000) Gold Credo (Credit) in lawful money. Constitution of Fund

Article 6 – Administrators of Ucadia Euro Union Estate

1. The Administrators of the Ucadia Euro Union Estate shall be the permanent Sunedrion, being the executive government of the Union: Administrators of Estate

(i) If the permanent Sunedrion has not yet convened, or is impeded or obstructed that it cannot properly exercise its supreme administrator responsibilities, then the Administrators shall temporarily be the prerogative Sunedrion of the Union; and

(ii) If a prerogative Sunedrion of the Union have not yet convened, or are impeded or obstructed that they cannot exercise temporary executive responsibility, then the Administrators shall temporarily be a probational Sunedrion of the Union; and

(iii) If a probational Sunedrion have not yet convened, or are impeded or obstructed that it cannot exercise its temporary governing responsibility, then the Administrators shall temporarily be union of Ucadia Foundations of the Union; and

(iv) If three or more Ucadia Foundations have not yet been established within the bounds of the Union, the Administrators shall temporarily be the Trustees of the three Great Faiths in accord with the most sacred Covenant *Pactum De Singularis Caelum*.

Article 7 – Assets, Funds and Money of Union

1. The primary purposes of the Assets of the Union shall be for the successful formation and function of the Union; and in fulfilling its Primary Objects; and the underwriting of any loans, obligations, charges or advances therein; and the underwriting of any subsidiaries or funds thereof; and the proper settlement and discharge of any and all debts, liabilities and obligations. Assets, Funds and Money of the Union

2. The Union shall at all times be the sole, ultimate and absolute owner of all Property and Assets in its name, or purchased by or on its behalf, or related to any body, fund, company or entity within its control or jurisdiction. Absolute Owner of Property & Assets

3. The Union and its related charitable bodies, funds, companies or entities shall be the sole, ultimate and absolute owner of all Property and Assets purchased within the jurisdiction of any foreign and non-Ucadian bodies in its name, or purchased by or on its behalf; and no Property or Asset shall be purchased directly in the name of one or more Members. Absolute Owner of Property & Assets in foreign & non-Ucadian jurisdictions

   The right of use, equity and lesser ownership of Property and Assets by Members of the Union purchased within the jurisdiction of any foreign and non-Ucadian body politic shall at all times be distinct and administered separately to the ultimate and absolute ownership of the Property and Asset in question.

4. The Universal Unit of Account and Measure of the Union shall be the Ucadia Moneta. Universal Unit of Account

5. The Income of the Union shall be applied toward the promotion and achievement of the Primary Objects and Ancillary Objects of the Union as first priority. Income & Objects of the Union

6. Unless it is otherwise deemed and approved by Members to be in the best interests of the Union in fulfilling its Primary Objects, all profits of the Union shall be retained and reinvested as Capital for the meeting and fulfilment of the Primary Objects and Ancillary Objects of the Union. Distribution of Profits of the Union

Article 8 – Taxes, Charges and Exemptions of Union

1. The Union, by innate and holy mandate, has absolute Authority and Power to Rate itself, including (but not limited to) the Valuation of all its Rights, Lands, Goods, Estates, Trusts, Funds, Property and Assets. All Valuations, Rates and Taxes shall then be duly recorded within the proper Registers of the Union, in accord with the present Articles. No other non-Ucadian or foreign body, or foreign power, or foreign entity, Tax, Rates and Valuation

or foreign person or foreign corporation has any right, or power, or authority whatsoever to Rate, or Value or Tax the Rights, Lands, Goods, Estates, Trusts, Funds, Property and Assets of Ucadia and the Union.

2. The Union, its property and its assets, wherever located and by whomsoever held, shall enjoy immunity from every form of judicial process except to the extent that it expressly waives its immunity for the purpose of any proceedings or by the terms of any contract. Immunity from Judicial Process

3. The Union, its trusts, estates, property, accounts, assets and all deposits and other funds entrusted to it shall be immune in time of peace and in time of war from any measure such as expropriation, requisition, seizure, confiscation, prohibition or restriction or any other similar measures; and to the extent necessary to carry out the Primary and Ancillary Objects provided for in the present Constitutional Charter, all property and assets of the Union shall be free from restrictions, regulations, controls, and moratorium of any nature. Immunity from Other Actions

4. Where certain Rights, Lands, Goods, Estates, Trusts, Funds, Property or Assets of Ucadia and the Union are being used by a non-Ucadian or foreign body, or foreign power, or foreign entity, or foreign person or foreign corporation, the Union shall have the full Authority and Power to offer a peaceful, amicable and harmonious resolution by licensing such Rights, Lands, Goods, Estates, Trusts, Funds, Property or Assets by Special Treaty with any Government or State within the jurisdiction of the Union and any clauses or separate Special Treaty with relevant non-Ucadian Taxation bodies. By such Treaty or Convention, the Union shall be empowered to consider any such non-Ucadian and foreign body "tax exempt" from payments to the Union; or other such arrangements that are considered conducive to peaceful, amicable and harmonious relations, without contradicting the present Articles. Tax Treaties and Status

5. Notwithstanding any other provision of these Articles, any attempt by any non-Ucadian or foreign body, or foreign power, or foreign entity, or foreign person or foreign corporation to Rate, or Value or establish a Tax Roll for certain Rights, Lands, Goods, Estates, Trusts, Funds, Property or Assets of Ucadia and the Union shall be an act of profanity, sacrilege and an abomination against all Heaven and Earth, as only Ucadian bodies possess the Divine Mandate to administer and hold in custody Sacred Circumscribed Space. Therefore, any such action to the contrary shall be considered a *Confession of Condemnation* whereby such a body, and all persons responsible shall be named in a *Writ;* and it shall be a moral obligation of every Ucadian Member to pursue by every and any means necessary to eliminate every temporal existence and manifestation of Any attempt to Rate, or Value or Tax a profanity, sacrilege and abomination against the Law

such profanity, sacrilege and abomination.

Article 9 – Liabilities, Debts and Obligations of Union

1. The Union shall seek at all times to be able to pay its debts as they become due in the normal course of business and to ensure the value of the assets of the Union is greater than the value of its liabilities, including contingent liabilities. *Reducing Solvency Risk*

2. No money shall be drawn from the Econos, being the Treasury of the Union, but in consequence of appropriations made by law; and a regular statement and account of the receipts and expenditures of all public money shall be published from time to time. *Appropriations by Law*

3. The Union shall devise, adopt and enforce sufficient procedures and measures to ensure that it possesses and controls adequate capital to support the relevant risks of its activities; and that the Union complies with its compliance obligations. *Capital Adequacy*

4. The Union shall hereby adopt and implement its own comprehensive internal capital adequacy assessment processes; and to ensure it has in place sound, effective and comprehensive strategies and processes to assess and maintain, on an ongoing basis: *Internal Capital Adequacy Assessment Processes*

   (i) The average risk weighting benchmarks in relation to compliance, best practice and reasonable market expectations; and whether such risk weights are "under" or "over" adequate capital planning; and

   (ii) The amounts, types and distribution of current financial resources allocated to risk management; and the re-alignment of such levels periodically in light of benchmarks, the changing nature and level of current risks and future risk contingencies.

5. The Union shall seek to comply with all reasonable requests and obligations, as defined and required by International Law; and shall honour its reporting duties, including but not limited to suspicious transactions, anti-money laundering reporting, capital and liquidity reporting. *Compliance and Reporting*

6. In the event that an agency or body of a body politic is found culpable of permitting a false action against the Union by seeking to wrongly gain advantage through the use of non-Ucadian Courts, then the Union reserves its absolute right, regardless of any claimed immunity or waivers or other protections claimed by such agencies or bodies or persons, to pursue to the full extent possible, every and any possible compensation, punishment, restitution, sanction, interdict, condemnation, conviction, seizure and satisfaction against each and *Unlimited Damages from false actions*

every institution responsible; and each and every individual person responsible; and every individual enjoined as culpable through omission, failure to act or tacit acceptance of such false action.

Article 10 – Solvency of the Union

1. Solvency is recognised as both the capacity of the Union to ensure it has sufficient Capital and liquid assets to satisfy its immediate debt obligations; and ownership, possession and use of sufficient Property to settle debts as they fall due. Solvency

2. The Union shall ensure a strong and stable position of Solvency is maintained, through the principles of prudent financial management and planning, namely: Optimum Solvency

   (i) *Sufficient Stock Capital* ensuring the Union has sufficient Stock Capital and Ucadia Monies in order to raise sufficient Cash through paid-up Capital; and

   (ii) *Prudent Cash Management* that obligations and expenditure match the ability of the business to meet its bills; and

   (iii) *Cash Offsets for Stocks* where it is possible to lower the demand for cash by offering Stocks in the Charitable Funds of the Union as a valid alternative, where appropriate.

3. The Union shall seek at all times to be able to pay its proper debts as they become due in the normal course of activities and to ensure the value of the Assets of the Union is greater than the value of its liabilities, including contingent liabilities. Reducing Solvency Risk

4. To ensure the Union is able to know and determine its solvency during the normal course of activities, and to assist in business plan and necessary compliance under the present Articles and International Law, the Union shall maintain at all times the highest Accounting Standards, Bookkeeping and periodic reporting and Audits of its activities. Solvency Test

5. The guaranteed prudential underwriting of the Union shall mean that the Union cannot technically or lawfully or legally be classed as Insolvent in respect of any debt or obligation owed between Ucadia Members, Ucadia Bodies or Societies. Instead, an event that cannot be supported by the existing Guaranteed and Capital Stock of the Union is grounds for the temporary suspension of those executives or officials; and the temporary appointment of suitable administrators to restore proper prudential and fiduciary management. Union cannot be Insolvent via Ucadia Obligations

6. A Legitimate Insolvency Event is when the following criteria exist: Legitimate Insolvency Event

(i) A valid and legitimate debt or obligation of the Union to a foreign body exists and is registered and acknowledged in writing in a valid Instrument by the Union to be settled in Lawful Money of a non-Ucadian body politic; and

via Foreign Obligation

(ii) The Union at the time of settlement has insufficient Public Money and Legal Ucadia Money as tender to discharge the valid and legitimate debt; and

(iii) The Union at the time of the settlement has insufficient Assets to offer an alternate settlement to the debt and obligation.

7. The lack of possession of certain reserves of Non-Ucadian and Foreign Fiat Notes of Foreign Banks shall be insufficient, unreasonable and false grounds alone to claim an Insolvency Event.

Lack of Foreign Fiat Notes not grounds for Insolvency

8. The assertion or demand for payment or settlement of a claim without merit, or reasonable grounds shall not be considered valid criteria in respect of solvency. The failure of claimants to follow due procedure as specified within these Articles, or to make gross and unreasonable demands shall instead be evidence of an offence and obligation due to the Union; and the acceptance by the false claimant(s) that the Union may use any, every and all means to pursue compensation, seizure of assets, punishment and imprisonment of the perpetrators and any other action deemed reasonable to prevent further false claims.

False Claim not a valid criteria

9. The rejection of two or more valid negotiations and reasonable offers made by the Union of Settlement of a valid foreign debt or obligation shall cause the associated foreign debt or obligation to be settled by the equal amount of the dishonour of such unreasonable and unfair rejection. Therefore, such rejection of valid and reasonable offers shall never be considered legitimate or legal grounds whatsoever of an insolvency event.

Rejection of valid Settlement not a valid criteria

10. Any move, proposal or action by the Board of Directors or group of Members to declare an Insolvency Event that contradicts these Articles is therefore a formal act of fraud, treachery and treason and immediate grounds for their suspension from any official capacity, the reversal of any or all decisions or actions taken by such Members in any official capacity and the pursuit of penalties against such Members and their actions.

False Insolvency Event

Article 11 – Society of Ucadia Euro Union

1. The Society of Ucadia Euro Union, also known simply as The *Society*, is the constituted body politic of the Ucadia Euro Union under the present Constitutional Charter, dedicated to the fulfilment of

Society of Ucadia Euro Union

sustainable peace and prosperity for all people and the respect of all life and our planet Earth.

2. The Society, in honouring the true nature of the Divine Creator, excludes no one purely upon their religion, race, sexuality, age or gender. Thus, the Society is truly a unity of Light. Society representing all persons

Article 12 – Sovereign Functions & Relations

1. The *Society of the Ucadia Euro Union* by its simple name as The *Society* and by its formal name and character is an independent ecclesiastical, sovereign and legal entity recognised by all constituted Ucadia Unions, Universities, Provinces, Campuses and related bodies. Sovereign Relations

2. The Society is a subject of Ucadian Law first and international law second; and innately exercises its sovereign functions. Sovereign Functions

3. In the Ucadia Euro Union, the Society and its Organs have sovereign immunity and may not be sued unless it has waived its immunity or consented to suit. The Society as a sovereign is immune from suit unless it unequivocally consents to being sued. Sovereign Immunity

4. Legislative, executive and judicial functions are reserved to the competent organs and bodies of the Society, according to the provisions of the present Constitutional Charter and approved Rules and Bylaws. Legislative Functions

5. The Society shall have diplomatic representation to all Ucadia bodies and to non-Ucadian bodies according to the norms of international law. Diplomatic Relations

6. All official and authorised representatives having diplomatic powers of the Union shall be immune from legal process with respect to acts performed by them in their official capacity except when the Union waives this immunity; and such officials of the Union shall be granted the same immunities from travelling facilities, immigration restrictions, alien registration requirements, and national service obligations and the same facilities as regards exchange restrictions as are accorded by members to the representatives, officials, and employees of comparable rank of Non-Ucadian nations and societies. Immunity of Officials

Article 13 – Impediment of Ucadia Euro Union

1. An Impediment is any action or event that may have a notable or significant effect of interfering with the Divine Mandate of the Union and its officials and authorised agents and representatives. Impediment

2. No impediment of the Ucadia Euro Union Society shall diminish, disqualify or dissolve the Ucadia Euro Union Estate or the Ucadia Impediment of Society

Euro Union Trust, even if such an impediment causes the temporary suspension of government or administration or the annexation of lands within the bounds of the Union.

3. Without prejudice to the rights of Persons under Ucadian Law of the Jurisdiction to commence an action against an agency, person or body of the Union, the Union shall take whatever lawful measure is necessary to defend and defeat any such action and pursue any available penalties, or prosecution, or charges or compensation upon the following types of actions:

Unreasonable Grounds

(i) Any action undertaken in bad faith, or with prejudice or vexation in such a manner as to deliberately hinder, damage, obstruct the Union and its Officers and Agents; or

(ii) Any action commenced by a party having previously rejected legal tender and lawful Money provided by the Union for the discharge of a debt or obligation of the Union; or

(iii) Any action commenced through non-Ucadian foreign courts and non-Ucadian foreign jurisdiction; or

(iv) Any action commenced by a party whereby no evidence exists of any debt or obligation owed by the said body or agency or person of the Union; or

(v) Any action for liquidation commenced by any creditor where there is clear *prima facie* evidence of an arrangement for the settlement of any outstanding debts and that the Union continues in good faith to honour such arrangements; or

(vi) Any Action by a Member in contravention to these Articles.

Article 14 – Dissolution of Ucadia Euro Union

1. The Union shall be dissolved upon the three thousand two hundred and tenth (3210th) anniversary of the date of its first formation, ensuring all debts and liabilities are satisfied. Any and all intellectual property that remains shall then be given to the Ucadia Universities within the bounds of the dissolved Union, to have and to hold in perpetuity. Dissolution

TITLE II: MEMBERS

Article 15 – Members

1. A "**Member**" is a Superior Person constituting a vital and integral part of the function of the body of the Union. There shall be four types of Member of the Union, being Ordinary, Company, Society and State: Members

   (i) An "**Ordinary Member**" is any living man or woman whose identity is duly validated and registered in the Member Rolls of the Union in accord with the conditions of the present Constitutional Charter. An Ordinary Member possesses the right of one Vote upon the redemption of their Membership Number; and

   (ii) A "**Company Member**" is any association, body, entity, aggregate or partnership duly validated and registered as a Company in the Company Rolls of the Union in accord with the conditions of the present Charter. A Company Member possesses one Vote, while its own members may be recognised as Ordinary Members upon their proper registration in the Member Rolls of the Union; and

   (iii) A "**Society Member**" is any non-profit, religious, social, body politic or fraternal association duly validated and registered as a Society in the Society Rolls of the Union in accord with the conditions of the present Charter. A Society Member possesses one Vote, while its own members may be recognised as Ordinary Members upon their proper registration in the Member Rolls of the Union; and

   (iv) A "**State Member**" is any existing body politic, country, territory or nation properly recognised by International Law as a sovereign body politic, country, territory or nation and duly validated and registered as a State in the State Rolls of the Union in accord with the conditions of the present Charter. A State Member duly recognised and accepted assumes the permanent government and authority of either a Ucadia University and all subdivisions or a Ucadia Province and all subdivisions upon ratification.

2. The conditions of admission, sanction and expulsion shall be defined by the present Constitutional Charter and any associated and approved Rules and Bylaws of the Union. Admission, Sanction & Expulsion

3. All valid Members of the Union shall be recognised through a Unique Member Number in both a long form of one hundred and forty four characters and a short form of eighteen characters:- Unique Member Number

(i) The "**Long Form Unique Membership Number**" of one hundred and forty-four (144) characters shall be constructed from eight by eighteen character numbers being Union Trust Identification, Ucadian Day-Time of Registration, Ucadia Form Identifier, Trust Identification for Registrar Office, Officer Trust Number, Location Identifier of Registration, Member Number and Certificate Number; and

(ii) The "**Short Form Unique Membership Number**" of eighteen (18) characters shall be the Member Number derived from the existing member number to One Heaven and replacing the first two characters with the letters EU. Therefore the Unique Membership Number of a member of the Union shall be in the form: EU0000-000000-000000.

4. The Union shall maintain Unique and Accurate Rolls listing all valid Members. There shall be three types of member Rolls being General, Redeemed and Electoral:- Member Roll

(i) The General Member Roll of the Union, also known as the Great Roll of Superior Persons shall be the official Member Roll which records each and every unique Membership Number issued in validation of the existence of a Divine Person associated with a living man or woman within the bounds and jurisdiction of the Union; and

(ii) The Redeemed Member Roll of the Union shall be the official Member Roll which records each and every unique Membership Number issued in validation of the existence of a living Member, to whom an Official Member Number has been assigned through a voluntary Act of Redemption; and

(iii) The Electoral Member Roll of the Union shall be the official Member Roll which records a copy of the Redeemed Member Roll for those Redeemed Members above the minimum age to vote. A Member not on the Electoral Roll is not permitted to participate in voting and elections.

5. For the purpose of consistency, membership of the Union shall be equitable to Citizenship of the Union, with any other definitions pertaining to Citizenship that imply a ceding of rights, or enemy of the state or some other deficiency null and void. Membership and Citizenship

6. In accord with membership of the Union being formed and derived from sacred consent to membership of One Heaven, membership and member registration to the Union takes precedence over all other memberships to inferior societies, except One Heaven. Member Precedence

Article 16 – Member Rights & Obligations

1. All Member Rights, Obligations and Privileges shall be sourced and subscribed through the Articles of the present Constitutional Charter. Member Rights & Obligations

2. A Member is a Superior Person and Member Rights are Positive Rights as defined by the present Charter. Member Rights may therefore be defined as Universal and Conditional:- Member Rights

   (i) "**Universal Rights**", also known as Universal Positive Rights, are a sub-class of Positive Rights whereby such valid Rights created, defined and bestowed to a Legal Person by the existence of an aggregate person, or community, or body politic, or association in accord with the Rule of Law through the most sacred Covenant *Pactum De Singularis Caelum* and the present Constitutional Charter are Peremptory, Permanent, Immutable and Indefeasible and once bestowed are not subject to any form or condition of waiver, abandonment, surrender, disqualification, incapacitation, seizure, capture, arrest, resignation, alienation, suspension, suppression, forfeiture or abrogation. Therefore Universal Positive Rights are the highest possible form of Universal Rights of any society or aggregate person; and

   (ii) "**Conditional Rights**", also known as Conditional Positive Rights, are a sub-class of Positive Rights whereby such valid Rights created, defined and delegated to a Legal Person by the existence of an aggregate person, or community, or body politic, or association in accord with the Rule of Law through the most sacred Covenant *Pactum De Singularis Caelum* and the present Charter upon acceptance of the associated obligations and duties attached to them. Furthermore, if such any such conditions and obligations are breached or repudiated, then the relevant Conditional Positive Right may be waived, surrendered, suspended, abandoned, resigned, disqualified, seized, captured, arrested, rescinded, suppressed, forfeited or revoked until such time as the fundamental breach of duty and obligation is repaired or such a Right is duly restored. A Legal Person to whom a Conditional Positive Right has been bestowed may also lawfully convey equitable title of such a Right to another person.

3. A "**Member Rights Advocate**" is a suitably authorised and qualified Trustee granted by a Member sufficient legal rights under Power of Attorney to represent the best interests of a Member and their Rights with any and all Non-Ucadian societies. Member Rights Advocate

4. The occupancy of a position of Member of the Union is held in trust and upon the performance of the occupant of such a position acting in accord with the functions and obligations of a Trustee as defined by the present Charter and associated Covenants and Laws. Obligations of Member

Therefore, a Member is expected to behave at all times in good faith, good conscience and good actions demonstrating the eight standard characteristics of a Trustee as Fiduciary being Integrity, Frugality, Prudence, Humility, Faculty, Competence, Accountability and Capacity.

The failure of a Member to act or perform in a manner becoming a Trustee and Fiduciary may cause such occupant of such a position to face disciplinary charges in relation to their conduct, or the suspension of certain Conditional Rights or Privileges.

5. The provision of services, support, technology, applications, forms, property, currency or any other assistance, other than education, emergency health or basic sustenance shall be considered privileges that remain in place so long as a Member continues to perform their agreed Obligations. Member Privileges

The Union reserves the right to temporarily withdraw one or more services or supports in the event of some conviction or as some ordered punishment in the event of a default and delinquency by a Member.

Article 17 – Member Terms & Conditions

1. The Union shall have the right to make and publish as binding to any agreement associated with one or more Services, a Statement of Terms and Conditions for fair use of such Services. Terms and Conditions

It shall be a condition of provision of any service by the Society that a related Statement of terms and conditions is included and made available to any user of that service prior to the service being used.

In the construction of a statement of terms and conditions, the following criteria shall always apply:-

(i) Nothing in a statement of Terms and Conditions may contradict one or more Articles of the present Constitutional Charter; and

(ii) The articles of the present Constitutional Charter shall always take precedence over any statement of Terms and Conditions and nothing written or implied in a statement of terms and conditions shall change this fact; and

(iii) A statement of Terms and Conditions may include such clauses not explicitly stated within the present Constitutional Charter provided such clauses are consistent with the intention of present Constitutional Charter and a related statement from the Supreme Executive exists ratifying such clauses as a legitimate regulation; and

(iv) All statements of Terms and Conditions must be lodged and approved by vote at the appropriate level of the organisation prior to use with a record kept.

2. An Individual is deemed a full Ordinary Member of the Society, when:-

Conditions for Ordinary Membership

(i) They have fulfilled the obligations associated with Registration and Validation as prescribed by the present Charter; and

(ii) They have acknowledged reading and accepting the Terms and Conditions of Association; and

(iii) They have openly pledged their loyalty and allegiance to the Society and they have signed, or indicated their agreement to this effect; and

(iv) They have not previously been expelled from the Society in the past five (5) years, or deemed ineligible due to membership of an organisation deemed "illegal" according to the by-laws of the Society.

3. Member Registration, Identity and Verification are vital and fundamental functions of due diligence to protect the integrity of information, to reduce the risk of fraud and misrepresentation and ultimately protect the well being and rights of all Members of the Society.

Member Registration, Identity and Verification

4. The Union and all Ucadia societies are invoked to use the tools of Registration carefully and respectfully lest an injury be created through the registration of property by a member of a Ucadia society or Union that does not have consent or does not properly hold title.

Ownership and Registration

The intention of Registration is not to make claims over the personal and private property of others, but to protect the intellectual property of Members and the Union itself. Thus the registration of a man or woman as a Member is actually (1) the recognition of the Natural Rights of the Office of Man or Office of Woman and (2) the granting of the Rights associated with the Superior Person being at all times the property of the Society.

Therefore, the Union reserves the right at all times to request proper registration including the request for the provision of such minimal information needed to verify the identity of the particular Member or Officer.

5. The Union shall require registration for a number of functions including (but not limited to) Ordinary Member Self Registration, Ordinary Member Relative Registration, Company Member Registration, Society Member Registration and Bulk Ordinary Member Registration:- General Categories of Registration

(i) *Ordinary Member Self Registration* refers to a living man or woman whom has reached Age of Majority and is of sound body and mind, who performs the act of Ordinary Membership redemption by registering their own particulars in the Great Register; and

(ii) *Ordinary Member Relative Registration* refers to a living man or woman whom has reached Age of Majority and is of sound body and mind, who performs the act of registering their ancestor or descendant particulars in the Great Register. All relative registrations are initially ledger entries in the Great Register and not active member accounts; and

(iii) *Company Member Registration* refers to one or more existing Ordinary Members performing the act of registering the particulars of a valid Company in accord with the Conditions of Registering a valid Company Member; and

(iv) *Society Member Registration* refers to three (3) or more existing Ordinary Members performing the act of registering the particulars of a valid Society in accord with the Conditions of Registering a valid Society Member; and

(v) *Bulk Ordinary Member Registration* refers to one or more officials of a society performing the act of registering the particulars of many members contained in a bulk datum, into the Great Register. All bulk registrations are initially ledger entries in the Great Register and not active member accounts.

6. Valid Registration is required to ensure a valid Member Redemption. Failure to provide the minimum necessary information or to intentionally or accidentally breach the terms and conditions of Member Registration may result in a failure to successfully redeem membership. The methods and options for Member Registration may also differ according to the different registration types of Membership. Valid Registration and Membership

7. The essential member registration data input information requirements for an Ordinary Member Self- Registration shall include (but may not be limited to):- Ordinary Member Self Registration Information

(i) *Current Legal Name* (lawful name currently used on legal documents) including (a)First Name (required); and (b) Middle Name (required only if member has a middle name(s)); and (c) Last Name (required); and

(ii) *Borne Name* (name used on birth documents) including (a)First Name (required); and (b) Middle Name (required only if member has a middle name(s)); and (c) Last Name (required); and

(iii) *Valid and Verified Digital Communication Address* (required for member accounts). Such addresses for member accounts must belong solely to the member, it should not be a group email alias where others may have access to it; an exception to this is for minor descendants during a descendant member account provisional period; and

(iv) *Borne Date* (required); and

(v) *Borne Location* (required).

8. All Ordinary Member accounts created via self registration may undergo a maximum twenty-eight (28) day grace period during which time a member may choose to rescind, cancel or delete their membership account by request. Ordinary Member Self Registration

During the grace period, use of certain tools may be limited such as: a member will not be able to publish gazette notices or other public records.

At the expiration of the grace period and identity is verified, automated notices will be published in the gazette regarding the member. The grace period also allows a member to make any typo corrections to their name via the member account terminal.

All member accounts created via Ordinary Self Registration require a valid functional and verified email address as a primary means of contact. Any account having an unconfirmed/unverified email address at the expiration of the grace period will be automatically deleted without further recourse or action.

Members are of course permitted to register again in this situation. In the event of a member desiring to rescind, cancel or delete membership after the expiration of the grace period, the matter will be referred to Article 38 (*Rights*) of the Covenant of One Heaven.

9. Ordinary Relative Registration refers to an Ordinary Member who has reached Age of Majority and is of sound body and mind, who performs Ordinary Member Relative Registration the act of registering their ancestor or descendant particulars in the Great Register. All relative registrations are initially ledger entries in the Great Register and not active member accounts.

All Ordinary Relative Registrations must use a registration tool designated for relatives, namely Ancestor Registration and Descendant Registration:-

(i) *Ancestor Registration* including (a) Registration of lawful deceased ancestors is permitted; and (b) Registration of an ancestor whom is still living and under lawful guardianship of the member performing the registration is permitted; and (c) Registration of an ancestor whom is still living and of sound body and mind is expressly forbidden; and

(ii) *Descendant Registration* including (a) Registration of minor descendants whom are under the immediate lawful guardianship of the member performing the registration is permitted; and (b) Registration of a descendant whom has reached age of majority and under lawful guardianship of the member performing the registration is permitted; and (c)Registration of a descendant whom has reached age of majority and is of sound body and mind is expressly forbidden.

10. When a minor descendant (child) whom has already been registered by a verified ancestor (parent or guardian), the following methods are made available to activate the descendant member account:- Ordinary Member Guardian Registration

(i) *Verified Ancestor/Lawful Guardian Activation* of Descendant Member Account, namely (a) Descendant must be at least twelve (12) years of age; and (b) Ancestor/Guardian uses descendant member account activation tool; and (c) Ancestor/Guardian provides any missing particulars needed for full member account activation, information requirements will be that of the same of self registration; and (d) Once account is active, it will be placed in a twenty-eight (28) day grace period thus giving the descendant the free will choice for full account redemption, at which time all rules of grace period fall under self registration; and (e) Descendant member account provisionally remains under the care of the Ancestor/Guardian until descendant reaches the Age of Majority and is of sound body and mind; and

(ii) *Descendant Self Activation* including (a) If not previously activated, a descendant is permitted to self activate their member account from their existing registration using a descendant self activation tool when descendant has reached the Age of Majority and is of sound body and mind; and (b) Descendant provides any missing particulars needed for member account activation, information requirements will be that of the same of self registration; and (c) Once account is active, it will be placed in a twenty-eight (28) day grace period thus giving the descendant the free will choice for full account redemption, at which time all rules of grace period fall under self registration; and

(iii) *Society Official Activation* including (a) Society Officials are permitted to activate a descendant member account upon request of the descendant; and (b) Once account is active, it will be placed in a twenty-eight (28) day grace period thus giving the descendant the free will choice for full account redemption, at which time all rules of grace period fall under self registration.

11. *Company Member Registration* refers to one (1) or more existing Members performing the act of registering a valid company particulars in the Great Register as a part in forming a valid Company Record on the Company Roll of the Union.

Company Member Registration

All company registrations must use the registration tools designated for such registration procedures and shall include (but may not be limited to):-

(i) *Current Legal Name* (lawful name currently used on legal documents); and

(ii) *Formation Date* (name used on incorporation documents); and

(iii) *Copy of Memorandum and Articles of Association* or Incorporation; and

(iv) *Digital Communication Address* (required for member accounts). Such addresses for member accounts must belong solely to the member, it should not be a group email alias; and

(v) *Director Details* (required); and

(vi) *Mailing Address* (required); and

(vii) *Registered Office Location* (required).

12. *Society Registration* refers to three (3) or more members performing the act of registering a society particulars in the Great Register as a part in forming a valid Society Record on the Society Roll of the Union.

Society Member Registration

All society registrations must use the registration tools designated for such registration procedures and shall include (but may not be limited to):-

(i) *Current Legal Name* (lawful name currently used on legal documents); and

(ii) *Formation Date* (name used on incorporation documents); and

(iii) *Copy of Memorandum and Articles of Association or Constitution*; and

(iv) *Digital Communication Address* (required for member accounts). Such an address for member accounts must belong solely to the member, it should not be a group email alias; and

(v) *Director or Elected Officers Details* (required); and

(vi) *Mailing Address* (required); and

(vii) *Registered Office Location* (required).

13. Bulk Member Registration refers to one (1) or more officials of a society performing the act of registering the particulars of many members contained in a bulk datum, into the Great Register. Bulk Member Registration

All bulk registrations are initially ledger entries in the Great Register and not active member accounts.

All members with particulars contained in a bulk registration must have given express consent to the official(s) performing the act of registration. Active Member Accounts as a result of bulk registration:

(i) It is permitted that bulk registrations contain particulars for member account activations; and

(ii) Bulk datum must specify if member particulars is registration only or with active member account; and

(iii) All further requirements and grace period henceforth will be referred to Self Registration laws; and

(iv) All bulk registrations must be performed with a registration tool designated for bulk.

Article 18 – Member Accounts & Services

1. All Accounts, Documents, Instruments and Benefits provided to Members shall be as Services, and considered as privileges subject to Member Service Contracts and appropriate fees and conditions. Excluding emergency relief, sustenance or health assistance, all other benefits provided to Members shall be subject to terms and conditions Member Accounts and Services and the reasonable conduct and behaviour of Members.

2. A "**Member Service Contract**" is any agreement between a Member and an entity, organisation, department or agency of the Union providing one or more services. All Services of the Union shall be provided to Members under Member Service Contracts. *Member Service Contracts*

3. The Union shall retain the absolute right to suspend or terminate one or more Services to a Member, in event that the Member refuses to honour the terms and conditions of the relevant Member Service Contract, or is belligerently delinquent. However, the Union shall not be permitted to unilaterally suspend or terminate unrelated Services of a Member, if a dispute or controversy exists on some other Service or Services. *Suspension or Termination of Services*

Article 19 – Member Records, Identification & Verification

1. The Union shall keep a Book or Folio called the Member Roll as a Register of one or more entries of Persons entitled as Members, to participate in the affairs of the Union according to the present Articles subject to the Jurisdiction of the Union. *Member Records*

   Each and every valid Member of the Union shall be entitled to be entered as a valid Record within the Member Roll for the purpose of identifying such entitlements and participation in the affairs of the Union. Where the name of the Ordinary Member is not clear, a Placeholder name may be used.

2. "**Vital Records**" are those Records of life events of Members, kept, held and managed under the full Authority and Powers of the Union, including but not limited to: Birth Certificates, Marriage Certificates and Death Certificates. The Union shall be tasked and mandated with the safekeeping of such Vital Records. The Original Copy of all Vital Records shall always be kept by the Union and can never be published, printed, transmitted, transferred, conveyed, surrendered, disclaimed, gifted, granted or registered to a Non-Ucadian body, foreign power or third party. However, the limited use of such information, rights and intellectual property contained within such Vital Records may be licensed from time to time, to such foreign powers under written Convention and Treaty. *Vital Records*

3. By virtue of the Divine Mandate of One Heaven through the Sacred Constitutional Charter of Incorporation of the Union, the Vital Records of the Union are the first, highest and original Records of such life events, with any and all other records by any and all other Non-Ucadian and foreign bodies being inferior and subordinate *Vital Records of Union as first, highest and original Records*

records, regardless of the alleged time of creation of such records.

4. In accord with the most sacred Covenant *Pactum De Singularis Caelum*, all life events as defined as Vital Records are duly recorded within the Great Register of One Heaven at the time such events occur, even if no record of such fact within the temporal realm exists. By virtue of the Divine Mandate of One Heaven granted to the Union through its Sacred Constitutional Charter, the Union possesses then a sacred and solemn obligation to ensure that those things bound and recorded in Heaven are properly recorded on Earth. Therefore, the proper, lawful and legal Space-Day-Time of recording and registering all life events as Vital Records is precisely the same day and time and place of the event, regardless of the day or time the record is subsequently entered. Sacred-Space-Day Time of Recording life event

5. Wherever and whenever a conflict arises between a claimed vital record, or derivative record of a foreign power, or Non-Ucadian entity and the Vital Records of the Union, the Vital Records of the Union as the original, first, and highest Records of all such life events, shall always take precedence. Vital Records of Union take precedence

6. A Foreign and Non-Ucadian Power, duly notified, shall be obliged to accept the superior standing of Vital Records and to make such corrections in their own records that may be in error and to seek a peaceful and amicable Convention and Treaty with the Union under license for the limited right of use of such names and information. Obligation to correct errors

7. A Foreign or Non-Ucadian Power that refuses to acknowledge the superior standing of Vital Records; and refuses to seek a peaceful and amicable Convention and Treaty with the Union, shall therefore acknowledge by such perfidy, dishonour, profanity, sacrilege and heresy the full spiritual, ecclesiastical, moral, financial, lawful and legal consequences of their actions as a formal and binding declaration of confession. By such a Declaration of Confession, each and every responsible minister and executive of the government of the Foreign Power shall be named and every administrator responsible shall be named jointly and severally. The Union shall then be solemnly bound to fulfil and pursue as a *Holy Writ* by every means in Heaven and upon the Earth, resulting in the full execution of such a Declaration of Confession against such members of the Foreign and Non-Ucadian Power. Declaration of Confession by a Foreign Power

8. Identity Verification shall be an essential function for the protection of the highest standards of integrity and trust that exists in the provision and use of services associated with any property, rights, instruments and transactions; and in the processing of applications for certification Member Identity Verification

of key Officers and bodies and divisions of the Union such as Campuses, Provinces and Universities. It shall be a condition of any Member seeking Office or to establish a new body in accord with the present Charter that they fully consent to the provision of necessary Proof of Identity requirements.

Similarly, it shall be a condition of the provision of any Member Services associated with currency, property, trusts, instruments or any other trusted financial service that a Member fully consent to the necessary Identity Requirements.

The administration and government of the Union shall at all times reserve the right to deny a Member their application as a candidate for Office or formation of a Body Politic should such Identity Verification procedures fail.

The administration and government of the Union shall at all times reserve the right to deny a Member the access and use of any service that requires Identity Verification should such Identity Verification procedures fail or the Member refuse to consent to such procedures.

Violations of verification and validation

9. The intentional and knowing provision of false information at the time of any verification or identification requirements by the Union or its associated agencies or bodies, shall be considered a serious criminal offence against the Union.

Upon sufficient evidence being available to reveal such a serious criminal offence, the Union and its authorised bodies and agencies shall retain the rights to pursue maximum damages and penalties against any such person or body, including but not limited to: suspension, termination of services, expulsion, interdict, confiscation of property, forfeiture, criminal indictment, public notice, civil damages and compensation.

Organised violations of verification and validation

10. The intentional and knowing provision of false information at the time of any verification or identification requirements by the Union or its associated agencies or bodies, by an organised group, body or entity shall be considered a declaration of belligerence and attack against the integrity, security and safety of the Union.

Upon detection and verification of such an organised and deliberate attack against the Union by any organisation, group, entity or body, such a body shall be duly recorded and prescribed by the Union, including the option to designate such an organisation, group, entity or body as an enemy combatant, terrorist organisation, criminal enterprise; and then to pursue through every means and all possible treaties and agreements with every possible law enforcement, financial, military, security and political body to ensure the prompt capture, seizure, disruption or neutralisation of any such threat.

Article 20 – Member Documents & Instruments

1. The Union shall issue from time to time official documents and instruments pertaining to its Members. Such documents and instruments shall remain at all times the property of the Union; and the Union shall retain the right at all times to charge fees for the production of such documents and instruments and to demand the return, cancellation or destruction of such documents and instruments if a Member fails to honour their obligations of proper care and use. Member Documents & Instruments

2. A *Member Live Borne Record*, is a Vital Record of the Union, issued under Official Seal in accord with Article 48 (*Member Records*) of the most sacred Covenant *Pactum De Singularis Caelum*, that attests to the accurate recording of a particular life event being the live birth of a Person; and gives further assurance as to the Ecclesiastical, Moral and Lawful Authority of the Union in the registration of such a life event. Member Live Borne Record

   A Member Live Borne Record relates to the *Proof of Live Birth* of a Ucadia Member as a True Person and a True Trust, possessing certain unalienable Rights as defined by the sacred Covenant *Pactum De Singularis Caelum* and the Constitutional Charter of the Union. Therefore no inferior foreign person, or foreign corporation may claim a superior position in respect of a Ucadia Member as a True Person and a True Trust; and all lesser records of foreign bodies are either a licensed derivative or unlawful, illegal and fraudulent.

   Any Foreign Birth Certificate issued under any presumption, or incomplete (inchoate) information implying that the new born or new person was still born, or property of the state, or chattel, or a slave, or a bastard, or the product of slaves, or a ward of the state shall automatically cause such a foreign record and registration to be null and void *ab initio* (from the beginning) upon such perfidy, deception, moral repugnancy, profanity, sacrilege and heresy against the people of the body politic, the Rule of Law and all civilised history and human decency.

   An Official Copy of a Member Live Borne Record shall only be issued upon the successful completion, review and authorised acceptance of a Member Live Borne Record Application when submitted with any appropriate fees by a suitably qualified Member of the Union.

3. A *Member Birth Certificate Record*, also known simply as a "Birth Certificate", is a Vital Record of the Union, issued under Official Seal, that attests to the accurate recording of a particular life event being the birth of a Person; and gives further assurance as to the Ecclesiastical, Member Birth Certificate

Moral and Lawful Authority of the Union in the registration of such a life event, as underwritten by a valid and legitimate Live Borne Record.

A Member Birth Certificate relates to the *Proof of Birth* of a Ucadia Member as a Superior Person, possessing certain unalienable Rights as defined by the sacred Covenant *Pactum De Singularis Caelum* and the Constitutional Charter of the Union. Therefore no inferior foreign person, or foreign corporation may claim a superior position in respect of a Ucadia Member as a Superior Person; and all lesser records of foreign bodies are either a licensed derivative or unlawful, illegal and fraudulent.

An Official Copy of a Member Birth Certificate Record shall only be issued upon the successful completion, review and authorised acceptance of a Member Birth Certificate Record Application when submitted with any appropriate fees by a suitably qualified Member of the Union.

4. A *Member Promised Land Record*, is a Vital Record of the Union, in accord with Article 48 (*Member Records*) of the most sacred Covenant *Pactum De Singularis Caelum*, that represents the fulfilment of an ancient sacred pledge by the Divine Creator that all Level 6 Life Forms who redeem themselves in recognition of their membership to One Heaven and Ucadia may lawfully assert their Divine Right and own their home in Trust upon the provision of a valid Certificate of Vacant Possession and Occupancy and then a Certificate of Survey and Title.

Member Promised Land Record

A valid Promised Land Record may only be issued to the custody of the appropriate Ucadia Foundation or Campus, Province or University associated with the Member as a right assigned to the particular Member, in accord with the most sacred Covenant *Pactum De Singularis Caelum.*

5. A *Member Identification Certificate*, also known simply as "Official Identification", is an Abstract of certain Records of the Union, issued under Official Seal, that attests to the accurate portrayal and likeness of the photo image, domicile information and signature of an Ordinary Member on the same Document; and grants through an attached *Certificate of Authority*, a limited license and "right of use" to a foreign power to record the existence of the Certificate and the information it contains.

Member Identification Certificate

A Member Identification Certificate shall only be issued upon the successful completion, review and authorised acceptance of a Member Identification Certificate Application when submitted with any appropriate fees by a suitably qualified Member of the Union.

6. A *Member Competency Certificate*, also known simply as "Proof of Competency", is an Abstract of certain Records of the Union, issued under Official Seal, that attests to the competency, training, education or level of skill and abilities of a particular Ordinary Member; and grants through an attached *Certificate of Authority*, a limited license and "right of use" to a foreign power to record the existence of the Certificate and the information it contains; and gives further assurance in the form by way of a *Professional Liability (Insurance) Bond* in the event of any claimed wrong, injury or liability arising as a direct result of the foreign power or agency acknowledging the particular Certificate. Member Competency Certificate

A Member Competency Certificate and associated *Certificate of Authority* and *Professional Liability (Insurance) Bond* shall only be issued upon the successful completion, review and authorised acceptance of a Member Competency Certificate Application when submitted with any appropriate fees by a suitably qualified Member of the Union.

7. A *Member Marriage Certificate*, also known simply as a "Marriage Certificate", is a Vital Record of the Union, issued under Official Seal, that attests to the accurate recording of a particular life event being the lawful union of two Ordinary Members under the Sacred Sacrament of Matrimony (of a man and woman), or Union (of two consenting adults); and gives further assurance as to the Ecclesiastical, Moral and Lawful Authority of the Union in the registration of such a life event. Member Marriage Certificate

A Member Marriage Certificate relates to the *Proof of Unities* of two Ucadia Members as Superior Persons, possessing certain unalienable Rights as defined by the sacred Covenant *Pactum De Singularis Caelum* and the Constitutional Charter of the Union. Therefore no inferior foreign person, or foreign corporation may claim a superior position in respect of such Ucadia Members as Superior Persons; and all lesser records of foreign bodies are either a licensed derivative or unlawful, illegal and fraudulent.

Any Foreign Marriage Certificate issued under any presumption, or incomplete (inchoate) information implying that the persons required a license to marry, or are property of the state, or chattel, or slaves, or bastards, or the product of slaves, or wards of the state shall automatically cause such a foreign record and registration to be null and void *ab initio* (from the beginning) upon such perfidy, deception, moral repugnancy, profanity, sacrilege and heresy against the people of the body politic, the Rule of Law and all civilised history and human decency.

An Official Copy of a Member Marriage Certificate shall only be issued upon the successful completion, review and authorised acceptance of a Member Marriage Certificate Application when submitted with any appropriate fees by a suitably qualified Member of the Union.

8. A *Member Death Certificate*, also known simply as a "Death Certificate", is a Vital Record of the Union, issued under Official Seal, that attests to the accurate recording of a particular life event being the civil and physical death of a Person; and gives further assurance as to the Ecclesiastical, Moral and Lawful Authority of the Union in the registration of such a life event.

Member Death Certificate

A Member Death Certificate relates to the *Proof of Death* of a Ucadia Member as a Superior Person, possessing certain unalienable Rights as defined by the sacred Covenant *Pactum De Singularis Caelum* and the Constitutional Charter of the Union. Therefore no inferior foreign person, or foreign corporation may claim a superior position in respect of a Ucadia Member as a Superior Person; and all lesser records of foreign bodies are either a licensed derivative or unlawful, illegal and fraudulent.

A Member Death Certificate is distinct and separate to any prior written notification or attestation by a competent witness or physician or examiner as to fact of the physical death of the body of a human being. A Member Death Certificate relates to the civil and actual death of a Person connected to the physical body and identity of a deceased human being. Therefore a Member Death Certificate and all forms of death certificates must, by reason of logic, only be issued after clear written evidence is presented from a competent authority as to the physical death of the body of a human being.

Any Foreign Death Certificate or any other instrument issued in such a manner to import, imply or function as a death certificate, particularly for the purpose of probate administration, under any presumption, or incomplete (inchoate) information implying that the deceased person remains the property of the state, or chattel, or a dead slave, or a dead bastard, or the deceased product of slaves, or a deceased ward of the state shall automatically cause such a foreign record and registration to be null and void *ab initio* (from the beginning) upon such perfidy, deception, moral repugnancy, profanity, sacrilege and heresy against the people of the body politic, the Rule of Law and all civilised history and human decency.

An Official Copy of a Member Death Certificate shall only be issued upon the successful completion, review and authorised acceptance of a

Member Death Certificate Application when submitted with any appropriate fees by a suitably qualified Member of the Union.

9. A *Member Driver Certificate*, also known simply as "Operator Certificate" or "Driver Certificate", is an Abstract of certain Records of the Union, issued under Official Seal, that attests to the competency, training, education and level of skill and abilities of a particular Ordinary Member in relation to a specific type of mechanical and motorised equipment, including (but not limited to) bikes, cars, trucks, lorries, boats, ships, planes and jets; and grants through an attached *Certificate of Authority*, a limited license and "right of use" to a foreign power to record the existence of the Certificate and the information it contains; and gives further assurance in the form of a *Public Liability (Insurance) Bond* in the event of any claimed wrong, injury or public liability arising as a direct result in the foreign power or agency acknowledging the particular Certificate. The issue of any potential damage arising to the motor vehicle is covered separately through a Catastrophe (Insurance) Bond associated with the documentation of the vehicle or vessel as part of any Transport Warrant or Travel Warrant. Member Driver Certificate

A Member Driver Certificate and associated Certificate of Authority and Insurance Bond shall only be issued upon the successful completion, review and authorised acceptance of a Member Driver Certificate Application when submitted with any appropriate fees by a suitably qualified Member of the Union.

The Union assures each approved Member issued a Driver Certificate against any loss or injury arising from professional negligence, omission or error through a Professional Insurance (Liability) Bond and that the Union shall make good any claims and charges by an injured party. However, the Union shall not make good any claim or charge in the absence of an injured party, or the automated issuance of fines and penalties, particularly via automated and computerised devices, where evidence of an act of professional negligence, omission or error reasonably exists and no genuine third party exists. Furthermore, any such false claims or charges issued by foreign bodies against a Member possessing a valid Driver Certificate shall be automatically converted into a debt ten times the value of the claim or charge as a Debt of Record owed by the foreign body to the Union in making such false claims or charges. The Union shall then pursue to the fullest extent the recovery of such valid debts by any and all means necessary.

10. A *Member Banking Warrant*, also known simply as "Bankers Warrant", is an Instrument of Authority of the Union, issued under Member Banking

Official Seal, authorising a foreign power or body to issue a Bankers Permit in the name of a Member of the Union; or for a foreign bank or foreign financial institution to open an account in the name of a Member of the Union; and for the foreign power or body or bank to then be granted the right to hold a particular *Completion (Insurance) Bond* of sufficient value, issued by the Union, in trust as insurance and security against any liability, injury, damages or contingency in performance of the Warrant. Warrant

A Member Banking Warrant and associated Bond shall only be issued upon the successful completion, review and authorised acceptance of a Member Banking Warrant Application when submitted with any appropriate fees by a suitably qualified Member of the Union.

11. A *Member Health Warrant*, also known simply as "Health Warrant", is an Instrument of Authority of the Union, issued under Official Seal, authorising a foreign health facility or hospital to provide emergency or elective health care services in the name of a Member of the Union; and for the foreign health facility or hospital to then be granted the right to hold a particular Bond of sufficient value, issued by the Union, in trust as insurance and security against any liability, costs, injury, damages or contingency in performance of the Warrant. Member Health Warrant

A Member Health Warrant and associated Bond shall only be issued upon the successful completion, review and authorised acceptance of a Member Health Warrant Application when submitted with any appropriate fees by a suitably qualified Member of the Union.

12. A *Member Distress Warrant*, also known simply as "Distress Warrant", is an Instrument of Authority of the Union, issued under Official Seal, authorising a foreign law enforcement agency or body to order the taking of goods and chattels out of the possession of a wrong-doer into the custody of the Member of the Union; and for the foreign law enforcement agency or body to then be granted the right to hold a particular Bond of sufficient value, issued by the Union, in trust as insurance and security against any liability, injury, claim, counter damages or contingency in performance of the Warrant. Member Distress Warrant

A Member Distress Warrant and associated Bond shall only be issued upon the successful completion, review and authorised acceptance of a Member Distress Warrant Application when submitted with any appropriate fees by a suitably qualified Member of the Union.

13. A *Member Travel Warrant*, also known simply as "Travel Warrant", is an Instrument of Authority of the Union, issued under Official Seal, authorising a foreign power or body to issue a Travel Permit or other such documentation in the name of a Member of the Union to enable Member Travel Warrant them to travel freely and without impediment upon the land; and for the foreign power or body to then be granted the right to hold a particular Bond of sufficient value, issued by the Union, in trust as insurance and security against any liability, injury, damages or contingency in performance of the Warrant.

A Member Travel Warrant and associated Bond shall only be issued upon the successful completion, review and authorised acceptance of a Member Travel Warrant Application when submitted with any appropriate fees by a suitably qualified Member of the Union.

14. A *Member Passport Warrant*, also known simply as a "Passport", is an Instrument of Authority of the Union, issued under Official Seal, authorising a foreign power or body to issue a Travel Permit or other such documentation in the name of a Member of the Union to enable them to travel freely and without impediment upon the water or in the air and through any port; and for the foreign power or body to then be granted the right to hold a particular Bond of sufficient value, issued by the Union, in trust as insurance and security against any liability, injury, damages or contingency in performance of the Warrant. Member Passport

A Member Passport Warrant and associated Bond shall only be issued upon the successful completion, review and authorised acceptance of a Member Passport Warrant Application when submitted with any appropriate fees by a suitably qualified Member of the Union.

15. A *Member Transport Warrant*, also known simply as a "Transport Warrant", is an Instrument of Authority of the Union, issued under Official Seal, authorising a foreign power or body to issue a Transport or Shipping Permit or other such documentation in the name of a Member of the Union to enable them to safely transport certain goods and services between one destination to another without impediment upon the land, or in water or in the air and through any port; and for the foreign power or body to then be granted the right to hold a particular Bond of sufficient value, issued by the Union, in trust as insurance and security against any liability, injury, damages or contingency in performance of the Warrant. Member Transport Warrant

A Member Transport Warrant and associated Bond shall only be issued upon the successful completion, review and authorised acceptance of a Member Transport Warrant Application when submitted with any appropriate fees by a suitably qualified Member of the Union.

Article 21 – Member Data, Privacy & Disclosure

1. Member Data, Privacy and Disclosure are the rules whereby the Union shall hold data related to members, and management and use such information consistent with the rights of Members and the Union itself.

Member Data Privacy & Disclosure

2. A "**Member Data Advocate**" is a suitably authorised and qualified Trustee granted by a Member sufficient legal rights under Power of Attorney to represent the best interests of a Member and their Data Protection and Data Privacy Rights with any Ucadia Societies and all Non-Ucadian societies.

Member Data Advocate

3. Data and Information created and formed by the Union shall at all times remain the property of the Union; and its use by Members or other parties shall in no way impute or waive such rights of ownership, nor imply any conveyance of such rights, unless the Union or an authorised officer or body explicitly waives such a right, on a case by case basis, consistent with the present Articles.

Data of Union remains property of Union

4. All Members are entitled as Members to the presumption of privacy and non-surveillance, unless clear evidence of one or more breaches of the laws of the Union demands a temporary suspension of such presumptions. Furthermore, all Members are entitled to know how information is collected and used about them and to be informed in a meaningful way as to the frequency and nature of use, unless a temporary condition of security or investigation necessitates such knowledge be reasonably held from disclosure.

Member Right to Privacy

Article 22 – Ordinary Member

1. An Ordinary Member is any living higher order being whose identity is duly registered in the Member Rolls of the Union. An Ordinary Member possesses the right of one (1) Vote upon the redemption of their Membership Number.

   In accordance with the most sacred Covenant *Pactum De Singularis Caelum*, all living men and women are perpetual members of One Heaven and therefore those that are domiciled within the bounds of the Union are *ipso facto* Ordinary Members of the Union as reflected in the General Roll of the Union.

Ordinary Member

2. A man or woman or youth or new born associated with a completed valid registration and was born within the jurisdiction and bounds of the Union, or permanently domiciled within the jurisdiction and bounds of the Union for seven years or more cannot be excluded from being recognised as a valid Ordinary Member.

Non Exclusion of Right to Ordinary Membership

3. An Ordinary Member may demonstrate their consent to being acknowledged as an Ordinary Member of the Union, through the Act of Redemption by redeeming their Membership Number either through association with One Heaven or through the Union itself. Redeemed Ordinary Member

Only Ordinary Members duly recorded as having redeemed their Membership Numbers may participate in voting within the Union and in the use of certain services and benefits of the Union prior to full independence of the Union.

4. A Person may apply to be an Ordinary Member of the Union, or to migrate to a place within the Union upon the grounds of Political, Climactic, Economic, Family Reunification or Business Reasons:- Immigration, Migration and Ordinary Members

(i) *Emergency Migration* is any Migration or Application on the strict basis of Political, Climactic or Economic Reasons. All Emergency Migration is Temporary with the expectation of Repatriation of Applicants after a limited and defined time; and

(ii) *Temporary Migration* is any Migration or Application that is not otherwise permanent; and

(iii) *Permanent Migration* is Migration or Application on the strict basis of Family Reunification, Economic or Business Reasons.

5. Any man or woman domiciled within the bounds of the Union, whether or not they have previously redeemed their Member Number may at any point abjure, reject and revoke their Ordinary Membership to the Union. Abrogation or Revokation of Member

When a man or woman, having demonstrated clearly their will and intent, without disability or incapacity to make such a decision, chooses to abjure, reject and revoke their Ordinary Membership, they become an exile and outcast to the Union and to all Ucadia Societies and may not receive any aid, or support or sustenance or assistance whatsoever, upon their own choice and solemn act.

Furthermore, any and all property or Rights owned, derived, sourced and within the jurisdiction of the Union shall remain wholly within the Ucadia Union and such a man or woman who chooses to abjure or revoke their Ordinary Membership shall abjure, disclaim, disavow and revoke by the same act any claim or right to any and all such Property.

6. An Abjurer or Revoker may seek clemency from the Union in requesting reconciliation by only one of two means of Confession being either Remorse or Incompetence:- Request of reconciliation by Abjurer or Revoker

(i) A ***Confession of Remorse*** is when any Abjurer or Revoker seeking reconciliation and reentry undertakes such a ceremony to withdraw and remove the blight of their previous abjuration and revocation. However, an Abjurer or Revoker may not receive any previous property otherwise disclaimed, surrendered, disavowed and rejected by their previous action; or

(ii) A ***Confession of Incompetence*** is when any Abjurer or Revoker seeking reconciliation and reentry undertakes such a ceremony to withdraw and remove the blight of their previous abjuration and revocation by admitting such an act be evidence of temporary incompetence. As a result, upon any acceptance of re-entry and reconciliation, such property rights may be restored but temporarily held within the guardianship of the society until a proper determination is made that the Ordinary Member is no longer incapacitated by incompetence.

Article 23 – Company Member

1. A Company Member is any association, body, entity, aggregate or partnership duly validated and registered as a Company in the Company Rolls of the Union in accord with the conditions of the present Charter. A Company Member possesses one (1) Vote, while its own members may be recognised as Ordinary Members upon their proper registration in the Member Rolls of the Union.

Company Member

2. Unless otherwise indicated, all services to Companies shall be for the exclusive benefit of Company Members.

Company Member use of Services

3. A Company registration within the Company Rolls of the Union takes precedence over any and all registrations in inferior rolls or registers of Non-Ucadian societies, whether or not the date of registration within the Company Rolls of the Union is at a later Sacred Space-Day-Time than the inferior registration of a Non-Ucadian society.

Precedence of Company Member Registration

4. Notwithstanding the information required as part of any application registration, the essential criteria for acceptance of a valid Company Member is *Permitted Registration, Unique Lawful Company Name, Legal Status, Company Born Date, Company Death Date, Constitution* and *ByLaws*:-

Essential Criteria for acceptance as Company Member

(i) *Permitted Registration* is that the Founders or Directors are not banned from holding such office or registering a Company and that such a Company is not banned or forbidden from registration; and

(ii) *Unique Lawful Company Name* is a valid and unique Company Name that does not infringe upon the rights, trademarks, patents and property of the Union or its valid subsidiaries, nor upon the pre-existing Company Members nor a name which is illegal and forbidden; and

(iii) *Legal Status* being the clear identification of the type of Company consistent with Ucadian Law then reflected within its foundation documents; and

(iv) *Company Born Date* being the clear date the founders of the Company first met in session and agreed to the founding principles and objects of the Company, as evidenced in its founding documents; and

(v) *Company Death Date* being the clear date of death at which the Company shall cease to exist, consistent with the type and Legal Status of the Company in accord with Ucadian law; and

(vi) *Constitution* being the founding principles and objects of the Company consistent with Ucadia Law, identifying its Organs and Purposes for existence; and

(vii) *ByLaws* are any ByLaws of the Company consistent with Ucadia Law as permitted by its Constitution. If no ByLaws are provided, then the Codes of the Union shall take first precedence as the default ByLaws.

5. Notwithstanding the Criminal Code of the Union and other Laws, Statutes and Regulations, a Company shall be forbidden from being duly registered if it engages in, or seeks to engage in any of the following objects, activities or practices being P*erfidious, Malevolent, Perverse* and *Repugnant*:- Banned or Forbidden Objects of Company

(i) *Perfidious* means any object, activity or practice which seeks to deliberately and intentionally cause harm to Ucadia, the Union or any Ucadia Societies, or its laws and systems or to injure, steal, threaten, the property, rights, copyright, trademarks and uses of Ucadia and the Union and any Ucadian Society; and

(ii) *Malevolent* means any object, activity or practice which seeks to deliberately and intentionally cause physical harm to others, particularly other members, or to promote hate-speech, or hostility, or venomous, or vicious, or vindictive, or vengeful behaviour against others, particularly upon racist, or bigotry based philosophies; and

(iii) *Perverse* means any object, activity or practice which seeks to deliberately and intentionally degrade, corrupt or deliberately obscure the accepted norms and bounds of decent moral behaviour within society, particularly in activities which target the young or vulnerable or seek to develop an unhealthy or negative dependence or negative self-image or addiction for then taking advantage of such artificially constructed dependence or self-image; and

(iv) *Repugnant* means any object, activity or practice which seeks to deliberately and intentionally promote repulsive, disgusting, offensive or averse information or activities in public.

6. The Union shall reserve the right to maintain a list of corporations and companies banned and forbidden from seeking registration based upon such entities being ill-suited and contrary in law to be recognised.

Exclusion of Banned and Illegal Corporate Entities

The entry of such companies or corporations must be based on justice and fair process, with any and all companies having the right to appeal. Furthermore, no ban may be permanent beyond ten years and therefore every ban must be renewed and the basis of such forbiddance re-investigated as to its efficacy.

Article 24 – Society Member

1. A Society Member is any non-profit, religious, social, body politic or fraternal association duly validated and registered as a Society in the Society Rolls of the Union in accord with the conditions of the present Charter.

Society Member

A Society Member possesses one (1) Vote, while its own members may be recognised as Ordinary Members upon their proper registration in the Member Rolls of the Union.

A Society Member is distinct from a State Member in that a Society is a recognised body wholly functioning within the bounds and laws of Ucadia and the present Charter.

2. Unless otherwise indicated, all services to Societies shall be for the exclusive benefit of Society Members.

Society Member use of Services

3. A Society registration within the Society Rolls of the Union takes precedence over any and all registrations in inferior rolls or registers of Non-Ucadian societies, whether or not the date of registration within the Society Rolls of the Union is at a later Sacred Space-Day-Time than the inferior registration of a Non-Ucadian society.

Precedence of Society Member Registration

4. Notwithstanding the information required as part of any application registration, the essential criteria for acceptance of a valid Society Member is *Permitted Registration, Unique Lawful Society Name, Legal Status, Society Born Date, Society Death Date, Constitution* and

Essential Criteria for acceptance as Society Member

ByLaws:-

(i) *Permitted Registration* is that the Founders or Directors are not banned from holding such office or registering a Society and that such a Society is not banned or forbidden from registration; and

(ii) *Unique Lawful Society Name* is a valid and unique Society Name that does not infringe upon the rights, trademarks, patents and property of the Union or its valid subsidiaries, nor upon the pre-existing Society Members nor a name which is illegal and forbidden; and

(iii) *Legal Status* being the clear identification of the type of Society consistent with Ucadian Law then reflected within its foundation documents; and

(iv) *Society Born Date* being the clear date the founders of the Society first met in session and agreed to the founding principles and objects of the Society, as evidenced in its founding documents; and

(v) *Society Death Date* being the clear date of death at which the Society shall cease to exist, consistent with the type and Legal Status of the Society in accord with Ucadian law; and

(vi) *Constitution* being the founding principles and objects of the Society consistent with Ucadia Law, identifying its Organs and Purposes for existence; and

(vii) *ByLaws* are any ByLaws of the Society consistent with Ucadia Law as permitted by its Constitution. If no ByLaws are provided, then the Codes of the Union shall take first precedence as the default ByLaws.

5. The Rights of Society Members are those Rights of Use granted to valid registered Society Members as defined by the present Constitutional Charter including (but not limited to) *Laws, Jurisdiction, Participation, Representation, Services* and *Finance*:- Rights of Society Members

(i) *Laws* means a Society Member is granted the right to use and apply the laws and systems of Ucadia in the governance of its own Members in accord with the conditions of such use as prescribed by the present Charter; and

(ii) *Jurisdiction* means a Society Member is able to seek the benefit of the Jurisdiction and superior position of Ucadia societies and Ucadia law in comparison to inferior systems and those structures without proper Rule of Law; and

(iii) *Participation* means a Society Member may participate in the voting and open, equal and fair process of seeking consent, direction, voting and governance of the Union; and

(iv) *Representation* means the elected leaders of a Society Member, being granted status as Ordinary Members may participate in elections, even in the registration of political parties for representation in official capacity within the electoral framework of the Union; and

(v) *Services* means a Society Member may utilise and enjoy those services provided to Society Members and Members at large; and

(vi) *Finance* means a Society Member may participate in the Ucadia Financial System, including (but not limited to) financial assistance and support to enable the society to achieve its objects and the objects of its members.

Society Member Rolls and Ucadia Member Rolls

6. The Society Member Rolls are those rolls, registers and records of a Society Member in contrast to the Member Rolls and Registers of the Union and other valid Ucadia societies. It is a fundamental condition of acceptance of any application to become a Society Member that the leadership and members of the said society accept the superior jurisdiction of Ucadia. Notwithstanding and further rules and regulations, the following principles shall apply with respect to the rolls and member records of any society being accepted as a Society Member:-

(i) *No Transfer of Ownership* means unless a society explicitly states it to be so, there is no transfer of ownership in respect of the member rolls of a society to Ucadia or the Union or vice versa as part of the registration process. The society retains its rights of ownership to its own members and such information after such valid registration as before; and

(ii) *Dual Membership of Ordinary Members* means that all members of the society upon approval of registration as a Society Member become dual redeemed members of Ucadia as Redeemed Ordinary Members. Therefore, the Society Member is required to periodically provide an extract of member rolls to provide such dual membership. The Union shall forbid secrecy, particularly in such key services as voting so the refusal or failure to enable members to be considered dual members shall preclude a society from being a valid Society Member; and

(iii) *Prescribed Contact* means that contact to dual members of the Society shall only be in accord with those services and activities as prescribed by the present Charter.

7. Notwithstanding the Criminal Code of the Union and other Laws, Statutes and Regulations, a Society shall be forbidden from being duly registered if it engages in, or seeks to engage in any of the following objects, activities or practices being *Perfidious, Malevolent, Perverse, Repugnant* and *Recalcitrant*:- Banned or Forbidden Objects of Society

(i) *Perfidious* means any object, activity or practice which seeks to deliberately and intentionally cause harm to Ucadia, the Union or any Ucadia Societies, or its laws and systems or to injure, steal, threaten, the property, rights, copyright, trademarks and uses of Ucadia and the Union and any Ucadian Society; and

(ii) *Malevolent* means any object, activity or practice which seeks to deliberately and intentionally cause physical harm to others, particularly other members, or to promote hate-speech, or hostility, or venomous, or vicious, or vindictive, or vengeful behaviour against others, particularly upon racist, or bigotry based philosophies; and

(iii) *Perverse* means any object, activity or practice which seeks to deliberately and intentionally degrade, corrupt or deliberately obscure the accepted norms and bounds of decent moral behaviour within society, particularly in activities which target the young or vulnerable or seek to develop an unhealthy or negative dependence or negative self-image or addiction for then taking advantage of such artificially constructed dependence or self-image; and

(iv) *Repugnant* means any object, activity or practice which seeks to deliberately and intentionally promote repulsive, disgusting, offensive or averse information or activities in public ; and

(v) *Recalcitrant* means any object, activity or practice which seeks to deliberately obstruct, delay, impede and defeat the principle obligations of Society Membership (such as the provision of member details for dual membership or other reporting information prescribed by law) without legal or just cause.

8. No Society Member once accepted as a full member of the Union shall be permitted to be expelled or excluded from the Union, even when the Executive Government of the society openly defies the primary of clauses of this Charter, unless they are seen to actively participate in banned and forbidden objects, activities and purposes without Society Member Exclusion recourse.

Instead, the Executive of the Union shall have such rights and powers to restrict the membership rights and economic rights bestowed under this Charter until such time that the society who is in breach of its obligations has willingly agreed to restore proper law and function.

This clause is in recognition of the inherent respect and honour bestowed to all the peoples of the Union that while they may be sometimes ill governed, it must never be an action of the Union to exclude the citizens of any society from their due rights to be recognised as part of the Union.

Furthermore, in knowing that a society may in no way have its membership revoked by this Constitutional Charter, it compels both the Executive Government of the Union and the state in breach to seek some resolution beyond acts of extreme isolation and provocation.

Article 25 – State Member

1. A State Member is any existing body politic, country, territory or nation properly recognised by International Law as a sovereign body politic, country, territory or nation and duly validated and registered as a State in the State Rolls of the Union in accord with the conditions of the present Charter. A State Member duly recognised and accepted assumes the permanent government and authority of either a Ucadia University and all subdivisions or a Ucadia Province and all subdivisions upon ratification. State Member

   A State Member is distinct from a Society Member in that a State is a recognised body functioning primarily according to its own body of laws and customs and secondly within the bounds and laws of Ucadia and the present Charter through amity, mutual recognition and treaty. A body not recognised as an existing body politic, country, territory or nation properly recognised by International Western-Roman Law may be registered as a Society Member of Ucadia.

2. A State Member may register as a Primary (State) Member if they are named according to the Constitutional Charter as a Primary Member. A State Member may only be a Primary Member of just one Ucadia Regional Union. Primary and Axillary State Member Registration

   A State Member may register as an Auxiliary (State) Member if they are named according to the Constitutional Charter as an Axillary Member. A State Member may only be an Auxiliary Member of just one Ucadia Regional Union providing: (a) The University is not one of the twenty largest economies; and (b) The University shares both a common cultural and geographic bond with the region.

3. A State registration within the State Rolls of the Union takes precedence over any and all registrations in inferior rolls or registers of Non-Ucadian societies, whether or not the date of registration within the State Rolls of the Union is at a later Sacred Space-Day-Time than the inferior registration of a Non-Ucadian State, given the acceptance of a valid State Member is the acceptance of the permanent and valid government of a Ucadia University or Ucadia Province; and where such a state is already recognised as a sovereign and independent state of the same bounds by international and Western-Roman law and a probational government is in place for the said Ucadia University or Ucadia Province.

Precedence of State Member Registration

Where a permanent government for the Ucadia University or Ucadia Province exists, the ratification of the State Member shall see the requirement of elections to coincide with both bodies for their proper alignment as all members become dual members and therefore Ordinary Members of Ucadia.

4. The Rights of State Members are those Rights of Use granted to valid registered State Members as defined by the present Charter including (but not limited to) *Laws, Jurisdiction, Participation, Representation, Services* and *Finance*:-

Rights of State Members

(i) *Laws* means a State Member is granted the right to use and apply the laws and systems of Ucadia in the governance of its own Members in accord with the conditions of such use as prescribed by the present Charter; and

(ii) *Jurisdiction* means a State Member is able to seek the benefit of the Jurisdiction and superior position of Ucadia societies and Ucadia law in comparison to inferior systems and those structures without proper Rule of Law; and

(iii) *Participation* means a State Member may participate in the voting and open, equal and fair process of seeking consent, direction, voting and governance of the Union; and

(iv) *Representation* means the elected leaders of a State Member, being granted status as Ordinary Members of the Union as the leadership of a University or Province with its existing legislative and administrative subdivisions also being recognised as the valid Ucadian subdivisions of Provinces or Campuses respectively; and

(v) *Services* means a State Member may utilise and enjoy those services provided to State Members and Members at large; and

(vi) *Finance* means a State Member may participate in the Ucadia Financial System, including (but not limited to) financial assistance and support to enable the State to achieve its objects and the objects of its members and in particular access to the account established for the permanent Universities and Provinces of the Union.

5. Notwithstanding the Criminal Code of the Union and other Laws, Statutes and Regulations, a State shall be forbidden from being duly registered if it engages in, or seeks to engage in any of the following objects, activities or practices being *Perfidious, Malevolent, Perverse, Repugnant* and *Recalcitrant*:-

Banned or Forbidden Objects of State

(i) *Perfidious* means any object, activity or practice which seeks to deliberately and intentionally cause harm to Ucadia, the Union or any Ucadia Societies, or its laws and systems or to injure, steal, threaten, the property, rights, copyright, trademarks and uses of Ucadia and the Union and any Ucadian State; and

(ii) *Malevolent* means any object, activity or practice which seeks to deliberately and intentionally cause physical harm to others, particularly other members, or to promote hate-speech, or hostility, or venomous, or vicious, or vindictive, or vengeful behaviour against others, particularly upon racist, or bigotry based philosophies; and

(iii) *Perverse* means any object, activity or practice which seeks to deliberately and intentionally degrade, corrupt or deliberately obscure the accepted norms and bounds of decent moral behaviour within a society of the Union, particularly in activities which target the young or vulnerable or seek to develop an unhealthy or negative dependence or negative self-image or addiction for then taking advantage of such artificially constructed dependence or self-image; and

(iv) *Repugnant* means any object, activity or practice which seeks to deliberately and intentionally promote repulsive, disgusting, offensive or averse information or activities in public; and

(v) *Recalcitrant* means any object, activity or practice which seeks to deliberately obstruct, delay, impede and defeat the principle obligations of State Membership (such as the provision of member details for dual membership or other reporting information prescribed by law) without legal or just cause.

6. No State Member once accepted as a full member of the Union shall be permitted to be expelled or excluded from the Union, even when the

State Member Exclusion

Executive Government of the member state openly defies the primary of clauses of this Charter, unless they are seen to actively participate in banned and forbidden objects, activities and purposes without recourse.

Instead, the Executive of the Union shall have such rights and powers to restrict the membership rights and economic rights bestowed under this Charter until such time that the member state who is in breach of its obligations has willingly agreed to restore proper law and function.

This clause is in recognition of the inherent respect and honour bestowed to all the peoples of the Union that while they may be sometimes ill governed, it must never be an action of the Union to exclude the citizens of any member nation from their due rights to be recognised as part of the Union.

Furthermore, in knowing that a member state may in no way have its membership revoked by this Charter, it compels both the Executive Government of the Union and the state in breach to seek some resolution beyond acts of extreme isolation and provocation.

7. While a State Member may not be expelled for any reason, a member state retains the absolute right to voluntarily resign from the Union, providing such action is lawful under its charter, that it is supported by two-thirds of the total eligible voting population, free from political intimidation and voting irregularities. Voluntary Resignation from the Union

Where such conditions have been met, the Executive Government and all agencies are instructed to undertake a comprehensive and clear process to disengage that member state from its obligations to the Union as well as withdraw all rights, title, property and privileges of membership according to the will of the free people of the State.

Where such conditions of voluntary resignation have not been met, then by this Charter such unilateral acts of a national executive government to resign from the Union shall be considered an illegitimate and illegal act in contravention of the will of the people of the member state. Where such an action occurs, the Executive Government by this clause is obliged to notify the Executive Government of the member state that their request is denied.

Article 26 – Member Dispute & Arbitration

1. All Members and all types of Members of the Union are subject first and at all times to the articles of the present Charter and all approved and valid laws of the Union. Members subject to laws of the Union

The operation of the laws of the Union in relation to member discipline shall always operate on the Golden Rule of Law and Supreme Confession of Law and therefore the principles of the presumption of innocence, the right to fair justice, rules of evidence and the conditional right of appeal.

2. By the present Constitutional Charter, an offence shall be any act or intended act by an individual or group that willingly contravenes the present Constitutional Charter and any subsequent laws having been ratified and upheld by the appropriate branches of the Union.

Offences against the Union

A Member may only face disciplinary action if the action is listed as an offence and a suit brought to hearing. By this Constitutional Charter, two broad classes of alleged offences shall exist:-

(i) Offences explicitly listed in the present Constitutional Charter, which may or may not result in automatic suspension of certain rights; and

(ii) Offences as defined by valid laws enacted and upheld by the appropriate branches of the Union.

3. The Union has first and higher claim of jurisdiction for all of its members against any claims of offences that may be brought against a member by an alternate Non-Ucadian Society.

Offences against an alternate Society

When any alleged offence is listed against a member of an alternate Non-Ucadian society, an equivalent suit must be initiated within the Courts of the Union to enable the Society to hear the allegations against the Society Member. All evidence and material held by the Non-Ucadian society must then be relinquished to the higher jurisdiction for review.

When a Union court has a matter listed for review and hearing against one or more allegations against a member, no Non-Ucadian society has any jurisdiction to usurp such authority and must yield to the higher jurisdiction.

However, should a suit fail to be created of equivalent charges and allegations by a Union court in a timely manner enabling the matter to be heard and resolved, then both the society and the member yield the claim of higher jurisdiction to the inferior Non-Ucadian society.

As a matter of law and justice, all allegations must be heard and resolved no matter what society they are issued. The quashing of a charge in one court of a Non-Ucadian society and jurisdiction does not automatically mean the matter cannot or should not be heard and resolved satisfactorily by the law within a court of the Union.

4. All members have the right to a fair appeal in accordance with the

Right to hearing

rules and procedures of the Union. and appeal

5. Where the government of a Ucadia University or Province is found to be in direct breach of an article of the present Charter and upon written notification has failed to indicate either a willingness to comply, or has failed to make necessary steps to comply within 120 days, it shall be a requirement of the government of the Union to pass such legislation that disciplines the member state as way of punishment for the non compliance. Disciplinary action against government of Ucadia University or Province

In the framing of such punitive actions, the government of the Union must make every effort to see that diplomatic representations are exhausted first before any economic action is considered.

Action to expel the government of a University or Province from the Union is expressly forbidden under this Charter and any such illegal act or motion shall be immediately deemed null and void, even if such action has the vote and support of other members.

6. While the Union by its legal status holds primacy over its members in relation to the articles of the present Charter, the sovereignty of University Society is without contest. Therefore any punitive action proposed against a member state that is in direct breach of one or more of the articles of this Charter must not consider military action as a course, unless it relates specifically to one of the following criteria:- Military action

(i) That an act of genocide against significant numbers of citizens of the member state is currently being undertaken with the knowing support of the Executive Government and that the Executive Government has refused to halt such actions after all other measures have been exhausted; or

(ii) That a coup has occurred removing a legitimately and duly elected Executive Government from power and that such leaders of the coup have refused after repeated requests to return democratic and legitimate rule to the people of the member state; or

(iii) That the law and order of the member state has failed to such an extent that the basic rule of law and institutions of civil society have broken or unable to operate properly.

Article 27 – Member Sanction & Discipline

1. Competent Members, by definition, are expected to be knowledgeable as to the expectations of Members; and sufficiently self-disciplined in ethical and proper behaviour for Members; and suitably capable in critical thinking by Members of the Union. Therefore, it is first and foremost the responsibility of Competent Members for their good conduct and the avoidance of errors, omissions and potential offences against the Union; and not for the Union to necessarily enforce or impose standards upon Members. Responsibility of Members

2. As it is first and foremost the responsibility of Competent Members for their own good conduct and the avoidance of errors, omissions, or injury against the present Constitutional Charter or the good name and standards of the Union, the Union shall extend the notion of Trust and Self-Accountability to all Members, whereby it is a prime responsibility for each and every Member to be self accountable and to confess if they feel they have committed an offence. It is then an obligation of the Union to mitigate any form of censure or penalty based upon such self accountability, whilst being mindful that the remorse and willingness of the Member not to repeat such an offence and to learn from such error is the key priority. Operation of Trust and Self Accountability

3. The right of Members to be secure in their persons, houses, papers, and effects, against unreasonable searches and seizures, shall not be violated; and no warrants shall issue but upon probable cause, supported by oath or affirmation, and particularly describing the place to be searched and the persons or things to be seized. Safety and Security of Members

4. No person shall be held to answer for a capital or otherwise infamous crime, unless on a presentment or indictment of a grand jury, except in cases arising in times of emergency, war or public danger; nor shall any person be subject for the same offence to be twice put in jeopardy of life or limb; nor be compelled, in any criminal case, to be a witness against himself; nor be deprived of life, liberty, or property without due process of law; nor shall private property be taken for public use, without just compensation. Indictments

5. In all criminal prosecutions the accused shall enjoy the right to a speedy and public trial, by an impartial jury of the State and district wherein the crime shall have been committed, which district shall have been previously ascertained by law, and to be informed of the nature and cause of the accusation; to be confronted with the witnesses against him; to have compulsory process for obtaining witnesses in his favour; and to have the assistance of counsel for his defence. Trial by Jury

6. In suits at law, where the value in controversy shall exceed one Right to Trial by

thousand Union Ucadia Moneta, the right of trial by jury shall be preserved; and no fact so tried by a jury shall be otherwise reexamined in any court of the Union, other than according to the rules of law. Jury

7. Excessive bail shall not be required, nor excessive fines imposed, nor cruel and unusual punishments inflicted. Against Excessive Bail

Article 28 – Member Suspension & Interdiction

1. Member Suspension is where one or more services may be suspended, turned off or disabled in respect of a Member. Member Suspension may be a form of Penalty, or Punishment or mandatory in light of an accusation and hearing concerning a serious offence. Member Suspension

While it is forbidden to expel a Member, a Member can nonetheless be punished for acts of Perfidy and other serious offences through Suspension whereby services and privileges are suspended.

2. Punishment is reserved solely for Members that are found to have committed serious offences against the Union and have openly and deliberately breached the Trust of other Members by failing to be Self Accountable and accurately confess their offences. Punishment therefore, always assumes a level of fraudulent and untruthful behaviour has been found against the Member. Punishment may only be issued by a properly constituted Court of the Union in accord with these Articles. Punishment

The Union is the First and Primary Court of Original Jurisdiction for any and every alleged offence or accusation against a Member, whether such allegations are derived within a Ucadia community or a foreign body or society. It is a rule that all serious accusations must be resolved and therefore, whenever an accusation is based within a Ucadia community or a foreign body against a Member, an Issue Number must be raised, following the proper recording of the alleged offence. Therefore, no foreign body, or foreign court may claim to ever be a Court of Original Jurisdiction against a Member of the Union.

TITLE III: OFFICES AND OFFICERS

Article 29 - Office

1. An "**Office**" is recognised as a form of *Sacred Circumscribed Space*, Position and Title given life, recognition and personality through the power and authority of *Officium* in accord with the most sacred Covenant *Pactum De Singularis Caelum*. An Office does not exist, nor possess any validity or legitimacy unless granted *Officium*. Furthermore, no legitimate or valid authority or power exists, without first the existence of valid Office. Office

2. In accord with the most sacred Covenant *Pactum De Singularis Caelum*, there exists only four (4) valid types of Office being Divine, True, Superior and Inferior:- Four types of Office

   (i) A "**Divine Office**" is an Office of One Heaven; and

   (ii) A "**True Office**" is an instance of *Sacred Circumscribed Space* in the form of the Great Divine Office of Man or the Great Divine Office of Woman as defined by the Divine Creator, whereby each and every Living Member is invested and commissioned from the time of their physical birth until their physical death. Therefore, a True Office can never be usurped, seized, sold or stolen; and

   (iii) A "**Superior Office**" is an instance of Sacred Circumscribed Space in the form of a Great Divine Office within a valid Ucadia Community, as formed through its identification and definition within an instrument, agreement, covenant or document given existence by law or regulation according to the present Constitutional Charter; and

   (iv) An "**Inferior Office**" is a non-Ucadian office or "Pseudo Office"; and are all non-Ucadian positions whereby a defective or inferior Oath or Vow has been offered, or no Oath provided or where the fiduciary obligations have been abrogated in favour of agent and commercial advantages. All Non-Ucadian Offices, including all claimed Ecclesiastical Offices are Inferior Offices and "Pseudo Offices".

3. The foundation of all civilised rule of law, begins with the acknowledgement that the highest law comes from the Divine Creator of all things in the Universe expressed through the laws of the Universe and then through the reason and spirit of man and woman to make Positive Laws. Valid Office and Divine Law

   An Office by definition is a form of movable or immovable *Sacred Circumscribed Space* in which is held certain rights, authorities, capacities and powers, conferred upon one who has pronounced one or more Oaths or Vows and Sacraments and preserved by their continued honour to the fiduciary principles of good faith, good actions and good conscience. One who holds an Office under such fiduciary capacity is called an Officer. An Agent can never legitimately hold an Office.

As all rights and property are by definition sacred, all clerical and professional obligations and responsibilities in relation to the administration, transference and conveyance of any rights or property must be concluded in a valid Office. Any and every transaction or claimed transference or conveyance of property or rights must be concluded within the sacred space and place of a valid Office to have ecclesiastical, moral, lawful and legal force and effect.

By definition, the authority, rights and powers of a Divine Office is superior to any and all other forms of Office, regardless of title or claimed status. No Inferior Office possesses any power, force, authority, right or ability to abrogate or usurp the decisions or authority of a Divine Office. Similarly, no Superior Office or Inferior Office possesses any force, authority, right or ability to abrogate or usurp the authority of a True Office to exercise any of the Natural Rights granted to it, unless the occupant of a True Office wilfully and deliberately repudiates the Golden Rule of Law and all forms of logic, reason and sense.

Furthermore, as the very meaning and purpose of the word "authority" is ecclesiastical, all legitimate authority of all officials of all valid governments of all societies on planet Earth depends upon the acknowledgement and recognition that all authority is ultimately derived from the most sacred Covenant *Pactum De Singularis Caelum* as the highest source of authority being the perfect expression of Divine Law of the Divine Creator of all things in the Universe.

4. There are sixteen (16) essential types of valid *Sacred Circumscribed Space* of Office for the conduct and conclusion of sacred, clerical and professional obligations and responsibilities being: Sanctuary, Oratory, Consistory, Sacristy, Penitentiary, Chancery, Depository, Dispensary, Treasury, Ministry, Registry, Library, Notary, Secretary, Vestry and Rectory:- Types of valid Sacred Circumscribed Space of Office

(i) A "**Sanctuary**" is any temporary or permanent sacred space (dimension) circumscribed by the performance of one or more valid Sacraments of Heaven. All valid sacred space (dimension) as an Office is first and foremost a Sanctuary; and

(ii) An "**Oratory**" is any valid Office that exists for the auricular exposition, discussion, relation, examination, disposition and conclusion of matters derived from Divine Law, Ecclesiastical Law and Positive Law and from which all other Offices in which the spoken word of Men and Women is translated to writing or vice versa is derived; and

(iii) A "**Consistory**" is any valid Office that exists for a solemn and sacred assembly or council or other democratic or representative body; and

(iv) A "**Sacristy**" is any valid Office that exists for the receiving and safe keeping of most sacred vessels, books, vestments and may also be used by clergy as valid Trustees for worship or meetings; and

(v) A "**Penitentiary**" is any valid Office that exists for the receiving and safe keeping of sacred vows, confessions, absolutions, dispensations and examinations of conscience and may also be used by clergy as valid Trustees for providing sanctuary and sustenance to penitents confessed; and

(vi) A "**Chancery**" (also Chancellery) is any valid Office that exists for the receiving and safe keeping all original instruments, registers, memoranda, forms and rolls and for the original creation of new forms and instruments by valid Trustees as Scriveners as well as the provision of certified and valid extracts of original instruments and records; and

(vii) A "**Depository**" is any valid Office that exists for the purpose of receiving the temporary assignment of goods and property for safe keeping, or security, or bailment or warehousing upon the issue of receipts and to be returned upon expiry of such conditions; and

(viii) A **Dispensary** is any valid Office that exists for the purpose of dispensing, or settling, or resolving, or exchanging, or measuring, or paying, or issuing or trading property, goods or rights; and

(ix) A "**Treasury**" is any valid Office that exists for the purpose of receiving and keeping safe any and all property that has been salvaged or claimed or surrendered upon being abandoned, lost (presumed dead), incapacitated, infirm or intestate; and

(x) A "**Ministry**" is any valid Office that exists for conducting sacred, clerical and professional obligations and responsibilities and the dispensation and determination of questions of rights and property; and

(xi) A "**Registry**" is a valid Office that exists for the recording of entries, enrolments and events into Books, Registers, Rolls, Memoranda, Accounts and Manifests and the subsequent issue of Certificates, or Receipts as well as the administrative management of Journals, Ledgers and Summaries; and

(xii) A "**Library**" is a valid Office that exists for the recording, entry, safe keeping of copies and acknowledgement and evidence of service and publication of all official Notices, Books, Gazettes, Newspapers, References, Periodicals as well as Audio Visual Material as well as other claimed works of copyright; and

(xiii) A "**Notary**" is a valid Office that exists for the purpose of recording, entry, safe keeping of copies and acknowledgement and evidence of service of official Notices as well as the safe keeping and custody "in due course" of all "public" originals and proofs of any surrender, gift, waiver, abandonment, resignation, novation of property or rights by the Trustor through Deed or Act such as wills, affidavits, land and property conveyances; and

(xiv) A "**Secretary**" is a valid Office that exists for the purpose of the private recording, entry, safe keeping of copies and acknowledgement and evidence of service of Official Notices, Claims and Rights and the "secret surrender" and "passing" of such private material to other parties as required or demanded; and

(xv) A "**Vestry**" is a valid Office that exists for the purpose of recording and keeping safe the essential records of a Parish or Parochial body for proper spiritual administration of members, otherwise referred to as the "Cure of Souls"; and

(xvi) A "**Rectory**" is a valid Office that exists for providing teaching and instruction to students.

Appointment to Office

5. In accord with the most sacred Covenant *Pactum De Singularis Caelum* being the highest rule of law concerning the valid appointment and function of Office, every and all valid appointments, commissions or investitures to Office must comply with the rite of Investiture.

Investiture is one of thirty-three (33) valid Sacred Gifts of Heaven granted and administered through the formal ceremony of the formal bestowal or presentation of a possessory or prescriptive right of Office to an incumbent, including taking possession of the insignia of Office and the power of *Officium* in accordance with the present Constitutional Charter and associated covenants.

All candidates, who seek to occupy an office legitimately must do so under documented proof of one or more oaths of office whereby they acknowledge the supremacy of Heaven, agree to be bound to honour and upholding the Rule of Law and finally to impartially, fairly and equally serve the interests of their community or Society or Members.

Under Investiture, a successful candidate is granted a sacred commission as a Trustee to lawfully occupy an appropriate Office.

All Members who are granted the same Office are equal to the same Office, with none higher and none lower. By the present Article, when one of the same Office speaks as one, the one speaks for all of the same Office. When one of the same Office calls for assistance, all from the same Office are obliged to assist their fellow Officer and when the highest good standing of an Officer is injured, all Officers and the Divine Law and all Law has been injured by such disrespect.

Article 30 - Officer

1. An "**Officer**" is a Trustee granted a sacred commission through the Rite of Investiture to occupy a valid Office. Only valid Trustees are Officers. All Officers of the Union are by default Trustees and bound under their sacred oath to perform in accord with the norms of good faith, good actions and good conscience. No person may occupy or hold Office, except by an Oath to Office as prescribed herein. *(Officer)*

2. The number of additional Officers of the Union shall depend upon the direction of the Synod, in accordance with the present Constitutional Charter. *(Officers of the Union)*

3. All appointments of Officers are to be made on the terms and conditions and at the remuneration (whether by way of salary, fee, commission, participation in profits or otherwise) that the Directors thinks fit and are subject to termination at the pleasure of the Directors. *(Remuneration and Terms of Appointment)*

4. In reference to Officers:- *(Trustee Office)*

   (i) The origin of the concept of Trustee and the fact that such an Officer cannot hold an Office except under sacred Oath and Vow is as old as the origin of civilised society and law itself; and has been one of the most constant concepts of law throughout every age and era; and

   (ii) The concept of Trustee is founded on the most basic principle that a Person cannot legitimately possess the Rights or Property of others, unless they demonstrate the most exemplary and scrupulous characters of good faith, good actions and good conscience; and

(iii) Any repudiation of these fundamental concepts is the repudiation of the Rule of Law and law itself; and

(iv) In the absence of a valid Oath and Vow, no legitimate or valid occupation of an Office may exist.

5. A valid Officer may be temporarily or permanently appointed to an Office under the circumstances of Foundation, Death, Abandonment, Resignation, Refusal or Contestation of the Office by another:- Appointment of Officer

(i) *Foundation* is when a new Office is formed and an Officer as Trustee is appointed in accordance with the Instrument or Covenant for the first time; or

(ii) *Death* is when an existing Officer dies and a vacancy is declared; or

(iii) *Abandonment* is when an existing Officer is away from the domicile of the Office for more than two (2) years without word or adequate response and so a surrogate Trustee must be appointed to the Office; or

(iv) *Resignation* is when an existing Officer applies for resignation of duties of Office, creating a Vacancy; or

(v) *Refusal* is when an existing Officer as Trustee refuses to act in the manner and characteristics required of such Office; or

(vi) *Contestation* is when the competency or legitimacy of an Officer is challenged and upheld by a Competent Forum of Law before three Justices, requiring the resignation of the Officer.

6. When a Person who claims to be an Officer, but evidence exists of one or more of the following elements, then such a person is an impostor with no such commission to Office or Trust existing:- Invalid Officer

(i) Where a Person belongs to a religion, religious rite, society, institute, entity or order that continues to perform any formal or sacred ritual to repudiate Oaths or Vows made in the past or into the future in direct contradiction to the present Constitutional Charter; or

(ii) Where a Person belongs to a religion, religious rite, society, institute, entity or order that continues to require the making of one or more Oaths or Vows that are contradictory to the Golden Rule and Rule of Law, Justice and Due Process and the present Constitutional Charter; or

(iii) Where a Person claiming to be an Officer refuses to produce their Oath or Vow of Office or evidence of their commission; or

(iv) Where a Person has clearly and unequivocally breached trust and demonstrated behaviour that is repugnant, malicious, perfidous or injurous against the law.

Legal Requirement of Oath to be Trustee

7. No judge, magistrate or justice of the peace as a proper Jurist may adjudicate any matter of Law within a competent forum of Law or oratory unless they are presently a valid Trustee under Oath and secondly prepared to demonstrate under Oath the exemplary characteristics of a valid Trustee or valid Fiduciary:-

(i) As a valid Oath is required to create and maintain the Office of judge, or magistrate or justice of the peace, the absence of a valid Oath of Office means such a person is the worst kind of impostor and without any legitimacy whatsoever; and

(ii) As any adjudication concerning rights or property requires exemplary character, any judge, magistrate or justice of the peace that is unwilling or refuses to be entrusted under Oath by all parties to perform in good faith, good actions and good conscience is not a valid Fiduciary; and

(iii) The disregard to such fundamental principles may be properly construed as a formal and official admission of the absence of any proper Rule of Law, Justice or Due Process.

Cessation of Trustee

8. The commission as an Officer and Trustee ceases:-

(i) At the dissolution or satisfaction or termination or cessation or annulment of the Trust; or

(ii) Upon the Death of the Trustee; or

(iii) Abandonment, when a Trustee is away from the domicile of the Trust for more than two (2) years without word or adequate response; or

(iv) Resignation, when a Trustee resigns from the of duties of such Office; or

(v) Refusal, when a Trustee refuses to act in the manner and characteristics required of such Office; or

(vi) Contestation, when the competency or legitimacy of a Trustee is challenged and upheld by a competent forum of Law.

9. In accord with the present Articles, a valid and legitimate Trustee is bound in *Good Faith, Good Actions* and *Good Conscience* to eight (8) Characteristics being *Integrity, Frugality, Prudence, Humility, Faculty, Competence, Accountability* and *Capacity*:- Trustee Fiduciary Obligations

(i) *Integrity* being the characteristic of possessing a strict moral or ethical code as exemplified by the Trinity of Virtue (Good Faith, Good Actions and Good Conscience); and

(ii) *Frugality* being the characteristic of being economical and thrifty in the good use of those resources in ones possession or custody. The opposite of waste; and

(iii) *Prudence* being the characteristic of being practical, cautious, discrete, judicious and wise in the management of the affairs of the trust; and

(iv) *Humility* being the characteristic of being modest, without pretension or loftiness; and

(v) *Faculty* being the characteristic of possessing skill and ability in order to perform the obligations of Trustee; and

(vi) *Competence* being the characteristic of being fit, proper and qualified to produce and argue reason through knowledge and skill of Law, Logic and Rhetoric; and

(vii) *Accountability* being the characteristic of being answerable and liable to faithfully render an account for all acts and transactions; and

(viii) *Capacity* being the characteristic of possessing the legal and moral authority to hold such Office, including demonstrating all the previous necessary characteristics.

10. In accord with the present Articles, a valid and legitimate Trustee is empowered and responsible for the following eleven (11) elements including (but not limited to) *Rules, Standards, Forms, Procedures, Instruments, Notices, Transactions, Certificates, Transfers, Conveyances* and *Computations:-* Trustee Administrative Powers

(i) *Rules* being the ordinances, regulations or bylaws of the Trust; and

(ii) *Standards* being all means and measures of excellence used to compare the results of all activities and administrative duties;

and

(iii) *Forms* being all templates, inchoate and completed Instruments prescribed by law or these present Articles; and the manner whereby such forms must be correctly completed, used and applied; and

(iv) *Procedures* being all ways and methods of performance of obligations and administrative duties, usually in association with one or more Forms; and

(v) *Instruments* being all legally formed documents received and issued by the Trust and any associated trusts, estates or funds held in Chancery; and

(vi) *Notices* being all Instruments or services of process whereby one or more Parties are made aware of any formal legal matter that may affect certain rights, obligations and duties; and

(vii) *Transactions* being all the communications, deals, exchanges, transfers, conveyances and proceedings of the Trust and any associated trusts, estates or funds; and

(viii) *Certificates* being all official, authorised and acknowledged extracts of Records of the Trust and any associated trusts, estates or funds; and

(ix) *Transfers* being all passing of possession and holding of certain rights, titles or objects of property of the Trust and any associated trusts, estates or funds; and

(x) *Conveyances* being the passing of ownership of certain rights, titles or objects of property of the Trust and any associated trusts, estates or funds; and

(xi) *Computations* being all summaries, calculations and reckoning of arithmetic numbers and values associated with the Trust and any associated trusts, estates or funds.

Trustee Administrative Obligations

11. In accord with the present Articles, a valid and legitimate Trustee is bound in *Good Faith*, *Good Actions* and *Good Conscience*:-

(i) To take administrative ownership of the Trust *Res* or Estate Inventory or Fund Property, including all existing obligations and to protect the will and intention of the Trustor; and

(ii) To support the existing administrative obligations already established in relation to any Trust, or Estate, or Fund, or Corporation and to ensure their competent, prudent and wise operation; and

(iii) To hold to account any person acting as an assumed agent or trustee in association with any Trust, or Estate, or Fund or Corporation under the control of the proper Trustee and to recover any and all monies, property owed to such Trusts, or Estates, or Funds or Companies, or ensure charges as compensation are settled.

Article 31 – Candidate

1. No Candidate may be appointed to an Office unless that Candidate is suitably qualified for the position that they are to occupy in accordance with these Articles. Excluding the Office of Member, no one person may hold more than one position as an Officer of the Union, unless such additional Office be honourary or as a direct consequence of holding the primary Office. Qualification and Capacity of Candidate

2. A Candidate shall provide all the necessary material and disclosure to assess their suitability and qualifications necessary to be appointed to one or more Offices, including but not limited to: Material Provided by Candidate

(i) Name and current domicile; and

(ii) Image photo and proof of identity; and

(iii) Brief summary of previous experience; and

(iv) Application Form for Position (where appropriate).

3. A Candidate that refuses or fails to provide the necessary material to assess their suitability and qualifications is automatically ineligible to be appointed to any Office of the Union. Failure or Refusal to provide Material

4. A Candidate shall be not eligible for appointment or election to Office: Ineligible for Office

(i) If the Candidate is currently a member of a secret organisation, association or fraternity that is fundamentally opposed to the Union and its ideals; or

(ii) If the Candidate refuses or fails to provide the necessary material to assess their suitability and qualifications for Office; or

(iii) If the Candidate is known to have been deliberately deceptive, or dishonest in failing to disclose truthfully certain information that would otherwise have rendered them ineligible to be a Candidate; or

(iv) If the Candidate is currently facing any criminal indictment or case before any courts where there is the possibility of a custodial sentence of two years or more; or

(v) If the Candidate has been previously convicted by any court of a serious sexual offence or violent crime carrying a custodial sentence of two years or more; or

(vi) If the Candidate has demonstrated a lack of good faith, or good conscience, or good actions toward the integrity of Ucadia and the Objects of the Union and there is the likelihood that such behaviour may continue even if appointed or elected to Office.

5. All proposed permanent positions of senior Officers of the Union shall require the approval by vote of a motion before the Synod whereby the motion includes for one or more Officers: Member Approval for all Positions of Office

(i) The title of each position; and

(ii) The Job description of each position; and

(iii) The performance measurement criteria for each position; and

(iv) The proposed remuneration package of each position; and

(v) The proposed length of commission or employment for each position.

Article 32 – Oath & Obligation of Office

1. The Oath of Office is an oath a person must take before assuming any Office of the Union and performing any duties therein. All persons who are Directors or holding an Executive position of the Union shall be required to pledge the Oath of Office as a condition of acceptance into such position. Oath of Office

2. The Oath of Office shall be in two parts, the first being the recital of the one administering the Oath and the second being the one giving their Oath, by placing the left hand on a copy of *Pactum De Singularis Caelum* whilst the right hand is open, facing the one administering the Oath: The Oath

> *Let Heaven and Earth be my witness, before all here present, that as a natural [man/woman] of sound mind and capacity, by reason of my own free will, I [name] do solemnly pledge my allegiance to the [Name of Union or Ucadia University or Province], and to honestly and faithfully execute the Office bestowed upon me, so help me God. Amen.*

3. Upon the completion of the Oath, the Officer will be required to sign, with the one who administered the Oath as witness as to the fact that a Certificate of Oath

valid Oath of Allegiance was taken on that particular Day and Time. The Member shall then be entitled to an Authenticated Duplicate with the Original in the possession of the Union.

Article 33 – Officer Commission

1. A valid and legitimate Officer occupies an Office by an Instrument of Commission. No Person may justly claim to occupy an Office by any other means. Officer Commission

2. A Commission, also known as an Instrument of Commission or Commissioning Scroll or Warrant, shall adhere to the following elements at a minimum: - Key Elements of Instrument of Commission

    (i) That the Instrument is issued under the capacity and authority of the Head of the appropriate organ, body, association, company or entity of the Union; and

    (ii) That the Office named in the Instrument is subject to and under the authority of the relevant Head of the appropriate organ, body, association, company or entity of the Union; and

    (iii) That the appropriate reference to the Covenant, Constitution, Bylaws or Resolution granting the powers of the particular Office is clearly listed; and

    (iv) That the Instrument names the Person granted occupancy of the Office; and

    (v) That the Instrument clearly states the condition of occupancy of such Office is subject to the binding effect of the sacred and solemn oath made by the Person listed; and

    (vi) That the Instrument clearly states the limit of time of Occupancy or limit until expiry of the Commission (whichever is appropriate); and

    (vii) That the Instrument is appropriately dated, witnessed, signed and sealed.

TITLE IV: AGENCIES AND AGENTS

Article 34 – Agency

1. An "**Agency**" is recognised as a form of Warranty, Security and Power given life through some instrument of authority whereby a duly authorised Fiduciary of a Principal Trustee may act for or represent the interests of another. An Agency does not exist, nor possesses any validity or legitimacy unless it is created by a valid instrument of authority. An Agency can never possess greater powers than the Office that created it. Agency

Article 35 – Agent

1. An "**Agent**" is recognised as one of suitable character, possessing necessary security and authorised by delegation in trust to act for or in place of a Principal. A valid and legitimate Agent always carries a higher burden than an Officer upon the necessary security or bond to perform and act, as well as the necessary warrant of authority. The Authority of an Agent is always in Trust as a Fiduciary, as the Trust itself is called an Agency and exists so long as the prescribed time, or the proper performance of the Agent. Agent
2. A "**Fiduciary**" is recognised as a Person holding the character of a valid Trustee as an Agent; and the scrupulous good faith and honesty required for a valid Agency. Fiduciary by tradition emphasises the three essential criteria necessary in the capacity and character of a proper Fiduciary being good faith (*bona fides*), good actions (*bona acta*) and good conscience (*bona conscientia*):- Fiduciary
   - (i) *Good Faith*, also known as *bona fides* is the ancient custom that a man or woman cannot be a Fiduciary except under proper Oath or Vow to a recognised Divinity upon some object or text representing a firm belief in the efficacy of some sacred and ethical standards of law existing in the same name as the Divinity; and
   - (ii) *Good Actions*, also known as *bona acta* is the ancient custom that a man or woman cannot act as a Fiduciary except by acting in accord with the highest virtues of honesty, impartiality, frugality and prudence, also sometimes known as "clean hands doctrine"; and
   - (iii) *Good Conscience*, also known as *bona conscientia* is the ancient custom that a man or woman cannot act in the best interests of another, or fairly under the Rule of Law if they seek a contrary or negative outcome.

3. The definition of an Officer in terms of being a Trustee and a Principal may be defined by the Rules of Principal-Agent Relation, namely:- Principal Agent Relation

(i) When a Trust instrument specifically names a person, or a Trustee who by their powers chooses to nominate a person as Beneficiary, this creates the Principal-Agent Relation; and

(ii) It is only when the Beneficiary accepts the offer of the Benefit does such a Relation become a formal Principal-Agent Relation. Thus, any claim that a Principal can be secret or unknown is morally repugnant, absurd and void in law; and

(iii) A Principal-Agent Relation does not exist in the case of an unnamed beneficiary. Instead, the relation when an unnamed Beneficiary relation is created is the Trustee as Debtor and the unnamed beneficiary as Creditor; and

(iv) An Agent is by extension a representative of the Principal and is therefore obligated to perform in accord with the conditions of accepting the Benefit. The moment an Agent breaches their obligations, they become liable for their actions and lose any form of limited liability; and

(v) As an Agent is an extension of the Office of Principal, a Principal is liable for the actions of his/her Agents. Thus Notice of an Agent is Notice to Principal and Notice to Principal is Notice to their Agents; and

(vi) An Agent can never have the capacity or authority to form a sub-agent relation within the original Principal-Agent relation. Any relation formed then by the Agent with a third party must be as a Trustee of some stable right and authority.

4. In respect of an Agent:- General Reference to Agent

(i) An Agent binds not himself but the Principal with the agreements made; and

(ii) An Agent is by extension a representative of the Principal and is therefore obligated to perform in accord with the conditions of accepting the Benefit; and

(iii) The moment an Agent breaches their obligations, they become liable for their actions and lose any form of limited liability; and

(iv) An Agent that handles any form of money, or property or rights on behalf of the Principal is automatically a Fiduciary and obligated to act with Fiduciary Capacity and Fiduciary Standards.

Article 36 – Nominee

1. No Nominee may be appointed to an Agency unless that Nominee is qualified for the position that they are to occupy in accordance with these Articles. One person may hold more than one position at one time as an Agent of the Union.

Qualification and Capacity of Nominee

2. A Nominee shall provide all the necessary material and disclosure to assess their suitability and qualifications necessary to be appointed to one or more Agencies, including but not limited to:

Material Provided by Nominee

   (i) Name and current domicile; and
   (ii) Image photo and proof of identity; and
   (iii) Brief summary of previous experience; and
   (iv) Application Form for Position (where appropriate).

3. A Nominee that refuses or fails to provide the necessary material to assess their suitability and qualifications is automatically ineligible to be appointed to any Agency or Office of the Union.

Failure or Refusal to provide Material

4. A Nominee shall not be eligible for appointment as an Agent:

Ineligible for Office

   (i) If the Nominee refuses or fails to provide the necessary material to assess their suitability and qualifications to be an Agent; and
   (ii) If the Nominee is currently facing any criminal indictment or case before any courts where there is the possibility of a custodial sentence of two years or more; and
   (iii) If the Nominee has been previously convicted by any court of a serious sexual offence or violent crime carrying a custodial sentence of two years or more; and
   (iv) If the Nominee has demonstrated a lack of good faith, or good conscience, or good actions toward the integrity of Ucadia and the Objects of the Union and there is the likelihood that such behaviour may continue even if appointed as an Agent or elected to Office.

Article 37 – Promise, Security & Duty of Agent

1. Every Agent must provide a clear Promise of their duties that is then underwritten by some valuable financial security. In the absence of suitable security, a Person shall be committing a serious offence if they conduct any business as an Agent.

Promise and Security of Agent

Article 38 – Agent Warrant

1. Every Agent must possess a valid Warrant to act in their duties as an Agent; and be capable of providing proper evidence as to the source and issuer of the Warrant. Agent Warrant

2. Any person acting in the capacity of an Agent shall be fully liable for any adverse claims against their actions in the absence of a valid warrant or the refusal to produce evidence of a current and valid warrant upon demand. The refusal itself shall be sufficient evidence in any adverse claim. Agent fully liable in absence or refusal of warrant

TITLE V: ORGANS

Article 39 – Organs

1. The Union as a Body Politic shall be defined by distinct structural elements or "**Organs**" representing its vital parts. All legislative, executive and judicial functions are reserved to the competent Organs and bodies of the Body Politic, according to the provisions enumerated within the present Articles. Organs

2. The Organs of the Union shall be:- Organs of Union

   (i) "**Synod**", being the supreme legislative body of the Union, comprised of members known as "**Archons**"; and

   (ii) "**Mediator**", being a corporation sole and ex-officio head of the Synod; and

   (iii) "**Academy**", being the supreme administrative body of the Union; and

   (iv) "**Alexander**", being a corporation sole and ex-officio head of the Academy; and

   (v) "**Basilica**", being the supreme juridical, plenary and appellate forum of law in all matters concerning the Union; and

   (vi) "**Basileus**", being a corporation sole and ex-officio head of the Basilica; and

   (vii) "**Econos**", being the supreme treasury for all revenue, banking and finances concerning the Union; and

   (viii) "**Economos**" being a corporation sole and ex-officio head of the Econos; and

   (ix) "**Stratos**", being the supreme military command resources concerning the Union; and

   (x) "**Stratagos**" being a corporation sole and ex-officio head of the Stratos; and

   (xi) "**Energeia**", being the supreme business and trade body of the Union; and

   (xii) "**Kephalos**", being a corporation sole and ex-officio head of the Energeia; and

   (xiii) "**Psyches**" being the supreme spiritual and ecclesial body of the Union; and

   (xiv) "**Mentor**", being a corporation sole and ex-officio head of the

Psyches; and

(xv) "**Sunedrion**", being the supreme governing body of the Union; and

(xvi) A number of Subsidiaries, Funds, Trusts and other Bodies, whether incorporated or unincorporated.

3. No person shall be an elected Representative of the Union who shall not have attained the age of twenty-five years or greater than the age of eighty-five years, and be a Member of the Union, and be an inhabitant of a University of the Union where they shall be chosen; but no elected representative of a non-Ucadian society, shall be allowed to hold any office, civil or political. Representation of Organs of Union

4. All elected Representatives shall receive compensation for their services, to be ascertained by law, and paid out of the Econos (Treasury) of the Union. No elected Representative shall, during the time they are elected, or appointed to any civil office under the authority of the Union accept any emoluments or gifts directly or in kind. Compensation to elected Representatives

Article 40 – Synod

1. All legislative powers of the Union shall be vested in a Synod (The Synod), that shall consist of one house of representatives. The Synod shall be made up of elected representatives, known as "**Archon**", being individual members from legitimate and valid Ucadia Universities within the bounds of the Union. The *ex officio* head of the Synod shall be the *Mediator* as the living embodiment and personification of the Synod as a corporation sole. Synod

2. The Synod shall, in addition to all the other powers vested to it by the Charter and these Articles, have the following powers and functions:- Synod Powers

(i) To form and maintain an **Oversight Committee** reflecting each and every one of the twenty-two (22) permanent and standard Systems and any other permanent Organ of the Union; and to determine by common rules consistent with the present Charter the appointment of the Chair and composition of each committee, and the times of meeting and conduct of business of every Oversight Committee; and to have the powers and authority of a court to summons any officer, agent or representative of an Agency, System, Entity or Organ of the Union; and to compel any such officer, agent, or representative to provide truthful testimony under oath; and to order the release to the appropriate Oversight Committee any document or instrument of any Agency, Office, System, Entity or Organ of the Union, without obstruction or delay; and to call any Members of staff or experts to give evidence before that Oversight Committee of any Union body; and to hold in criminal contempt any such officer, agent, member or representative that intentionally obstructs or defies the rights, powers and authority of a relevant Oversight Committee; and

(ii) To form an **Appointment Commission** subject to the rules and procedures of the present Constitutional Charter to investigate, interview, debate and vote on the approval of all senior positions nominated by the Sunedrion; and

(iii) To form an **Inquiry Commission** to investigate any matter, subject to the rules and procedures of the present Constitutional Charter referred by a majority of an Oversight Committee on sufficient and clear evidence of potential systemic criminal conduct by any officer, agent, member or representative of the Union or any agency, entity, department, division, system or organ of the Union; and to refer any evidence to prosecutors for criminal proceedings, or to form an Impeachment Commission; and

(iv) To form an **Impeachment Commission** to conduct a trial upon sufficient evidence being found by an Inquiry Commission for the forced removal from office of any elected official within the jurisdiction of the Union; and

(v) To Create new Laws and amend existing Laws for review, amendment or repeal. The Synod shall not have the power to block money Acts required for the general operation and function of the Union; and

3. Once formed, the Synod shall exist in one continuous, unbroken and perpetual state of trust and existence for the life of the Union:- Perpetual State

(i) The business of the Synod shall be divided into "**Sessions**" being a period of fixed days corresponding to the requirement of elected members of the Synod to attend; and

(ii) It shall be the commissions to office of elected members of the Synod that are dissolved, not the offices themselves they hold, nor the Synod itself.

4. Excepting a Union election year, every year there shall be two (2) sessions of fixed days corresponding to equal divisions of the year whereby Members of the Synod are summonsed to attend:- Synod Sessions

(i) Each session shall be named for the season to which they correspond, namely Summer and Winter. A day within a session when Members of the Synod are summonsed to sit shall be called a Sitting Session Day; and

(ii) A day within a session when Members are not summonsed to sit shall be called a Non-Sitting Session Day. During a year in which a Union election is to be called the last session of Union before it is dissolved shall be the Winter session; and

(iii) The total length of a Union Synod session shall be determined by the Synod Mediator and shall not be permitted to exceed twenty eight (28) Sitting Session Days; and

(iv) The Synod Mediator shall be responsible for the issuing of summons to individual Archons for their attendance to Synod; and

(v) Excepting special leave granted by the Synod Moderator due to matters of Union security, health or extended personal matters, all Archons shall be required to attend the Sitting Session Days as listed in the summons; and

(vi) Failure of an Archon to attend six (6) or more Session Sitting Days within one Session shall be deemed a failure to discharge the duties of their office and the Synod Moderator shall be responsible for immediately initiating a Synod Expulsion Motion; and

(vii) The minimum number of Members (quorum) required to be present within the Synod to permit the full exercise of its powers shall be two thirds (2/3) the total number of Members of the Synod; and

(viii) All Proposed Acts shall be listed in the tradition of "Epistle" or "Epi." for short in consecutive order from all previous Acts, with each Act requiring both an abbreviated Title and a brief description in one sentence as to its primary purpose; and

(ix) Voting in the Synod shall be by open vote expressed as either Yes or No to the proposition before the chamber. Voting shall always require a quorum and shall follow the standard procedures listed in this Charter; and

(x) Total votes shall be tallied as either Yes, or No to the proposition expressed by the Act. A higher total number of Yes votes to No votes shall deem the Act or proposition has been passed. A higher total number of No votes to Yes votes shall deem the Act or proposition has been defeated; and

(xi) The record, attendance and vote of all Members of The Synod shall be recorded on the public record; and

(xii) The sessions on the floor of the Synod shall be open for the public record with all speeches, debates, motions, votes and documents recorded; and

(xiii) Furthermore, all committee meetings and special sessions of reviews shall also be open for the public record, except those proceedings deemed as being regular meetings of Union security. An expenditure related review may never be closed to public scrutiny.

5. Archons shall be appointed by commission for a term of six (6) years before such commission shall expire:- Archons

(i) During their Attendance at the Session of the Synod, and in going to and returning from the same, all Members of the Synod shall be privileged from arrest except in matters of Treason, Felony and Breach of the Peace. Such privilege does not extend to their property or office which shall fall under the normal course of law and investigation and right to search by issued Warrant; and

(ii) During debate in the Synod, all spoken and written material presented and entered into the Public Record of proceedings shall be privileged and immune from civil liability.

6. The Synod shall be the judge of the returns, and qualifications of its own members, and a majority of each shall constitute a quorum to do business; but a smaller number may adjourn from day to day, and may be authorised to compel the attendance of absent members, in such manner and under such penalties as the Synod may provide:- Qualifications & Rules of Synod

(i) The Synod may determine the rules of its proceedings, punish its members for disorderly behaviour, and, with the concurrence of two-thirds of the whole number, expel a member; and

(ii) The Synod shall keep a journal of its proceedings, and from time to time publish the same, excepting such parts as may in their judgement require secrecy; and the yeas and nays of the Members of the Synod, on any question, shall, at the desire of one-fifth of those present, be entered on the journal.

7. The form and full powers of the Synod shall be according to its form Synod Form and status:-

(i) A "**Provisional Synod**" shall consist of those spiritual forces presently occupying and possessing the spiritual and temporal bounds of the Union; and

(ii) A "**Preliminary Synod**" shall consist of a minimum of fourteen elected representatives being not less than seven representatives from each Preliminary, Probational, Prerogative or Permanent Ucadia University; and

(iii) A "**Probational Synod**" shall consist of a minimum of seventy two elected representatives being not less than seven representatives from each Preliminary, Probational, Prerogative or Permanent Ucadia University; and

(iv) A "**Prerogative Synod**" shall consist of a minimum of one hundred and forty four elected representatives being not less than seven representatives from each Preliminary, Probational, Prerogative or Permanent Ucadia University; and

(v) A "**Permanent Synod**" shall consist of a minimum of one hundred and forty four elected representatives being not less than seven representatives from each Prerogative or Permanent Ucadia University.

Article 41 – Mediator

1. The "**Mediator**", being a corporation sole, shall be the ex-officio head of the Synod and a member (Exarch) of the Sunedrion. Mediator

2. By virtue of the authority vested in the Office of Mediator, subject to the provisions of these Articles, the Mediator shall have the following consolidated powers:- Mediator Powers

(i) To appoint, suspend or remove the General Secretary to the Office of Mediator; and

(ii) To preside as Chair over any and all Synod convocations; and co-ordinate the agenda and minutes of such convocations; and overrule, suspend or set-aside any motion before a Synod convocation, other than a matter of Supply, Probity or Security or Treason; and

(iii) To oversee the Synod Rules of Order as well as Synod regulations of the Union; and

(iv) To institute Synod Committees of oversight, ensuring that all

Divisions and Systems of the Union are held to account, by sittings of such Committees with the authority of subpoena, question and sanction to any Officers less than an Exarch.

First Office reserved to Founding Ordinary Members

3. The Office of Mediator shall be reserved to the first Synod of Founding Ordinary Members as the embodiment of the said Office, for a period of not exceeding three years or less, until such time as it is deemed appropriate by the first Synod of Founding Ordinary Members to elect the first Mediator.

Mediator

4. The successors to the first Mediator shall be elected by a simple majority vote of Ordinary Members, either during the normal cycle of Elections or at a By-election specially called for such a vacancy within eight weeks of such occurrence.

Term

5. The successors to the first Mediator shall hold office for a period of four years or until resignation, or until removal in accordance with the powers of impeachment of the Synod; and unless so removed shall be eligible for re-appointment for a maximum of three terms.

Vacancy of Office

6. The Office of Mediator shall be declared vacant upon the death or resignation or removal of an Officer. The Mediator may resign by handing their resignation in writing to the Sunedrion.

Removal or Death of Officer

7. The death or removal or resignation of the Mediator shall not dissolve the Office. Instead the Office of Mediator shall continue *Sedes Vacante* until a suitable candidate has been vested into Office.

Article 42 – Academy

Academy

1. All administrative powers and functions of the Union shall be vested in an "**Academy**" (The Academy), being the supreme administrative body of the Union. The *ex officio* head of the Academy shall be the *Alexander* as the living embodiment and personification of the administrative services as a corporation sole.

Academy Powers

2. By virtue of the authority vested in the Academy, subject to the provisions of these Articles, the Academy shall have the following consolidated powers:-

    (i) To oversee the operational, human resources, logistical and administrative needs of the Systems of the Union; and

    (ii) To manage all technology, tools, methods and information needs of the Systems of the Union; and

    (iii) To keep, hold, classify, protect and manage all official contracts, agreements and treaties of the Union; and

(iv) To manage, oversee and review the training, qualification, vetting and development of skills of all administrative personnel appointed to the Systems of the Union.

Article 43 – Alexander

1. The "**Alexander**", being a corporation sole, shall be the ex-officio head of the Academy and a member (Exarch) of the Sunedrion. Alexander

2. By virtue of the authority vested in the Office of Alexander, subject to the provisions of these Articles, the Alexander shall have the following consolidated powers:- Alexander Powers

   (i) To oversee the general administrative, document and archival policies as well as documentation regulations of the Union; and

   (ii) To head the administrative Office of Alexander, including all staffing, facilities, administrative procedures and functions; and

   (iii) To assist in the vetting process of all senior Secretaries of the Union, with the power to veto a proposed appointment, if such a nomination is wholly unsuited to the qualifications or character necessary for the Union; and

   (iv) To preside as Chairperson over any and all meetings of the Academy of Secretaries of the Union and select the agenda and minutes of such meetings; and overrule, suspend or set-aside any motion before an Academy meeting, other than a matter of Supply, Discipline, Probity or Security or Treason.

3. The Office of Alexander shall be reserved to the first Synod of Founding Ordinary Members as the embodiment of the said Office, for a period of not exceeding six years or less, until such time as it is deemed appropriate by the first Synod of Founding Ordinary Members to elect the first Alexander. First Office reserved to Founding Ordinary Members

4. The successors to the first Alexander shall be elected by a simple majority vote of Ordinary Members, either during the normal cycle of Elections or at a By-election specially called for such a vacancy within eight weeks of such occurrence. Alexander

5. The successors to the first Alexander shall hold office for a period of four years or until resignation, or until removal in accordance with the powers of impeachment of the Union; and unless so removed shall be eligible for re-appointment for a maximum of three terms. Term

6. The Office of Alexander shall be declared vacant upon the death or resignation or removal of an Officer. The Alexander may resign by Vacancy of Office

handing their resignation in writing to the Sunedrion.

7. The death or removal or resignation of the Alexander shall not dissolve the Office. Instead the Office of Alexander shall continue *Sedes Vacante* until a suitable candidate has been vested into Office. Removal or Death of Officer

Article 44 – Basilica

1. All judicial powers of the Union shall be vested in a "**Basilica**" (The Basilica), being the supreme juridical, plenary and appellate forum of law in all matters concerning the Union, that shall consist of several courts that shall be united and consolidated together; and shall constitute and be subject to the provisions of these Articles and related *Union Judicial Charter*, one Supreme Court, within the bounds and Jurisdiction of the Union. The *ex officio* head of the Basilica shall be the *Basileus* as the living embodiment and personification of the law as a corporation sole. Basilica

2. As Constituted by the present Articles and related *Union Judicial Charter*, the one Supreme Court shall consist of two permanent *Dicastery*: one under the name *Supreme Court of Justice* that shall have and exercise original jurisdiction; and the other under the name *Supreme Court of Judicature* that shall have and exercise appellate jurisdiction with such original jurisdiction in respect of the examination, judgement and determinative powers of lesser courts: Constitution of Supreme Court

   (i) The Dicastery known as the *Supreme Court of Justice* shall be further divided into six Divisions called respectively the *Ecclesiastical Division*, the *Chancery Division*, the *Common Law Division*, the *Exchequer Division*, the *Administrative Division* and the *Admiralty Division*; and

   (ii) The Dicastery known as the *Supreme Court of Judicature* shall be further divided into six Divisions called respectively the *Penitentiary Division*, the *Records Division*, the *Procedures Division*, the *Legislative Division*, the *Fiduciary Division* and the *International Division*.

3 The highest Officers of the Supreme Court shall be constituted as follows:- Constitution of Judges of Supreme Court

   (i) The highest judicial Officers of Dicastery known as the *Supreme Court of Justice* shall be: the *Basileus*, the *Chancellor*, the *Exchequer*, the *Plenipotentiary*, the *Prefect*, the *Justiciar* as the Chief Justice of the Supreme Court of Justice, the *Custodian* as the Deputy Chief Justice of the Supreme Court of Justice and such Justices as are appointed by the Sunedrion, with the consent of the Synod; and

(ii) The highest *ex officio* judicial Officers of Dicastery known as the *Supreme Court of Judicature* shall be: the *Basileus*, the *Chancellor*, the *Exchequer*, the *Plenipotentiary*, the *Prefect*, the *Justiciar* as the Chief Justice of the Supreme Court of Appeal, the *Censor* as the Deputy Chief Justice of the Supreme Court of Judicature and such Appellate Justices as are appointed by Letters Patent, with the consent of Members by General or Extraordinary Meeting; and

(iii) The highest enforcement Officer of the Supreme Court shall be the *Marshal* and those Deputies and Agents appointed under valid Warrant issued by the Court; and

(iv) The highest clerical Officer of the Supreme Court shall be the *Narrator* and those Clerks and Agents appointed under valid Letters Patent as issued by the Court.

4. In respect of the Terms and Conditions of Officers of the Supreme Court: Terms and Conditions of Officers

(i) The Terms and Conditions of tenure as a Justice of the Supreme Court of a valid holder of an Office shall be the same as is specified for an Office and shall end upon the date and time the Person ceases to hold the Office; and

(ii) The Terms and Conditions of tenure as a Justice by Letters Patent, shall be in accord with the present Articles and the rules of Officers; and shall not exceed six years; and

(iii) The Terms and Conditions of tenure by Warrant or other official Instrument shall be subject to the terms of the Warrant or other official Instrument and the present Articles.

5. All causes and matters that may be commenced in, or that shall be transferred to the Supreme Court, shall be distributed among the several Divisions and Judges of the said Supreme Court in such manner as may from time to time be determined by the *Rules of Court* made under the authority of the present Articles and related *Union Judicial Charter*. Every Instrument whereby any cause or matter may be commenced in the said Supreme Court of Justice shall be marked with the name of the Division or with the name of the Judge to whom the cause or matter is assigned. Rules of Court

6. In respect of the Jurisdiction, Authority and Power of Ucadia and Ucadia Courts: Jurisdiction of Ucadia and Ucadia Courts

(i) Ucadia is judged by no one. Ucadia is the embodiment and personification of the Divine Creator of all Existence, of all Heaven, of the entire Universe and all the Earth. Therefore any person, or body politic, or society, or entity or corporation that claims such jurisdiction to judge Ucadia, or higher jurisdiction than Ucadia automatically confesses to be Insane, Incompetent and disqualified from holding any position of trust or office; and

(ii) All judicial plenary authority of Heaven, the Galaxy, the Solar System and Earth is vested in one supreme spiritual body, court of record and competent forum of Law known as the *Oratorium*, also known as the *Supreme Court* and also known as the *Supreme Court of One Heaven* in accord with the most sacred Covenant *Pactum De Singularis Caelum*. The Oratorium is by definition the highest See and is judged by no one. It is the sole right of the Oratorium itself to judge in all matters of Law upon any claim of Law, or Rights or Justice or Jurisdiction being spoken or written. All other judicial bodies, forums, assemblies, courts and tribunals are subject to the supreme jurisdiction of the Oratorium; and

(iii) The *Oratorium* as the One Heaven Supreme Court shall exist both spiritually and temporally whenever and wherever a Special Session or Ordinary Session is properly invoked and called. A ***Special Session*** of the Oratorium is called when three or more Authorised and Legitimate Members of Ucadia individually and collectively invoke and memorialise a proper Oath and Vow to the Golden Rule of Law and the Laws of Ucadia and becomes an *Authorised Tribunal* representing the True Rule of Law. When such an action occurs in good trust, good action and good intention, a valid Divine Court (*Curiam Divina*) is convened within the temporal realm as the highest possible court of appeal, the second highest court of original jurisdiction and forum of law, also known as the Curia Iuris (Court of Justice). No other competent forum, or court within temporal existence may claim higher appellate jurisdiction in all matters of law; and

(iv) The *Forum*, also known as the Globe Court of Justice, also known as the Globe Union Supreme Court and also known as the Globe Court shall be the first, principal and highest judicial organ of the Ucadia Globe Union in accord with the constitutional charter known as *Cartae Sacrorum De Congregatio Globus*. No other judicial body, excluding those competent forums of the Society of One Heaven, may ecclesiastically, legally or lawfully claim higher jurisdiction over the Globe Court of Justice. In the absence of a constituted sitting Forum, a proper constituted Union Supreme Court shall be temporarily vested with the powers of the Forum; and

(v) The judicial powers of the Union shall be vested in one Supreme Court; and

(vi) The one Supreme Court of the Union shall be the highest Competent Forum of Law of any foreign or domestic body within the bounds of the Union; and

(vii) The rejection of the absolute authority, power and jurisdiction of the Supreme Court by any foreign or domestic body within the bounds of the Union, shall be a confession that such a body and all officers of such a body are excommunicated and disqualified from hearing any matter of Law.

Jurisdiction of Basilica as Supreme Court of Justice

7. The Dicastery known as the *Supreme Court of Justice* shall be a Superior Court of Record. The Supreme Court of Justice as an original Court of Record and Competent Forum of Law shall have first, supreme, immediate and final jurisdiction in all matters within the bounds of the Union:-

(i) Arising under any *Right of Entry and Action* or *Right of Exemption* or *Right of Close* as prescribed by Ucadian Law, or the Constitution of the Union or the present Charter of the Union; and

(ii) Arising as an Original Action under a valid Superior Writ of *Recto Originalis, Recto Investigationis, Recto Capionis, Recto Custodiae* or *Recto Interdico*; and

(iii) Arising under the Enforcement of any Ucadian Law, or the Enforcement of the Constitution of the Union or the present Charter of the Union; and

(iv) Arising under any office, or agency or position of trust claiming any form of power or authority under a form of law within the bounds of the Union; and

(v) Arising under any form of trust, or estate, or fund of any company, or corporation, or body politic, or Union, or aggregate within the bounds of the Union; and

(vi) Arising under any treaty within the bounds of the Union; and

(vii) Arising under any claimed law, or rule, or authority, or custom of the See, or Sea, or Admiralty; and

(viii) Arising where the Union, or a Person suing or being sued on behalf of the Union is a Party; and

(ix) Arising from a dispute between bodies of Ucadia Members or the Union, or between members of different or lesser bodies within the bounds and jurisdiction of the Union; and

(x) Affecting consuls or other representatives; and

(xi) Arising under any claim of Ecclesiastical authority, or power, or law, or rule or custom; and

(xii) Arising from any statutes, laws and historic instruments of any foreign and non Ucadian society that is based upon a claimed treaty with any higher order spirit(s) or the Divine Creator, or claimed Rule of Law.

8. The Dicastery known as the *Supreme Court of Judicature* shall be a Superior Court of Record. The Supreme Court of Judicature shall represent the final and conclusive competent forum and court of appeal in all matters determined from all matters of law, judgements, records, decrees, procedures, orders, or sentences within the bounds of the Union:

Jurisdiction of Basilica as Supreme Court of Appeals

(i) Arising under any Right of Petition as prescribed by Ucadian Law, or the Constitution of the Union or these present Articles of the Union; and

(ii) Arising as an Original Action under a valid Superior Writ of *Recto Petitionis*, *Recto Documentis*, *Recto Expungo*, *Recto Abrogationis* or *Recto Restitutio*; and

(iii) Arising under the Constitution of the Union or these present Articles of the Union, or involving their interpretation; and

(iv) Arising under any laws, or rights or jurisdiction, or claimed laws, or rights or jurisdiction of any and all bodies politic, aggregates, entities, estates, companies or corporations within the bounds of the Union involving their interpretation, review and conduct; and

(v) Arising under any circumstance that a foreign body or claimed forum of law initiates an action against a Ucadia Member and such proceeding is to be properly transferred to the one Supreme Court; and

(vi) Of any question of bias, or breach of trust, or

maladministration, or incompetence or corruption concerning any office, or agency or position of trust claiming any form of power or authority under a form of law within the bounds of the Union; and

(vii) Of any question and appeal of sentence, or penalties or outcome arising from a previous proceeding within any claimed forum of law and court of record within the bounds of the Union; and

(viii) Of any question of accuracy of records managed by any office, or agency or position of trust claiming any form of power or authority under a form of law within the bounds of the Union; and

(ix) Of any question of Divine Law, Ecclesiastical Jurisdiction, Moral or Spiritual Authority; and

(x) Of any question or challenge of Supreme and Ultimate Jurisdiction or Challenge of Authority and Mandate against Ucadia, or a Ucadia Society or the Union.

Article 45 – Basileus

1. The "**Basileus**", being a corporation sole, shall be the ex-officio head of the Basilica and a member (Exarch) of the Sunedrion. Basileus

2. By virtue of the authority vested in the Office of Basileus, subject to the provisions of these Articles, the Basileus shall have the following consolidated powers:- Basileus Powers

(i) To appoint, suspend or remove the General Secretary to the Office of Basileus, subject to the advice and consent of the Secretary of the Union; and

(ii) To oversee the judicial policies as well as legal regulations of the Union; and

(iii) To preside as Chief Jurist over the Full Court and to confer with fellow Jurists as to the optimum operation and function of its processes and rules; and

(iv) To allocate suits, move suits or otherwise co-ordinate the business of the Court and the judicial activities and schedules of all Jurists.

3. The Office of Basileus shall be reserved to the first Synod of Founding Ordinary Members as the embodiment of the said Office, for a period of not exceeding three years or less, until such time as it is deemed First Office reserved to Founding Ordinary appropriate by the first Synod of Founding Ordinary Members to elect the first Basileus. — Members

4. The successors to the first Basileus shall be elected by a simple majority vote of Ordinary Members, either during the normal cycle of Elections or at a ByElection specially called for such a vacancy within eight weeks of such occurrence. — Basileus

5. The successors to the first Basileus shall hold office for a period of four years or until resignation, or until removal in accordance with the powers of impeachment of the Synod; and unless so removed shall be eligible for re-appointment for a maximum of three terms. — Term

6. The Office of Basileus shall be declared vacant upon the death or resignation or removal of an Officer. The Basileus may resign by handing their resignation in writing to the Sunedrion. — Vacancy of Office

7. The death or removal or resignation of the Basileus shall not dissolve the Office. Instead the Office of Basileus shall continue *Sedes Vacante* until a suitable candidate has been vested into Office. — Removal or Death of Officer

Article 46 – Econos

1. All treasury, revenue and finance powers of the Union shall be vested in an "**Econos**" (The Econos), being the supreme treasury for all revenue, banking and finances concerning the Union. The *ex officio* head of the Econos shall be the *Economos* as the living embodiment and personification of the treasury as a corporation sole. — Econos

2. By virtue of the authority vested in the Econos, subject to the provisions of these Articles, the Econos shall have the following consolidated powers:- — Econos Powers

   (i) To receive and store safely all precious items in the possession of the Union, including but not limited to those items posited in trust with the Treasury and ensure that such transactions are properly recorded and acknowledged; and

   (ii) To possess and hold in reserve sufficient Gold Credo (Credit) underwritten by Supreme Credo (Credits) to meet the long term need for financial stability and capital liquidity by the people and enterprises within the bounds of the Union; and

   (iii) To grant for the benefit of the Euro Union Reserve Bank sufficient Gold Credo (Credit) that enable sufficient Silver Credo (Credit) to be formed by the Bank as underwriting to a single regional currency unit and means of physical and digital exchange; and

(iv) To provide receipt and right of use of the necessary instruments of underwriting and mechanisms to maintain a single universal currency unit known as the Euro Union Moneta and fulfil the needs of the Euro Union. To enable all financial matters and transactions for all Member States to be able to be defined according to this single Union currency unit; and

(v) To provide cash and valuables management facilities for the receipt, posit, deposit, store, withdrawal, payment and conversion requirements of the government of the Euro Union; and

(vi) To provide treasury facilities on behalf of Society Members and State Members as Members of the Treasury for their storage, safe keeping and cash management needs; and

(vii) To cooperate with the Globe Union Treasury and regional Union Treasuries in honouring the framework of the Supreme Financial System; and

(viii) To provide a cooperative framework between the principle Treasury and Financial organs of each Member of the Treasury such that optimum and stable policies may be in place for each state in regards to prices, wages, unemployment, growth, debt and investment; and

(ix) To help facilitate the expansion and balanced growth of trade, and to contribute thereby to the promotion and maintenance of high levels of employment and real income and to the development of the productive resources of all Member States as primary objectives of economic policy of the Union; and

(x) In accordance with the above, to assist the Union in the achievement of its purposes and principle objectives.

Article 47 – Economos

1. The "**Economos**", being a corporation sole, shall be the ex-officio head of the Econos and a member (Exarch) of the Sunedrion. Economos

2. By virtue of the authority vested in the Office of Economos, subject to the provisions of these Articles, the Economos shall have the following consolidated powers:- Economos Powers

(i) To appoint, suspend or remove the General Secretary to the Office of Economos; and

(ii) To oversee the economic, fiscal and monetary policies as well as financial regulations of the Union; and

(iii) To oversee all fundraising, capital and operational government expenditure of the Union, subject to the audit functions of the Comptroller; and

(iv) To oversee, hold and be accountable for the administrative functions of the Union relating to fundraising, capital, money, currency and operational expenditure; and

(v) To oversee and control all cash management accounts, external financial relations, debt and foreign exchange holdings and securities; and

(vi) To fix and regulate all fees; and

(vii) To govern, manage and regulate the finances, accounts, investments, property, business and all affairs whatsoever of the Union and for that purpose to appoint Bankers and any other officers or agents whom it may seem expedient to appoint; and

(viii) To invest any moneys belonging to the Union, including any unapplied income, in the purchase of or subscription for or at interest upon the security of such stock, funds, shares or securities as it shall think fit, whether within or outside the Union, or in the purchase of freehold or leasehold hereditaments in the Union, including rents, with the like power of varying such investments; and

(ix) To sell, buy, exchange, lease and accept leases of real and personal property on behalf of the Union; and

(x) To provide and maintain the buildings, premises, furniture and apparatus, and other means needed for carrying on the work of the Union and to license lodgings, apartments and other places of residence, whether maintained by the Union or not so maintained, and upon and subject to such terms and conditions as the Sunedrion shall think fit; and

(xi) To make provision for schemes of superannuation, pensions or retirement benefits for all salaried officers and, so far as the Sunedrion shall think fit, for other employees of the Union, or their dependants or relatives.

3. The Office of Economos shall be reserved to the first Synod of Founding Ordinary Members as the embodiment of the said Office, for

First Office reserved to Founding

a period of not exceeding six years or less, until such time as it is deemed appropriate by the first Synod of Founding Ordinary Members to elect the first Economos. Ordinary Members

4. The successors to the first Economos shall be elected by a simple majority vote of Ordinary Members, either during the normal cycle of Elections or at a By-election specially called for such a vacancy within eight weeks of such occurrence. Economos

5. The successors to the first Economos shall hold office for a period of four years or until resignation, or until removal in accordance with the powers of impeachment of the Synod; and unless so removed shall be eligible for re-appointment for a maximum of three terms. Term

6. The Office of Economos shall be declared vacant upon the death or resignation or removal of an Officer. The Economos may resign by handing their resignation in writing to the Sunedrion. Vacancy of Office

7. The death or removal or resignation of the Economos shall not dissolve the Office. Instead the Office of Economos shall continue *Sedes Vacante* until a suitable candidate has been vested into Office. Removal or Death of Officer

Article 48 – Stratos

1. All military, security and intelligence powers of the Union shall be vested in a "**Stratos**" (The Stratos), being the supreme military command resources concerning the Union. The *ex officio* head of the Stratos shall be the *Stratagos* as the living embodiment and personification of the protection and security of the Union as a corporation sole. Stratos

2. By virtue of the authority vested in the Stratos, subject to the provisions of these Articles, the Stratos shall have the following consolidated powers:- Stratos Powers

   (i) To protect the security of the Union and its elected officials and staff from external and internal threats; and

   (ii) To provide ongoing security and protection of all Union initiatives and programs; and

   (iii) To provide the necessary instruments and mechanisms to maintain a single security and criminal investigation authority. To enable all regional security, police and criminal investigation matters for all Society Members and State Members to be able to be defined according to this single system; and

   (iv) To promote international and regional security cooperation through a permanent institution representing all Society Members and State Members and all Ordinary Members which provides the machinery for consultation and collaboration on international security and police problems; and

(v) To promote and ensure the highest standards of police integrity and security procedures for all Society Members and State Members and to assist in training, education and certification; and

(vi) To assist the Union Supreme Court in the recording and investigation of all matters; and

(vii) To assist the Union Supreme Court in the effect of warrants and subpoena to attend including the arrest and detainment of persons as deemed by the Union Supreme Court and ratified by the House and Synod of the Union; and

(viii) To provide short term, semi-permanent and permanent personnel as contracted and requested by State Member or Society Member for support of internal law and order and education programs; and

(ix) To provide elite military personnel and units capable of assisting in any matter requiring a highly mobile and effective intervention force within hours to any part of the region or world; and

(x) To provide permanent, highly trained land, sea and air units capable of assisting in any significant matter requiring a substantial intervention force within weeks to any part of the region or world; and

(xi) To provide permanent military posts and defenses in areas of disputed territory and aggression as designated by specific agreements of the House and Synod of the Union; and

(xii) In accordance with the above, to assist the Union in the achievement of its purposes and principle objectives.

Article 49 – Stratagos

1. The "**Stratagos**", being a corporation sole, shall be the ex-officio head of the Stratos and a member (Exarch) of the Sunedrion. Stratagos

2. By virtue of the authority vested in the Office of Stratagos, subject to the provisions of these Articles, the Stratagos shall have the following consolidated powers:- Stratagos Powers

(i) To appoint, suspend or remove the General Secretary to the Office of Stratagos; and

(ii) To oversee the security and protection policies as well as security regulations of the Union; and

(iii) To enforce and commit resources to all actions of writs, warrants by Officers of the Union in the performance of their authorised duties and powers; and

(iv) To protect the security of the Union and its officials and employees from external and internal threats; and

(v) To recruit, manage and provide ongoing security and protection of all Foundation initiatives and programs; and

(vi) To recruit, manage and provide an elite unit capable of assisting in any matter requiring a highly mobile and effective intervention force when an official of the Union is in danger.

3. The Office of Stratagos shall be reserved to the first Synod of Founding Ordinary Members as the embodiment of the said Office, for a period of not exceeding six years or less, until such time as it is deemed appropriate by the first Synod of Founding Ordinary Members to elect the first Stratagos. First Office reserved to Founding Ordinary Members

4. The successors to the first Stratagos shall be elected by a simple majority vote of Ordinary Members, either during the normal cycle of Elections or at a By-election specially called for such a vacancy within eight weeks of such occurrence. Stratagos

5. The successors to the first Stratagos shall hold office for a period of four years or until resignation, or until removal in accordance with the powers of impeachment of the Synod; and unless so removed shall be eligible for re-appointment for a maximum of three terms. Term

6. The Office of Stratagos shall be declared vacant upon the death or resignation or removal of an Officer. The Stratagos may resign by handing their resignation in writing to the Sunedrion. Vacancy of Office

7. The death or removal or resignation of the Stratagos shall not dissolve the Office. Instead the Office of Stratagos shall continue *Sedes Vacante* until a suitable candidate has been vested into Office. Removal or Death of Officer

Article 50 – Energeia

1. All business, corporate and trading powers of the Union shall be vested in an "**Energeia**" (The Energeia), being the supreme business Energeia

and trade body of the Union. The *ex officio* head of the Energeia shall be the *Kephalos* as the living embodiment and personification of business, trade and employment prosperity of the Union as a corporation sole.

2. By virtue of the authority vested in the Energeia, subject to the provisions of these Articles, the Energeia shall have the following consolidated powers:- Energeia Powers

(i) To hold, inspect or quarantine any cargo, goods for export or import within the bounds of the Union; and

(ii) To hold and demand the payment of any duties or tariffs required upon any imported goods; and

(iii) To seize or confiscate any cargo, goods or materials suspected of being imported to artificially depress the standard prices of a market, or contrary to the laws of the Union; and

(iv) To establish and negotiate standard prices and wages for essential goods and services; and

(v) To establish, monitor and enforce open pricing in all markets where national security permits.

Article 51 – Kephalos

1. The "**Kephalos**", being a corporation sole, shall be the ex-officio head of the Energeia and a member (Exarch) of the Sunedrion. Kephalos

2. The Office of Kephalos shall be reserved to the first Synod of Founding Ordinary Members as the embodiment of the said Office, for a period of not exceeding six years or less, until such time as it is deemed appropriate by the first Synod of Founding Ordinary Members to elect the first Kephalos. First Office reserved to Founding Ordinary Members

3. The successors to the first Kephalos shall be elected by a simple majority vote of Ordinary Members, either during the normal cycle of Elections or at a By-election specially called for such a vacancy within eight weeks of such occurrence. Kephalos

4. The successors to the first Kephalos shall hold office for a period of four years or until resignation, or until removal in accordance with the powers of impeachment of the Synod; and unless so removed shall be eligible for re-appointment for a maximum of three terms. Term

6. The Office of Kephalos shall be declared vacant upon the death or resignation or removal of an Officer. The Kephalos may resign by handing their resignation in writing to the Sunedrion. Vacancy of Office

7. The death or removal or resignation of the Kephalos shall not dissolve the Office. Instead the Office of Kephalos shall continue *Sedes Vacante* until a suitable candidate has been vested into Office. Removal or Death of Officer

Article 52 – Psyches

1. All spiritual, ceremonial and ecclesiastical affairs of the Union shall be vested in a "**Psyches**" (The Psyches), being the supreme spiritual and ecclesial body, representing all the major faiths of the Union. The *ex officio* head of the Psyches shall be the *Mentor* as the living embodiment and personification of the spiritual unity, respect and harmony of the Union as a corporation sole. Psyches

Article 53 – Mentor

1. The "**Mentor**", being a corporation sole, shall be the ex-officio head of the Psyches and a member (Exarch) of the Sunedrion. Mentor
2. The Office of Mentor shall be reserved to the first Synod of Founding Ordinary Members as the embodiment of the said Office, for a period of not exceeding six years or less, until such time as it is deemed appropriate by the first Synod of Founding Ordinary Members to elect the first Mentor. First Office reserved to Founding Ordinary Members
3. The successors to the first Mentor shall be elected by a simple majority vote of Ordinary Members, either during the normal cycle of Elections or at a By-election specially called for such a vacancy within eight weeks of such occurrence. Mentor
4. The successors to the first Mentor shall hold office for a period of four years or until resignation, or until removal in accordance with the powers of impeachment of the Synod; and unless so removed shall be eligible for re-appointment for a maximum of three terms. Term
5. The Office of Mentor shall be declared vacant upon the death or resignation or removal of an Officer. The Mentor may resign by handing their resignation in writing to the Sunedrion. Vacancy of Office
6. The death or removal or resignation of the Mentor shall not dissolve the Office. Instead the Office of Mentor shall continue *Sedes Vacante* until a suitable candidate has been vested into Office. Removal or Death of Officer

Article 54 – Sunedrion

1. All executive powers of the Union shall be vested in a Sunedrion (The Sunedrion) being the supreme governing body of the Union. The Sunedrion shall be made up of the seven supreme Officers known as "**Exarchs**", including the Mediator, the Alexander, the Basileus, the Economos, the Stratagos, the Kephalos and the Mentor. Sunedrion

2. The full powers of the Sunedrion shall be according to its status:- Sunedrion Status

   (i) A "**Provisional Sunedrion**" shall consist of the commanders of those spiritual forces presently occupying and possessing the spiritual and temporal bounds of the Union; and

   (ii) A "**Preliminary Sunedrion**" shall consist of a maximum of one elected representative from each Ucadia Foundation within the jurisdiction of each Ucadia University; and

   (iii) A "**Probational Sunedrion**" shall consist of a maximum of one elected representative from each Preliminary, Probational, Prerogative or Permanent Ucadia University within the Union; and

   (iv) A "**Prerogative Sunedrion**" shall consist of active office holders being the Mediator, the Alexander, the Basileus, the Economos, the Stratagos, the Kephalos and the Mentor, elected by the Prerogative Synod; and

   (v) A "**Permanent Sunedrion**" shall consist of official office holders being the Mediator, the Alexander, the Basileus, the Economos, the Stratagos, the Kephalos and the Mentor, elected by the Permanent Synod.

3. By virtue of the powers vested in the Sunedrion, subject to the provisions of the present Articles, the Sunedrion shall have the following consolidated powers:- Sunedrion Powers

   (i) To appoint, suspend or remove any office holder less than an Exarch, subject to the advice and consent of the Synod; and

   (ii) To preside over any and all executive meetings, conferences, committees and business; and select the agenda and minutes of any such activities, through the advice, support and counsel of the appropriate Secretary; and overrule, suspend or set-aside any motion before any executive meeting, conference, or committee, except a motion concerning probity; and

   (iii) To make public or secret treaties or agreements with non-Ucadian and foreign states and bodies, by and with the Advice of the Sunedrion and Consent of the Synod; and

(iv) To submit proposed bills for review and upon a simple majority vote, to then order the bill to the Synod for review and vote; and

(v) To assent any legislation into law as a Statute within thirty days of its receipt, providing such legislation has been presented and approved by vote of the Synod; and

(vi) To veto any legislation within thirty days of its receipt, providing such legislation has been presented once and passed by less than two thirds majority vote in the Synod. However, the Sunedrion may not veto legislation having been passed by two thirds majority vote; and

(vii) To declare a state of emergency in times of clear disaster or major crisis, for not more than sixty days, before having to submit an account to the Synod for such action and a bill for its approval or extension for not longer than six months, whereby the Sunedrion shall have full strategic command for the commitment of the forces and resources of the Union, and the power to temporarily suspend certain procedures and rules, upon the agreed counsel of an Emergency Sunedrion; and

(viii) To nominate and appoint, subject to the advice and consent of the Synod, the candidate for any and all Offices less than an Exarch. However, any motion to suspend or remove such office holders shall be subject to the Synod; and

(ix) To publish in print and multimedia form an Annual Plan of the Government, subject to the advice and approval of the Synod, that states the financial, moral, strategic and well-being of the Union to all Members, Officers, Agents, Employees and Contractors; and

(x) To publish in print and multimedia form an Annual Message outlining the key messages, guidance, inspiration and comfort to all Members, Officers, Agents, Employees and Contractors of the Union.

TITLE VI: UCADIA GLOBE UNION

Article 55 – Ucadia Globe Union

1. The "**Ucadia Globe Union**" or simply the "Globe Union" is the highest civil society, body, entity, body politic, aggregate, association and union of all Ucadia and Non-Ucadia Societies for planet Earth and the entire Solar System. Ucadia Globe Union

Only the Supernatural and Spiritual Societies of One Heaven, One Christ, One Islam and One Spirit may properly claim higher status than the Global Union Society of the Whole Earth and Sea, in accord with the most sacred Covenants *Pactum De Singularis Caelum*, *Pactum De Singularis Christus*, *Pactum De Singularis Islam* and *Pactum De Singularis Spiritus*.

2. The eleven (11) primary Organs of the Ucadia Globe Union are:- The Organs of the Globe Union

(i) Globe Senate; and

(ii) Supreme (Globe) Council; and

(iii) Global Secretariat; and

(iv) Globe Court of Justice; and

(v) Globe Treasury; and

(vi) Global Guard; and

(vii) Global Defence Council; and

(viii) Globe Economic Council; and

(ix) Globe Ecologic Council; and

(x) Globe Cultural Council; and

(xi) Global Space Council.

Article 56 – Gold Credo (Credit)

1. "**Gold Credo (Credit)**" is the second highest possible form of valid and legitimate Money, issued under the exclusive Divine Rights: *Ius Divinum Moneta* and *Ius Divinum Vectigalis Moneta*, in accord with the most sacred Covenants *Pactum De Singularis Caelum, Pactum De Singularis Christus, Pactum De Singularis Islam, Pactum De Singularis Spiritus, Carta Sacrum De Congregationis Globus* and the seven (7) Constitutional Charters of the Ucadia Regional Unions. Gold Credo (Credit)

Gold Credo (Credit) is the primary lawful and legal currency and asset class used by Ucadia Union Banks and Funds to underwrite the ownership, use and exchange of all goods, services, assets and obligations.

2. A Gold Credo (Credit) shall have the following permanent value relationships:- Face value relationships of a Gold Credo (Credit)

   (i) 100 gold credo (credit) = 1 supreme credo (credit); and

   (ii) 1 gold credo (credit)= 10,000 silver credo (credit); and

   (iii) 1 gold credo (credit)= 10,000,000 union moneta; and

   (iv) 1 gold credo (credit)= 10,000,000 university moneta.

3. In accord with the most sacred Covenants *Pactum De Singularis Caelum, Pactum De Singularis Christus, Pactum De Singularis Islam, Pactum De Singularis Spiritus, Carta Sacrum De Congregationis Globus and the seven (7) Constitutional Charters of the Ucadia Regional Unions,* the exclusive Divine Right of *Ius Divinum Templum* to form, control and administer Gold Credo (Credit) Registers and Accounts shall be permanently vested to the Ucadia Globe Union Treasury as Trustee of the **Ucadia Gold Credo (Credit) Monetary System**. Formation, Control and Oversight of Gold Credo (Credit) Register and Accounts

4. Qualification for the right to ultimately hold, own and manage Gold Credo (Credit) Accounts shall be granted only to those valid Ucadia Union Banks and Funds listed as beneficiaries of one or more Gold Credo (Credit) Accounts. Qualification for Gold Credo (Credit) Account

5. All rights, rules, qualifications, procedures, instruments, registers, accounts, transactions, settlements and systems pertaining to Ucadia Gold Credo (Credit) shall be subject to the *Ucadia Gold Credo (Credit) Monetary System* administered by the Ucadia Globe Union Treasury, consistent with *Carta Sacrum De Congregationis Globus (Globe Union Charter)* and *Carta Economia De Congregationis Globus (Globe Union Economic Charter)* and *Carta Iudicialis De Congregationis Globus (Globe Union Judicial Charter).* Ucadia Gold Credo (Credit) Monetary System

6. While the principle value of a Supreme Credo (Credit) is upon the equality of all men and women, regardless of race, colour, creed, gender or religion, the principle value and purpose of Gold Credo (Credit) is to recognise the value a society places on the education and knowledge of its people, as well as the collective investment by Ucadia societies in fulfilling the core obligations of humanity to the future of life on planet Earth and within the Solar System. Principle Value Purpose of Ucadia Gold Credo (Credit)

7. In accord with the most sacred Covenant *Pactum De Singularis Caelum*, Gold Credo represents the permanent ecclesiastical, lawful and legal extraction of the essence of all spiritual and temporal value Non use of physical gold as currency

of Gold from all the existing physical and elemental material into Ucadia Gold Credo (Credit).

Any and all ecclesiastical and official ceremonies, rites and rituals concerning physical gold and gold reserves are hereby prohibited, suppressed and never permitted to be revived.

The historical spiritual and temporal value of Gold through Ucadia Gold Credo (Credo) may continue to be used in underwriting legitimate currencies, however the physical material of gold is only permitted to be treated as a useful commodity or ceremonial event of significance.

Subject to *Carta Economia De Congregationis Globus (Globe Union Economic Charter)*, Physical Gold henceforth is strictly forbidden to be generally used as currency, money or the underwriting of money.

8. Subject to *Carta Sacrum De Congregationis Globus (Globe Union Charter)* and *Carta Economia De Congregationis Globus (Globe Union Economic Charter)*, a new Gold Credo (Credit) Register shall be formed and published every eight (8) years. Gold Credo (Credit) Register

If the total value of transactions between Gold Credo (Credit) Accounts during the eight (8) year period reflects less than ten (10 %) of the total value of the Register, no recalculations are required and the Register may be re-issued under new Instrument Numbers for the following eight (8) years.

9. Subject to *Carta Sacrum De Congregationis Globus (Globe Union Charter)* and *Carta Economia De Congregationis Globus (Globe Union Economic Charter)*, the following eight (8) criteria are recognised and ratified as the essential requirements of a valid Gold Credo (Credit) Instrument listed in the Gold Credo (Credit) Register:- Structure of a Gold Credo (Credit)

(i) At least one valid unit of universal value evidenced by the existence of a unique eighteen (18) digit serial number representing the valid existence of the Gold Credo (Credit) belonging to the Great Ledger of Gold Credo (Credit) serial numbers for all Gold Credo (Credit) created and issued; and

(ii) The eighteen (18) digit Great Register number representing the valid Master Account Number into which the one or more Gold Credo (Credit) have been placed; and

(iii) A single beneficiary Master Account Number to whom the Gold Credo (Credit) is granted being the Ucadia Globe Union Reserve Bank or one of the seven (7) valid Ucadia Regional Union Reserve Banks; and

(iv) A record of the valid eighteen (18) digit Great Register number of the authorised office of the Union Treasury that first created the Gold Credo (Credit); and

(v) A record of the valid eighteen (18) digit Great Register number of the Member commissioned to the office of the Union Treasury that first created the Gold Credo (Credit); and

(vi) The eighteen (18) digit Great Register number of the instrument to which the one or more Gold Credo (Credit) have been assigned; and

(vii) The Ucadian Time at which the Gold Credo (Credit) was legitimately created and assigned to its particular instrument; and

(viii) The eighteen (18) digit Great Register number representing the valid Supreme Credo (Credit) instrument specifically underwriting the issue of these one or more Gold Credo (Credit).

10. Subject to *Carta Sacrum De Congregationis Globus (Globe Union Charter)* and *Carta Economia De Congregationis Globus (Globe Union Economic Charter)*, the calculation of any gift, grant or conveyance of Gold Credo (Credits), underwritten by Supreme Credo (Credits) at the commencement of the first Gold Credo Register shall be according to the following criteria under the principal that all people are borne equal and should have equal access to knowledge and the right to a competent, complete and comprehensive education to tertiary level skills and abilities:- Start Up Calculation Methodology Gold Credo (Credits)

(i) *Regional Ucadia Unions*: One Gold Credo (Credit) per living person between the ages of 18 and 80 having accomplished at least 10 years primary and secondary school and completed at least one tertiary degree or qualification - whether or not home school - through duly recognised education institutions and valid education methods at the time of the calculation; and

(ii) *Ucadia Foundations*: A Fund of eight million (8,000,000) Gold Credo (Credits) to the Ucadia Foundation Treasury, created by multiplying the total number of Ucadia Universities by the base number twenty four thousand, with eligibility per Ucadia Foundation based on weighting the total population of the relevant Ucadia University as a percentage of total world population; and

(iii) *Original Nations*: A Fund of sixteen million (16,000,000) Gold Credo (Credits) to the Original Nations Treasury, with eligibility per Ucadia Original Nations Society based on weighting the total indigenous and disenfranchised populations of each relevant internationally recognised state and country as a percentage of total world population of indigenous and disenfranchised; and

(iv) *Fixed Funds:* Individual Funds of twenty six million (26,000,000) Gold Credo (Credit) allocated to Treasury of One Christ, Treasury of One Islam, Treasury of One Spirit, Ucadia Moon Federation Treasury and Ucadia Mars Federation Treasury; and

(v) *Fixed Funds*: Individual Funds of sixteen million five hundred thousand (16,500,000) Gold Credo (Credit) allocated to Ucadia Europa-Jupiter Federation Treasury and Ucadia Titan-Saturn Federation Treasury; and

(vi) *Reserve*: Fund of at least eighty two million (82,000,000) Gold Credo (Credit) allocated to Ucadia Globe Union Treasury.

11. Subject to *Carta Sacrum De Congregationis Globus (Globe Union Charter)* and *Carta Economia De Congregationis Globus (Globe Union Economic Charter)*, once a Gold Credo (Credit) has been formed, it exists as a most sacred object representing a living embodiment of the spirit of a Supreme Credo (Credit) and the pure essence of value of gold. Once created, no Gold Credo (Credit) may be uncreated.

Forbiddance to deface, destroy a Gold Credo (Credit)

The existence of all Gold Credo (Credit) is to be validated and verified via a Register of Currency in accord with the most sacred Covenant *Pactum De Singularis Caelum* and published once every eight (8) years.

12. Subject to *Carta Sacrum De Congregationis Globus (Globe Union Charter)* and *Carta Economia De Congregationis Globus (Globe Union Economic Charter)*, the Gold Credo (Credit) Register reflecting the base stock of Gold Credo (Credit) may be increased upon the expiry of the previous register every eight (8) years according to these conditions:-

Expansion of Gold Credo (Credit)

(i) If the total number of Gold Credo (Credit) entitled to be issued based on the total number of registered secondary school graduates and tertiary students or qualified and competent residents increases within the bounds of the Ucadia Union; and

(ii) One new Gold Credo shall then be issued for every additional education enrolment since the previous calculation for that particular Union.

13. As a Gold Credo (Credit) once created cannot be uncreated, in the event that the total number of secondary school graduates and tertiary students and total qualified and competent members of population decreases, then the excess number shall return to the benefit of the Globe Union Treasury. Contraction of Gold Credo (Credit)

14. In respect of the Start-Up Calculations as at GAIA E8:Y3209:A1:S1:M6:D1, also known as [21 December 2009], to determine the proportion and entitlements of the Ucadia Union Treasuries being the determination of the number of people within the bounds of each regional Union between the ages of 17 and 80 having completed at least ten years primary and secondary education and having undertaken either a tertiary degree, or qualification or home school equivalent:- Founding Start Up Calculation

(i) Approximately thirty million, five hundred and seventeen thousand (30,517,000) people were identified within the bounds of the Africans Union between the ages of 17 and 80, after applying the benchmark factors allowing for literacy and numeracy standards of the region; and

(ii) Approximately three hundred and forty six million, five hundred and twenty one thousand (346,521,000) people were identified within the bounds of the Americas Union between the ages of 17 and 80, after applying the benchmark factors allowing for literacy and numeracy standards of the region; and

(iii) Approximately fifty nine million, nine hundred and twelve thousand (59,912,000) people were identified within the bounds of the Arabian Union between the ages of 17 and 80, after applying the benchmark factors allowing for literacy and numeracy standards of the region; and

(iv) Approximately three hundred and ninety nine million, seven hundred and thirty four thousand (399,734,000) people were identified within the bounds of the Asia Union between the ages of 17 and 80, after applying the benchmark factors allowing for literacy and numeracy standards of the region; and

(v) Approximately two hundred and eighty eight million and ninety one thousand (288,091,000) people were identified within the bounds of the Euro Union between the ages of 17 and 80, after applying the benchmark factors allowing for literacy and numeracy standards of the region; and

(vi) Approximately seventeen million and nine hundred and eighty one thousand (17,981,000) people were identified within the bounds of the Oceanic Union between the ages of 17 and 80, after applying the benchmark factors allowing for literacy and numeracy standards of the region; and

(vii) Approximately twenty seven million, four hundred and thirty seven thousand (27,437,000) people were identified within the bounds of the Levant Union between the ages of 17 and 80, after applying the benchmark factors allowing for literacy and numeracy standards of the region.

Gold Credo (Credo) Accounts

15. Consistent with *Carta Sacrum De Congregationis Globus (Globe Union Charter)* and *Carta Economia De Congregationis Globus (Globe Union Economic Charter)*, there shall be only two possible types of Gold Credo (Credit) Accounts being Fund and Sovereign held by valid Ucadia Union Treasuries:-

(i) A *Gold Credo Fund Account* identified by the letters "GF" is the primary account for holding Gold Credo and the first Account into which any new Gold Credo are deposited. While the value of Gold Credo (Credit) are not used to underwrite further assets, the value of a Gold Credo (Credit) Fund Account represents the full faith and credit of Sovereign and Independent bodies, associations and societies; and

(ii) A *Gold Credo Sovereign Account* identified by the letters "GS" provides the underlying asset value and underwriting to the issuance of Silver Credo (Credits). A Silver Credo cannot be issued and circulated as currency unless a value of similar amount exists in an associated Gold Credo Sovereign Account. Once Gold Credo are deposited into a Gold Credo Sovereign Account, the amount of Gold Credo is held and locked for a period of four years corresponding to the length of time a Silver Credo Register is in circulation.

Foundation Capital Stock of Gold Credo (Credit)

16. Consistent with *Carta Sacrum De Congregationis Globus (Globe Union Charter)* and *Carta Economia De Congregationis Globus (Globe Union Economic Charter)*, the Foundation Capital Stock of Gold Credo (Credit) created by the Ucadia Globe Union Treasury and the seven (7) Ucadia Regional Union Treasuries issued on GAIA E8:Y3209:A1:S1:M6:D1, also known as [21 December 2009], is one billion four hundred forty million (1,440,000,000) for the benefit of the following Union Treasuries:-

(i) Twenty six million (26,000,000) Gold Credo (Credit) deposited for the Treasury of One Christ into Account Number GU7100-999999-999999 formed through the conversion and activation of two hundred and sixty thousand (260,000) Supreme Credo

(Credit) from Account Number OH7100-999999- 999999; and

(ii) Twenty six million (26,000,000) Gold Credo (Credit) deposited for the Treasury of One Islam into Account Number GU8100-999999-999999 formed through the conversion and activation of two hundred and sixty thousand (260,000) Supreme Credo (Credit) from Account Number OH8100-999999- 999999; and

(iii) Twenty six million (26,000,000) Gold Credo (Credit) deposited for the Treasury of One Spirit into Account Number GU9100-999999-999999 formed through the conversion and activation of two hundred and sixty thousand (260,000) Supreme Credo (Credit) from Account Number OH9100-999999-999999; and

(iv) Thirty million, five hundred and seventeen thousand (30,517,000) Gold Credo (Credit) deposited for the Ucadia Africans Union Treasury into Account Number GU1100-999999-999999 formed through the conversion and activation of three hundred and five thousand, one hundred and seventy (305,170) Supreme Credo (Credit) from Account Number OH1100-999999-999999; and

(v) Three hundred and forty six million, five hundred twenty one thousand (346,521,000) Gold Credo (Credit) deposited for the Ucadia Americas Union Treasury into Account Number GU2100-999999-999999 formed through the conversion and activation of three million, four hundred and sixty five thousand and two hundred and ten (3,465,210) Supreme Credo (Credit) from Account Number OH2100-999999-999999; and

(vi) Fifty nine million, nine hundred and twelve thousand (59,912,000) Gold Credo (Credit) deposited for the Ucadia Arabian Union Treasury into Account Number GU3100-999999-999999 formed through the conversion and activation of five hundred and ninety nine thousand, one hundred and twenty (599,120) Supreme Credo (Credit) from Account Number OH3100-999999-999999; and

(vii) Three hundred and ninety nine million, seven hundred and thirty four thousand (399,734,000) Gold Credo (Credit) deposited for the Ucadia Asia Union Treasury into Account Number GU4100-999999-999999 formed through the conversion and activation of three million, nine hundred and ninety seven thousand and three hundred and forty (3,997,340) Supreme Credo (Credit) from Account Number OH4100-999999-999999; and

(viii) Two hundred and eighty eight million, ninety one thousand (288,091,000) Gold Credo (Credit) deposited for the Ucadia Euro Union Treasury into Account Number GU5100-999999-999999 formed through the conversion and activation of two million, eight hundred and eighty thousand and nine hundred and ten (2,880,910) Supreme Credo (Credit) from Account Number OH5100-999999-999999; and

(ix) Seventeen million, nine hundred and eighty one thousand (17,981,000) Gold Credo (Credit) deposited for the Ucadia Oceanic Union Treasury into Account Number GU6100-999999-999999 formed through the conversion and activation of one hundred and seventy nine thousand and eight hundred and ten (179,810) Supreme Credo (Credit) from Account Number OH6100-999999-999999; and

(x) Twenty seven million, four hundred and thirty seven thousand (27,437,000) Gold Credo (Credit) deposited for the Ucadia Levant Union Treasury into Account Number GUL100-999999-999999 formed through the conversion and activation of two hundred and seventy four thousand, three hundred and seventy (274,370) Supreme Credo (Credit) from Account Number OHL100-999999-999999; and

(xi) Eighty two million, eight hundred and seven thousand (82,807,000) Gold Credo (Credit) deposited for the Ucadia Globe Union Treasury into Account Number GU0100-999999-999999 formed through the conversion and activation of eight hundred and twenty eight thousand and seventy (828,070) Supreme Credo (Credit) from Account Number OH0100-999999-999999; and

(xii) Sixteen million (16,000,000) Gold Credo (Credit) deposited for the Original Nations Treasury into Account Number GUZ100-999999-999999 formed through the conversion and activation of one hundred and sixty thousand (160,000) Supreme Credo (Credit) from Account Number OHZ100-999999-999999; and

(xiii) Eight million (8,000,000) Gold Credo (Credit) deposited for the Ucadia Foundations Treasury into Account Number GUF100-999999-999999 formed through the conversion and activation of eighty thousand (80,000) Supreme Credo (Credit) from Account Number OHF100-999999-999999; and

(xiv) Twenty six million (26,000,000) Gold Credo (Credit) deposited for the Ucadia Moon Federation Treasury into Account Number GUX100-999999-999999 formed through the conversion and activation of two hundred and sixty thousand (260,000) Supreme Credo (Credit) from Account Number OHX100-999999-999999; and

(xv) Twenty six million (26,000,000) Gold Credo (Credit) deposited for the Ucadia Mars Federation Treasury into Account Number GUM100-999999-999999 formed through the conversion and activation of two hundred and sixty thousand (260,000) Supreme Credo (Credit) from Account Number OHM100-999999-999999; and

(xvi) Sixteen million five hundred thousand (16,500,000) Gold Credo (Credit) deposited for the Ucadia Europa-Jupiter Federation Treasury into Account Number GUJ100-999999-999999 formed through the conversion and activation of one hundred and sixty five thousand (165,000) Supreme Credo (Credit) from Account Number OHJ100-999999-999999; and

(xvii) Sixteen million five hundred thousand (16,500,000) Gold Credo (Credit) deposited for the Ucadia Titan-Saturn Federation Treasury into Account Number GUT100-999999-999999 formed through the conversion and activation of one hundred and sixty five thousand (165,000) Supreme Credo (Credit) from Account Number OHT100-999999-999999.

17. Consistent with *Carta Sacrum De Congregationis Globus (Globe Union Charter)* and *Carta Economia De Congregationis Globus (Globe Union Economic Charter)*, no Interest or rent may be charged by any central bank or financial institution on the manufacture and distribution of currency supported by the face value of the given Gold Credo (Credit) in circulation. Forbiddance of Compound Interest

The calculation of any fee based on a derivative of a sum value is banned by any entity being charged on the release of credits into circulation upon the certification of a valid loan. Only flat fees as a reflection of service, with no imputed attempt to hide Interest as a fee is permitted.

The reason that compound Interest shall be banned is that it directly attacks the integrity and fabric of currency value and therefore wealth and commerce. This has been an ancient and fundamental understanding by civilisations using monetary systems for thousands of years.

18. A valid Ucadian Union Treasury may gift, grant, exchange or convey Gold Credo only to another valid Ucadian Union Treasury. The rules for any gift, grant, exchange or conveyance of Gold Credo (Credit) Gift, Grant, Exchange or Conveyance of Gold Credo between valid Ucadia Union Treasuries shall be the following:-

(i) A valid Ucadia Union Treasury may only gift, grant, exchange or convey existing Gold Credo (Credit) formed by the initial calculation of conversion of Supreme Credo (Credits) or subsequent conversions as stated by the present Article; and

(ii) Excluding the Globe Union Treasury, all other valid Ucadia Union Treasuries may only gift or grant a maximum of five percent (5%) of their Gold Credo (Credit) reserves to other valid Ucadia Union Treasuries between each Gold Credo Account Settlement Period of once every eight (8) years. The Globe Union Treasury may gift or grant a maximum of ten percent (10%) of its Gold Credo (Credit) reserves; and

(iii) A valid Ucadia Union Treasury may exchange or convey Gold Credo (Credits) as payment and settlement of obligations and debts with another Treasury at the conclusion of a Gold Credo Account Settlement Period once every eight (8) years as part of the function of a Ucadia Union Treasury Resolution Convention and the acceptance and clearance of certain valid obligations and debts.

19. The *Account Settlement Period* for all Gold Credo (Credit) transactions between valid Ucadia Union Treasuries shall be once every eight (8) years. All accounts in Gold Credo (Credit) shall be settled at the conclusion of this eight (8) year period at a Ucadia Union Treasury Resolution Convention according to the following criteria:- Gold Credo (Credit) Account Settlement Period

(i) All valid Ucadia Union Treasuries are required to attend the Convention; and

(ii) All Treasuries submit claims and obligations in terms of Gold Credo (Credits) at the commencement of the Convention; and

(iii) All debts and obligations are cross matched, cleared and net redemptions or obligations made clear before final settlement and the required payment of any outstanding Gold Credo (Credit).

20. In the event that the capital stock of a valid Ucadian Union Treasury should become greater than a ratio of more than one Gold Credo per one Ordinary Member or less than one Gold Credo for every thirty (30) Ordinary Members then a Special Redemption Convention shall be called upon the time of renewal for the currency register of Gold Credo (Credit) to hold a Special Redemption Convention whereby the following steps shall be mandatory and take place:- Gold Credo (Credit) Special Redemption Convention

(i) Any Ucadia Union Treasury with a ratio of greater than one Gold Credo per one Ordinary Members shall surrender as a gift a minimum of ten (10%) percent of its reserves in Gold Credo (Credit) to the Globe Union Treasury or greater if insufficient to lessen the ratio from one Gold Credo per one Ordinary Member; and

(ii) Any Ucadia Union Treasury with a ratio of less than one Gold Credo for every thirty (30) Ordinary Members, shall be given a gift by the Globe Union Treasury of sufficient Gold Credo (Credit) so that the ratio is not less than one Gold Credo for every ten (10) Ordinary Members of the particular Union.

21. The issue of Gold Credo (Credit) and the management of its various Registers, Manifests and Accounts are governed by the Rules of the *Ucadia Gold Credo (Credit) Monetary System* consistent with the most sacred Covenant *Pactum De Singularis Caelum, Carta Sacrum De Congregationis Globus,* this present Charter and its associated Economic Charter. Autonomy of Gold Credo (Credit) Rules

These Rules are so designed to create an Autonomous and self-correcting system that forbids the necessity for intervention or manual correction. Therefore, at no point is there any lawful requirement for direct intervention in the autonomous rules conducting the creation, management or use of Gold Credo (Credits).

The Globe Union Treasury shall be empowered to provide additional guidelines and policies towards the Ucadia Gold Credo (Credit) Monetary System as an automated and self regulating system.

Article 57 – Silver Credo (Credit)

1. "**Silver Credo (Credit)**" is the third highest possible form of valid and legitimate Money, issued under the exclusive Ecclesiastical Rights *Ius Ecclesiae Moneta* and *Ius Ecclesiae Vectigalis Moneta*, in accord with the most sacred Covenants *Pactum De Singularis Caelum, Pactum De Singularis Christus, Pactum De Singularis Islam, Pactum De Singularis Spiritus, Carta Sacrum De Congregationis Globus* and the seven (7) Constitutional Charters of the Ucadia Regional Unions. Silver Credo (Credit)

It is the primary lawful and legal currency used by Ucadia Unions, Universities, Provinces, Campuses and Medium-Large Companies for the exchange of goods, services and obligations.

2. Consistent with *Carta Sacrum De Congregationis Globus (Globe Union Charter)* and *Carta Economia De Congregationis Globus (Globe Union Economic Charter)*, a Silver Credo (Credit) shall have Face value relationships of a Silver Credo (Credit)

the following permanent value relationships:-

(i) 1,000,000 silver credo (credit) = 1 supreme credo (credit); and

(ii) 10,000 silver credo (credit) = 1 gold credo (credit); and

(iii) 1 silver credo (credit) = 1,000 union moneta; and

(iv) 1 silver credo (credit) = 1,000 university moneta.

3. In accord with the most sacred Covenants *Pactum De Singularis Caelum, Pactum De Singularis Christus, Pactum De Singularis Islam, Pactum De Singularis Spiritus, Carta Sacrum De Congregationis Globus and the seven (7) Constitutional Charters of the Ucadia Regional Unions,* the exclusive Ecclesiastical Right of *Ius Ecclesiae Templum* to form, control and administer Silver Credo (Credit) Registers and Accounts shall be permanently vested to those valid Ucadia Union Banks and Funds listed as owners of one or more Silver Credo (Credits), with the Globe Union Bank as Trustee of the **Ucadia Silver Credo (Credit) Monetary System**.

Formation, Control and Oversight of Silver Credo (Credit) Register and Accounts

4. Qualification for the right to ultimately hold, own and manage Silver Credo (Credit) Accounts shall be granted only to those valid Ucadia Unions, Universities, Provinces, Campuses and Medium-Large Companies listed as beneficiaries of one or more Silver Credo (Credit) Accounts.

Qualification for Silver Credo (Credit) Account

5. All rights, rules, qualifications, procedures, instruments, registers, accounts, transactions, settlements and systems pertaining to Ucadia Silver Credo (Credit) shall be subject to the *Ucadia Silver Credo (Credit) Monetary System* administered by the Ucadia Globe Union Bank, consistent with *Carta Sacrum De Congregationis Globus (Globe Union Charter), Carta Economia De Congregationis Globus (Globe Union Economic Charter)* and *Carta Iudicialis De Congregationis Globus (Globe Union Judicial Charter).*

Ucadia Silver Credo (Credit) Monetary System

6. While the principle value purpose of Gold Credo (Credit) is to recognise the value a society places on the education and knowledge of its people, as well as the collective investment by Ucadia societies in fulfilling the core obligations of humanity to the future of life on planet Earth and within the Solar System, the principle value purpose of Ucadia Silver Credo (Credit) is to recognise the positive and empowering employment and fair payment and compensation of people within each Ucadia society, through the use and application of their education, knowledge and skills, as well as the collective investment by Ucadia societies in fulfilling the core obligations of humanity to the future of life on planet Earth and within the Solar System.

Principle Value Purpose of Ucadia Silver Credo (Credit)

7. In accord with the most sacred Covenant *Pactum De Singularis Caelum*, Silver Credo represents the permanent ecclesiastical, lawful and legal extraction of the essence of all spiritual and temporal value of Silver from all the physical and elemental material into Ucadia Silver Credo (Credit). Non use of physical silver as currency

Any and all ecclesiastical and official ceremonies, rites and rituals concerning physical silver and silver reserves are hereby prohibited, suppressed and never permitted to be revived.

The historical spiritual and temporal value of Silver through Ucadia Silver Credo (Credo) may continue to be used in underwriting legitimate currencies, however the physical material of silver is only permitted be treated as a useful commodity.

8. Consistent with *Carta Sacrum De Congregationis Globus (Globe Union Charter)* and *Carta Economia De Congregationis Globus (Globe Union Economic Charter)*, a new Silver Credo (Credit) Register shall be formed and published every four (4) years. Silver Credo (Credit) Register

If the total value of transactions between Silver Credo (Credit) Accounts during the four (4) year period reflects less than ten (10 %) of the total value of the Register, no recalculations are required and the Register may be re-issued under new Instrument Numbers for the following four (4) years.

9. Consistent with *Carta Sacrum De Congregationis Globus (Globe Union Charter)* and *Carta Economia De Congregationis Globus (Globe Union Economic Charter)*, the following eight (8) criteria are recognised and ratified as the essential requirements of a valid Silver Credo (Credit) Instrument listed in the Silver Credo (Credit) Register:- Structure of a Silver Credo (Credit)

(i) At least one valid unit of universal value evidenced by the existence of a unique eighteen (18) digit serial number representing the valid existence of the Silver Credo (Credit) belonging to the Great Ledger of Silver Credo (Credit) serial numbers for all Silver Credo (Credit) ever created and issued; and

(ii) The eighteen (18) digit Great Register number representing the valid Master Account Number into which the one or more Silver Credo (Credit) have been placed; and

(iii) A single beneficiary Master Account Number to whom the Silver Credo (Credit) is granted being a valid Union Reserve Bank, valid Ucadia University Reserve Bank, Ucadia Province Community Bank, Ucadia Campus Community Bank, Ucadia Fund or Registered Ucadia Medium-Large Company; and

(iv) A record of the valid eighteen (18) digit Great Register number of the authorised office of the Union Reserve Bank that first created the Silver Credo (Credit); and

(v) A record of the valid eighteen (18) digit Great Register number of the Member commissioned to the office of the Union Reserve Bank that first created the Silver Credo (Credit); and

(vi) The eighteen (18) digit Great Register number of the instrument to which the one or more Silver Credo (Credit) have been assigned; and

(vii) The Ucadian Time at which the Silver Credo (Credit) was legitimately created and assigned to its particular instrument; and

(viii) The eighteen (18) digit Great Register number representing the valid Gold Credo (Credit) instrument specifically underwriting the issue of these one or more Silver Credo (Credit).

10. The calculation of any gift, grant or conveyance of Silver Credo (Credits), underwritten by Gold Credo (Credits) at the commencement of the first Silver Credo Register shall be according to the following criteria under the principle that such entitlements to Ucadia Universities, Provinces, Campuses, Foundations and Medium-Large Companies shall reflect a fair, reasonable and realistic valuation of existing Non-Ucadian money reserves, deposits, obligation values, capital and asset values, transactions, trade and productivity:-

Start Up Calculation Methodology of Silver Credo (Credits)

(i) *GDP Calculation*: The initial measure used to determine the valid entitlement of Silver Credo (Credit) for each Ucadia University, Province and Campus shall be the estimated Gross Domestic Product (GDP) multiplied by fourteen (14) times for each Ucadia University at parity prices as at the Sacred Space Day Time being GAIA E8:Y3209:A29:S3:M27:D1, also known as [Monday, 10 May 2010]; and

(ii) Fixed Funds: representing approximately the maximum underwriting of fifty four percent (54%) of the value of Gold Credo (Credit) underwriting the funds associated with One Christ, One Islam, One Spirit, Original Nations, Ucadia Foundations, Ucadia Moon Federation, Ucadia Mars Federation, Ucadia Europa-Jupiter Federation and Ucadia Titan-Saturn Federation.

11. Once created, no Silver Credo (Credit) may be uncreated. Once a Silver Credo (Credit) has been formed, it exists as a most sacred object representing both an extraction from the spirit and essence of a Gold

Forbiddance to deface, destroy a Silver Credo

Credo (Credit) and the pure essence of value and nature of silver. (Credit)

The existence of all Silver Credo (Credit) is to be validated and verified via a Register of Currency that in accord with the most sacred Covenant *Pactum De Singularis Caelum* is to be published once every four (4) years.

12. The Silver Credo (Credit) Register reflecting the base stock of Silver Credo (Credit) may be increased upon the expiry of the previous register every four (4) years according to these conditions:- Expansion of Silver Credo (Credit)

(i) That the total number of employed and average wages for the particular Union has risen since the last review and issue of a new Silver Credo (Credit) Register; and

(ii) That a fair, reasonable and objective assessment of projected asset and transactional values within a Ucadia Union produces a figure larger than the Silver Credo (Credits) currently allocated to such accounts by the particular Union Reserve Bank.

13. While a Silver Credo (Credit) once created cannot be uncreated, the total number of Silver Credo (Credits) may be reduced every four years by returning excess Silver Credo to the Globe Union Reserve Bank upon the following criteria:- Reduction of Silver Credo (Credit)

(i) That the total number of employed and average wage for the particular Union has fallen since the last review and issue of a new Silver Credo (Credit) Register; and

(ii) That a fair, reasonable and objective assessment of projected asset and transactional values within a Ucadia Union produces a figure substantially lower than the Silver Credo (Credits) currently allocated to such accounts by the particular Union Reserve Bank.

14. The Foundation Capital Stock of Silver Credo (Credit) for the Ucadia Euro Union and all Universities, Provinces and Campuses therein shall be one trillion and six hundred billion (1,600,000,000,000) Silver Credos (Credits). Foundation Capital Stock of Silver Credo (Credit)

15. Consistent with *Carta Sacrum De Congregationis Globus (Globe Union Charter)* and *Carta Economia De Congregationis Globus (Globe Union Economic Charter)*, there shall be twenty (20) different types of Ucadia Silver Credo (Credit) Accounts, including:- Silver Credo (Credit) Accounts

(i) *Silver Credo (Credit) Bond Account* is an account potentially bringing New Silver Credo (Credit) into Circulation transferred from a Silver Credo (Credit) Sovereign Account as underwriting to an issued bond, so that no bond ever issued under Ucadia can ever possibly be in default. Conversion to foreign currency is a separate right and issue. When the certificate is "redeemed" the account is settled and cleared to a Silver Credo (Credit) Cash Account; and

(ii) *Silver Credo (Credit) Budget Account* is an account holding an unrealised amount of proposed Silver Credo (Credit) for a specific purpose. Once approved the Budget Account is cleared and the funds released into the appropriate accounts; and

(iii) *Silver Credo (Credit) Capital Account* is an account holding a certain amount of Silver Credo (Credit) transferred from a Silver Credo (Credit) Cash Account as effectively "paid up capital" against a specific asset; and

(iv) *Silver Credo (Credit) Cash Account*, also known as a "clearing account" as the primary Silver Credo (Credit) Account for clearing obligations. Every Silver Credo (Credit) Account holder always has one Silver Credo (Credit) Cash Account; and

(v) *Silver Credo (Credit) Coin Account* is an account bringing New Silver Credo (Credit) into Circulation transferred from a Silver Credo (Credit) Sovereign Account as underwriting to a negotiable Coin Certificate or actual minted batch of Silver Credo (Credit) Coins. When the certificate is "redeemed" the account is settled and cleared to a Silver Credo (Credit) Cash Account; and

(vi) *Silver Credo (Credit) Contingency Account* is an account holding a certain amount of Silver Credo (Credit) transferred from a Silver Credo (Credit) Cash Account as contingency against an incomplete contract, or risk, or option or contract to complete or come into effect on conditions; and

(vii) *Silver Credo (Credit) Credit Account* is an account potentially bringing New Silver Credo (Credit) into Circulation transferred from a Silver Credo (Credit) Sovereign Account as an advance "on demand" of new Silver Credo (Credit) on the agreement of a repayment or deposit of other valuable considerations, including the payment of non-Ucadian currencies and provision of some form of collateral; and

(viii) *Silver Credo (Credit) Demand Account* is an account holding an unrealised Demand and Debt for Silver Credo (Credit) that is due on account of one or more breaches and failures of contract and *bona fide* losses; and

(ix) *Silver Credo (Credit) Donation Account* is an account bringing New Silver Credo (Credit) into Circulation transferred from a Silver Credo (Credit) Sovereign Account as recognition for any historic foreign (non-Ucadian) currency finalisation, whether the person intended to exchange for Silver Credo (Credit) or not, or whether a formal loan or credit agreement was ever considered; and

(x) *Silver Credo (Credit) Exchange Account*, also known as a "settlement account" as the primary Silver Credo (Credit) Account for settling market obligations; and

(xi) *Silver Credo (Credit) Fund Account*, is an account potentially bringing New Silver Credo (Credit) into Circulation transferred from a Silver Credo (Credit) Sovereign Account as valuation to some other fixed corpus (body) of assets held in trust for a fixed term and assigned to the control of a valid Ucadia entity; and

(xii) *Silver Credo (Credit) Gain Account* is an account holding an unrealised Claim for Silver Credo (Credit) that is due on account of a *bona fide* profit against one or more registered assets with previous values; and

(xiii) *Silver Credo (Credit) Loss Account* is an account holding an unrealised Claim for Silver Credo (Credit) that is due on account of a *bona fide* loss against one or more registered assets with previous values; and

(xiv) *Silver Credo (Credit) Payment Account* is an account holding repayments in Silver Credo (Credit); and

(xv) *Silver Credo (Credit) Penalty Account* is an account holding the voluntary or assigned Silver Credo (Credit) payments as charge of penalties against breaches of contract; and

(xvi) *Silver Credo (Credit) Sovereign Account* is an account bringing New Silver Credo (Credit) into Circulation created upon the underwriting of Ucadia Gold (Credit) Credo held in trust. Only valid Ucadia entities hold Sovereign Accounts. Ucadia Silver Credo (Credit) is never transferred from a Silver Credo (Credit) Sovereign Account into another account, unless there is a corresponding valid trigger and event. In this sense, all Silver Credo (Credit) is effectively "spent" into circulation one transaction at a time based upon some key economic activity rather than arbitrary releases of large amounts that can disrupt the effectiveness of Silver Credo (Credit) in circulation; and

(xvii) *Silver Credo (Credit) Stamp Account* is an account bringing New Silver Credo (Credit) into Circulation transferred from a Silver Credo (Credit) Sovereign Account as underwriting to a negotiable Stamp Certificate or actual minted batch of Silver Credo (Credit) Stamps. When the certificate is "redeemed" the account is settled and cleared to a Silver Credo (Credit) Cash Account; and

(xviii) *Silver Credo (Credit) Suspension Account* is an account holding a certain amount of Silver Credo (Credit) transferred from other Silver Credo (Credit) Accounts of an individual or company in respect to disputed assets,or agreements or an unpaid demand of debt; and

(xix) *Silver Credo (Credit) Surety Account* is an account holding a certain amount of Silver Credo (Credit) transferred from a Silver Credo (Credit) Cash Account as effectively "insurance" against a specific contract; and

(xx) *Silver Credo (Credit) Valuation Account* is an account holding an unrealised Valuation of an asset in Silver Credo (Credit).

Qualification for Ucadia Silver Credo (Credit) Accounts

16. Only a registered and *bona fide* organ of a Ucadia Union, University, Province, Campus, or Foundation, Fund or Medium-Large Company may hold one or more Ucadia Silver Credo (Credit) Accounts:-

(i) *Ucadia Foundations for Universities* may hold and use Silver Credo (Credit) Accounts once their Board of Directors are ratified; and they have concluded the mandatory probational period without sanction or prohibition; and

(ii) *Ucadia Registered Companies* with an average revenue of twelve million (12,000,000) Ucadia Moneta (or greater) may hold and use Silver Credo (Credit) Accounts once their Board of Directors are ratified; and they have concluded the mandatory probational period without sanction or prohibition; and

(iii) *Prerogative and Permanent Ucadia Universities, Provinces and Campuses* may hold and use Silver Credo (Credit) Accounts if they have an average revenue of twelve million (12,000,000) Ucadia Moneta (or greater), once their executive government is ratified; and they have concluded the mandatory probational period without sanction or prohibition; and

(iv) Ucadia Federations and Funds possessing Ucadia Gold Credo (Credit) Rights may hold and use Silver Credo (Credit)

Accounts once their Board of Directors are ratified; and they have concluded the mandatory probational period without sanction or prohibition.

17. Consistent with *Carta Sacrum De Congregationis Globus (Globe Union Charter)* and *Carta Economia De Congregationis Globus (Globe Union Economic Charter)*, it shall be mandatory that all *Prerogative* and *Permanent* Ucadia Unions, Universities, Provinces, Campuses and Medium-Large Companies to settle their accounts between one another using Silver Credo (Credits) where the value of such transactions is equal to or exceeds one million (1,000,000) Ucadia Moneta.

Mandatory Use of Silver Credo (Credit) to settle accounts

18. No Interest or rent may be charged by any central or reserve bank or financial institution on the manufacture and distribution of currency supported by the face value of the given Silver Credo (Credit) in circulation.

Forbiddence of Compound Interest

The calculation of any fee based on a derivative of a sum value is banned by any entity being charged on the release of credits into circulation upon the certification of a valid loan. Only flat fees as a reflection of service, with no imputed attempt to hide Interest as a fee is permitted.

19. A valid Ucadian Union Reserve Bank or Ucadian University Reserve Bank or Ucadia Province Community Bank may gift, grant, exchange or convey Silver Credo only to another valid Ucadian Union or University Reserve Bank or Province Community Bank. Notwithstanding any further rules defined by the associated *Union Economic Constitutional Charter* to this present Charter, the rules for any gift, grant, exchange or conveyance of Silver Credo (Credit) between valid Ucadia Union Treasuries shall be the following:-

Gift, Grant, Exchange or Conveyance of Silver Credo

(i) A valid Ucadian Union or University Reserve Bank may only gift, grant, exchange or convey existing Silver Credo (Credit) formed by the initial calculation of conversion of Gold Credo (Credits) or subsequent expansions of the supply of Silver Credo (Credit) as stated by the present Article; and

(ii) Excluding the Union Reserve Banks, all Ucadian University Reserve Banks may only gift or grant a maximum of two percent (2%) of their Silver Credo (Credit) reserves to other valid Ucadian Union or University Reserve Banks per year. The Globe Union Reserve Bank may gift or grant a maximum of eight percent (8%) of its Silver Credo (Credit) reserves, while Ucadia Regional Reserve Banks may gift or grant a maximum of four percent (4%) of their Silver Credo (Credit) reserves; and

(iii) A valid Ucadian Union or University Reserve Bank may exchange or convey Silver Credo (Credits) as payment and settlement of obligations and debts with another valid Ucadian Union or University Reserve Bank at the conclusion of a Silver Credo Account Settlement Period once every four (4) years as part of the function of a Ucadia Reserve Bank Resolution Convention and the acceptance and clearance of certain valid obligations and debts.

20. The Account Settlement Period for all Silver Credo (Credit) transactions between valid Ucadian Union and University Reserve Banks and Ucadia Province Community Banks across the planet Earth shall be once every four years, prior to the re-issue of the new Silver Credo (Credit) Register. All accounts in Silver Credo (Credits) shall be settled at the conclusion of this four year period at a Ucadia Banks Resolution Convention according to the following criteria:-

Silver Credo (Credit) Account Settlement Period

(i) All valid Ucadia Union and University Reserve Banks and Ucadia Provincial Community Banks are required to attend the global Convention. The Convention shall be held in a different region (Union) every four years; and

(ii) All Ucadia Union and University Reserve Banks and Ucadia Provincial Community Banks must submit claims and obligations in terms of Silver Credo (Credits) prior to the commencement of the Convention; and

(iii) All regional and international debts and obligations of Campuses, Provinces and University Governments, their Agencies and Administration must have been submitted to the appropriate University Reserve Bank or Ucadia Provincial Community Bank at least ninety (90) days prior to the Global Convention; and

(iv) All regional and international debts and obligations of registered commercial and non-profit Companies, Associations and Entities must have been submitted to the appropriate University Reserve Bank at least ninety (90) days prior to the Global Convention; and

(v) All holdings in University Credits and Union Moneta of Union Reserve Banks and University Reserve Banks must be submitted at least ninety (90) days prior to the Global Convention; and

(vi) The first session of the Global Convention shall be the Government Obligations Settlement Session whereby the obligations and debts between governments are unwound and cleared and technically settled, with any balances to be repatriated at the conclusion of the Convention; and

(vii) The second session of the Global Convention shall be the Trade and Commercial Settlement Session whereby the trade and commercial debts owed by companies between Universities, regions and Unions are unwound and cleared and technically settled, with any balances to be repatriated at the conclusion of the Convention; and

(viii) The third and final session of the Global Convention shall be the Currency Repatriation Session whereby the holdings of Credit and Moneta currencies by each Reserve Bank are repatriated to the home Reserve Bank through unwinding, clearance and settlement. Any outstanding balances may then be used as payment of outstanding obligations from Session One or Session Two, or cleared by direct purchase through available Silver Credits of the Bank itself.

Silver Credo (Credit) Special Redemption Convention

21. In the event that the capital stock or holdings of Silver Credo (Credit) of a valid Ucadian Union Reserve Bank or Ucadia University Reserve Bank or Ucadia Province Community Bank should become greater than a ratio of more than one hundred thousand (100,000) Silver Credo per one Ordinary Member or less than one thousand (1,000) Silver Credo per one Ordinary Member then a Special Redemption Convention shall be called anytime prior the time of renewal for the currency register of Silver Credo (Credits) to hold a Special Redemption Convention whereby the following steps shall be mandatory and take place:-

(i) Any Ucadia University Reserve Bank or Ucadia Province Community Bank with a ratio of greater than one hundred thousand (100,000) Silver Credo (Credit) per one Ordinary Member shall surrender as a gift a minimum of ten (10%) percent of its reserves in Silver Credo (Credit) to its appropriate Union Reserve Bank and donate a greater amount if insufficient to lessen the ratio to below one hundred thousand (100,000) Silver Credo (Credit) per (1) Ordinary Member; and

(ii) Any Ucadia Union Reserve Bank with a ratio of greater than one hundred thousand (100,000) Silver Credo (Credit) per one Ordinary Member shall surrender as a gift a minimum of ten (10%) percent of its reserves in Silver Credo (Credit) to the Globe Union Reserve Bank and donate a greater amount if insufficient to lessen the ratio to below one hundred thousand

(100,000) Silver Credo (Credit) per (1) Ordinary Member; and

(iii) Any University Reserve Bank with a ratio of less than ten thousand (10,000) Silver Credo per one Ordinary Member, shall be given a gift by the appropriate Union Reserve Bank sufficient Silver Credo (Credit) so that the ratio is not more or less than ten thousand (10,000) Silver Credo per one Ordinary Member; and

(iv) Any Union Reserve Bank with a ratio of less than ten thousand (10,000) Silver Credo per one Ordinary Member, shall be given a gift by the Globe Union Reserve Bank of sufficient Silver Credo (Credit) so that the ratio is not more or less than ten thousand (10,000) Silver Credo per one Ordinary Member.

22. The issue of Silver Credo (Credit) and the management of its various Registers, Manifests and Accounts are governed by the Rules of the *Ucadia Silver Credo (Credit) Monetary System* consistent with the most sacred Covenant *Pactum De Singularis Caelum, Carta Sacrum De Congregationis Globus (Globe Union Charter) and Carta Economia De Congregationis Globus (Globe Union Economic Charter).* Autonomy of Silver Credo (Credit) Rules

These Rules are so designed to create an Autonomous and self-correcting system that forbids the necessity for intervention or manual correction. Therefore, at no point is there any lawful requirement for direct intervention in the autonomous rules conducting the creation, management or use of Silver Credo (Credits).

The Globe Union Reserve Bank shall be empowered to provide additional guidelines and policies towards the Ucadia Silver Credo (Credit) Monetary System as an automated and self regulating system.

Article 58 – Great Seal & Symbols of Globe Union

1. By the power and authority of the Charter of the Globe Union a great seal shall be forged and shall be known as the Great Seal of the Globe Union. Great Seal of Globe Union

It shall be entrusted to the Global Council and the Global Secretariat to protect and honour The Great Seal of Globe Union, for its imprint shall represent nothing less than the existence of the word and law of the Globe Union Free Society of Free Societies.

As such, it is only upon the approval of the Global Council that The Great Seal of the Globe Union shall be instanced on a document or instrument, excepting those documents prescribed as mandatory for the Secretary-General, Global Council and Globe Senate by this

Charter.

2. In recognition of the general elections of the Global Council every five (5) years, the The Great Seal of the Globe Union shall reflect the unique term of the Global Council. Unique Design of the Seal

At the conclusion of a General Election for the Global Council, a new Great Seal shall be forged reflecting the new officials and leadership of the Union.

3. The Global Council of the Union is to provide for the safe custody of the Seal, which may only be used by the authority of the Global Council excepting those documents listed as mandatory for Secretariat, Global Board and Global Council by this Charter. Affixing the Great Seal

Every instrument to which the Seal is affixed is to be signed by either the Secretary-General, or countersigned by at least two (2) Globe Councillors of the Global Council or by another Member appointed by the Global Council for the purpose.

The Global Council may determine either generally or in any particular case that a signature may be affixed by a mechanical means specified in the determination.

4. The organisation of the Union may have one (1) or more duplicates of the Seal which are to be facsimiles of the Seal with the addition on their faces of the words "Certificate Seal" and which are to be known as Certificate Seals. Any certificate for shares, membership, certification, qualification or financial instruments issued under a Certificate Seal is deemed to be sealed with the Great Seal. Certificate Seal

5. The flag of the Globe Union shall be the seven (7) Seals of the Ucadia Regional Unions arranged as the wheel and tree of Life on a white coloured background. The Flag

The flag represents the breaking and ending of the seven (7) Seals of Tyranny and the birth of the seven (7) seals of freedom whereby men and women are legally considered sovereign beings. On the outside, each seal represents a different Union, the top being the Africans Union, then clockwise the Americas Union, Asia Union, Arabian Union, Euro Union and Oceanic Union. At the centre is the seal of the Levant Union.

6. The anthem of the Union shall be commissioned and confirmed by the First Session of the Globe Senate. The Anthem

7. The motto of the Union shall be confirmed by the First Session of the Permanent Globe Senate. The Motto

8. The currency of the Globe Union shall be the Ucadia Moneta. The Currency

9. United Earth Day shall be confirmed by the First Session of the Globe Senate. — Union Day

Article 59 – Globe Senate

1. All legislative Powers of the Globe Union Free Society of Societies shall be vested in a **Senate** (The Senate), that shall consist of one house – a Senate. The Senate shall be made up of living representatives as Senators from each of the following types of Members and Organs:- — The Globe Senate

(i) Three (3) elected representatives from each Union Society Member including Africans Union, Americas Union, Asia Union, Arabian Union, Euro Union, Oceanic Union and Levant Union; and

(ii) Three (3) elected representatives from each of the three (3) great faiths including One Christ, One Islam and One Spirit; and

(iii) one elected representative from each of the specialised Free Societies including (but not limited to): One Jerusalem Free Society, Heal The Earth Society, Protect The Earth Society, Give Mars Life Society, Psygos Society, Civila Society, Ekelos Society, Teknas Society; and

(iv) Each of the Executor-Generals of Globe Resources and Systems being a Senator for the duration of their tenure of office; and

(v) one elected representative from each University Society Member.

2. Excluding Globe Senators holding their position by fact of their office, Globe Senators shall be appointed for a term of six (6) years. Provisional and suspended Members may attend Senate sessions but may not vote or originate new questions or matters before the Senate. — Terms of Globe Senate

Article 60 – Supreme (Globe) Council

1. The Executive Power of the Globe Union shall be vested in an executive government comprising a **Supreme** (Globe) **Council**, a Secretariat (Secretary-General) and the Global Board of Executors of Agencies (Global Board of Executors). The Supreme (Globe) Council shall consist of a minimum of fifteen (15) Members being:- — Supreme (Globe) Council

(i) One (1) representative for each of the Union Free Societies and Permanent Space Colonies; and

(ii) The nine (9) ex-officio heads of key Organs of the Globe Union, including: Prefect of Globe Senate, General Secretary, General Justice, General Treasurer, General Marshal, General Architect, General Ecologist, General Conservator and General Surveyor.

2. The non-permanent Members of the Supreme Council shall be elected for a term of six (6) years. An elected Member having been represented in two (2) successive Supreme Councils shall be ineligible for election the following term. The ex-officio heads of Key Organs shall hold their position on the Supreme Council only during their tenure of office. The Supreme Council shall elect a chair from their own ranks of ex-officio heads of key Organs for a period of one year, reflecting the qualities best needed for the time. No person may be chair for two years in a row, except in global states of emergency and no person may be chair for more than eight (8) individual years. Terms of Supreme Council

Article 61 – Global Secretariat

1. The Supreme (Globe) Council grants the day to day executive authority and responsibility of the Globe Union to a Secretary-General and Global Board of Executors of Agencies. Global Secretariat

Article 62 – Global Court of Justice

1. The Forum, also known as the **Globe Court of Justice**, also known as the Globe Union Supreme Court and also known as the Globe Court shall be the first, principal and highest judicial organ of the Globe Union. Global Court of Justice

The Globe Court of Justice shall function in accordance with *Carta Sacrum De Congregationis Globus (Globe Union Charter)* and *Carta Iudicialis De Congregationis Globus (Globe Union Judicial Charter)* and annexed codes of law in particular the Judicial Code. No other judicial body, excluding those competent forums of the Society of One Heaven, may ecclesiastically, legally or lawfully claim higher jurisdiction over the Globe Court of Justice.

Therefore, any matter adjudicated by the full bench of The Court shall be final and irrevocable, except by appeal to one (1) of the higher competent forums of the Society of One Heaven in accordance with the sacred Covenant known as *Pactum De Singularis Caelum*.

The Trust Number for The Globe Court is:

920000-000000-000000

Article 63 – Globe Treasury

1. The **Globe Union Treasury** is the principal and primary office, place, chamber, storehouse, vault, penitentiary and temple for the recording and safe keeping of all precious items in the possession of the Globe Union. Globe Treasury

Globe Union Treasury shall be the primary civil financial entity of all lesser societies on Earth on behalf of the Treasuries of One Christ, One Islam and One Spirit. No other public financial entity or body shall have higher standing on planet Earth, except the Treasuries of One Christ, One Islam and One Spirit.

The Trust Number for the Globe Union Treasury is:

940100-999999-999999

2. The purposes of the Globe Union Treasury are:- Purposes of Globe Union Treasury

(i) To receive and store safely all precious items in the possession of the Globe Union, including but not limited to those items posited in trust with the Treasury and ensure that such transactions are properly recorded and acknowledged; and

(ii) To possess and hold safely all Supreme Credo (Credit) conveyed by the Treasuries of One Christ, One Islam and One Spirit for the benefit of all humanity through the regional treasuries being the Africans Union Treasury, Americas Union Treasury, Asia Union Treasury, Arabian Union Treasury, Euro Union Treasury, Oceanic Union Treasury and Levant Union Treasury; and

(iii) To Create, update and maintain sufficient stock of Gold Credo (Credit) underwritten by Supreme Credo (Credits) for the benefit of the regional treasuries granted the benefit use of the value of Gold Credo (Credits) to meet the long term need for financial stability and capital liquidity by the people and enterprises of planet Earth; and

(iv) To Create, update and maintain sufficient stock of Silver Credo (Credit) underwritten by Gold Credo (Credits) for the benefit of regional, national, provincial and community banks granted the benefit use of the value of Silver Credo (Credits) to meet the long term need for financial stability and capital liquidity by the governments and enterprises of planet Earth; and

(v) To provide cash and valuables management facilities for the receipt, posit, deposit, store, withdrawal, payment and conversion requirements of the government and organs of the Globe Union; and

(vi) To provide receipt and right of use of the necessary instruments of underwriting and mechanisms to maintain a single universal currency unit known as the **Ucadia Moneta** and fulfil the needs of the Globe Union. To enable all financial matters and transactions for all Member States to be able to be defined according to this single Union currency unit; and

(vii) To provide treasury facilities on behalf of Society Members and State Members as Members of the Treasury for their storage, safe keeping and cash management needs; and

(viii) To cooperate with the regional Union Treasuries and regional Reserve Banks in honouring the framework of the Supreme Financial System; and

(ix) To provide a cooperative framework between the principle Treasury and Financial organs of each Member of the Treasury such that optimum and stable policies may be in place for each state in regards to prices, wages, unemployment, growth, debt and investment; and

(x) To help facilitate the expansion and balanced growth of trade, and to contribute thereby to the promotion and maintenance of high levels of employment and real income and to the development of the productive resources of all Member States as primary objectives of economic policy of the Globe Union; and

(xi) In accordance with the above, to assist the Union in the achievement of its purposes and principle objectives.

3. Be it known to all those future and present that the Trustees of the Treasury of the Globe Union did receive the conveyance of One Hundred Forty Four Million (144,000,000) Supreme Credo (Credit) on UCA E8:Y3208:A17: S2:M18:D4, also known as [14 March 2009], for the benefit of the following Union Treasuries:-

Valuables held by Globe Union Treasury

(i) One million six hundred thousand (1,600,000) Supreme Credo (Credits) conveyed for the benefit of the Treasury of One Christ [Trust No. GU7100-999999-999999] with the transaction reflected in the balance of [Account No. OH7100-999999-999999]; and

(ii) One million six hundred thousand (1,600,000) Supreme Credo (Credits) conveyed for the benefit of the Treasury of One Islam

[Trust No. GU8100-999999-999999] with the transaction reflected in the balance of [Account No. OH8100-999999-999999]; and

(iii) One million six hundred thousand (1,600,000) Supreme Credo (Credits) conveyed for the benefit of the Treasury of One Spirit [Trust No. GU9100-999999-999999] with the transaction reflected in the balance of [Account No. OH9100-999999-999999]; and

(iv) Eleven million forty-one thousand (11,041,000) Supreme Credo (Credits) conveyed for the benefit of the Africans Union Treasury [Trust No. GU1100-999999-999999] with the transaction reflected in the balance of [Account No. OH1100-999999-999999]; and

(v) Five million fifty-eight thousand (5,058,000) Supreme Credo (Credits) conveyed for the benefit of the Americas Union Treasury [Trust No. GU2100-999999-999999] with the transaction reflected in the balance of [Account No. OH2100-999999-999999]; and

(vi) One million six hundred and thirty thousand (1,630,000) Supreme Credo (Credits) conveyed for the benefit of the Arabian Union Treasury [Trust No. GU3100-999999-999999] with the transaction reflected in the balance of [Account No. OH3100-999999-999999]; and

(vii) One million one hundred thousand (1,100,000) Supreme Credo (Credits) conveyed for the benefit of the Levant Union Treasury [Trust No. GUL100-999999-999999] with the transaction reflected in the balance of [Account No. OHL100-999999-999999]; and

(viii) Forty million five thousand (40,005,000) Supreme Credo (Credits) conveyed for the benefit of the Asia Union Treasury [Trust No. GU4100-999999-999999] with the transaction reflected in the balance of [Account No. OH4100-999999-999999]; and

(ix) Thirteen million five hundred thousand (13,500,000) Supreme Credo (Credits) conveyed for the benefit of the Euro Union Treasury [Trust No. GU5100-999999-999999] with the transaction reflected in the balance of [Account No. OH5100-999999-999999]; and

(x) Eight hundred and sixty-six thousand (866,000) Supreme

Credo (Credits) conveyed for the benefit of the Oceanic Union Treasury [Trust No. GU6100-999999-999999] with the transaction reflected in the balance of [Account No. OH6100-999999-999999]; and

(xi) Fifty-eight million (58,000,000) Supreme Credo (Credits) to the Globe Union Treasury [Trust No. GU0100-999999-999999] with the transaction reflected in the balance of [Account No. OH0100-999999-999999]; and

(xii) One million four hundred thousand (1,400,000) Supreme Credo (Credits) to the Original Nations Treasury [Trust No. GUZ100-999999-999999] with the transaction reflected in the balance of [Account No. OHZ100-999999-999999]; and

(xiii) Six hundred thousand (600,000) Supreme Credo (Credits) to the Council of Ucadia Foundations Treasury [Trust No. GUF100-999999-999999] with the transaction reflected in the balance of [Account No. OHF100-999999-999999]; and

(xiv) Two million (2,000,000) Supreme Credo (Credits) to the Ucadia Moon Federation Treasury [Trust No. GUX100-999999-999999] with the transaction reflected in the balance of [Account No. OHX100-999999-999999]; and

(xv) Two million (2,000,000) Supreme Credo (Credits) to the Ucadia Mars Federation Treasury [Trust No. GUM100-999999-999999] with the transaction reflected in the balance of [Account No. OHM100-999999-999999]; and

(xvi) One million (1,000,000) Supreme Credo (Credits) to the Ucadia Jupiter-Europa Federation Treasury [Trust No. GUJ100-999999-999999] with the transaction reflected in the balance of [Account No. OHJ100-999999-999999]; and

(xvii) One million (1,000,000) Supreme Credo (Credits) to the Ucadia Saturn-Titan Federation Treasury [Trust No. GUT100-999999-999999] with the transaction reflected in the balance of [Account No. OHT100-999999-999999].

4. In order to fulfil its primary objectives, the Globe Union Treasury shall comprise of the following permanent organs and any such other organs deemed necessary by amendment to this Charter:- Organs of Globe Union Treasury

(i) Globe Union Reserve Bank; and

(ii) Globe Union Exchange; and

(iii) Globe Union Disaster Relief Fund; and

(iv) Globe Union Bank for Reconstruction and Development; and

(v) Globe Union Insurance Fund; and

(vi) Globe Union Government Budget Agency; and

(vii) Globe Union Finance Company; and

(viii) Globe Union Centre for Settlement of Investment Disputes (GCSID).

Article 64 – Globe Guard

1. A permanent military and police force shall be established and known as the **Globe Guard**. The Globe Guard

The supplying and cost of personnel for the Guard shall be met by compulsory and fair contribution from all Society and Union Members of the Globe Union.

Article 65 – Global Defence Council

1. All matters of policy, planning, campaigns, budgets and resources concerning the Globe Guard, global planetary defences, peacekeeping and emergency logistics shall be vested in a **Global Defence Council**, headed by the General Marshal. Global Defence Council

The Global Defence Council shall consist of thirty six (36) Members elected from the Globe Senate.

All Members of the Global Defence Council shall be elected for a term of six (6) years corresponding to the same election cycle as election to the Globe Senate. Each Member of the Globe Defence Council shall have one (1) representative.

Article 66 – Globe Economic Council

1. All matters of economic policy, planning, budgets, infrastructure development, building and resources concerning the Globe Union shall be vested in a **Globe Economic Council**, headed by the General Architect. Globe Economic Council

The Globe Economic Council shall consist of thirty six (36) Members elected from the Globe Senate.

All Members of the Globe Economic Council shall be elected for a term of six (6) years corresponding to the same election cycle as election to the Globe Senate. Each Member of the Globe Economic Council shall have one (1) representative.

Article 67 – Globe Ecological Council

1. All matters of environmental policy, planning, laws, treaties, standards, budgets and programs including (but not limited to) emissions targets, pollution reduction, recycling, endangered species, temporary protected habitat zones, ecology conservation and regeneration concerning the Globe Union shall be vested in a **Globe Ecological Council**, headed by the General Ecologist. Globe Ecological Council

The Globe Ecological Council shall consist of thirty six (36) Members elected from the Globe Senate.

All Members of the Globe Ecological Council shall be elected for a term of six (6) years corresponding to the same election cycle as election to the Globe Senate. Each Member of the Globe Ecological Council shall have one (1) representative.

Article 68 – Globe Cultural Council

1. All matters of cultural policy, planning, laws, treaties, standards, budgets and programs including (but not limited to) indigenous culture preservation, traditional cultures, world heritage sites, artefacts, museums, digital archives, cultural tolerance and education concerning the Globe Union shall be vested in a **Globe Cultural Council**, headed by the General Conservator. Globe Cultural Council

The Globe Cultural Council shall consist of thirty six (36) Members elected from the Globe Senate.

All Members of the Globe Cultural Council shall be elected for a term of six (6) years corresponding to the same election cycle as election to the Globe Senate. Each Member of the Globe Cultural Council shall have one (1) representative.

Article 69 – Global Space Council

1. All matters of space policy, planning, budgets, laws, treaties, geo-spatial position rights, satellites, earth launch stations, launch vehicle construction, military activities in space, mining in space and on moons and planets, space stations, permanent moon bases, colonies, transport, infrastructure development, building and resources concerning the Globe Union shall be vested in a **Global Space Council**, headed by the General Surveyor. Global Space Council

The Global Space Council shall consist of thirty six (36) Members elected from the Globe Senate.

All Members of the Global Space Council shall be elected for a term of six (6) years corresponding to the same election cycle as election to the Globe Senate. Each Member of the Global Space Council shall have one (1) representative.

Article 70 – One Christ

1. The most sacred Universal Ecclesia of One Christ, also known as the One Holy Apostolic Universal Ecclesia, also known as the Sol Ecclesia, also known as the Authentic Body of Christ, is the first, highest and supreme association, aggregate, fraternity, body, entity and society of Members sharing spiritual heritage associated with all forms of Christian and Jewish faiths. One Christ

In accord with the most sacred Covenant *Pactum De Singularis Caelum*, no Christian or Jewish person, association, aggregate, institute, body, entity or society may assert or claim higher jurisdiction or authority than the Universal Ecclesia of One Christ.

All living Higher Life Forms who profess to be Christian or Jewish are ipso facto (as a matter of fact) subject first to the laws of One Heaven and second to the laws of the Universal Body of Christ above any other lesser society, association, aggregate, institute, fraternity, society, entity or body.

Furthermore, every and all ordained, acknowledged, commissioned or certified clergy of any Christian or Jewish body are also officers of One Christ; and subject to the laws and obligations of One Christ first above any other lesser society, association, aggregate, institute, fraternity, society, entity or body.

Article 71 – One Islam

1. The most sacred Holy Society of One Islam, also known as the One True Way of Allah, also known as the One Umma, is the first, highest and supreme association, aggregate, fraternity, body, entity and society of Members sharing spiritual heritage associated with all forms of Islamic faiths. One Islam

In accord with the most sacred Covenant *Pactum De Singularis Caelum*, no Muslim person, association, aggregate, institute, body, entity or society may assert or claim higher jurisdiction or authority than the Holy Society of One Islam.

All living Higher Life Forms who profess to be Muslim are ipso facto (as a matter of fact) subject first to the laws of One Heaven and second to the laws of the Universal Body of One Umma above any other lesser society, association, aggregate, institute, fraternity, society, entity or body.

Furthermore, every and all ordained, acknowledged, commissioned or certified clergy of any Muslim body are also officers of One Islam; and subject to the laws and obligations of One Islam first above any other lesser society, association, aggregate, institute, fraternity, society, entity or body.

Article 72 – One Spirit

1. The most sacred Sacred Society of One Spirit, also known as the One Holy Apostolic Spirit, also known as the One Spirit Tribe, also known as the One Spirit, is the first, highest and supreme association, aggregate, fraternity, body, entity and society of Members sharing spiritual heritage associated with traditional, indigenous, Earth based, meditative and eastern customary faiths. One Spirit

In accord with the most sacred Covenant *Pactum De Singularis Caelum*, no Hindu, Buddhist or other traditional spiritual body, person, association, aggregate, institute, body, entity or society may assert or claim higher jurisdiction or authority than the Sacred Society of One Spirit.

All living Higher Life Forms who profess to be Hindu or Buddhist or Daoist or Jain or traditional indigenous faith are ipso facto (as a matter of fact) subject first to the laws of One Heaven and second to the laws of the Sacred Society of One Spirit above any other lesser society, association, aggregate, institute, fraternity, society, entity or body.

Furthermore, every and all ordained, acknowledged, commissioned or certified clergy of any Hindu, Buddhist or other traditional spiritual body are also officers of One Spirit; and subject to the laws and obligations of One Spirit first above any other lesser society, association, aggregate, institute, fraternity, society, entity or body.

TITLE VII: UCADIA UNIVERSITIES

Article 73 – Ucadia University

1. A *Ucadia University* is the second largest administrative division of government and administration of the Union. A University is an ecclesiastical, sovereign, official, lawful, legal and administratively constituted subdivision of the Union and is equivalent to a "politia", "sovereign state", "dominion" or "independent sovereign nation". Ucadia University

   Under Ucadia Trust and Ucadia Company Law, a valid Ucadia University is recognised as a Superior Civil Trust and Ecclesiastical Capital Company.

2. Each and every valid Ucadia University was first formed as the second largest operational division of the occupational forces of One Heaven on Earth following the complete conquest of all land, sea, earth, space, time, atmosphere and spirit within the boundaries of the Union; and lawful possession and occupation of all rights, property, title and uses within the same bounds. Therefore a Ucadia University is first and foremost a spiritual and supernatural body that cannot be extinguished merely by one or more temporal means. Origin, Life and Existence of Ucadia University

   In accord with the most sacred covenant Pactum De Singularis Caelum, a Ucadia University possesses a Life not exceeding one complete standard Age of one thousand and seventy (1,070) years or approximately one third the life expectancy of the Union.

   The Life of a valid Ucadia University is then divided into Terms, being the period of time that certain elected officials may hold particular office, before general elections to elect new office holders. Excluding the first Term of three years, all subsequent Terms are six years.

   Within each Term, the legislative body known as the Parliament as well as the Courts shall sit at several times during the year, or "Sessions". Each given year, there must be at least one Session.

3. A Ucadia University may also be formed by Treaty and Commonwealth of Original Nations (Tribes) under one (or more) of the Thirty Three (33) *Sacred Covenants of Original Law, Original People* and *Original Land* as recognised through the most Sacred Covenant *Pactum De Singularis Caelum*. Original Nations and Treaty and Commonwealth of Original Nations

   An **Original Nation** is a significant community of people originating from a traditional bounded area of land, having long standing continuous human habitation and association to an ancient Covenant of Law, Culture and Rights recognised under Ucadia and Non-Ucadia Law. Under the present Charter, a properly registered body claiming to be an Original Nation (Tribe) possessing a current mandate under Ucadia Law is a valid Sovereign Body and Community, possessing its own unique bounds within the University, or corresponding to either a Campus or Province. A claimed Original Nation (Tribe) without proper mandate or registration under the Union has no legitimacy or validity in law.

4. The Founding Ucadia Universities of the Union, in alphabetic order are: Founding Ucadia Universities of Union

(i) Ucadia Albania (University) [Trust No.945000-100000-000000]; and

(ii) Ucadia Andorra (University) [Trust No.945000-200000-000000]; and

(iii) Ucadia Armenia (University) [Trust No.945000-300000-000000]; and

(iv) Ucadia Austria (University) [Trust No.945000-400000-000000]; and

(v) Ucadia Belarus (University) [Trust No.945000-500000-000000]; and

(vi) Ucadia Belgium (University) [Trust No.945000-600000-000000]; and

(vii) Ucadia Bosnia and Herzegovina (University) [Trust No.945000-700000-000000]; and

(viii) Ucadia Bulgaria (University) [Trust No.945000-800000-000000]; and

(ix) Ucadia Croatia (University) [Trust No.945000-900000-000000]; and

(x) Ucadia Cyprus (University) [Trust No.945001-000000-000000]; and

(xi) Ucadia Czech Republic (University) [Trust No.945001-100000-000000]; and

(xii) Ucadia Denmark (University) [Trust No.945001-200000-000000]; and

(xiii) Ucadia Estonia (University) [Trust No.945001-300000-000000]; and

(xiv) Ucadia Faroe Islands (University) [Trust No.945001-400000-000000]; and

(xv) Ucadia Finland (University) [Trust No.945001-500000-

000000]; and

(xvi) Ucadia France (University) [Trust No.945001-600000-000000]; and

(xvii) Ucadia Georgia (University) [Trust No.945001-700000-000000]; and

(xviii) Ucadia Germany (University) [Trust No.945001-800000-000000]; and

(xix) Ucadia Gibraltar (University) [Trust No.945001-900000-000000]; and

(xx) Ucadia Greece (University) [Trust No.945002-000000-000000]; and

(xxi) Ucadia Greenland (University) [Trust No.945002-100000-000000]; and

(xxii) Ucadia Vatican (University) [Trust No.945002-200000-000000]; and

(xxiii) Ucadia Hungary (University) [Trust No.945002-300000-000000]; and

(xxiv) Ucadia Iceland (University) [Trust No.945002-400000-000000]; and

(xxv) Ucadia Ireland (University) [Trust No.945002-500000-000000]; and

(xxvi) Ucadia Israel (University) [Trust No.945002-600000-000000]; and

(xxvii) Ucadia Italy (University) [Trust No.945002-700000-000000]; and

(xxviii) Ucadia Latvia (University) [Trust No.945002-800000-000000]; and

(xxix) Ucadia Liechtenstein (University) [Trust No.945002-900000-000000]; and

(xxx) Ucadia Lithuania (University) [Trust No.945003-000000-000000]; and

(xxxi) Ucadia Luxembourg (University) [Trust No.945003-100000-000000]; and

(xxxii) Ucadia Macedonia (University) [Trust No.945003-200000-

000000]; and

(xxxiii) Ucadia Malta (University) [Trust No.945003-300000-000000]; and

(xxxiv) Ucadia Moldova (University) [Trust No.945003-400000-000000]; and

(xxxv) Ucadia Monaco (University) [Trust No.945003-500000-000000]; and

(xxxvi) Ucadia Netherlands (University) [Trust No.945003-600000-000000]; and

(xxxvii) Ucadia Norway (University) [Trust No.945003-700000-000000]; and

(xxxviii) Ucadia Poland (University) [Trust No.945003-800000-000000]; and

(xxxix) Ucadia Portugal (University) [Trust No.945003-900000-000000]; and

(xl) Ucadia Romania (University) [Trust No.945004-000000-000000]; and

(xli) Ucadia Russia (University) [Trust No.945004-100000-000000]; and

(xlii) Ucadia San Marino (University) [Trust No.945004-200000-000000]; and

(xliii) Ucadia Slovakia (University) [Trust No.945004-300000-000000]; and

(xliv) Ucadia Slovenia (University) [Trust No.945004-400000-000000]; and

(xlv) Ucadia Spain (University) [Trust No.945004-500000-000000]; and

(xlvi) Ucadia Svalbard and Jan Mayen (University) [Trust No.945004-600000-000000]; and

(xlvii) Ucadia Sweden (University) [Trust No.945004-700000-000000]; and

(xlviii) Ucadia Switzerland (University) [Trust No.945004-800000-000000]; and

(xlix) Ucadia Ukraine (University) [Trust No.945004-900000-

000000]; and

(l) Ucadia United Kingdom (University) [Trust No.945005-000000-000000]; and

(li) Ucadia Serbia (University) [Trust No.945005-100000-000000]; and

(lii) Ucadia Åland Islands (University) [Trust No.945005-200000-000000]; and

(liii) Ucadia Guernsey (University) [Trust No.945005-300000-000000]; and

(liv) Ucadia Isle of Man (University) [Trust No.945005-400000-000000]; and

(lv) Ucadia Jersey (University) [Trust No.945005-500000-000000]; and

(lvi) Ucadia Kosovo (University) [Trust No.945005-600000-000000]; and

(lvii) Ucadia Montenegro (University) [Trust No.945005-700000-000000].

5. There shall be established as the principal Organs of each Ucadia University:- Organs of Ucadia University

(i) A *Parliament*, being the primary legislative Organ of the University, legally embodied and personified through the Great Office of Prefect; and

(ii) A *Supreme Court*, being the primary judicial Organ of the University, legally embodied and personified through the Great Office of Justiciar; and

(iii) A *Cabinet*, being the primary executive Organ of the University as the executive meeting of all the Director-Generals of Ucadia Systems of the University, legally embodied and personified through the Great Office of Chamberlain; and

(iv) A *College*, being the primary institutional Organ of the University, legally embodied and personified through the Great Office of Dean; and

(v) A *Militia*, being the primary military and security Organ of the University, legally embodied and personified through the Great Office of Marshal; and

(vi) A *Chancery Court*, being the primary administrative Organ of Rights, Trusts, Estates, Land and Wards of the University, legally embodied and personified through the Great Office of Chancellor; and

(vii) An *Exchequer Court*, being the primary administrative Organ of Taxation, Revenues, Funds and Securities of the University, legally embodied and personified through the Great Office of Exchequer; and

(viii) A *Sacristy*, being the primary administrative Organ of Vital and Sacred Records, Events, Covenants, Treaties, Deeds and Titles of the University, legally embodied and personified through the Great Office of Plenipotentiary; and

(ix) A *Vestry*, being the primary administrative Organ of Rolls of the University, legally embodied and personified through the Great Office of Custodian; and

(x) An *Archive*, being the primary administrative Organ of Historic Records, Primary Sources and Files of the University, legally embodied and personified through the Great Office of Censor; and

(xi) A *Library*, being the primary administrative Organ of Collections, Information and Knowledge Resources of the University, legally embodied and personified through the Great Office of Narrator.

6. The Great Offices of State are by tradition, the embodiment of the Sovereign Rights and Authorities, as Sovereign Ministers of the Ucadia University. The Sovereign, by definition, is the State and represents the legal embodiment of executive, legislative and judicial governance of the Ucadia University. The Great Offices of State

In accord with the most sacred Covenant *Pactum De Singularis Caelum* the twelve Great Offices of State are: *President, Dean, Chancellor (Domestic Vice-President), Exchequer (Treasurer), Plenipotentiary (International Vice-President), Prefect, Justiciar (Chief Justice), Chamberlain, Marshal, Narrator, Custodian* and *Censor (Inspector)*:

(i) *President*, as the supreme leader, the head of state and the living embodiment and personification of the University as a corporation sole. The Office of President is equivalent to the Office of Minister-General of a Ucadia Foundation of the same University jurisdiction; and

(ii) *Dean*, as the head and living embodiment of the University College as a corporation sole; and

(iii) *Chancellor*, as the Domestic Vice-President and head and living embodiment of the University Court of Chancery as a corporation sole; and

(iv) *Exchequer*, as the Treasurer and head and living embodiment of the University Court of the Exchequer (Treasury) as a corporation sole; and

(v) *Plenipotentiary*, as the International Vice-President and the head and living embodiment of the University Sacristy as a corporation sole; and

(vi) *Prefect*, as the head and living embodiment of the University Parliament as a corporation sole; and

(vii) *Justiciar*, as the Chief Justice and head and living embodiment of the University Supreme Court as a corporation sole; and

(viii) *Chamberlain*, as the head and living embodiment of the University Cabinet as a corporation sole; and

(ix) *Marshal*, as the head and living embodiment of the University Militia as a corporation sole; and

(x) *Narrator*, as the head and living embodiment of the University Library as a corporation sole; and

(xi) *Custodian*, as the head and living embodiment of the University Vestry as a corporation sole; and

(xii) *Censor*, as the Inspector and head and living embodiment of the University Archives as a corporation sole.

Collection of Ius Ucadia Universitas (University Rights)

7. *Ius Ucadia Universitas* (Ucadia University Rights) is the third collection of seven *Ucadia Sovereign Entity Rights*; and may be explicitly invoked or referenced by Sovereign Right of Action through registration and possession of a proper Mandate associated with a Ucadia Sovereign Entity in Ucadia or Non-Ucadia Jurisdiction. The collection of Ucadia University Rights of *Ius Ucadia Universitas* contains twenty Rights being:-

(i) *Ius Ucadia Universitas* as the Superior Rights associated with a University administrative division, body politic and government; and

(ii) *Ius Ucadia Universitas Existentiae* as the Superior Right for the Existence of Ucadia as inherited from *Ius Ucadia Unionis*;

and

(iii) *Ius Ucadia Universitas Mandati* as the Superior Right of Mandate of Ucadia as inherited from *Ius Ucadia Unionis*; and

(iv) *Ius Ucadia Universitas Hereditatis* as the Superior Right of Inheritance as inherited from *Ius Ucadia Unionis*; and

(v) *Ius Ucadia Universitas Dominionis* as the Superior Right of Dominion of Ucadia as inherited from *Ius Ucadia Unionis*; and

(vi) *Ius Ucadia Universitas Proprietatis* as the Superior Right of Property of Ucadia as inherited from *Ius Ucadia Unionis*; and

(vii) *Ius Ucadia Universitas Moneta* as the Superior Right of Money of Ucadia as inherited from *Ius Ucadia Unionis*; and

(viii) *Ius Ucadia Universitas Potestatis* as the Superior Right of Authority and Power of Ucadia as inherited from *Ius Ucadia Unionis*; and

(ix) *Ius Ucadia Universitas Registrum* as the Superior Right of Registers and Rolls as inherited from *Ius Ucadia Unionis*; and

(x) *Ius Ucadia Universitas Nomenis* as the Superior Right to Name, Title and Reputation as inherited from *Ius Ucadia Unionis*; and

(xi) *Ius Ucadia Universitas Fecerim* as the Superior Right of the University to invent, create and make seals, arms, heralds, instruments and other property of value as inherited from *Ius Ucadia Unionis*; and

(xii) *Ius Ucadia Universitas Sociari* as Superior Right of Membership as inherited from *Ius Ucadia Unionis*; and

(xiii) *Ius Ucadia Universitas Terram* as the Superior Right of the Province Assembly to grant a Right or Title to Land defined and surveyed within its metes and bounds as inherited from *Ius Ucadia Unionis*; and

(xiv) *Ius Ucadia Universitas Usum Terram* as the Superior Right of Use to Land defined and surveyed within its metes and bounds as inherited from *Ius Ucadia Unionis*; and

(xv) *Ius Ucadia Universitas Mutat Terram* as the Superior Right to Alter the (Top of the) of Land defined and surveyed within its metes and bounds as inherited from *Ius Ucadia Unionis*; and

(xvi) *Ius Ucadia Universitas Fodere Terram* as the Superior Right to Dig (or Mine) the Land defined and surveyed within its metes and bounds as inherited from *Ius Ucadia Unionis*; and

(xvii) *Ius Ucadia Universitas Alienum Subcriptio* as the Superior Right to register a subsidiary within the jurisdiction of a foreign estate, body, person or entity as inherited from *Ius Ucadia Unionis*; and

(xviii) *Ius Ucadia Universitas Audit* as the Superior Right of the Province Assembly to review any books, or any information, or any accounts of any officer operating within the bounds of the University as inherited from *Ius Ucadia Unionis*; and

(xix) *Ius Ucadia Universitas Inspectionis* as the Superior Right to establish a Commission of Investigation with the power to call any registered Member and any information held by within the bounds of the University as inherited from *Ius Ucadia Unionis*; and

(xx) *Ius Ucadia Universitas Anathema* as the Superior Right to commission a Province Impeachment for the forced removal of any elected official to any position within any branch of government within the bounds of the University as inherited from *Ius Ucadia Unionis*.

8. The Executive Government of a valid Preliminary or Probational University may be granted by Sacred Charter, the Right to form a Religious and Charitable Corporation Sole for the purpose of interfacing with non-Ucadian societies, entities, bodies politic, companies and persons. Such an entity shall be called the Ucadia Foundation of the particular University. The President in the ecclesiastical capacity of Minister-General shall be the embodiment and personification of the Corporation Sole. Ucadia Foundation

As each and every valid Ucadia Foundation shall first be formed under the laws of Ucadia, any registration, or recording or notification with a non-Ucadian society, body politic, entity, state, company or person must be done clearly so no imputation of transfer or surrender or alienation or donation of property or rights is imputed or implied. The grant of the first Sacred Charter to form a Ucadia Foundation shall be for one year, subject to the achievement of criteria to form a valid Probational University Status and the holding of first Member wide general elections. Thereafter, the maximum life of a Ucadia Foundation granted by Sacred Charter shall be seventy years and shall not be permitted to continue to exist beyond the end of the first Term of the first Permanent University Parliament.

Subject to formal approval, a Ucadia Foundation may be approved and formed and then recorded with a foreign estate, foreign nation or foreign body politic on the following eight conditions:-

(i) That the said foreign non-Ucadian body is duly recognised by at least twenty other non-Ucadian foreign bodies as a valid entity of a size equal or larger than the bounds of the said Ucadia University; and

(ii) The executive of the Ucadia University making such foreign registration are duly recognised and possess valid credentials and registration and have not been banned from holding office, nor are presently subject to active criminal action within the courts of Ucadia nor the foreign courts in which registration is sought; and

(iii) The instance to be recorded with a foreign body is as the Ucadia Foundation for the said University as a Foreign Corporation Sole or Body Corporate for Charitable Purposes; and

(iv) That the formal name of the Ucadia Foundation for the said University has been duly enrolled within the Charter Rolls of the Ucadia Union and such Charter Rights promulgated and made patent, including a valid Certificate of such Charter and Rights; and

(v) The President of the said Ucadia University is registered within the *Directorium Ecclesiam Ucadia* (Directory of Ecclesiastical Persons of Ucadia) as having the character and personality of a Cleric; and

(vi) A Constitution for the instance of foreign recording as the Ucadia Foundation for the said University has been formed, promulgated and approved in acceptance of the Charter and Rights granted to the said Ucadia Foundation; and

(vii) The Bylaws for the Ucadia Foundation for the said University whereby the instance of the Ucadia University shall function in amity and harmony with the foreign body have been formed, promulgated and approved in accord with the Constitutional Charter of the said Ucadia Foundation; and

(viii) That the Office Holders as defined within the approved Constitutional Charter have been duly elected and that such elections are certified, including the Certificate of Divine Commission of the President in their capacity as a Cleric.

If one or more of these items cannot be fully demonstrated, then a foreign registration of an instance of a Ucadia University, or part thereof, is not valid.

9. In accord with the present Constitution and Charter there shall be five possible "states" or "types" of Legal Status for a Ucadia University being *Provisional, Preliminary, Probational, Prerogative* and *Permanent*:- University Legal Status

(i) *Provisional University* is the first of five types of states of a valid Ucadia University. All Provisional Universities within the Union were formed between GAIA E8:Y3209:A1:S1:M6:D1 [Mon 21 Dec 2009] and GAIA E8:Y3210:A1:S1:M17:D1 [Tue 21 Dec 2010] as the second largest operational division of the occupational forces of One Heaven following the complete conquest of all land, sea, earth, space, time, atmosphere and spirit within the boundaries of the Union; and lawful possession and occupation of all rights, property, title and uses within the same bounds; and the investiture of a unique and individual spiritual member into each of the Twelve Great Offices of State. Under the terms of spiritual military occupation, the boundaries and Cadastral features of each University within each Union have been properly surveyed with the Survey and Charter for each Province registered within the Great Register of the Union and the event published in the Globe Union Gazette and Ucadia Gazette; and

(ii) *Preliminary University* is the second of five types of states of a valid Ucadia University formed when not less than twelve (12) Ordinary Ucadia Members domiciled within the bounds of the University elect an interim University Embassy and Government instituted through a Convention for the formation of a Ucadia Foundation for the University, with each Founding Member having invoked and recorded an Oath of Allegiance and an Oath of Office; in accord with the Criteria for the Foundation of a Preliminary University. All applications and approvals of Preliminary Universities shall be under the temporary administration of the Ucadia Foundation of the Union subject to the fact that no Preliminary, Probational or Prerogative or Permanent University Administration yet exists; and

(iii) *Probational University* is the third of five types of states of a valid Ucadia University formed when not less than fifty (50) percent of all Provinces within the bounds of the University have been formed as Probational or Prerogative or Permanent;

and with such application recognised and approved subject to appointments of Officers to the positions of the Twelve Great Offices of State duly published in the Ucadia Gazette and certified in accord with the Criteria for the Foundation of a Probational University. All applications and approvals of Probational Universities are superior to any pre-existing Preliminary University Administration and upon such approval, all rights, powers and authorities must be duly conveyed to the new administration; and

(iv) *Prerogative University* is the fourth of five types of states of a valid Ucadia University formed when a State Member of Ucadia, representing the internationally recognised government sharing the same bounds of the University agrees to adopt the Ucadia Model and systems of effective administration for the benefit of its Members. As a Ucadia State Member is an existing body politic, nation, state or country duly recognised by international Western-Roman bodies and having duly elected its government by its Members, a State Member therefore holds a prerogative right and privilege, subject to the conditions of the present Constitution and Charter and the Criteria for the Foundation of a Prerogative University. All applications and approvals of Prerogative Universities are superior to any pre-existing Preliminary or Probational University Administration and upon such approval, all rights, powers and authorities must be duly conveyed to the new administration; and

(v) *Permanent University* is the fifth type of state of a valid Ucadia University formed when not less than eighty (80) percent of all Provinces within the bounds of the University have been formed as Probational or Prerogative or Permanent with at least fifty (50) percent as Permanent Provinces; and with such application recognised and approved subject to election of Officers to the positions of the Twelve Great Offices of State duly gazetted and certified in accord with the Criteria for the Foundation of a Permanent University. All applications and approvals of Permanent Universities are superior to any and all pre-existing Preliminary or Probational or Prerogative University Administration and upon such approval, all rights, powers and authorities must be duly conveyed to the new administration.

10. In accord with the most sacred Covenant *Pactum De Singularis Caelum*, the principal headquarters for the University is a Ucadia

Ucadia Embassy and Diplomatic Status

Embassy ("Ucadia Embassy") being the highest Embassy of ecclesiastical and ordinary power of all Heaven and Earth, all sanctuaries and clergy and all bodies and persons claiming any form of ecclesiastical authority, office, power or right within the bounds of a Ucadia University. A Ucadia Embassy holds plenary authority as the one holy universal and apostolic Politia (Politic or Body Politic).

11. A Great Seal as the highest symbol and sign of ordinary plenary and legislative authority shall be made, cast and minted for each University every six (6) years. The Great Seal shall reflect the unique term and character of the University Parliament. At the conclusion of a University General Election, a new Great Seal shall be made, cast and minted reflecting the new officials and leadership of the University. Great Seal

The Great Seal shall be entrusted to the Legislature and the Executive of each University to protect and honour their Great Seal. It shall be only upon the approval of Parliament or the Executive Government of the University that the Great Seal be instanced on an instrument, excepting those documents prescribed as mandatory under the particular Constitutional Charter of the University. Every Instrument whereby the Seal is affixed is to be signed by either a member of the Executive, or countersigned by at least two (2) Members of the Parliament appointed by Parliament for the purpose. Parliament may determine either generally or in any particular case that a signature may be affixed by a mechanical means specified in the determination.

12. The organisation of the Ucadia University may have one (1) or more duplicates of the Seal, that are to be facsimiles of the Seal with the addition on their faces of the words "Certificate Seal" and are to be known as Certificate Seals. Any certificate for shares, membership, certification, qualification or financial instruments issued under a Certificate Seal is deemed to be sealed with the Great Seal. Certificate Seal

13. Each Ucadia University shall have a unique Flag. The Parliament and College of a University may choose to use an existing Flag representing by tradition the same bounds of the University as its official flag or another. The final design of the Flag shall, for each University, be determined and ratified by the First Session of the Parliament of each respective Ucadia Permanent University. The Flag

14. The Anthem of the University shall be commissioned and confirmed by the First Session of the Parliament of each respective Ucadia Permanent University. The Anthem

15. The Currency of each University within the bounds of the Union shall be the Ucadia Moneta (Money) for the store of value and payment of wages and as the unit of standard exchange and the means of trade. The Currency

16. The primary administrative Organ of Historic Records, Primary Sources and Files of the University, legally embodied and personified through the Great Office of Censor, shall be the Official Archives. University Archive

17. The primary administrative Organ of Collections, Information and Knowledge Resources of the University, legally embodied and personified through the Great Office of Narrator, shall be the Library. University Library

Article 74 – University Parliament

1. All legislative Powers of the University shall be vested in a Parliament (The Parliament), that shall consist of one house - a Parliament. The Parliament shall be made up of seven (7) elected representatives from each Provincial Assembly and the University Director-Generals, as defined by the present Charter. University Parliament

   Parliamentarians shall be appointed for a Term of six (6) years corresponding to the fixed terms of the University College (Executive Branch). Where a Parliamentarian is a Parliamentarian by being a University Director, their term shall be the same as their tenure as University Director.

2. The Parliament shall be first called to Life within the first year of formation of a Preliminary University when all valid Members within the jurisdiction and bounds of the University shall be granted the right to vote for all Offices at the first General Election; and thereafter shall continue to be convened, constituted, sitting, existing and possessing Life for a further one thousand and seventy years, until the time appointed for the death and transition of the University itself into some new form. Origin and Life of Parliament

   Therefore, at no point during its Life, shall Parliament be dissolved, impeded or suspended. Therefore, all laws having been passed by Parliament and assented into law, shall remain in effect for the Life of the Parliament, unless otherwise repealed, amended or expired.

   When representatives are elected, the period of time within the Life of the Parliament they are commissioned to be present shall be called a Term and at the expiry of the Term, any such commission of a representative shall expire, yet the Parliament shall continue to live. When representatives are called to meet within a Term, the period of time of such meetings shall be called a Session and at the end of a Session, the Parliament shall be in recess until the next beginning of the next Session.

3. Vested by the present Constitution and Charter, each properly constituted Parliament of a Ucadia University shall possess, hold and own certain Rights, Powers and Authorities derived from the consent Rights, Powers and Authority of Parliament

of all Members as the source of all Rights, Powers and Authorities of Government. Therefore, all Rights, Powers and Authority of the College (Executive Branch) and Systems and Services of Government shall be sourced from these Rights and no other.

4. All Parliament Instruments shall be in accord with the official forms defined by the present Sacred Charter and associated Codes. All agreements of the Parliament shall be made in accord with the Rights and within the limits of the Rights prescribed by the present Charter. All Acts of Law shall be debated and passed or rejected based upon the procedures defined by the present Constitutional Charter. The first Act of Law passed by the first Session of the first Term of the first Parliament shall be the present Constitutional Charter. The second and subsequent Acts of Law passed by the first Session of the first Term of the first Parliament shall be each of the thirty three Codes of Law in the order prescribed.

Parliament Instruments and Acts as Law

All Acts of Law shall be uniquely identified and recorded in the following manner based upon the procedures defined by the present Constitutional Charter and associated Codes:

(i) Life means that as Parliament possesses only one life and cannot be dissolved, impeded or suspended, any attempt to identify statutes according to the reign, or time, or period of a government, or head of state is redundant; and

(ii) Term Number is the primary identifier for any and all acts of Parliament whereby each and every Term is uniquely numbered and represents the first component of the unique identifier of a Bill or Act; and

(iii) Session Number is the second identifier for any and all acts of Parliament, whereby each and every Session is uniquely numbered and represents the second component of the unique identifier of a Bill or Act; and

(iv) Title of Act is the short title of the Act defining its principal relation to one Code of Law or Constitution or Body; and

(v) Singular Purpose means a proposed Bill or Act cannot relate to two or more Codes of Law, or Constitutions within the same Bill or Act. Instead, separate Bills or Acts must be passed for each and every Code of Law or Constitution or major Statutory Body it refers; and

(vi) Singular Action means that a proposed Bill or Act cannot seek to undertake multiple Actions such as funding and rights and restrictions and remedies in one form. A separate proposed Bill or Act must be presented for each Action in logical order and sequence of proposed amendments or enhancements.

5. The Parliament shall exist for a fixed period of life not less than one complete standard Age of one thousand and seventy (1070) years, corresponding to the life of the University. Members of Parliament shall be appointed for a Term of six years and have their commissions dissolved every six years and shall be required to resign from office ahead of University Elections for new Members. Life of Parliament

6. Excepting a University election year, every year there shall be four (4) Sessions of fixed days corresponding to equal divisions of the year, whereby Members of Parliament are summonsed to attend. Parliamentary Sessions

Each of these sessions shall be named for the season that they correspond, namely Summer, Autumn, Winter and Spring Session. A day within a session when Members of Parliament are summonsed to sit in Parliament shall be called a Sitting Session Day.

A day within a session when Members of Parliament are not summonsed to sit in Parliament shall be called a Non-Sitting Session Day. During a year that a University election is to be called, the Parliament shall not sit for the Spring session. Instead the last Session of Parliament shall be the Winter session.

7. Responsibility for good conduct and control of the Parliament and the scheduling of business within the chamber shall be vested in the Office of Prefect of the Parliament (Parliament Prefect). The Prefect of the Parliament shall be an independent role, free from political party preferences. The candidate shall be elected by new Parliamentarians themselves on the first day of sitting of Parliament following a University Election. Prefect of the Parliament (Parliament Prefect)

8. Excluding the election of Office Holders, voting in University Parliament shall be by open vote expressed as either Yes or No to the proposition before the chamber. Voting shall always require a quorum and shall follow the standard procedures listed in this Charter. Parliament Voting and Elections

Total votes shall be tallied as either Yes, or No to the proposition expressed by the proposed Ordinance. A higher total number of Yes votes to No votes shall deem the proposed Ordinance or proposition has been passed. A higher total number of No votes to Yes votes shall deem the proposed Ordinance or proposition has been defeated.

The record, attendance and vote of all Members of University Parliament shall be recorded on the public record.

9. Each Session of Parliament shall be a minimum of twelve days and a maximum of forty days, with the precise number and dates set by the Parliament session length

Parliament Prefect.

10. The Parliament Prefect shall be responsible for the issuing of summons to individual Parliamentarians for their attendance to Parliament. Excepting special leave granted by the Parliament Prefect due to matters of University security, health or extended personal matters, all Parliamentarians shall be required to attend the Sitting Session Days as listed in the summons.

Parliament attendance

Failure of a Parliamentarian to attend six (6) or more Session Sitting Days within one (1) Session shall be deemed a failure to discharge the duties of their office and the Parliament Prefect shall be responsible for immediately initiating a Parliament Expulsion Motion or a Director Expulsion Motion should the Parliamentarian be a University Director-General.

Both Vice-Presidents shall be immune from any action for non-attendance breaches.

11. The Commissions of Members of Parliament to sit in Parliament shall be dissolved every six (6) years following that last day of the Winter Session for Parliament.

Dissolution of Commissions of Members of Parliament

12. The date of a University Election shall always occur within the Spring months, allowing forty (40) days prior to the date of the election for the official campaign period.

Date of University Election

13. The formation of new commissions for Parliamentarians shall occur within fourteen (14) days after the University Election day following the count and verification of all votes.

New Commissions of Elected Members

The instrument of formation of a new Parliament shall be three (3) declarations from the University Director of the University Election Commission:

(i) To each successful candidate for election to the Parliament confirming their validity as the rightful representative of their constituency representing their commission; and

(ii) To the successful candidate for election as President and the two (2) Vice-Presidents confirming their validity as the rightful executive to form government; and

(iii) To the caretaker President that the election result has been verified and that writs to summons successful candidates to be invoked into Parliament and form the new Executive must now be issued.

Upon receipt of the declaration, the caretaker President shall be required to issue writs within seven (7) days for the summonsing to

Parliament of successful candidates to form the new Parliament and Executive.

14. The minimum number of Members (quorum) required to be present within the Parliament to permit the full exercise of its powers shall be two thirds (2/3) the total number of Members of that house. Quorum

Parliament shall not be permitted to undertake procedures that require a quorum if the total number of Members in the Parliament is not equal or greater to the quorum.

15. The sessions on the floor of the Parliament shall be open for the public record with all speeches, debates, motions, votes and documents recorded in a public record. Public record of proceedings

Furthermore, all committee meetings and special sessions of reviews shall also be open for the public record, except those proceedings voted and passed by the house as being regular meetings of University security. An expenditure related review may never be closed to public scrutiny.

16. During their attendance at the Session of the Parliament, and in going to and returning from the same, all Members of the Parliament shall be privileged from arrest except in matters of Treason, Felony and Breach of the Peace. Such privilege does not extend to their property or office that shall fall under the normal course of law and investigation and right to search by issued Warrant. Legal privilege

During debate in the Parliament, all spoken and written material presented and entered into the Public Record of proceedings shall be privileged and immune from civil liability.

17. The Permanent Parliament shall have the right and power to commission a University Commission of Investigation with the power to call any registered Member within the University and any information held by the University Executive to review. Parliament Investigations and Actions

The Permanent Parliament also has vested by this Charter the power to commission a University Impeachment for the forced removal of any elected official from the President to any position within any branch of government in the University.

A University Commission of Investigation must be called by the Permanent Parliament when a call to expel one or more members is made, excluding cases where the grounds of the charge are based on an automatic expulsion.

18. The Censure of a Parliament is when the Permanent Synod and Sunedrion of the Union exercise their Right of Jurisdiction over a Censure of Parliament

University in accord with the Rule of Law, Justice and Due Process to admonish or order the suspension of all commissions of a Parliament in accord with the conditions set forth herein.

No body, person, aggregate or entity has the power or right to dissolve a Parliament and University other than the Members of a Permanent University themselves. However, when the Permanent Union Synod and Sunedrion that the University belongs proves one or more of the following grounds for Censure, then the members of Parliament may be lawfully Censured or Suspended for a period of not less than ninety (90) days and not more than three hundred and sixty (360) days:

(i) That the Parliament has been found to have deliberately and wilfully exceeded its rights in engaging in activities that have brought disrepute or harm to Ucadia, or University or Union; or

(ii) That the Parliament has entered into agreements with other parties that it has no right or authority to do, or such agreements that contradict good faith, good actions and good conscience; or

(iii) That the Parliament has wilfully and deliberately taken actions that are considered Criminal in nature by the Criminal Code of the Union.

Article 75 – University College

1. The primary Organ of Institutional Power and Authority of a Ucadia University shall be vested in an aggregate called the University College, comprising the President, the Twelve Great Divine Offices of State and the University Cabinet of Directors-General of Systems of the University. *University College*

   The head of the College shall be embodied and personified in the ceremonial Office of Dean as a Corporation Sole. The Vice President of Domestic Affairs shall always be vested into this position and dignity.

2. The primary Organ of Executive Power and Authority of a Ucadia University shall be vested in an executive committee called the Cabinet, comprising a President and the University Directors-General of Systems. *University Cabinet*

   The word Cabinet originates from the ancient Anglaise (Old French) word of the same name meaning a small office or study, particularly in reference to government officials.

   The secretary of the Cabinet, being the most senior public servant and Chief of Staff of the President, shall be embodied and personified in the Office of Chamberlain as a Corporation Sole.

3. The President is the supreme leader of the Society, its head of state, the highest elected office and the living embodiment and personification of the University as a Corporation Sole. The Office of President is equivalent to the Office of Minister-General in respect of any Ucadia Foundation duly formed for a Preliminary or Probational University. The President

The President is vested with the sovereign and executive authority to manage the needs and affairs of the University through the selection or dismissal of wise counsel in the form of their University Cabinet of Directors-General, the agencies, officials and administration of the Government.

The President shall have the authority of Commander in Chief of the Militia and all the armed security forces in times of declared disaster or war. The President shall have during both declared times, the power to command marshal law. In matters of war, the President shall have full strategic command for the commitment of the forces of the University upon the agreed counsel of the University Security Council.

In times of declared national disaster or request by other societies, the President shall have the power to commit the nation's forces on the agreed counsel of the University Disaster Relief Council for such national or foreign assistance requests.

The President shall have the authority over all agencies and University Directors-General as Chairman and Head of the Cabinet. As Chairman, the President may choose to overrule motions of the Cabinet and select the agenda and minutes of the meetings, through the advice and counsel of the Chamberlain.

The President shall have Power, by and with the Advice and Consent of the Parliament, to make Treaties, and he shall nominate, and by and with the Advice and Consent of the Parliament, shall appoint Ambassadors, other public Ministers and Consuls, Judges of the Supreme Court, and all other Officers of the University, whose Appointments are not herein otherwise provided for, that shall be established by Law: but the Parliament may by Law vest the Appointment of such inferior Officers, as they think proper, in the President alone, in the Courts of Law, or in the Heads of Departments.

The President shall have the power to submit bills to the Parliament for review and vote and shall have the power to veto any legislation having been presented once and passed not having two thirds majority votes in the Parliament. The President may not veto legislation having been passed without major amendment by the Parliament for the second time.

The President shall be responsible upon the passing of bills by the Parliament and not having been vetoed to sign such bills into law within thirty (30) days of their approval by the Parliament. The President having unreasonably delayed the ascent of two (2) or more Bills and without due notification of veto shall be liable for grounds of Impeachment.

The President shall have the Power by virtue of this Charter to pardon any convicted criminal and stay the sentence of any court imposed sentence for any lesser court than the Supreme Court of the University. The President does not have the power to amend a judgement of the Supreme Court.

Monarch as President

4. In certain jurisdictions, the living embodiment and personification of a state is recognised as a Monarch. Thus, the body of a reigning sovereign may hold two distinct yet coexisting personas: the first being that of a natural person as Monarch and that of a State or "crown", as a Corporation Sole as accorded through law. Where Members choose by a majority of two-thirds or greater, to recognise the head of state as a Monarch, or where an existing Monarch of an internationally recognised Constitutional Monarchy older than one hundred years chooses to exercise their prerogative in seeking to form a Prerogative University Status, the present Constitutional Charter acknowledges such Rights and freedom of choice. In both cases the President as Monarch shall be exempt from the maximum six year Terms.

However, in all cases of recognised rule of a University by Constitutional Monarchy, any claimed successor according to proper rules of succession must be endorsed by a vote of confidence of two-thirds or greater by the Parliament upon ascending the throne. Furthermore, the Parliament must re- endorse their confidence by a vote in favour of the Monarch at least every twelve years. A Monarch that fails to hold the confidence of Parliament must abdicate. Finally, a Monarch is forbidden to continue to hold power if seriously incapacitated by virtue of reason, age or serious infirmary.

Oath of the President

5. Prior to the commencement of their term of office, the President shall make the following public oath - "I do solemnly promise before the Divine Creator and all Heaven and Earth that I will faithfully execute the Office of President of (University), and will to the best of my ability, preserve, protect and defend the Charter of (University)."

Term of the President

6. The President shall hold their Office during the Term of six (6) Years, and, together with two (2) Vice Presidents, chosen for the same Term, be elected by the people following the procedures for general and

University elections contained within this Charter. A President is ineligible to serve beyond a total of two (2) terms, twelve (12) years.

7. The President shall, at stated times, receive for their services, a Compensation, that shall neither be increased nor diminished during the period that they shall have been elected, and shall not receive any other income during their term. Payment of the President

8. The Vice-President of Foreign Affairs shall be one (1) of two (2) Vice-Presidents elected together with the President for the same term, once every six (6) years. Vice-President of Foreign Affairs

The Vice-President of Foreign Affairs shall be the second most senior elected official for the planning, management and good governance of all International issues and business on behalf of the nation. The International Vice-President shall be the nation's most senior foreign diplomat.

9. The Vice-President of Domestic Affairs shall be one (1) of two (2) Vice-Presidents elected together with the President for the same term, once every six (6) years. Vice-President of Domestic Affairs

The Vice-President of Domestic Affairs shall be the second most senior elected official for the planning, management and good governance of all University issues. The University Vice-President is the nation's most senior public servant.

10. In accord with the present Constitutional Charter, only a man or woman meeting all of the following criteria shall be permitted to stand for election to the office of President and / or Vice President: Minimum Qualifications of President, Vice Presidents

(i) Currently holds the office of President, or Vice-President, or Governor or Parliamentarian of the University; and

(ii) Aged between thirty five (35) and sixty five (65) and in generally good health; and

(iii) They are not otherwise ineligible to hold the office of President or Vice President.

11. Both Vice-Presidents shall, at stated times, receive for their services, a Compensation, that shall neither be increased nor diminished during the period that they shall have been elected, and shall not receive any other income during their term. Payment of a Vice President

12. By this Charter an Executive Code shall be formed. All existing and new laws providing for effective function and oversight of executive government and executive responsibility shall be subject to inclusion in the Executive Code. Executive, Service and Emergency Codes

By this Charter a Service Code shall be formed. All existing and new laws providing for public service and administration responsibility shall be subject to inclusion in the Service Code. By this Charter an Emergency Code shall be formed. All existing and new laws providing for local, university and international emergencies shall be subject to inclusion in the Emergency Code.

By this Charter, the Office of President holds an additional and unique honour and responsibility as the Living ambassador of the Executive, Service and Emergency laws of the Society.

The President represents the legal and living embodiment of these laws in person, such that any injury to this body of laws also represents an injury to the person, represented by living flesh and blood.

As ambassador and living representative of these laws, the President is bound to protect these laws from injury by their own actions or through any failure of due process or lack of respect of the law.

13. In the good management of the University, its affairs and requirements can be compared to the good conduct of a company with its Members as shareholders.

Function and Operation of University Cabinet

The University Cabinet shall be a board of individuals selected by the President to head the permanent statutory authorities and uphold the laws regarding the critical systems of the University. The tenure of a Director-General shall be at the sole discretion of the President.

The Chamberlain shall be responsible for the operation of the Cabinet, its agendas and documentation, as well as reporting duties of Directors-General as well as permanent secretaries to agencies. The Chamberlain shall also be head of the public service.

Given the importance of each system within our Society functioning to its optimum, the position of a University Director-General should reflect the very best of the community with the knowledge, experience and respect relating to the system they manage.

14. In respect to the high office of the President, by the power of this Charter, an official seal shall be forged and it shall be known as the Official Seal of the President.

The Official Seal of the President

Each President shall have their own unique official seal based on the common seal of office. All official acts of the President shall require this Seal to be affixed as verification of its authenticity.

15. Upon election to the office of President, it is their solemn duty to publish two (2) documents to Members each and every year of their office. These documents shall be:

Documents of the President

(i) The President shall be required publish an annual plan (subject to the approval of the University Board and Parliament) that shall state the financial, moral and well being position of the University. The Annual Plan shall also outline the plans of the President to help the Members of the Society and how the contributions of the Members are being used to better all Members; and

(ii) The President shall be required to publish an annual message to all the Members that the President outlines his / her key message, guidance, inspiration and comfort to all Members of the University.

Article 76 – University Chancery

1. The primary administrative Organ of Rights, Trusts, Estates, Warrants, Patents, Land and Wards of the University, legally embodied and personified through the Great Office of Chancellor as a Corporation Sole, shall be known as the Chancery Court, also known as the *Forum Cancellariae*. University Chancery

2. The primary administrative Organ of Rolls of the University, legally embodied and personified through the Great Office of Custodian as a Corporation Sole, shall be known as the Vestry. All original Rolls shall be held within the Vestry with the Custodian being the sole *Custos Rotolorum* of the University. University Vestry

3. The primary administrative Organ of Vital and Sacred Records, Events, Covenants, Treaties, Deeds and Titles of the University, legally embodied and personified through the Great Office of Plenipotentiary, shall be known as the Sacristy. The Vice-President for Foreign Affairs as Secretary of State shall be vested into the Great Office of Plenipotentiary. University Sacristy

4. The primary purposes and responsibilities of the Chancery are: Powers, Authority and Responsibilities of the Chancery

   (i) To provide a secure and centralised repository and archive of all original instruments and official documents of the University and other manuscripts of importance; and

   (ii) To maintain, update, secure and protect the Great Ledger and Great Register and Public Record of the University including but not limited to all documents associated with such entries; and

   (iii) To maintain, update, publish, secure and protect the official Gazette of the University including but not limited to all documents associated with such public notices; and

(iv) To maintain, develop and support the library of official forms of the University ensuring their easy availability and use for all Members; and

(v) To administer all Rights in respect of Trusts, Estates, Warrants, Patents, Land and Companies within the jurisdiction of the University; and

(vi) To administer the needs and affairs of all wards of the University, including, but not limited all trusts and estates held for the benefit of Members; and

(vii) The coordination of all official receipts, acknowledgements and certificates derived from valid extracts of original records held in trust by the Chancery.

5. The Vestry of the University is the first of two most sacred and solemn chamber for the safe and secure keeping of sacred items, such as the Rolls of the University. It is also the term used for any authorised tribunal of persons, having been convened to administer the Rolls of the University themselves, or associated ledgers and registers of rights. Thus, when the term is used in the context of such an authorised committee, the Vestry (meeting) shall be equivalent to the convening of an authorised Parochial Church Council.

Powers, Authority and Responsibilities of the Vestry

The primary purposes and responsibilities of the Vestry are:

(i) To provide a secure and centralised repository and archive of all original Rolls of the University and other sacred instruments of importance; and

(ii) To maintain, update, secure and protect the Rolls of the University, ensuring the enrolment, entry and formation of records of Persons is free of error; and

(iii) To maintain, update, publish, secure and protect official extracts of the Rolls for the purpose of Administration, including but not limited to Members, Electors, Companies, Officers and Agents.

6. The Sacristy of the University is the second of two most sacred and solemn chamber for the safe and secure keeping of sacred items, such as Vital and Sacred Records, Event Registers, Covenants, Treaties, Deeds and Titles of the University. When such records are entered into the sacred space of the Sacristy, then such records and documents are therefore consecrated before all Heaven and Earth in the name of the

Powers, Authority and Responsibilities of the Sacristy

Divine Creator. Thus, any lesser body or non-Ucadian entity that disputes such sacred records as the Vital and Sacred Records of Live Borne Records is therefore culpable of profanity and sacrilege as well as perfidy, fallacy and dishonour.

All Live Borne Records and official Certificates of the Plenipotentiary are issued from the Sacristy.

Article 77 – University Judiciary

1. The primary judicial Organ of the University, legally embodied and personified through the Great Office of Justiciar, shall be the Supreme Court as the highest court of the University, having Jurisdiction over all Members and associated matters, citations, claims, petitions and controversies. University Judiciary

2. The primary military and security Organ of the University, legally embodied and personified through the Great Office of Marshal, shall be the Militia as the highest civilian security and military force of the University, having Jurisdiction in the defence of all Members and the rule of law. University Militia

3. In the conduct of law and the hearing of matters, the Supreme Court shall have first, original and complete jurisdiction over all matters pertaining to Members and the Courts of a Member State. Recognition of the Superiority of the Supreme Court

Article 78 – University Exchequer

1. The primary administrative Organ of Taxation, Revenues, Funds and Securities, legally embodied and personified through the Great Office of Exchequer, shall be the Exchequer Court, also known as the Curia Scaccarium, as the principal office, place, chamber, storehouse, vault, penitentiary and temple for the recording and safe keeping of all University Moneta, cash, funds, securities, records and ledgers of University revenue, expenses and other obligations. University Exchequer

2. In order to fulfil its primary objectives, the University Exchequer shall comprise of the following permanent organs and any such other organs deemed necessary by amendment to this Charter: Organs of the University Exchequer

   (i) University Treasury; and

   (ii) University Community Bank; and

   (iii) University Disaster Relief Fund; and

   (iv) University Bank for Reconstruction and Development; and

(v) University Insurance Fund; and

(vi) University Budget Agency; and

(vii) University Finance Company.

3. Ucadia Moneta as University Sovereigns represents the ecclesiastical, lawful and legal units of currency and means of exchange of the Union.

Ucadia Moneta and University Sovereign (Money)

The primary purpose and function of Ucadia Moneta is to create the most consistent unit of measure, most stable store of value that can then be utilised for the purchase and consumption of goods and services as well as the conversion into assets as equivalent stores of value.

University Sovereigns may be formed by valid Ucadian Universities of the Union on the underwriting of a certain set amount of Silver Credos (Credits) held in trust for the University against the value of the stock of Moneta (money) by the University Reserve Bank. In turn, the stock of Silver Credos (Credits) are underwritten by a stock of Gold Credos (Credits) held in trust by the Union Treasury, that are ultimately underwritten by Supreme Credos (Credits) held in trust by the Temple, also known as the Globe Union Treasury.

One thousand (1,000) University Sovereigns are equivalent to one (1) Silver Credo (Credit). A University Sovereign (Money) and Ucadia Moneta (Money) have the same value.

4. During the period that a Ucadia University is at the Preliminary or Probational Status, the University Exchequer, University Parliament and University Executive shall only have access to Ucadia Currency Accounts managed by the Council and Secretariat of Ucadia Foundations.

Temporary and Development Ucadia Currency Accounts

This temporary status concerning Ucadia Currency Accounts shall similarly apply to all Ucadia Provinces and Campuses within the jurisdiction of the said Ucadia University, unless by special exemption of the Council and Secretariat of Ucadia Foundations, a Prerogative or Permanent Campus or Province is granted full access to its Ucadia Currency Accounts prior to the University itself gaining similar status.

The University Exchequer, University Parliament and University Executive shall not be granted full authority and access to its permanent accounts until the status of the Ucadia University is lawfully and legitimately recognised at the status of Prerogative or Permanent.

Article 79 – Ucadia (Temporary) Foundation

1. In accord with Article 104 (Ucadia Foundations & Charitable Funds) of the most sacred Covenant *Pactum De Singularis Caelum*, the Right to form Executive Government of a valid Preliminary or Probational University shall be granted by Constitutional Charter to an association of a minimum of twelve (12) competent, valid and registered Ucadia Members, to form a properly Ucadia registered body politic and corporate for the purpose of developing a permanent Ucadia political presence and interfacing with non-Ucadian societies, entities, bodies politic, companies and persons. Ucadia (Temporary) Foundation

   The body formed shall be known as a "**Ucadia Foundation**" of the particular University with its initial constitutional charter granted for a maximum of four (4) years, before a new constitutional charter must be registered and issued for each and every additional four (4) years. Each valid Ucadia Foundation shall constitute the preliminary executive government of the relevant Ucadia University.

2. The primary purpose of a Ucadia Foundation being formed as the preliminary Executive Government of a Ucadia University is to assist in the development of a permanent Ucadia political presence and interfacing with non-Ucadian societies, entities, bodies politic, companies and persons. Purpose and Operation of Ucadia Foundation

   A Ucadia Foundation is therefore always a temporary body registered within Ucadia Law, but never registered within a non-Ucadian or foreign jurisdiction. Once fifty (50 %) percent or more of the Provinces within the jurisdiction of a Ucadia University have reached Probational or Prerogative status, a Ucadia Foundation must transition power within one hundred and eighty (180) days to a Probational or Prerogative Executive Government for the Ucadia University.

3. *Ius Ucadia Fundationis* (Ucadia Foundation Rights) is the sixth collection of seven *Ucadia Sovereign Entity Rights*; and may be explicitly invoked or referenced by Sovereign Right of Action through registration and possession of a proper Mandate associated with a Ucadia Sovereign Entity in Ucadia or Non-Ucadia Jurisdiction. The collection of Sovereign Rights of *Ius Ucadia Fundationis* (Custody, Guardianship & Preservation) contains eight (8) Rights being:- Collection of Ius Ucadia Fundationis (Foundation Rights)

   (i) *Ius Ucadia Fundationis* as the collection of Superior Rights associated with a Ucadia Foundation as inherited from *Ius Ucadia Universitas*; and

   (ii) *Ius Ucadia Fundationis Existentiae* as the Superior Right for the Existence of Ucadia as inherited from *Ius Ucadia Fundationis*; and

(iii) *Ius Ucadia Fundationis Mandati* as the Superior Right of Mandate of Ucadia as inherited from *Ius Ucadia Fundationis*; and

(iv) *Ius Ucadia Fundationis Proprietatis* as the Superior Right of Property of Ucadia as inherited from *Ius Ucadia Fundationis*; and

(v) *Ius Ucadia Fundationis Potestatis* as the Superior Right of Authority and Power of Ucadia as inherited from *Ius Ucadia Fundationis*; and

(vi) *Ius Ucadia Fundationis Registrum* as the Superior Right of Registers and Rolls as inherited from *Ius Ucadia Fundationis*; and

(vii) *Ius Ucadia Fundationis Nomenis* as the Superior Right to Name, Title and Reputation as inherited from *Ius Ucadia Fundationis*; and

(viii) *Ius Ucadia Fundationis Fecerim* as the Superior Right of the Foundation to invent, create and make seals, arms, heralds, instruments and other property of value as inherited from *Ius Ucadia Fundationis*.

4. The first one hundred and eight days after a Ucadia Foundation is granted its Constitutional Charter shall be known as an interim period, wherein, the Council of Ucadia Foundations, upon advice of the Secretariat and Visitor and Architect, if still living and capable, may elect to immediately rescind the charter and rights of a particular Ucadia Foundation, if behaviour and actions have been established that run contrary to the agreements upon founding such a body.

180 Day Interim Period

Thereafter the interim period, the Council of Ucadia Foundations may only vote to have a Ucadia Foundation investigated for malfeasance and poor management first, before any proposed action of sanction or dissolving a Ucadia Foundation is permissible.

5. The Constitutional Charter granted to a Ucadia Foundation shall not exceed four (4) years, before it must be renewed for a further four (4) years maximum. The first year of any initial granted Constitutional Charter shall be probational, whereby the particular Ucadia Foundation may be issued with a dissolution notice, upon clear evidence of gross maladministration, malfeasance or misrepresentation, without sufficient remedy demonstrated to rectify such serious breaches of trust.

Expiry and Renewal of Constitutional Charter

Whilst the initial grant of a Constitutional Charter to a Ucadia

University requires a minimum association of twelve (12) suitably qualified Ucadia Members, it shall be permissible that a Foundation has its charter renewed at the time with a minimum of four (4) suitably qualified Ucadia Members.

Previous Ucadia Foundation Members that have resigned, or expelled, or have abrogated their rights of membership shall automatically be ineligible to be recognised or registered as Foundation Members upon any renewal of the relevant Ucadia Foundation Constitutional Charter. Furthermore, any outstanding rights or obligations associated with previous Foundation Members shall also cease at the expiry of the previous Constitutional Charter for the particular Ucadia Foundation, unless rolled over by unanimous vote of Foundation Members registered under the renewed Constitutional Charter.

6. All valid and registered Ucadia Foundations for all Ucadia Universities shall ipso facto (as a matter of fact) be members of the Council of Ucadia Foundations. Council of Ucadia Foundations

The Council of Ucadia Foundations shall comprise of a maximum of two nominated representative from each valid and registered Ucadia Foundation for each Ucadia University, as the temporary executive government of Ucadia, subject to oversight from the Visitor and Architect, if still living and capable. Each nominated representative shall hold such temporary office for a maximum of six months, before either being re-elected or a new member of each Ucadia Foundation is nominated.

The Council of Ucadia Foundations shall meet via digital video conferencing at least once every quarter, with the Secretariat of the Ucadia Foundations responsible for managing the agenda, voting records and minutes.

7. All temporary administrative management of procedural and executive actions shall be vested in the Secretariat of Ucadia Foundations as a single body representing the interests of all Ucadia Foundations equally. Secretariat of Ucadia Foundations

The Secretariat of Ucadia Foundations shall report directly to a Secretary and in turn the Visitor and Architect, if still living and capable.

8. Budgeting, finance and funding of Ucadia Foundations shall be vested in the Treasury of Council of Ucadia Foundations, with budgeting decisions held by the Council and day to day management held by the Secretariat of Ucadia Foundations. Treasury of Council of Ucadia Foundations

9. The following shall be the minimum qualification criteria for the formation of a valid Ucadia Foundation within the jurisdiction of a Qualification Criteria for

Ucadia University:-

Formation of Ucadia Foundation

(i) A probational Ucadia University Executive Government does not currently exist for the particular University at the time of the application; and

(ii) The conditions to recognise a probational Ucadia University Executive Government are unlikely to be met within the next sixty (60) to ninety (90) days; and

(iii) No valid and properly registered Ucadia Foundation currently exists for the Ucadia University at the time of the application; and

(iv) A minimum of twelve (12) suitable and qualified Ucadia Members living within the jurisdiction of the Ucadia University have put their names to the application; and

(v) The applicants to the formation of a Ucadia Foundation have contributed the appropriate amounts required to form an individual bond for each Ucadia Foundation Member; and

(vi) There exists no other cause or reason not to delay or deny the application at the time of its filing.

Qualification Criteria for Ucadia Foundation Members

10. The following shall be the minimum qualification criteria to be regarded as a suitable and qualified Ucadia Member capable of being accepted as a Ucadia Foundation Member:-

(i) That the Person is a Ucadia Member, having redeemed their Member number and received their Live Borne Record; and

(ii) That the Person has read the present most sacred Covenant and the Essential Ucadia Reading Material required for any potential Ucadia Foundation Member and has acknowledged their subscription to the material in writing; and

(iii) That the Person has participated in at least one verified Ucadia training session or workshop and has been suitably tested on their knowledge and support of the Ucadia Model; and

(iv) That the Person has deposited sufficient contribution in good faith toward the necessary bond as a Ucadia Foundation Member; and

(v) That the Person is not otherwise facing active legal actions or personal issues that would preclude how much time and effort they may be able to invest as a Ucadia Foundation Member; and

(vi) That the Person is a valid inhabitant of the jurisdiction of the Ucadia University related to the proposed Ucadia Foundation; and

(vii) No other issue exists that would otherwise render the Person ineligible.

11. By definition, being a Ucadia Foundation Member is different and separate to being a Ucadia Member. A Ucadia Member is not automatically a Ucadia Foundation Member within the Ucadia University jurisdiction where they are domiciled. Ucadia Members and Ucadia Foundation Members

Being a Ucadia Foundation Member is both a privilege and a solemn obligation, to help manifest a permanent presence of Ucadia within the jurisdiction of a particular Ucadia University, as well as help support the services and operations to other Ucadia Members. As a consequence, they are required to have a stronger and deeper knowledge of the Ucadia Model and to dedicate a regular portion of their time to fulfil this prime objective.

Finally, because Ucadia Foundation Members agree to be honourable representatives of Ucadia and Ucadia Members, they are bound by a solemn oath and bond to act accordingly. Ucadia Members are not required to make such a significant contribution to become a Ucadia Member.

12. The relevant Council and Secretariat of Ucadia Foundations shall institute policies and guidelines in the interim, before the establishment of probational, prerogative and permanent bodies, concerning the appropriate types and levels of bonds associated with Ucadia Foundation Membership and Ucadia Officers. Foundation Member Bonds

13. A valid Ucadia Foundation constituted for longer than twelve (12) months, shall be granted upon application, the right to register a Charitable Fund with the non-Ucadian and foreign state associated with the jurisdiction of the relevant Ucadia University. Registered Charitable Fund

14. All Ucadia Foundation Members are bound by their oath to refrain from directly acquiring or receiving any form of assets, shares, Ucadia Money or objects of significant financial value during their time as a Ucadia Foundation Member. Other than fair financial compensation for their contribution of time and the reimbursement of any costs, Ucadia Foundation Members are forbidden from profiting or appearing to profit from such a position of trust. This rule applies equally to the Visitor and Architect. Foundation Member Property Interests and Payment

Any records created previously in relation to Ucadia Foundation Members stating a direct pecuniary interest or receipt of any asset must be corrected and recorded within the minutes of official meetings of the relevant Ucadia Foundation. The prior ownership of assets by a Ucadia Foundation Member, or the acquisition of assets associated with the utilisation of services and goods of Ucadia, does not apply to the above rule, providing there is clear evidence such transactions and benefits were done with clean hands and without undue bias.

Article 80 – University Foundation

1. The foundation of a valid Ucadia University of the Union shall be in accord with the criteria and terms defined by the present Article and the five possible "states" or "types" of Legal Status for a Ucadia University being Provisional, Preliminary, Probational, Prerogative and Permanent. University Foundation

2. A *Provisional University* is is the first of five types of states of a valid Ucadia University. All Provisional Universities within the Union were formed between GAIA E8:Y3209:A1:S1:M6:D1 [Mon 21 Dec 2009] and GAIA E8:Y3210:A1:S1:M17:D1 [Tue 21 Dec 2010] as the second largest operational division of the occupational forces of One Heaven following the complete conquest of all land, sea, earth, space, time, atmosphere and spirit within the boundaries of the Union; and lawful possession and occupation of all rights, property, title and uses within the same bounds; and the investiture of a unique and individual spiritual member into each of the Twelve Great Offices of State. Under the terms of spiritual military occupation, the boundaries and Cadastral features of each University within each Union have been properly surveyed with the Survey and Charter for each Province registered within the Great Register of the Union and the event published in the Globe Union Gazette and Ucadia Gazette. Provisional University Foundation

3. A *Preliminary University* is the second of five types of states of a valid Ucadia University formed when not less than twelve (12) Ordinary Ucadia Members domiciled within the bounds of the University elect an interim University Embassy and Government instituted through a Convention for the formation of a Ucadia Foundation for the University, with each Ordinary Member having invoked and recorded an Oath of Allegiance and an Oath of Office; in accord with the Criteria for the Foundation of a Preliminary University. All applications and approvals of Preliminary Universities shall be under the temporary administration of the Council and Secretariat of Ucadia Foundations subject to the fact that no Preliminary, Probational or Prerogative or Permanent University Administration yet exists within the said bounds of the University. Preliminary University Foundation

4. The following twelve (12) criteria are the essential structural Criteria for the

components and properties of a valid Preliminary University:

Foundation of a Preliminary University

(i) A unique and valid name and unique eighteen (18) digit University Location Trust Number and unique eighteen (18) digit University Society Trust Number exists for the Province within the bounds of the Union; and

(ii) That no existing Preliminary, Probational, Prerogative or Permanent University of the same name and same unique University Location Trust Number and University Society Trust Number exists and is currently recognised and officially registered as active; and

(iii) That at least five (5) candidates make and sign the petition for recognition of a Preliminary University; and that all candidates are Ordinary Ucadia Members of good actions, good conscience with good trust; and have not previously been refused, denied, banned or prevented in any way from holding any office of the Union, or University or Province or Campus; and that all candidates agree for their names and Member numbers to be included within the Ucadia Gazette notice recognising the formation of the Preliminary University as well as the granting of a Temporary Charter to form an Ucadia Foundation within the bounds of the University; and

(iv) That the candidates making the petition for recognition of a Preliminary University do so free from any duress, or any coercion, or any motive of fraud and misrepresentation, or to act as a foreign agent, or for other negative and improper motive; and the candidates making the petition for recognition of a Preliminary University have not petitioned for recognition of any other Preliminary, Probational, Prerogative or Permanent University; and

(v) That all candidates making the petition for recognition of a Preliminary University have been domiciled in the same location as the University for at least three (3) months; and the candidates making the petition for recognition of a Preliminary University are competent and capable and willing to perform the obligations and duties required of an Officer of a Ucadia University; and

(vi) That upon the issue of the Ucadia Gazette in acknowledgement of the Preliminary University and the granting of the Mandate and Right to form an Ucadia Foundation that the Members convene a Constitutional Convention to agree to accept the Charter and discuss and form a Constitution for the University;

and that such records are duly provided to be published as a Gazette notice and Register Record; and

(vii) That upon the conclusion of the Constitutional Convention, that the members of the Preliminary University meet and ratify the Constitution for the Ucadia University as well as discuss and agree to the proposed bylaws of the University Foundation; and that such records of Covenant of Ratification and agreement are duly provided to be published as a Gazette notice and Register Record; and

(viii) That upon the conclusion of the Ratification Meeting, that the members of the Preliminary University convene a General Election for the election of the first Office Holders of the Preliminary University and does ratify the bylaws and elect the key Office holders to the positions of President, Dean, Chancellor, Exchequer and Plenipotentiary; and that such records of ratification and elections are duly provided to be published as a Gazette notice and Register Record; and

(ix) That each elected Office Holder takes a valid Oath of Allegiance to the University and executes an Agreement of Office for their Position; and that such copies of agreements are provided within seven (7) days for recording; and

(x) That the Ucadia University duly register and record itself as an existing and valid Foreign Body Corporate for Religious and Charitable Purposes with the appropriate foreign state and/or national governments operating within the same region; and

(xi) That every effort is made to ensure the University properly qualifies to be a Probational University within twelve months; and

(xii) That General Elections are held within twelve months whereby all Members may participate to elect Office Holders as a *bona fide* Probational University.

Probational University Foundation

5. A *Probational University* is the third of five types of states of a valid Ucadia University formed when not less than fifty (50) percent of all Provinces within the bounds of the University have been formed as Probational or Prerogative or Permanent; and with such application recognised and approved subject to appointments of Officers to the positions of the Twelve Great Offices of State duly gazetted and certified in accord with the Criteria for the Foundation of a Probational University. All applications and approvals of Probational Universities are superior to any pre-existing Preliminary University

Administration and upon such approval, all rights, powers and authorities must be duly conveyed to the new administration.

6. The following ten (10) criteria are the essential structural components and properties of a valid Probational University:- Criteria for the Foundation of a Probational University

(i) A unique and valid name and unique eighteen (18) digit University Location Trust Number and and unique eighteen (18) digit University Society Trust Number exists for the University within the bounds of a unique Location Trust of the Union and that one hundred and forty-four Ordinary Members are recorded within the bounds of the University; and

(ii) That no existing Probational, Prerogative or Permanent University of the same name and same unique University Location Trust Number and University Society Trust Number exists and is currently recognised as active; and

(iii) That there are at least one hundred and forty four (144) or more living Ordinary Members domiciled within the bounds of the University; and

(iv) That at least three candidates make and sign the petition for recognition of a Probational University and that all three are existing Governors of their respective Provinces within the bounds of the University and are Ordinary Members of good actions, good conscience with good faith and has not previously been refused, denied, banned or prevented in any way from holding any office of the Union, or University or Province or Campus; and that the three candidates making the petition for recognition of a Probational University do so free from any duress, or any coercion, or any motive of fraud and misrepresentation, or to act as a foreign agent, or for other negative and improper motive; and

(v) That the three candidates have been domiciled in the same location as the University for at least three (3) months and no other person living within the same domicile has petitioned for recognition of the same Probational University in the past twelve months; and

(vi) The candidates making the petition for recognition of a Probational University have not petitioned for recognition of any other Preliminary, Probational, Prerogative or Permanent University; and

(vii) The candidates making the petition for recognition of a Probational University are competent and capable and willing to perform the obligations and duties required of a President of a University; and

(viii) The candidates making the petition for recognition of a Probational University invoke the Oath of Allegiance to the Union as attested, witnessed and recorded in writing; and

(ix) The candidates making the petition for recognition of a Probational University accept the obligations and duties of Office of the University pronouncing upon the sacred Covenant *Pactum De Singularis Caelum* as attested, witnessed and recorded in writing; and

(x) That written notice of the recorded Oath of Allegiance, the name and University Location Trust Number and University Society Trust Number of the Probational University, are provided within fourteen (14) days to any and all existing Provincial and University administrations of the Union to which the University belongs as well as to each and every Province and Campus within the same University; and that the President within thirty (30) days of assuming Office of President makes provision for a permanent Post Office mailing address, a permanent phone contact number, a contact email address and a means by which the Governors and administration of the Provinces of the University may receive regular paper and/or electronic communication and information.

7. A *Prerogative University* is the fourth of five types of states of a valid Ucadia University formed when a State Member of Ucadia, representing the internationally recognised government sharing the same bounds of the University agrees to adopt the Ucadia Model and systems of effective administration for the benefit of its Members. As a Ucadia State Member is an existing body politic, nation, state or country duly recognised by international Western-Roman bodies and having duly elected its government by its Members, a State Member therefore holds a prerogative right and privilege, subject to the conditions of the present Constitution and Charter and the Criteria for the Foundation of a Prerogative University. All applications and approvals of Prerogative Universities are superior to any pre-existing Preliminary or Probational University Administration and upon such approval, all rights, powers and authorities must be duly conveyed to the new administration. Prerogative University Foundation

8. The following ten (10) criteria are the essential structural components and properties of a valid Prerogative University: Criteria for the Foundation of a Prerogative

(i) That the University is already a valid Preliminary or Probational University making the application for recognition as a Prerogative University; and University

(ii) That the Petitioner is a duly authorised official of a Ucadia State Member as plenipotentiary with the power to act on behalf of the government and people in relation to such a petition; and

(iii) That the particular Ucadia State Member is recognised by international Western-Roman bodies as an existing body politic, or state corresponding to the boundaries of the relevant University; and

(iv) That no existing Prerogative or Permanent University of the same name and same unique University Location Trust Number and University Society Trust Number exists and is currently recognised and registered as active; and

(v) That the particular Ucadia State Member making the petition for recognition of a Prerogative University is a Member of good actions, good conscience with good faith and has not previously been refused, denied, banned or prevented in any way from holding any office or government of the Union, or University or Province or Campus; and

(vi) That the particular Ucadia State Member making the petition for recognition of a Prerogative University has not petitioned for recognition of any other Prerogative University in the past twelve months; and

(vii) That the particular Ucadia State Member making the petition for recognition of a Prerogative University is competent and capable and willing to perform the obligations and duties required of the government of a valid Ucadia University; and

(viii) That the executive of the particular Ucadia State Member making the petition for recognition of a Prerogative University invokes the Oath of Allegiance to the Union as witnessed, attested and recorded in writing; and

(ix) That written notice of the petition and recorded Oath of Allegiance, the name and University Location Trust Number and University Society Trust Number of the Prerogative University, are Gazetted within the Ucadia Gazette with fourteen (14) days given for any official notice of objection; and

(x) That the present Charter and Covenant are ratified by the elected assembly of the Ucadia State Member within ninety

(90) days of receiving confirmation of recognition as the government of the particular Prerogative University.

9. A *Permanent University* is the fifth type of state of a valid Ucadia University formed when not less than eighty (80) percent of all Provinces within the bounds of the University have been formed as Probational or Prerogative or Permanent with at least fifty (50) percent as Permanent Provinces; and with such application recognised and approved subject to election of Officers to the positions of the Twelve Great Offices of State duly gazetted and certified in accord with the Criteria for the Foundation of a Permanent University. All applications and approvals of Permanent Universities are superior to any and all pre-existing Preliminary or Probational or Prerogative University Administration and upon such approval, all rights, powers and authorities must be duly conveyed to the new administration. Permanent University Foundation

10. The following ten (10) criteria are the essential structural components and properties of a valid Permanent University: Criteria for the Foundation of a Permanent University

(i) That the University is a valid existing Probational or Prerogative University making the application for permanent recognition; and

(ii) That a minimum of one thousand two hundred and thirty four (1234) living Ordinary Members are registered as domiciled within the bounds of the University; and

(iii) That peace and amity is declared within the bounds of the University and not less than eighty percent (80%) of all Provinces of the University are duly constituted as Probational or Permanent with at least fifty percent (50%) of these as Permanent Provinces; and

(iv) That three (3) candidates make the petition for recognition of a Permanent University and are existing Governors of Permanent Provinces or Commissioners of Permanent Campuses within the bounds of the University and are Ordinary Members of good actions, good conscience with good faith and have not previously been refused, denied, banned or prevented in any way from holding any office of the Union, or University or Province or Campus; and that the candidates making the petition for recognition of a Permanent University do so free from any duress, or any coercion, or any motive of fraud and misrepresentation, or to act as a foreign agent, or for other negative and improper motive; and

(v) The candidates making the petition for recognition of a

Permanent University have been domiciled in the same location as the University for at least twelve (12) months and no other person living within the same domicile has petitioned for recognition of a Permanent University; and

(vi) The candidates making the petition for recognition of a Permanent University have not petitioned for recognition of any other Permanent University; and

(vii) The candidates making the petition for recognition of a Permanent University are competent and capable and willing to perform the obligations and duties required of a President of a University; and

(viii) The candidates making the petition for recognition of a Permanent University invokes the Oath of Allegiance to the Union in the physical presence of at least two (2) other Governors of Provinces of the same University as attested, witnessed and recorded in writing; and

(ix) The candidate making the petition for recognition of a Permanent University accepts the obligations and duties of Office of President and invokes upon the sacred Covenant *Pactum De Singularis Caelum* the Oath of President of a University in the physical presence of at least two (2) other Governors of Provinces of the same University as attested, witnessed and recorded in writing; and

(x) That written notice of the recorded Oath of Allegiance, Oath of President, the name and University Location Trust Number and University Society Trust Number of the Permanent University, the full name and contact details of the President are provided within fourteen (14) days to any and all existing Provincial and University administrations of the Union to which the University belongs as well as to each and every Province and Campus within the same University; and that the President within thirty (30) days of assuming Office of President makes provision for a permanent Post Office mailing address, a permanent phone contact number, a contact email address and a means by which the Governors and administration of the Provinces of the University may receive regular paper and/or electronic communication and information.

TITLE VIII: UCADIA PROVINCES

Article 81 – Ucadia Province

1. A *Ucadia Province* is the second smallest operational division of government and administration of the Union. A Province is an ecclesiastically, legally and lawfully constituted subdivision of a University and is equivalent to a "state government area" or "state" or "region". Ucadia Province

   A valid Ucadia Province is a Superior Civil Trust and Ecclesiastical Capital Company having a mortal life not exceeding one complete standard Age of one thousand and seventy (1,070) years or approximately one third the life expectancy of the Union.

   An Ordinary Member may only belong to one Province according to the location of their current primary living location also known as domicile address.

2. When the organic boundaries of an Original Nation (Tribe), as defined and registered in accord with the present Charter and the most sacred Covenant *Pactum De Singularis Caelum*, match the same boundaries of a Province under the Union, then the government and administration of the Original Nation and Province shall be one and the same. Under such circumstances, the Offices of the Province shall be the Official Government and the Offices of the Original Nation shall be honorific and ceremonial. Province as Original Nation

3. In accord with the present Constitution and Charter there shall be five possible "states" or "types" of Legal Status for a Ucadia Province being Provisional, Preliminary, Probational, Prerogative and Permanent:- Province Legal Status

   (i) *Provisional Province* is the first of five types of states of a valid Ucadia Province. All Provisional Provinces within each University of the Union were formed between VENUS E8:Y3210:A0:S1:M27:D6 [21st of December 2011] and GAIA E1:Y1:A1:S1:M9:D1 [21st December 2012] as the second smallest operational divisions of occupational forces of One Heaven following the complete conquest of all land, sea, earth, space, time, atmosphere and spirit within the boundaries of the University; and lawful possession and occupation of all rights, property, title and uses within the same bounds; and the investiture of a unique and individual spiritual member into each of the Major Offices of Governor, Deputy Governor, Counsel, Procurator , Speaker and Comptroller for each and every Province on planet Earth. Under the terms of spiritual military occupation, the boundaries and Cadastral features of each Province within each University within each Union have been properly surveyed with the Survey and Charter for each Province registered within the Great Register of the Union and the event published in the Globe Union Gazette and Ucadia Gazette; and

(ii) *Preliminary Province* is the second of five types of states of a valid Ucadia Province. A Preliminary Province is formed when not less than six (6) Ordinary Members domiciled within the bounds of the Province elect an interim Provincial Consulate and Government instituted through a Convention for its formation, subject to the approval of the Ucadia Foundation for the relevant University, with each Ordinary Member having invoked and recorded an Oath of Allegiance and an Oath of Office; and the fulfilment of the Criteria for the Foundation of a Preliminary Province; and

(iii) *Probational Province* is the third of five types of states of a valid Ucadia Province. A Probational Province is formed when not less than seventy-two (72) Ordinary Members domiciled within the bounds of the Province elect an interim Provincial Consulate and Government instituted through a Treaty between not less than one third of the total Campuses of the Province and the six Major Offices being elected, with each incumbent having invoked and recorded an Oath of Allegiance and an Oath of Office; and the fulfilment of the Criteria for the Foundation of a Probational Province. All applications and approvals of Probational Provinces are superior to any pre-existing Preliminary Province Administration and upon such approval, all rights, powers and authorities must be duly conveyed to the new administration within 20 days; and

(iv) *Prerogative Province* is the fourth of five types of states of a valid Ucadia Province formed when a State Member of Ucadia, representing an internationally recognised state government sharing the same bounds of the Province agrees to adopt the Ucadia Model and systems of effective administration for the benefit of its Members. As a Ucadia State Member is an existing body politic, or state duly recognised by international Western-Roman bodies and having duly elected its government by its Members, a State Member therefore holds a prerogative right and privilege, subject to the conditions of the present Constitution and Charter and the Criteria for the Foundation of a Prerogative Province. All applications and approvals of Prerogative Provinces are superior to any pre-existing Probational Province Administration and upon such approval, all rights, powers and authorities must be duly conveyed to the new administration within 40 days; and

(v) *Permanent Province* is the fifth type of state of a valid Ucadia Province formed when not less than fifty percent (50) percent of all living men and women over the age of eighteen, domiciled within the bounds of the Province redeem their status as Ordinary Members and elect a permanent leadership and not less than sixty percent (60%) of all Campuses of the Province are duly constituted as Probational or Permanent with at least forty-percent (40%) of these as Permanent Campuses in accord with the Criteria for the Foundation of a Permanent Province. All applications and approvals of Permanent Provinces are superior to any and all pre-existing Probational or Prerogative Province Administration and upon such approval, all rights, powers and authorities must be duly conveyed to the new administration within 60 days.

Foreign Registration of a Ucadia Province

4. A Provisional or Permanent Province administration is forbidden to register or record any instance of itself with any foreign estates, foreign nations and body politics sharing the same or similar bounds.

However, a Preliminary, Probational or Prerogative Province administration may record an instance of itself with a foreign estate, foreign nation or foreign body politic on the conditions:-

(i) That the said foreign body is duly recognised by at least twenty other foreign bodies as a valid entity of a size equal or larger than the bounds of the said Ucadia Province; and

(ii) The executive of the Ucadia Province making such foreign recording are duly recognised and possess valid credentials and registration and have not been banned from holding office, nor are presently subject to active criminal action within the courts of Ucadia nor the foreign courts in which registration is sought; and

(iii) The instance to be recorded with a foreign body is as the Ucadia Foundation for the said Province as a Foreign Corporation Sole or Body Corporate for Religious and Charitable Purposes; and

(iv) That the formal name of the Ucadia Foundation for the said Province has been duly enrolled within the Charter Rolls of the Union and Ucadia and such Charter Rights promulgated and made patent, including a valid Certificate of such Charter and Rights; and

(v) The Governor of the said Ucadia Province is registered within the *Directorium Ecclesiam Ucadia* (Directory of Ecclesiastical Persons of Ucadia); and

(vi) A Constitution for the instance of foreign recording as the Ucadia Foundation for the said Province has been formed, promulgated and approved in acceptance of the Charter and Rights granted to the said Ucadia Foundation; and

(vii) The Bylaws for the Ucadia Foundation for the said Province whereby the instance of the Ucadia Province shall function in amity and harmony with the foreign body have been formed, promulgated and approved in accord with the Constitutional Charter; and

(viii) That the Office Holders as defined within the approved Constitutional Charter have been duly elected and that such elections are certified, including the Certificate of Divine Commission of the Governor.

5. The primary administrative Organ of Historic Records, Primary Sources and Files of each Ucadia Province, legally embodied and personified through the Great Office of Censor, shall be the Official Archives. Ucadia Province Archive

6. The primary administrative Organ of Collections, Information and Knowledge Resources of each Ucadia Province, legally embodied and personified through the Great Office of Narrator, shall be the Library. Ucadia Province Library

Article 82 – Province Assembly

1. All legislative powers of a Province shall be vested in an Assembly of Elected Members ("Assembly") which shall consist of elected representatives from each Convention of each Campus within the bounds of the Province:- Province Assembly

(i) A *Provisional Assembly* shall consist of those spiritual forces presently occupying and possessing the spiritual and temporal bounds of the Province; and

(ii) A *Probational Assembly* shall consist of a minimum of fifteen elected representatives being not less than five representatives from each Probational or Permanent Campus; and

(iii) A *Prerogative Assembly* shall consist of not less than five representatives from each Probational or Permanent Campus within the bounds of the Province in accord with the Criteria for the Foundation of a Prerogative Province; and

(iv) A *Permanent Assembly* shall consist of not less than five representatives from each Permanent Campus only within the bounds of the Province in accord with the Criteria for the Foundation of a Permanent Province.

Name of the Assembly

2. The name of the Assembly shall be the unique geographic name of the location plus the words "Ucadia Province". Where a Permanent Assembly votes in favour to register a subsidiary of itself with a foreign society or entity, the words "Ucadia Assembly" shall be used with the unique geographic name of the location to reflect both the purpose and mission of the Assembly and Province.

Rights, Powers and Authority of Permanent Assembly

3. Vested by the present sacred Charter, a Province Assembly shall possess, hold and own certain Positive Rights in accord with the most sacred Covenant *Pactum De Singularis Caelum* derived from the consent of Ordinary Members of the Province. All Powers and Authority of a Province Government, Services and Administration are sourced from these Rights. Therefore, it is through the grants of the Province Assembly of some or all of these rights that the Province Executive governs. There are three (3) types of Rights associated with a Province Assembly of a Province being *Universal, Conditional* and *Ucadia*:-

(i) *Universal Rights*, also known as Universal Positive Rights, are a sub-class of Positive Rights whereby such valid Rights are created, defined and bestowed to a Province Assembly through the existence of the University to which the Province belongs and are Peremptory, Permanent, Immutable and Indefeasible once bestowed are not subject to any form or condition of waiver, abandonment, surrender, disqualification, incapacitation, seizure, capture, arrest, resignation, alienation, suspension, suppression, forfeiture or abrogation. Universal Rights granted to a Province Assembly cannot exceed the power or authority of the University that granted such Rights; and

(ii) *Conditional Rights*, also known as Conditional Positive Rights, are a sub-class of Positive Rights whereby such valid Rights are created, defined and bestowed to a Province Assembly through the existence of the University to which the Province belongs upon acceptance of the associated obligations and duties attached to them. Furthermore, if any such conditions and obligations are breached or repudiated, then the relevant Conditional Positive Right may be waived, surrendered, suspended, abandoned, resigned, disqualified, seized, captured, arrested, rescinded, suppressed, forfeited or revoked until such time as the fundamental breach of duty and obligation is repaired or such a Right is duly restored. Conditional Rights granted to a Province Assembly cannot exceed the power or authority of the University that granted such Rights. A Province Assembly to whom a Conditional Positive Right has been bestowed may also lawfully convey equitable title of such a Right to another person; and

(iii) *Ucadia Rights* are unique Positive Rights associated with Ucadia itself and when bestowed, granted, given, delegated or assigned to a Province Assembly representing the lawful possession, holding or ownership of some Ucadian Right.

4. The following forty-four (44) valid bodies of Universal Positive Rights of a Province Assembly of a Province are recognised in accord with the most sacred Covenant *Pactum De Singularis Caelum* and the present Constitutional Charter:- Universal Positive Rights of Assembly

(i) *Ius Provinciae Iuris* as the Universal Right of the Province Assembly to Rights as inherited from *Ius Universitas Iuris*; and

(ii) *Ius Provinciae Definire* as the Universal Right of the Province Assembly to Define Rights as inherited from *Ius Universitas Definire*; and

(iii) *Ius Provinciae Concedere* as the Universal Right of the Province Assembly to Grant Rights as inherited from *Ius Universitas Concedere*; and

(iv) *Ius Provinciae Hereditatis* as the Universal Right of the Province Assembly of Inheritance as inherited from *Ius Universitas Hereditatis*; and

(v) *Ius Provinciae Nascendi* as the Universal Right of the Province Assembly to be Born as inherited from *Ius Universitas Nascendi*; and

(vi) *Ius Provinciae Vitam* as the Universal Right to Life of the Province Assembly as inherited from *Ius Universitas Vitam*; and

(vii) *Ius Provinciae Mori Eligate* as the Universal Right of a Province Assembly to vote unanimously to dissolve the Province back to the status of a Provisional Province as inherited from *Ius Universitas Mori Eligate*; and

(viii) *Ius Provinciae Victus* as the Universal Right of Ordinary Members of a Province Assembly to receive sustenance as inherited from *Ius Universitas Victus*; and

(ix) *Ius Provinciae Tectum* as the Universal Right of Ordinary Members of a Province Assembly to be provided shelter as inherited from *Ius Universitas Tectum*; and

(x) *Ius Provinciae Salutus* as the Universal Right of Ordinary Members of a Province Assembly of being provided (physical) safety from harm as inherited from *Ius Universitas Salutus*; and

(xi) *Ius Provinciae Possessionis* as the Universal Right of the Province Assembly to have, possess and hold property as inherited from *Ius Universitas Possessionis*; and

(xii) *Ius Provinciae Habendi* as the Universal Right of the Province Assembly to have, possess and hold a thing as inherited from *Ius Universitas Habendi*; and

(xiii) *Ius Provinciae Propritetatis* as the Universal Right of the Province Assembly of dominion, ownership, occupation and title as distinct from possession as inherited from *Ius Universitas Proprietatis*; and

(xiv) *Ius Provinciae Registrum* as the Universal Right of the Province Assembly for Registers of Rights and Possession of Property as inherited from *Ius Universitas Registrum*; and

(xv) *Ius Provinciae Album* as Universal Right of the Province Assembly to Record Rights and Possessions of Property as inherited from *Ius Universitas Album*; and

(xvi) *Ius Provinciae Nomenis* as the Universal Right of the Province Assembly to Name, Title and Reputation as inherited from *Ius Universitas Nomenis*; and

(xvii) *Ius Provinciae Fecerim* as the Universal Right of the Province Assembly to invent, create and make seals, arms, heralds, instruments and other property of value as inherited from *Ius Universitas Fecerim*; and

(xviii) *Ius Provinciae Indicium* as the Universal Right of Freedom of Knowledge and Information of the Province Assembly as inherited from *Ius Universitas Indicium*; and

(xix) *Ius Provinciae Honeste Conveniendi* as the Universal Right of the Province Assembly to Peaceful Assembly as inherited from *Ius Universitas Honeste Conveniendi*; and

(xx) *Ius Provinciae Sociari* as Universal Right of Membership of the Province Assembly to the Province in which it is born as inherited from *Ius Universitas Sodalis*; and

(xxi) *Ius Provinciae Terram* as the Universal Right of the Province Assembly to grant a Right or Title to Land defined and surveyed within its metes and bounds as inherited from *Ius Universitas Terram*; and

(xxii) *Ius Provinciae Usum Terram* as the Universal Right of Use of the Province Assembly of grant a Right of Use and Possession to Land defined and surveyed within its metes and bounds as inherited from *Ius Universitas Usum Terram*; and

(xxiii) *Ius Provinciae Mutat Terram* as the Universal Right of the Province Assembly to grant a Right or Title to Alter the (Top of the) of Land defined and surveyed within its metes and bounds as inherited from *Ius Universitas Mutat Terram*; and

(xxiv) *Ius Provinciae Fodere Terram* as the Universal Right of the Province Assembly to grant a Right or Title to Dig (or Mine) the Land defined and surveyed within its metes and bounds as inherited from *Ius Universitas Fodere Terram*; and

(xxv) *Ius Provinciae Aqua* as the Universal Right of the Province Assembly to grant a Right or Title to Water of the Province Assembly as inherited from *Ius Universitas Aqua*; and

(xxvi) *Ius Provinciae Concordia* as the Universal Right of the Province Assembly to make Agreements as inherited from *Ius Universitas Concordia*; and

(xxvii) *Ius Provinciae Concordia Honorari* as the Universal Right of the Province Assembly to have Agreements Honored as inherited from *Ius Universitas Concordia Honorari*; and

(xxviii) *Ius Provinciae Concordia Fraudulenta* as the Universal Right of the Province Assembly to have Fraudulent Agreements Annulled, Voided and Expunged as inherited from *Ius Universitas Concordia Fraudulenta;* and

(xxix) *Ius Provinciae Concordia Terminare* as the Universal Right of the Province Assembly to Terminate Agreements that fail to be Honored as inherited from *Ius Universitas Concordia Terminare*; and

(xxx) *Ius Provinciae Perfungor* as the Universal Right of the Province Assembly to commission work to be performed as inherited from *Ius Universitas Perfungor*; and

(xxxi) *Ius Provinciae Nolle Perfungor* as the Universal Right of the

Province Assembly to Refuse to have work performed as inherited from *Ius Universitas Nolle Perfungor*; and

(xxxii) *Ius Provinciae Fructibus* as the Universal Right of the Province Assembly to the fruits, energy, results and product of performance, work and effort of work commissioned by the Province Assembly as inherited from *Ius Universitas Fructibus*; and

(xxxiii) *Ius Provinciae Solutionis Perfungor* as the Universal Right of the Province Assembly to receive fair payment in exchange for fruits, energy, results and product of performance, work and effort commissioned by the Province as inherited from *Ius Universitas Solutionis Perfungor*; and

(xxxiv) *Ius Provinciae Commercium* as the Universal Right of the Province Assembly to trade and exchange as inherited from *Ius Universitas Commercium*; and

(xxxv) *Ius Provinciae Pecuniam* as the Universal Right of the Province Assembly to make and use Money for Trade as inherited from *Ius Universitas Pecuniam*; and

(xxxvi) *Ius Provinciae Imaginis* as the Universal Right of the Province Assembly to make an image, reflection, portrait, likeness, imitation, representation or copy as inherited from *Ius Universitas Imaginis*; and

(xxxvii) *Ius Provinciae Praedicamus* as the Universal Right of the Province Assembly to make public, publish, transmit, distribute, broadcast and preach as inherited from *Ius Universitas Praedicamus*; and

(xxxviii) Ius Provinciae Suffragii as the Universal Right of the Province Assembly to vote and have such choice counted in the democratic process of electing officials of society as inherited from *Ius Universitas Suffragii*; and

(xxxix) *Ius Provinciae Leges Sciri* as the Universal Right of the Province Assembly that all Laws be known and none secret as inherited from *Ius Universitas Leges Sciri*; and

(xl) *Ius Provinciae Alienum Subcriptio* as the Universal Right of the Province Assembly to register a subsidiary within the jurisdiction of a foreign estate, body, person or entity as inherited from *Ius Universitas Alienum Subcriptio*; and

(xli) *Ius Provinciae Rationem Alienum* as the Universal Right of the

Province Assembly to register and establish a bank account for any subsidiary within the jurisdiction of a foreign estate, body, person or entity as inherited from I*us Universitas Rationem Alienum*; and

(xlii) *Ius Provinciae Audit* as the Universal Right of the Province Assembly to review any books, or any information, or any accounts of any officer operating within the bounds of the Province as inherited from *Ius Universitas Audit*; and

(xliii) *Ius Provinciae Inspectionis* as the Universal Right of the Province Assembly to establish a Commission of Investigation with the power to call any registered Member within the Province and any information held by the Province Executive to review as inherited from *Ius Universitas Inspectionis*; and

(xliv) *Ius Provinciae Anathema* as the Universal Right of the Province Assembly to commission a Province Impeachment for the forced removal of any elected official from the Governor to any position within any branch of government within the Province as inherited from *Ius Universitas Anathema*.

5. The Assembly shall exist for a fixed period of life not less than one complete standard Age of one thousand and seventy (1070) years, corresponding to the life of the Province. Members of the Assembly shall have their commissions dissolved every four years and shall resign from office ahead of Province Elections for new Members. Life of Assembly

6. Excepting a provincial election year, every year there shall be four (4) sessions of fixed days corresponding to equal divisions of the year whereby Members of Assembly are summonsed to attend. Assembly Sessions

Each of these sessions shall be named for the season to which they correspond, namely Summer, Autumn, Winter and Spring Session. A day within a session when Members are summonsed to sit in Assembly shall be called a Province Sitting Session Day.

A day within a session when Members of the Assembly are not summonsed to sit shall be called a Non-Sitting Session Day.

During a year in which a provincial election is to be called, the Province Assembly shall not sit for the Spring session. Instead the last session of Province Assembly before it is dissolved shall be the Winter session.

7. Responsibility for good conduct and control of the Province Assembly and the scheduling of business within the chamber shall be vested in the Office of Speaker of Province Assembly (Province Speaker). Office of Speaker of Province Assembly (Province

The Speaker of a Province Assembly shall be an independent role, free from political party preferences. The candidate shall be elected by the new Assembly themselves on the first day of sitting of the new Assembly after a Province Election. Speaker)

8. The date of a provincial election shall always occur within the Spring months, allowing forty (40) days prior to the date of the election for the official campaign period. Date of Province Election

9. The minimum number of Members (quorum) required to be present within the chamber of Assembly to permit the full exercise of its powers shall be two thirds (2/3) the total number of elected Members of that house. Quorum

Assembly shall not be permitted to undertake procedures that require a quorum if the total number of Members is not equal or greater to the quorum.

10. The total length of an Assembly session shall be determined by the Province Speaker and shall not be permitted to exceed fourteen (14) Ordinary Sitting Session Days in a month. However, the Speaker is permitted to call an emergency session of Assembly to a maximum of five (5) days within a month other than Ordinary Sitting Session Days. Assembly session length

11. The Province Speaker shall be responsible for the issuing of summons to individual Province Assembly representatives for their attendance. Assembly attendance

Excepting special leave granted by the Province Speaker due to matters of national security, health or extended personal matters, all Assembly representatives shall be required to attend the Sitting Session Days as listed in the summons.

Failure of a Province Assembly representative to attend five (5) or more Session Sitting Days within one (1) Session shall be deemed a failure to discharge the duties of their office and the Province Speaker shall be responsible for immediately initiating an Assembly Member Expulsion Motion or a Director Expulsion Motion should the Assembly representative be a Provincial-General.

12. The sessions on the floor of the Assembly shall be open for the public record with all speeches, debates, motions, votes and documents recorded in a Journal. Public record of proceedings

Furthermore, all committee meetings and special sessions of reviews shall also be open for the public record, except those proceedings concerning matters of security or active law enforcement investigations. An expenditure related review may never be closed to public scrutiny.

13. During their attendance at the Session of the Assembly, and in going Legal privilege to and returning from the same, all Members of the Assembly shall be privileged from arrest except in matters of Treason, Felony and Breach of the Peace. Such privilege does not extend to their property or office which shall fall under the normal course of law and investigation and right to search by issued Warrant.

During debate in the Assembly, all spoken and written material presented and entered into the Public Record of proceedings shall be privileged and immune from civil liability.

14. The Permanent Assembly shall have the right and power to commission a Province Commission of Investigation with the power to call any registered Member within the Province and any information held by the Province Executive to review. Assembly Investigations and Actions

The Permanent Assembly also has vested by this Charter the power to commission a Province Impeachment for the forced removal of any elected official from the Governor to any position within any branch of government in the Province.

A Province Commission of Investigation must be called by the Probational or Prerogative or Permanent Assembly when a call to expel one or more members is made, excluding cases where the grounds of the charge are based on an automatic expulsion.

15. The Censure or Suspension of an Assembly is when the permanent University Parliament under which the Province Assembly is bound exercises their right in accord with the Rule of Law, Justice and Due Process to admonish or order the suspension of all operations. Censure or Suspension of Assembly

No body, person, aggregate or entity has the power or right to dissolve or disband a permanent Assembly and Province other than the Members of the Assembly themselves. However, when the permanent University Parliament to which the Province belongs proves one or more of the following grounds for Censure or Suspension, then the Assembly may be lawfully Censured or Suspended for a period of not less than 40 days and not more than 160 days:

(i) That the Assembly has been found to have deliberately and wilfully exceeded its rights in engaging in activities that have brought disrepute or harm to Ucadia, or the Province or University or Union; or

(ii) That the Assembly has entered into agreements with other parties for which it has no right or authority to do, or such agreements that contradict good faith, good actions and good conscience; or

(iii) That the Assembly has wilfully and deliberately taken actions that are considered Criminal in nature by the Criminal Code of the Union.

16. The dissolution and wind-up of a Permanent Assembly is when a three-quarters of all Ordinary Members of the permanent Province vote in Session in favour of its dissolution and wind-up as a permanent Province. If approved, then the Province shall revert to the status of a Preliminary Province as no Province may be lawfully dissolved, abandoned, conveyed, surrendered, disqualified, seized, captured, arrested, alienated, suppressed, forfeited or abrogated.

Dissolution and Wind-up of a Permanent Assembly

Article 83 – Province Council

1. The Executive Power and Authority of the Province shall be vested in an executive government known as the Provincial Council comprising the Major Offices of Governor, Deputy Governor, Counsel, Procurator, Speaker and Comptroller and the Board of Provincial-Generals.

Province Council

2. By virtue of this Charter, a Governor is vested with the executive authority to manage the needs and affairs of the Province through the selection or dismissal of wise counsel in the form of their Province Board of Provincial-Generals, the agencies, officials and administration of the Province Government.

The Governor

The Governor shall have the authority of Province Commander in Chief in time of declared disaster with the power to command marshal law.

In times of declared State disaster, the Governor shall have the power to commit the State forces on the agreed counsel of the Province Disaster Relief Council.

The Governor shall have the authority over all agencies and Provincial-Generals as Chairman of the Board of Provincial-Generals. As Chairman, the Governor may choose to overrule motions of the Board and select the agenda and minutes of the Board meetings.

The Governor shall have Power, by and with the advice and consent of the Province Assembly, to make Treaties; and shall nominate, and by and with the advice and consent of the Province Assembly, shall appoint public Ministers and Consuls, Judges of the Provincial Court, and all other Officers of the Province, whose Appointments are not herein otherwise provided for, and which shall be established by Law: but the Province Assembly may by Law vest the Appointment of such inferior Officers, as they think proper, in the Governor alone, in the Courts of Law, or in the Heads of Departments.

The Governor shall have the Power by virtue of this Charter to pardon any convicted criminal and stay the sentence of any court imposed sentence for any lesser court than the Provincial Court. The Governor does not have the power to amend a judgement of the Provincial Court.

3. Prior to the commencement of their term of office, the Governor shall make the following public oath- "I [full name of new Governor] do solemnly invoke (or affirm) that I will faithfully execute the Office of Governor of (Province), and will to the best of my Ability, preserve, protect and defend the Province of (Province) and the Charter of (University)." Oath of the Governor

4. Excluding the 1st term of the 1st permanent Governor of a Province, the Governor shall hold their Office during the term of four (4) Years, and be elected by provincial election following the procedures for general, provincial and university elections contained within this Charter. Term of the Governor

   The 1st term of the 1st permanent Governor shall be a maximum of two (2) years. Thereafter, all terms shall be the standard length.

   By this Charter a Governor is ineligible to serve beyond a total of four (4) terms, sixteen (16) years. A Governor having served the Province for greater than fourteen (14) years shall be known as a Grand Governor.

5. The Governor shall, at stated Times, receive for their Services, a Compensation, which shall neither be increased nor diminished during the Period for which they shall have been elected, and shall not receive any other income during their term. Payment of the Governor

6. In the good management of the Province, its affairs and requirements can be compared to the good conduct of a company with its Members as shareholders. The Board of Provincial-Generals (Provincial Board) shall be a board of individuals selected by the Governor to head the permanent statutory authorities and uphold the laws regarding the critical systems of the state. The tenure of a Director shall be at the sole discretion of the Governor. The Board of Provincial - Generals (Provincial Board)

   Given the importance of each system within our society functioning to its optimum, the position of a Provincial-General should reflect the very best of the community with the knowledge, experience and respect relating to the system they manage.

7. The Domestic Affairs Committee shall be a permanent subcommittee of the Provincial Board. The purpose of the Domestic Affairs Committee shall be the coordination of all systems associated with domestic functions enabling optimum provincial planning. Domestic Affairs Committee

The Domestic Affairs Committee shall be permanently chaired by the Domestic Deputy-Governor. The committee shall be permanently attended by the Directors of the following systems:-

(i) Planning System; and

(ii) Knowledge System; and

(iii) Justice System; and

(iv) Power System; and

(v) Sanitation System; and

(vi) Security System; and

(vii) Industry System; and

(viii) Employment System; and

(ix) Education System; and

(x) Health System; and

(xi) Temporary Assistance System; and

(xii) Constructions System; and

(xiii) Entertainment System; and

(xiv) Natural Ecosystem.

8. The Diplomatic Affairs Committee shall be a permanent subcommittee of the Provincial Board. The purpose of the Diplomatic Affairs Committee shall be the coordination of all systems associated with diplomatic and inter provincial agreements. Diplomatic Affairs Committee

The Diplomatic Affairs Committee shall be permanently chaired by the Diplomatic Deputy Governor. The committee shall be permanently attended by the Directors of the following systems:-

(i) Planning System; and

(ii) Knowledge System; and

(iii) Justice system; and

(iv) Security System; and

(v) Finance System; and

(vi) Trade System; and

(vii) Technology Development.

9. By this Constitutional Charter, the provincial government operations of a Province is recognised as the public servants and officials supporting the actions of the Province Assembly and the Province Council. Province Management

Article 84 – Province Judiciary & Law Enforcement

1. The judicial power of the Province shall be vested in one (1) Provincial Court and those inferior courts named and defined in this Charter. Province Judiciary and Law Enforcement

   The Assembly may itself introduce further inferior courts as is deemed necessary to establish on condition that it does not conflict, corrupt or diminish the primary courts listed in this Charter.

2. The Provincial Court shall consist of twelve (12) Justices appointed by the Governor upon the approval of Congress at a time of vacancy of position to the Provincial Court. Construction of the Provincial Court

   The tenure of a Justice of the Provincial Court shall be for a period of not greater than eight (8) years and subject to their good conduct and the confidence of the Assembly. A Justice shall be required to resign within thirty (30) days of their eightieth (80th) birthday, regardless the remaining length of their tenure.

3. The Provincial Court shall have Original Jurisdiction in all matters:- Original Jurisdiction

   (i) In relation to criminal proceedings relating to alleged breaches of law of a serious Level 4 Criminal Offence or above status; and

   (ii) In relation to commercial matters relating to disputed property rights and contracts valued at greater than twenty five thousand (25,000) units of Union currency; and

   (iii) In which the Province, or a person suing or being sued on behalf of the Province, is a party; and

   (iv) Between Campuses, or between residents of different Campuses, or between a District and a resident of another Campus; and

   (v) In which a Great Writ or an injunction is sought against an officer of the Province.

4. The Provincial Court shall represent the final and conclusive court of appeal in all matters determined from all judgements, decrees, orders, and sentences:- Appellate Jurisdiction

   (i) of any Magistrate, Justice or Justices exercising the Original

Jurisdiction of the Provincial Court; and

(ii) of any other local court, or court exercising Provincial Jurisdiction.

5. By virtue of the powers and functions defined in this Charter, it shall be a principle purpose of Province Assembly to make laws and a principle purpose of the Provincial Court to preside and judge over cases brought in regards to these laws. This is a principle of the separation of powers. Principle of separation of powers and the Provincial Court

In so far as judgements of the Provincial Court affect the function and effect of the laws of Province Assembly, the Court shall not be permitted to use its verdicts as an alternative means of creating new law or regulation. Nor is a Provincial Court permitted to impose its jurisdiction in matters that are clearly identified as having jurisdiction in the University Supreme Court.

However, it shall be considered a primary role of the Provincial Court to ensure that the laws of the Province at all levels reflect the good principles of this Charter and the fair principles of justice.

Where laws by the Province Government or by the Province Assembly in anyway contradict the principles of this Charter and / or fail to execute effectively its function or purpose it shall be considered a requirement of the Provincial Court to ensure that such laws and regulations are properly read down and rendered ineffective in their enforcement.

6. In relation to all matters of original jurisdiction, the minimum number of justices required to preside shall be one (1), excepting in matters of Charter and Provincial law where all twelve (12) justices shall be required to preside. Quorum of the Provincial Court

In relation to all matters of appellate jurisdiction, the minimum number of justices required to preside shall be three (3), except in any case involving the appeal or review of a previous Provincial Court ruling, where all twelve (12) justices shall be required to preside.

7. By this Charter, the Province defence and law enforcement of a Member Province is recognised as the Province based organisations reporting to a Province Executive Government which itself is a subordinate government to the University Government. Province law enforcement

Article 85 – Province Foundation

1. The foundation of a valid Ucadia Province of the Union shall be in Province Foundation

accord with the criteria and terms defined by the present Article and the five possible "states" or "types" of Legal Status for a Ucadia Province being *Provisional, Preliminary, Probational, Prerogative* and *Permanent*.

A Preliminary Province may not be formed until a duly constituted and valid Ucadia Foundation has been first formed for the relevant Ucadia University.

2. A *Provisional Province* is the first of five types of states of a valid Ucadia Province. All Provisional Provinces within each University of the Union were formed between VENUS E8:Y3210:A0:S1:M27:D6 [21st of December 2011] and GAIA E1:Y1:A1:S1:M9:D1 [21st December 2012] as the second smallest operational divisions of occupational forces of One Heaven following the complete conquest of all land, sea, earth, space, time, atmosphere and spirit within the boundaries of the University; and lawful possession and occupation of all rights, property, title and uses within the same bounds; and the investiture of a unique and individual spiritual member into each of the Twelve (12) Master Offices of the See being: Governor, Captain, Master, Protonotary, Procurator, Justice, Navigator, Rector, Registrar, Speaker, Treasurer and Comptroller for each and every Province on planet Earth. Provisional Province Foundation

Under the terms of spiritual military occupation, the boundaries and Cadastral features of each Province within each University within each Union have been properly surveyed with the Survey and Charter for each Province registered within the Great Register of the Union and the event published in the Globe Union Gazette and Ucadia Gazette.

3. A *Preliminary Province* is the second of five types of states of a valid Ucadia Province. A Preliminary Province is formed when not less than six (6) Ordinary Members domiciled within the bounds of the Province elect an interim Provincial Consulate and Government instituted through a Convention, subject to the approval of the Ucadia Foundation for the relevant University, with each Ordinary Member having invoked and recorded an Oath of Allegiance and an Oath of Office; and the fulfilment of the Criteria for the Foundation of a Preliminary Province. All applications and approvals of Preliminary Provinces shall be under the temporary administration of the relevant Ucadia Foundation. Preliminary Province Foundation

4. The following twelve (12) criteria are the essential structural components and properties of a valid Preliminary Province:- Criteria for the Foundation of a Preliminary Province

(i) A unique and valid name and unique eighteen (18) digit Province Location Trust Number and unique eighteen (18) digit

Province Society Trust Number exists for the Province within the bounds of a unique University Location Trust of the Union; and

(ii) That no existing Preliminary, Probational Province or Permanent Province of the same name and same unique Province Location Trust Number and Province Society Trust Number exists and is currently recognised and officially registered as active; and

(iii) The six candidates making the petition for recognition of a Preliminary Province are Ordinary Members of good actions, good conscience with good trust and have not previously been refused, denied, banned or prevented in any way from holding any office of the Union, or University or Province or Campus; and

(iv) The candidates making the petition for recognition of a Preliminary Province do so free from any duress, or any coercion, or any motive of fraud and misrepresentation, or to act as foreign agents, or for other negative and improper motive; and

(v) The candidates making the petition for recognition of a Preliminary Province have been domiciled in the same location as the Province for at least three (3) months; and

(vi) The candidates making the petition for recognition of a Preliminary Province have not petitioned for recognition of any other Preliminary, Probational, Prerogative or Permanent Province in the past twelve months; and

(vii) The candidates making the petition for recognition of a Preliminary Province is competent and capable and willing to perform the obligations and duties required of a Province and has the support of at least two (2) other Commissioners of the same Province; and

(viii) The candidates making the petition for recognition of a Preliminary Province invoke the Oath of Allegiance to the Union in the physical presence of at least two other Members of the same Province as witnesses to the event as attested, witnessed and recorded in writing; and

(ix) The candidates making the petition for recognition of a Preliminary Province accept the obligations and duties of Office of Governor and invokes upon the sacred Covenant *Pactum De*

Singularis Caelum the Oath of Governor of a Province in the physical presence of at least two other Members of the same Province as witnesses to the event as attested, witnessed and recorded in writing; and

(x) That written notice of the recorded Oath of Allegiance, the name and Province Location Trust Number and Province Society Trust Number of the Preliminary Province, the full name and contact details of the Office Holder are provided within fourteen (14) days to any and all Provincial administrations of Universities of the Union to which the Province belongs as well as to each and every Campus within the same Province with a permanent Post Office mailing address, a permanent phone contact number, a contact email address and a means whereby administration of the Campuses of the Province may receive regular paper and/or electronic communication and information; and

(xi) That upon the Issue of Official Recognition of the Preliminary Province, a Constitution for the Province to operate as a Ucadia Foundation is prepared, and approved by the Members; and

(xii) That the Province duly register and record itself as a valid Foreign Body Corporate for Religious and Charitable Purposes with the appropriate foreign state and/or national governments operating within the same region.

5. A *Probational Province* is the third of five types of states of a valid Ucadia Province. A Probational Province is formed when not less than seventy-two (72) Ordinary Members domiciled within the bounds of the Province elect an interim Provincial Consulate and Government instituted through a Treaty between not less than one third of the total Campuses of the Province and the six Major Offices being elected, with each incumbent having invoked and recorded an Oath of Allegiance and an Oath of Office; and the fulfilment of the Criteria for the Foundation of a Probational Province. Probational Province Foundation

6. The following ten (10) criteria are the essential structural components and properties of a valid Probational Province:- Criteria for the Foundation of a Probational Province

(i) A unique and valid name and unique eighteen (18) digit Province Location Trust Number and unique eighteen (18) digit Province Society Trust Number exists for the Province within the bounds of a unique University Location Trust of the Union; and

(ii) That no existing Probational, Prerogative or Permanent

Province of the same name and same unique Province Location Trust Number and Province Society Trust Number exists and is currently recognised as active; and

(iii) That there are at least seventy-two (72) or more living Ordinary Members domiciled within the bounds of the Province; and

(iv) The candidate making the petition for recognition of a Probational Province is an existing Commissioner of a Permanent Campus within the bounds of the Province and is an Ordinary Member of good actions, good conscience with good faith and has not previously been refused, denied, banned or prevented in any way from holding any office of the Union, or University or Province or Campus; and that the candidate making the petition for recognition of a Probational Province does so free from any duress, or any coercion, or any motive of fraud and misrepresentation, or to act as a foreign agent, or for other negative and improper motive; and

(v) The candidate making the petition for recognition of a Probational Province has been domiciled in the same location as the Province for at least three (3) months and no other person living within the same domicile has petitioned for recognition of a Probational Province in the past twelve months; and

(vi) The candidate making the petition for recognition of a Probational Province has not petitioned for recognition of any other Probational Province in the past twelve months; and

(vii) The candidate making the petition for recognition of a Probational Province is competent and capable and willing to perform the obligations and duties required of a Governor of a Province and has the support of at least two (2) other Commissioners of the same Province; and

(viii) The candidate making the petition for recognition of a Probational Province invokes the Oath of Allegiance to the Union in the physical presence of at least two other Members of the same Province as witnesses to the event as attested, witnessed and recorded in writing; and

(ix) The candidate making the petition for recognition of a Probational Province accepts the obligations and duties of Office of Governor and invokes upon the sacred Covenant *Pactum De Singularis Caelum* the Oath of Governor of a Province in the physical presence of at least two other Members of the same Province as witnesses to the event as attested, witnessed and recorded in writing; and

(x) That written notice of the recorded Oath of Allegiance, Oath of Governor, the name and Province Location Trust Number and Province Society Trust Number of the Probational Province, the full name and contact details of the Governor are provided within fourteen (14) days to any and all Provincial administrations of Universities of the Union to which the Province belongs as well as to each and every Campus within the same Province with a permanent Post Office mailing address, a permanent phone contact number, a contact email address and a means by which the Commissioners and administration of the Campuses of the Province may receive regular paper and/or electronic communication and information.

Prerogative Province Foundation

7. A *Prerogative Province* is the fourth of five types of states of a valid Ucadia Province formed when a State Member of Ucadia, representing an internationally recognised state government sharing the same bounds of the Province agrees to adopt the Ucadia Model and systems of effective administration for the benefit of its Members. As a Ucadia State Member is an existing body politic, or state duly recognised by international Western-Roman bodies and having duly elected its government by its Members, a State Member therefore holds a prerogative right and privilege, subject to the conditions of the present Constitution and Charter and the Criteria for the Foundation of a Prerogative Province. All applications and approvals of Prerogative Provinces are superior to any preexisting Probational Province Administration and upon such approval, all rights, powers and authorities must be duly conveyed to the new administration.

Criteria for the Foundation of a Prerogative Province

8. The following ten (10) criteria are the essential structural components and properties of a valid Prerogative Province:-

(i) That the Province is already a valid Preliminary or Probational Province making the application for recognition as a Prerogative Province; and

(ii) That the Petitioner is a duly authorised official of a Ucadia State Member as plenipotentiary with the power to act on behalf of the government and people in relation to such a petition; and

(iii) That the particular Ucadia State Member is recognised by international Western-Roman bodies as an existing body politic, or state corresponding to the boundaries of the relevant Province; and

(iv) That no existing Prerogative or Permanent Province of the same name and same unique Province Location Trust Number and Province Society Trust Number exists and is currently recognised and registered as active; and

(v) That the particular Ucadia State Member making the petition for recognition of a Prerogative Province is a Member of good actions, good conscience with good faith and has not previously been refused, denied, banned or prevented in any way from holding any office or government of the Union, or University or Province or Campus; and

(vi) That the particular Ucadia State Member making the petition for recognition of a Prerogative Province has not petitioned for recognition of any other Prerogative Province in the past twelve months; and

(vii) That the particular Ucadia State Member making the petition for recognition of a Prerogative Province is competent and capable and willing to perform the obligations and duties required of the government of a valid Ucadia Province; and

(viii) That the executive of the particular Ucadia State Member making the petition for recognition of a Prerogative Province invokes the Oath of Allegiance to the Union as witnessed, attested and recorded in writing; and

(ix) That written notice of the petition and recorded Oath of Allegiance, the name and Province Location Trust Number and Province Society Trust Number of the Prerogative Province, are Gazetted within the Ucadia Gazette with 14 days given for any official notice of objection; and

(x) That the present Charter and Covenant are ratified by the elected assembly of the Ucadia State Member within 90 days of receiving confirmation of recognition as the government of the particular Prerogative Province.

Permanent Province Foundation

9. A *Permanent Province* is the fifth type of state of a valid Ucadia Province formed when not less than fifty percent (50) percent of all living men and women over the age of eighteen, domiciled within the bounds of the Province redeem their status as Ordinary Members and elect a permanent leadership and not less than sixty percent (60%) of all Campuses of the Province are duly constituted as Probational or Permanent with at least forty-percent (40%) of these as Permanent Campuses in accord with the Criteria for the Foundation of a Permanent Province. All applications and approvals of Permanent

Provinces are superior to any and all pre-existing Probational or Prerogative Province Administration and upon such approval, all rights, powers and authorities must be duly conveyed to the new administration.

Criteria for the Foundation of a Permanent Province

10. The following ten (10) criteria are the essential structural components and properties of a valid Permanent Province:-

(i) That the Province is a valid existing Probational or Prerogative Province making the application for permanent recognition; and

(ii) That a minimum of four hundred and thirty two (432) living Ordinary Members are registered as domiciled within the bounds of the Province; and

(iii) That peace and amity is declared within the Province and not less than sixty percent (60%) of all Campuses of the Province are duly constituted as Probational or Permanent with at least forty- percent (40%) of these as Permanent Campuses; and

(iv) That three (3) candidates make the petition for recognition of a Permanent Province and are existing Commissioners of Permanent Campuses within the bounds of the Province and are Ordinary Members of good actions, good conscience with good faith and have not previously been refused, denied, banned or prevented in any way from holding any office of the Union, or University or Province or Campus; and that the candidates making the petition for recognition of a Permanent Province do so free from any duress, or any coercion, or any motive of fraud and misrepresentation, or to act as a foreign agent, or for other negative and improper motive; and

(v) The candidates making the petition for recognition of a Permanent Province have been domiciled in the same location as the Province for at least three (3) months and no other person living within the same domicile has petitioned for recognition of a Permanent Province in the past twelve months; and

(vi) The candidates making the petition for recognition of a Permanent Province have not petitioned for recognition of any other Permanent Province in the past twelve months; and

(vii) The candidates making the petition for recognition of a Permanent Province are competent and capable and willing to perform the obligations and duties of a Permanent Province;

and

(viii) The candidates making the petition for recognition of a Permanent Province invoke the Oath of Allegiance to the Union in the physical presence of at least two other Members of the same Province as witnesses to the event as attested, witnessed and recorded in writing; and

(ix) The nominated candidates making the petition for recognition of a Permanent Province accept the obligations and duties of Office of Governor and invokes upon the sacred Covenant *Pactum De Singularis Caelum* the Oath of Governor of a Province in the physical presence of at least two other Members of the same Province as witnesses to the event as attested, witnessed and recorded in writing; and

(x) That written notice of the recorded Oath of Allegiance, Oath of Governor, the name and Province Location Trust Number and Province Society Trust Number of the Permanent Province, the full name and contact details of the Governor are provided within fourteen (14) days to any and all Provincial administrations of Universities of the Union to which the Province belongs as well as to each and every Campus within the same Province with a permanent Post Office mailing address, a permanent phone contact number, a contact email address and a means by which the Commissioners and administration of the Campuses of the Province may receive regular paper and/or electronic communication and information.

TITLE IX: UCADIA CAMPUSES

Article 86 – Ucadia Campus

1. A *Ucadia Campus* is the smallest administrative division of government and administration of the Union. A Campus is an ecclesiastically, legally and lawfully constituted administrative subdivision of a Province and is equivalent to a "local government area", and a "council", "city", "municipality", "borough", "shire" or "county". A Campus shall be named and defined according to the pre-existing legislative and geographic subdivision of a state or region or province into individual districts, postcodes or boroughs. Ucadia Campus

   A valid Ucadia Campus is a Superior Civil Trust and Ecclesiastical Capital Company having a mortal life not exceeding one complete standard Age of one thousand and seventy (1,070) years or approximately one third the life expectancy of the Union. An Ordinary Member may only belong to one (1) Campus according to the location of their current primary living location also known as domicile address.

2. When the organic boundaries of an Original Nation (Tribe) match the same boundaries of a Province under the Union, then the government and administration of the Original Nation and Campus shall be one and the same. Under such circumstances, the Offices of the Campus shall be the Official Government and the Offices of the Original Nation shall be honorific and ceremonial. Campus as Original Nation

3. In accord with the present Constitution and Charter there shall be five possible "states" or "types" of Legal Status for a Ucadia Campus being *Provisional, Preliminary, Probational, Prerogative* and *Permanent*:- Campus Legal Status

   (i) *Provisional Campus* is the first of five types of states of a valid Ucadia Campus. All Provisional Campuses within each Province of each University of the Union were formed between VENUS E8:Y3210:A0:S1:M27:D6 [21st of December 2011] and GAIA E1:Y1:A1:S1:M9:D1 [21st December 2012] as the smallest operational divisions of occupational forces of One Heaven following the complete conquest of all land, sea, earth, space, time, atmosphere and spirit within the boundaries of the Campus; and lawful possession and occupation of all rights, property, title and uses within the same bounds; and the investiture of a unique and individual spiritual member into each of the twelve Original Offices of the Land being Commissioner, Accountant, Secretary, Reader, Jurist, Proctor, Notary, Scrivener, Steward, Postmaster, Bailiff and Sheriff for each and every Campus on planet Earth. Under the terms of spiritual military occupation, the boundaries and Cadastral features of each University within each Union have been properly surveyed with the Survey and Charter for each Province registered within the Great Register of the Union and the event published in the Globe Union Gazette and Ucadia Gazette; and

(ii) *Preliminary Campus* is the second of five types of states of a valid Ucadia Campus. A Preliminary Campus is formed when not less than three (3) living Ordinary Members domiciled within the same bounds of the Campus come together as the Preliminary Commissioner, Accountant and Secretary, each having invoked and recorded an Oath of Allegiance and an Oath of Office; and the fulfilment of the Criteria for the Foundation of a Preliminary Campus; and

(iii) *Probational Campus* is the third of five types of states of a valid Ucadia Campus. A Probational Campus is formed when not less than thirty three (33) living Ordinary Members domiciled within the same bounds of the Campus come together as a Probational Convention and elect and ratify twelve of their own into the twelve Original Offices of the Land, each having invoked and recorded an Oath of Allegiance and an Oath of Office; and the fulfilment of the Criteria for the Foundation of a Probational Campus. All applications and approvals of Probational Campuses are superior to any pre-existing Preliminary Campus Administration and upon such approval, all rights, powers and authorities must be duly conveyed to the new administration; and

(iv) *Prerogative Campus* is the fourth of five types of states of a valid Ucadia Campus formed when a State Member of Ucadia, representing an internationally recognised local government or county or council sharing the same bounds of the Campus agrees to adopt the Ucadia Model and systems of effective administration for the benefit of its Members. As a Ucadia State Member is an existing body politic, or council or county or borough duly recognised by international Western-Roman bodies and having duly elected its government by its Members, a State Member therefore holds a prerogative right and privilege, subject to the conditions of the present Constitution and Charter and the Criteria for the Foundation of a Prerogative Campus. All applications and approvals of Prerogative Campuses are superior to any pre-existing Preliminary or Probational Campus Administration and upon such approval, all rights, powers and authorities must be duly conveyed to the new administration; and

(v) *Permanent Campus* is the fifth type of state of a valid Ucadia Campus formed when not less than fifty percent (50%) of all living men and women over the age of eighteen, domiciled within the bounds of the Campus redeem their status as Ordinary Members and elect a permanent leadership in accord with the Criteria for the Foundation of a Permanent Campus. All applications and approvals of Permanent Campuses are superior to any and all pre-existing Probational or Prerogative Campus Administration and upon such approval, all rights, powers and authorities must be duly conveyed to the new administration.

Foreign Registration of a Ucadia Campus

4. A Provisional or Permanent Campus administration is forbidden to register or record any instance of itself with any foreign estates, foreign nations and body politics sharing the same or similar bounds. However, a Preliminary, Probational or Prerogative Campus administration may record an instance of itself with a foreign estate, foreign nation or foreign body politic on the conditions:-

(i) That the said foreign body is duly recognised by at least twenty other foreign bodies as a valid entity of a size equal or larger than the bounds of the said Ucadia Campus; and

(ii) The executive of the Ucadia Campus making such foreign recording are duly recognised and possess valid credentials and registration and have not been banned from holding office, nor are presently subject to active criminal action within the courts of Ucadia nor the foreign courts in which registration is sought; and

(iii) The instance to be recorded with a foreign body is as the Ucadia Foundation for the said Campus as a Foreign Corporation Sole or Body Corporate for Religious and Charitable Purposes; and

(iv) That the formal name of the Ucadia Foundation for the said Campus has been duly enrolled within the Charter Rolls of the Union and Ucadia and such Charter Rights promulgated and made patent, including a valid Certificate of such Charter and Rights; and

(v) The Commissioner of the said Ucadia Campus is registered within the *Ucadia Foundation* (Directory of Official Persons of Ucadia); and

(vi) A Constitution for the instance of foreign recording as the Ucadia Foundation for the said Campus has been formed, promulgated and approved in acceptance of the Charter and Rights granted to the said Ucadia Foundation; and

(vii) The Bylaws for the Ucadia Foundation for the said Campus whereby the instance of the Ucadia Campus shall function in amity and harmony with the foreign body have been formed, promulgated and approved in accord with the Constitutional Charter; and

(viii) That the Office Holders as defined within the approved Constitutional Charter have been duly elected and that such elections are certified, including the Certificate of Divine Commission of the Commissioner.

5. The primary administrative Organ of Historic Records, Primary Sources and Files of the Campus, legally embodied and personified through the Great Office of Censor, shall be the Official Archives. Ucadia Campus Archive

6. The primary administrative Organ of Collections, Information and Knowledge Resources of the Campus, legally embodied and personified through the Great Office of Narrator, shall be the Library. Ucadia Campus Library

Article 87 – Campus Convention

1. All legislative powers of a Campus shall be vested in a Convention of Members ("Convention") which shall consist of all men and women who are members of One-Heaven and recognised as Ordinary Members of the Union currently domiciled within the bounds of the Campus:- Campus Convention

(i) A Provisional Convention shall consist of those spiritual forces presently occupying and possessing the spiritual and temporal bounds of the Campus; and

(ii) A Preliminary Convention shall consist of a minimum of three (3) Ordinary Members who are also recognised as the Preliminary Campus Board in accord with the Criteria for the Foundation of a Preliminary Campus; and

(iii) A Probational Convention shall consist of a minimum of thirty three (33) Ordinary Members who are also recognised as the Probational Campus Board in accord with the Criteria for the Foundation of a Probational Campus; and

(iv) A Prerogative Convention shall consist of not less than all men and women over the minimum voting age, duly registered to vote within the rules of the State Member in accord with the Criteria for the Foundation of a Prerogative Campus ;and

(v) A Permanent Convention shall consist of not less than all men and women over the age of eighteen, domiciled within the bounds of the Campus in accord with the Criteria for the Foundation of a Permanent Campus.

Name of the Convention

2. The name of the Convention shall be the unique geographic name of the location plus the words “Ucadia Campus”. Where a Permanent Convention votes in favour to register a subsidiary of itself with a foreign society or entity, the words “Ucadia Mission” shall be used with the unique geographic name of the location to reflect both the purpose and mission of the Convention and Campus.

Rights, Powers and Authority of Permanent Convention

3. Vested by the present sacred Charter, a Permanent Convention shall possess, hold and own certain Positive Rights in accord with the most sacred Covenant *Pactum De Singularis Caelum*. All Powers and Authority of a Permanent Convention are sourced from these Rights. There are three (3) types of Rights associated with a Permanent Convention of a Campus being Universal, Conditional and Ucadia:-

(i) Universal Rights, also known as Universal Positive Rights, are a sub-class of Positive Rights whereby such valid Rights are created, defined and bestowed to a Permanent Convention through the existence of the Province to which the Campus belongs and are Peremptory, Permanent, Immutable and Indefeasible once bestowed are not subject to any form or condition of waiver, abandonment, surrender, disqualification, incapacitation, seizure, capture, arrest, resignation, alienation, suspension, suppression, forfeiture or abrogation. Universal Rights granted to a Permanent Convention cannot exceed the power or authority of the Province that granted such Rights; and

(ii) Conditional Rights, also known as Conditional Positive Rights, are a sub-class of Positive Rights whereby such valid Rights are created, defined and bestowed to a Permanent Convention through the existence of the Province to which the Campus belongs upon acceptance of the associated obligations and duties attached to them. Furthermore, if any such conditions and obligations are breached or repudiated, then the relevant Conditional Positive Right may be waived, surrendered, suspended, abandoned, resigned, disqualified, seized, captured, arrested, rescinded, suppressed, forfeited or revoked until such time as the fundamental breach of duty and obligation is repaired or such a Right is duly restored. Conditional Rights granted to a Permanent Convention cannot exceed the power or authority of the Province that granted such Rights. A

Permanent Convention to whom a Conditional Positive Right has been bestowed may also lawfully convey equitable title of such a Right to another person; and

(iii) Ucadia Rights are unique Positive Rights associated with Ucadia itself and when bestowed, granted, given, delegated or assigned to a Permanent Convention represents the lawful possession, holding or ownership of some Ucadian Right.

4. All Convention Instruments shall be in accord with the official forms defined by the present Sacred Charter and associated Codes. All agreements of the Convention shall be made in accord with the Rights and within the limits of the Rights prescribed by the present Charter. Convention Instruments and Agreements

5. Excluding the election of Office Holders, voting in Campus Convention shall be by open vote expressed as either Yes or No to the proposition before the chamber. Convention Voting and Elections

Voting shall always require a quorum and shall follow the standard procedures listed in this Charter. Total votes shall be tallied as either Yes, or No to the proposition expressed by the proposed Ordinance. A higher total number of Yes votes to No votes shall deem the proposed Ordinance or proposition has been passed. A higher total number of No votes to Yes votes shall deem the proposed Ordinance or proposition has been defeated.

The record, attendance and vote of all Members of Campus Convention shall be recorded on the public record.

6. The Convention shall exist for a fixed period of one thousand and seventy (1070) years. Life of Convention

7. Every year, there shall be a minimum of three (3) Ordinary Sessions and one (1) Annual Session whereby such Sessions are evenly spread so that they occur not less than sixty (60) days apart and not more than one hundred (100) days apart in a building suitable for such a purpose whereby all registered local Ordinary Members may attend. Convention Sessions

The Agenda of Business ("General Business") of the Convention shall be according to the rules of the present Article, subject to the management of proceedings by the Campus Executive with the length of the Session not less than two (2) hours and not exceeding four (4) hours, including a mandatory break of a minimum of half an hour where the planned session is longer than two hours.

The General Business of an Ordinary Session shall always be considered different to the General Business of an Annual Session. The procedures for General Business shall be defined and recorded in the

Legislative Code.

8. The date of a campus election shall always occur at least fourteen (14) days prior to the commencement of an Annual Session allowing forty (40) days prior to the date of the election for the official campaign period.

Date of Campus Convention Elections

9. The minimum number of Members (quorum) required to be present within the chamber of a Campus Convention to permit the full exercise of its powers shall be two thirds (2/3) the total number of Members of that Convention. The Convention shall not be permitted to undertake procedures that require a quorum if the total number of Members in that House is not equal or greater to the quorum.

Quorum

10. Responsibility for good conduct and control of the Convention and the scheduling of business within the chamber shall be vested in the Office of Speaker of Campus Convention (Convention Speaker).

Office of Speaker of Campus Convention (Convention Speaker)

The Speaker of a Campus Convention shall be an independent role, free from political party preferences. The candidate shall be elected by the new Campus themselves on the first day of sitting of the new Campus Convention after a Campus Election.

11. The Convention shall have the right and power to commission a Campus Commission of Investigation with the power to call any registered Member within the Campus and any information held by the Campus Executive to review.

Convention Investigations and Actions

The Convention also has vested by this Charter the power to commission a Campus Impeachment for the forced removal of any elected official from the Commissioner to any position within any branch of government in the Campus. A Campus Commission of Investigation must be called by the Convention when a call to expel one or more members is made, excluding cases where the grounds of the charge are based on an automatic expulsion.

12. Accordingly, a Campus Convention shall not be permitted to grow beyond one hundred thousand (100,000) households or two hundred and fifty thousand permanent population. This is in recognition of the practical limitations placed on the Commissioner to be able to properly support a community.

Maximum size of Convention

Communities that grow to this limit or beyond must institute within six months of reaching this number a Community sub-division whereby the community is divided into two-equal halves based on the geographic distribution of Members.

13. If by three hundred and sixty (360) Days since the formation of a Probationary Convention one or more of the conditions of the Criteria

Disbanding of Probationary

for the Foundation of a Permanent Campus are not met, the appropriate permanent Province Assembly shall have the right to disband the Probational Convention and revoke its status. If no permanent Province Assembly yet exists, the University Parliament shall have such right. If no permanent University Parliament exists, it shall be the responsibility of the Union Senate. Convention

Upon disbandment, the persons originally making the application for a Probationary Convention are not permitted to directly re-apply for a new Campus, nor hold office for a period of not less than six (6) months.

14. The Censure or Suspension of a Permanent Convention is when the Permanent Province Assembly under which the Campus Convention is bound exercises their right in accord with the Rule of Law, Justice and Due Process to admonish or order the suspension of all operations. Censure or Suspension of Convention

No body, person, aggregate or entity has the power or right to dissolve or disband a Permanent Convention and Campus other than the Ordinary Members of the Convention themselves.

However, when the Permanent Province Assembly to which the Campus belongs proves one or more of the following grounds for Censure or Suspension, then the Convention may be lawfully Censured or Suspended for a period of not less than forty (40) days and not more than one hundred and sixty (160) days:-

(i) That the Convention has been found to have deliberately and willfully exceeded its rights in engaging in activities that have brought disrepute or harm to Ucadia, or the Province or University or Union; or

(ii) That the Convention has entered into agreements with other parties for which it has no right or authority to do, or such agreements that contradict good faith, good actions and good conscience; or

(iii) That the Convention has willfully and deliberately taken actions that are considered Criminal in nature by the Criminal Code of the Union.

15. The dissolution and wind-up of a Permanent Convention is when a three-quarters of all Ordinary Members of the Campus vote in Session in favour of its dissolution and wind-up as a Permanent Convention upon the existence of one of the following conditions. If approved, then the Convention shall revert to the status of a Preliminary Convention as no Convention may be lawfully dissolved, abandoned, conveyed, surrendered, disqualified, seized, captured, arrested, Dissolution and Wind-up of a Permanent Convention

alienated, suppressed, forfeited or abrogated.

The list of conditions by which one is necessary for any valid dissolution and wind-up of a Permanent Convention are:-

(i) That the total active living membership of the Convention has been less than thirty-six (36) for twelve months or more; or

(ii) That the Convention is bankrupt and unable to continue to pay its financial obligations with no prospect of independent financial income in the future to meet its ongoing obligations; or

(iii) That the entire Executive has been expelled from the Union and that the majority of remaining members represent members and supporters of their former network.

Article 88 – Campus Commissioner

1. The Commissioner is the supreme leader of the Campus, its head and prime representative. The office of the Commissioner is the highest elected office of a district and at all times should be considered with the greatest dignity and respect. *Campus Commissioner*

2. By virtue of this Charter, a Commissioner is vested with the executive authority to manage the needs and affairs of the Campus through the selection or dismissal of wise counsel in the form of their Campus Board of Directors, the agencies, officials and administration of the Campus Government. *Rights, Powers and Authority of the Commissioner*

   The Commissioner shall have the authority over all agencies and Campus Directors as Chairman of the Board of Directors. As Chairman, the Commissioner may choose to overrule motions of the Board and select the agenda and minutes of the Board meetings.

   The Commissioner shall have Power, by and with the Advice and Consent of the Convention, shall appoint public officials and magistrates, and all other Officers of the Campus, whose Appointments are not herein otherwise provided for, and which shall be established by Law: but the Convention may by Law vest the Appointment of such inferior Officers, as they think proper, in the Commissioner alone, in the Courts of Law, or in the Heads of Departments.

3. The Oath of Commissioner is a sacred Oath of a member of the government of a Campus. Prior to the commencement of their term of office, an Officer of the government of a Campus shall make the following public oath - *Oath of Commissioner*

I (name) do solemnly invoke before the One True Divine Creator of All Heaven and Earth and all here present as credible witnesses that in Good Faith and with Good Actions and Good Conscience I will faithfully, truly and honorarily execute the Office of [Name of Office] of [Campus] Campus of [Province] of [University] of [Union] and will duly serve, protect and defend the Campus of [Campus] and the Charter of the Union.

4. The Commissioner shall hold their Office during the Term of two (2) Years, and be elected by Campus election following the procedures for general, provincial and university elections contained within this Charter. Term of Commissioner

By this Charter a Commissioner is ineligible to serve beyond a total of four terms (8) years. A Commissioner having served the nation for greater than eight (8) years shall be known as a Grand Commissioner.

5. The Commissioner shall, at stated Times, receive for their services, a compensation, which shall neither be increased nor diminished during the Period for which they shall have been elected, and shall not receive any other income during their term. Payment of the Commissioner

6. In the good management of the Campus, its affairs and requirements can be compared to the good conduct of a corporation with its Members as shareholders. Campus Board of Directors (Campus Board)

The Campus Board of Directors shall be a board of individuals selected by the Commissioner to head the permanent statutory authorities and uphold the laws regarding the critical systems of the district. The tenure of a Director shall be at the sole discretion of the Commissioner.

Given the importance of each system within our society functioning to its optimum, the position of a Campus Director should reflect the very best of the community with the knowledge, experience and respect relating to the system they manage.

7. The local civil service includes every officer and employee of a local county body or agency, except as otherwise provided in this Charter for a Campus. All positions in the civil service shall be subject to the terms and conditions of employment as specified by the civil service statutes of the State to which the county belongs. Campus Management & Operations

In the civil service, permanent appointment and promotion shall be made under a general system based on merit ascertained by competitive examination.

8. While a Campus Convention is free to make laws and regulations which are in the best interests of the Members of the Campus, the Local Laws and Regulations

following conditions must always be met for each and every Ordinance. A failure of a law of a Campus to meet this criteria shall deem that law illegal, whether or not it has been passed by the Campus Convention and/or Commissioner or not:-

(i) Best interests of the Campus: That in relation to legislation and regulations concerning the creation, disposal and/or management of assets of the Campus, that the law serves the best interests of the Campus first and any special interests and third parties last; and

(ii) Consistency with Charter: That the proposed law does not directly contradict any of the articles of this Charter.

Article 89 – Campus Judiciary & Law Enforcement

1. The judicial power of the Campus shall be vested in one Local Court being the Campus Convention as Grand Jury and duly appointed judicial officials. The Local Court shall consist of three (3) Magistrates appointed by the Commissioner and Board of Directors upon the approval of the Convention at a time of vacancy of position to the Local Court. *Campus Judiciary & Law Enforcement*

The tenure of a Magistrate of the Local Court shall be for a period of not greater than eight (8) years and subject to their good conduct and the confidence of the Convention. A Magistrate shall be required to resign within 30 days of their 80th birthday, regardless the remaining length of their tenure.

2. Vested by this Charter, the Local Court shall have the following powers of Original Jurisdiction: *Original Jurisdiction*

(i) In relation to criminal proceedings relating to alleged breaches of law, excluding major and serious offences carrying a penalty of ten years or more; and

(ii) In relation to commercial matters relating to disputed property rights and contracts valued less than twenty five thousand (25,000) units of Union currency; and

(iii) In which the Campus, or a person suing or being sued on behalf of the Campus, is a party; and

(iv) In which a Great Writ or an injunction is sought against an officer of the Campus.

3. By this Charter, all law enforcement of the Campus shall be vested in the Office of Sheriff as the highest authority of law enforcement within *Campus law enforcement*

the bounds of the Campus.

Article 90 – Campus Foundation

1. The foundation of a valid Ucadia Campus of the Union shall be in accord with the criteria and terms defined by the present Article and the five possible "states" or "types" of Legal Status for a Ucadia Campus being Provisional, Preliminary, Probational, Prerogative and Permanent. Campus Foundation

   A Preliminary Campus may not be formed until a duly constituted and valid Ucadia Foundation has been first formed for the relevant Ucadia University, and then a duly constituted and valid Ucadia Province for the relevant Ucadia Province.

2. A *Provisional Campus* is the first of five types of states of a valid Ucadia Campus. All Provisional Campus within each Province of each University of the Union were formed between VENUS E8:Y0:A0:S1:M27:D6 [21st of December 2011] and GAIA E1:Y1:A1:S1:M9:D1 [21st December 2012] as the smallest operational divisions of occupational forces of One Heaven following the complete conquest of all land, sea, earth, space, time, atmosphere and spirit within the boundaries of the Campus; and lawful possession and occupation of all rights, property, title and uses within the same bounds; and the investiture of a unique and individual spiritual member into each of the Original Twelve (12) Offices of the Land being: Commissioner, Sheriff, Proctor, Reader, Steward, Secretary, Scrivener, Jurist, Postmaster, Notary, Bailiff and Accountant for each and every Campus on planet Earth. Under the terms of spiritual military occupation, the boundaries and Cadastral features of each University within each Union have been properly surveyed with the Survey and Charter for each Province registered within the Great Register of the Union and the event published in the Globe Union Gazette and Ucadia Gazette. Provisional Campus Foundation

3. A *Preliminary Campus* is the second of five types of states of a valid Ucadia Campus. A Preliminary Campus is formed when not less than three (3) living Ordinary Members domiciled within the same bounds of the Campus come together as the Preliminary Commissioner, Accountant and Secretary, each having invoked and recorded an Oath of Allegiance and an Oath of Office; and the fulfilment of the Criteria for the Foundation of a Preliminary Campus. Preliminary Campus Foundation

4. The following ten (10) criteria are the essential structural components and properties of a valid Preliminary Campus:- Criteria for the Foundation of a Preliminary Campus

   (i) A unique and valid name and unique eighteen (18) digit

Campus Location Trust Number and Campus Society Trust Number exist for the Campus within the bounds of a unique Province Location Trust of the Union; and

(ii) That no existing Preliminary, Probational, Prerogative or Permanent Campus of the same name and same unique Campus Location Trust Number and Campus Society Trust Number exists and is currently recognised and officially registered as active; and

(iii) The candidate making the petition for recognition of a Preliminary Campus is an Ordinary Member of good actions, good conscience with good faith and has not previously been refused, denied, banned or prevented in any way from holding any office of the Union or Province or Campus; and

(iv) The candidate making the petition for recognition of a Preliminary Campus does so free from any duress, or any coercion, or any motive of fraud and misrepresentation, or to act as a foreign agent, or for other negative and improper motive; and

(v) The candidate making the petition for recognition of a Preliminary Campus has been domiciled in the same location as the Campus for at least three (3) months and no other person living within the same domicile has petitioned for recognition of the same Preliminary Campus in the past twelve months; and

(vi) The candidate making the petition for recognition of a Preliminary Campus has not petitioned for recognition of any other Preliminary, Probational, Prerogative or Permanent Campus in the past twelve (12) months; and

(vii) The candidate making the petition for recognition of a Preliminary Campus is competent and capable and willing to perform the obligations and duties required of an Officer of a Campus; and

(viii) The candidate making the petition for recognition of a Preliminary Campus invokes the Oath of Allegiance to the Union in the presence of at least two witnesses with such an event and fact is attested, witnessed and recorded in writing; and

(ix) The candidate making the petition for recognition of a Preliminary Campus accepts the obligations and duties of Office of Commissioner and invokes upon the sacred Covenant

Pactum De Singularis Caelum the Oath of Commissioner of a Campus in the presence of at least two witnesses with such an event and fact is attested, witnessed and recorded in writing; and

(x) That written notice of the recorded Oath of Allegiance, Oath of Commissioner, the name and Campus Location Trust Number and Campus Society Trust Number of the Preliminary Campus, the full name and contact details of the Commissioner are provided within fourteen (14) days to any existing Province and Union to which the Campus belongs as well as to each and every Campus within the same Province where such contact details are known by the new Commissioner.

Probational Campus Foundation

5. A *Probational Campus* is the third of five types of states of a valid Ucadia Campus. A Probational Campus is formed when not less than thirty three (33) living Ordinary Members domiciled within the same bounds of the Campus come together as a Probational Convention and elect and ratify twelve (12) of their own into the twelve Original Offices of the Land, each having invoked and recorded an Oath of Allegiance and an Oath of Office; and the fulfilment of the Criteria for the Foundation of a Probational Campus. All applications and approvals of Probational Campuses are superior to any pre-existing Preliminary Campus Administration and upon such approval, all rights, powers and authorities must be duly conveyed to the new administration.

Criteria for the Foundation of a Probational Campus

6. The following ten (10) criteria are the essential structural components and properties of a valid Probational Campus:-

(i) A unique and valid name and unique eighteen (18) digit Campus Location Trust Number and Campus Society Trust Number exist for the Campus within the bounds of a unique Province Location Trust of the Union; and

(ii) That no existing Probational, Prerogative or Permanent Campus of the same name and same unique Campus Location Trust Number and Campus Society Trust Number exists and is currently recognised as active; and

(iii) That there are at least thirty three (33) or more living Ordinary Members domiciled within the bounds of the Campus; and

(iv) The candidate making the petition for recognition of a Probational Campus is an Ordinary Member of good actions, good conscience with good faith and has not previously been refused, denied, banned or prevented in any way from holding any office of the Union or Province or Campus; and that the candidate making the petition for recognition of a Probational Campus does so free from any duress, or any coercion, or any motive of fraud and misrepresentation, or to act as a foreign agent, or for other negative and improper motive; and

(v) The candidate making the petition for recognition of a Probational Campus has been domiciled in the same location as the Campus for at least three (3) months and no other person living within the same domicile has petitioned for recognition of a Probational Campus in the past twelve months; and

(vi) The candidate making the petition for recognition of a Probational Campus has not petitioned for recognition of any other Probational Campus in the past twelve (12) months and other than being an Ordinary Member does not currently hold any other Office of the Union as defined by the present Charter; and

(vii) The candidate making the petition for recognition of a Probational Campus is competent and capable and willing to perform the obligations and duties required of a Commissioner of a Campus; and

(viii) The candidate making the petition for recognition of a Probational Campus invokes the Oath of Allegiance to the Union in the presence of at least two witnesses with such an event and fact is attested, witnessed and recorded in writing; and

(ix) The candidate making the petition for recognition of a Probational Campus accepts the obligations and duties of Office of Commissioner and invokes upon the sacred Covenant *Pactum De Singularis Caelum* the Oath of Commissioner of a Campus in the presence of at least two witnesses with such an event and fact is attested, witnessed and recorded in writing; and

(x) That written notice of the recorded Oath of Allegiance, Oath of Commissioner, the name and Campus Location Trust Number and Campus Society Trust Number of the Probational Campus, the full name and contact details of the Commissioner are provided within fourteen (14) days to any existing Province and Union to which the Campus belongs as well as to each and every Campus within the same Province where such contact details are known by the new Commissioner.

7. A *Prerogative Campus* is the fourth of five types of states of a valid Prerogative

Campus Foundation

Ucadia Campus formed when a State Member of Ucadia, representing an internationally recognised local government or county or council sharing the same bounds of the Campus agrees to adopt the Ucadia Model and systems of effective administration for the benefit of its Members. As a Ucadia State Member is an existing body politic, or council or county or borough duly recognised by international Western-Roman bodies and having duly elected its government by its Members, a State Member therefore holds a prerogative right and privilege, subject to the conditions of the present Constitution and Charter and the Criteria for the Foundation of a Prerogative Campus.

All applications and approvals of Prerogative Campuses are superior to any pre-existing Preliminary or Probational Campus Administration and upon such approval, all rights, powers and authorities must be duly conveyed to the new administration.

Criteria for the Foundation of a Prerogative Campus

8. The following ten (10) criteria are the essential structural components and properties of a valid Prerogative Campus:-

(i) That the Campus is already a valid Preliminary or Probational Campus making the application for recognition as a Prerogative Campus; and

(ii) That the Petitioner is a duly authorized official of a Ucadia State Member as plenipotentiary with the power to act on behalf of the government and people in relation to such a petition; and

(iii) That the particular Ucadia State Member is recognised by international Western-Roman bodies as an existing body politic, or state corresponding to the boundaries of the relevant Campus; and

(iv) That no existing Prerogative or Permanent Campus of the same name and same unique Campus Location Trust Number and Campus Society Trust Number exists and is currently recognised and registered as active; and

(v) That the particular Ucadia State Member making the petition for recognition of a Prerogative Campus is a Member of good actions, good conscience with good faith and has not previously been refused, denied, banned or prevented in any way from holding any office or government of the Union, or University or Province or Campus; and

(vi) That the particular Ucadia State Member making the petition for recognition of a Prerogative Campus has not petitioned for recognition of any other Prerogative Campus in the past twelve months; and

(vii) That the particular Ucadia State Member making the petition for recognition of a Prerogative Campus is competent and capable and willing to perform the obligations and duties required of the government of a valid Ucadia Campus; and

(viii) That the executive of the particular Ucadia State Member making the petition for recognition of a Prerogative Campus invokes the Oath of Allegiance to the Union as witnessed, attested and recorded in writing; and

(ix) That written notice of the petition and recorded Oath of Allegiance, the name and Campus Location Trust Number and Campus Society Trust Number of the Prerogative Campus, are Gazetted within the Ucadia Gazette with 14 days given for any official notice of objection; and

(x) That the present Charter and Covenant are ratified by the elected assembly of the Ucadia State Member within 90 days of receiving confirmation of recognition as the government of the particular Prerogative Campus.

Permanent Campus Foundation

9. A *Permanent Campus* is the fifth type of state of a valid Ucadia Campus formed when not less than fifty percent (50%) of all living men and women over the age of eighteen, domiciled within the bounds of the Campus redeem their status as Ordinary Members and elect a permanent leadership in accord with the Criteria for the Foundation of a Permanent Campus. All applications and approvals of Permanent Campuses are superior to any and all pre-existing Probational or Prerogative Campus Administration and upon such approval, all rights, powers and authorities must be duly conveyed to the new administration.

Criteria for the Foundation of a Permanent Campus

10. The following ten (10) criteria are the essential structural components and properties of a valid Permanent Campus:-

(i) That the Campus is a valid existing Probational or Prerogative Campus making the application for permanent recognition; and

(ii) That a minimum of one hundred and forty four (144) living Ordinary Members are registered as domiciled within the bounds of the Campus; and

(iii) That three (3) candidates make the petition for recognition of a Permanent Campus and are Ordinary Members of good actions, good conscience with good faith and has not previously been refused, denied, banned or prevented in any way from holding any office of the Union or Province or Campus; and

(iv) The candidates making the petition for recognition of a Permanent Campus do so free from any duress, or any coercion, or any motive of fraud and misrepresentation, or to act as foreign agents, or for other negative and improper motive; and

(v) That the candidates making the petition for recognition of a Permanent Campus have been domiciled in the same location as the Campus for at least three (3) months and no other person living within the same domicile has petitioned for recognition of a Permanent Campus in the past twelve months; and

(vi) The candidates making the petition for recognition of a Permanent Campus have not petitioned for recognition of any other Campus in the past twelve (12) months; and

(vii) The candidates making the petition for recognition of a Permanent Campus are competent and capable and willing to perform the obligations and duties required of a Permanent Campus; and

(viii) The candidates making the petition for recognition of a Permanent Campus invoke the Oath of Allegiance to the Union in the presence of at least two witnesses with such an event and fact is attested, witnessed and recorded in writing; and

(ix) The candidate making the petition for recognition of a Permanent Campus accepts the obligations and duties of Office of Commissioner and invokes upon the sacred Covenant *Pactum De Singularis Caelum* the Oath of Commissioner of a Campus in the presence of at least two witnesses with such an event and fact is attested, witnessed and recorded in writing; and

(x) That written notice of the recorded Oath of Allegiance, Oath of Commissioner, the name and Campus Location Trust Number and Campus Society Trust Number of the Permanent Campus, the full name and contact details of the Executive are provided within fourteen (14) days to any existing Province and Union to which the Campus belongs as well as to each and every Campus within the same Province.

TITLE X: SYSTEMS

Article 91 – Systems

1. All administrative agencies and related services, skills and resources of the Union shall be divided into twenty-two (22) permanent and standard "**Systems**", in accord with the present Constitutional Charter. Systems

   The permanent and standard Systems shall reflect and compliment the fourteen standard categories of all economic activity, namely:-

   Primary

   (i) Primary: Energy, Water & Infrastructure; and

   (ii) Primary: Buildings & Construction; and

   (iii) Primary: Products: Agriculture, Food, Drugs & Biosafety; and

   (iv) Primary: Products: Primary Elements & Materials; and

   Industry

   (v) Industry: Products: Materials Manufacture & Wholesale; and

   (vi) Industry: Products: Machine Manufacture & Wholesale; and

   (vii) Industry: Logistics, Transport, Vehicles, & Space; and

   (viii) Industry: Communications, Data, Information & Media ; and

   Services

   (ix) Services: Products: Retail, Online & Direct Sales; and

   (x) Services: Government, Societies & Charities; and

   (xi) Services: Business & Corporate; and

   (xii) Services: Personal, Wellbeing & Professional; and

   (xiii) Services: Scientific, Cultural & Creative; and

   (xiv) Services: General, Fiduciary & Non-Classifiable.

2. The eight (8) "**Primary Systems**" of the Union shall be:- Primary Systems

   (i) Clean Energy, Water & Infrastructure Systems; and

   (ii) Buildings, Construction & Facilities Management Systems; and

   (iii) Harmonic Agriculture & Organic Systems; and

   (iv) Ethical Food & Therapeutic Systems; and

(v) Environmental Protection and Preservation Systems; and

(vi) Disease Prevention & Sanitation Systems; and

(vii) Security & Emergency Systems; and

(viii) Advanced Elements & Materials Production Systems.

3. The four (4) "**Industry Systems**" of the Union shall be:- Industry Systems

(i) Logistics, Transport & Space Systems; and

(ii) Industry, Innovation and Workflow Systems; and

(iii) Communications, Networks and Media Systems; and

(iv) Technology Development & Research Systems.

4. The ten (10) "**Services Systems**" of the Union shall be:- Services Systems

(i) Member Support Services & Charitable Systems; and

(ii) Knowledge and Intellectual Property Systems; and

(iii) Vocation, Skills and Productivity Systems; and

(iv) Market Solutions and Settlement Systems; and

(v) Arts, Culture & Creative Systems; and

(vi) Health Support & Wellbeing Systems; and

(vii) Banking, Finance and Revenue Systems; and

(viii) Justice & Legal Support Systems; and

(ix) Administrative Support & Electoral Systems; and

(x) Entities, Agreements & Securities Systems.

5. Excluding Secretariats, all Systems of the Union shall follow the same rules of Organisational Structure in defining subdivisions within itself:- Organisational Structures of Systems

(i) "**Team**" shall be a subdivision of a Unit whereby two (2) or more people, to a maximum of thirty (30) people function according to some technical function and mandate; and

(ii) "**Unit**" shall be a subdivision of a Section whereby ten (10) or more people, to a maximum of one hundred and twenty (120) people function according to some technical function and mandate; and

(iii) "**Section**" shall be a subdivision of a Department whereby twenty (20) or more people, to a maximum of three hundred and sixty (360) people function according to some technical function and mandate; and

(iv) "**Department**" shall be a subdivision of a Division whereby thirty (30) or more people, to a maximum of two thousand (2,000) people function according to some general division of services; and

(v) "**Division**" shall be a primary subdivision of one of the twenty-two Systems of six hundred (600) or more people, to a maximum of twenty thousand (20,000) people according to a primary division of responsibilities of a System.

Systems Political Structures

6. The Systems of the Union shall be fully integrated and organised across each and every level and division of the Union to optimise communication, administration and effective use of resources:-

(i) *Executor-General and Global Resources* - Global resources, decisions and policies concerning each System shall be in the hands of a duly appointed Executor-General; and

(ii) *Regional-General and Union Resources* - Union resources, decisions and policies concerning each System shall be in the hands of a duly appointed Regional-General with all Union Regional-Generals being members of the Globe Council of the appropriate System with the Executor-General as Chairman; and

(iii) *Director-General and University Resources* - University resources, decisions and policies concerning each System shall be in the hands of a duly appointed Director-General with all University Director-Generals being members of the Union Council of the appropriate System with the Regional-General as Chairman; and

(iv) *Provincial-General and Province Resources* - Province resources, decisions and policies concerning each System shall be in the hands of a duly appointed Provincial-General with all Provincial-Generals being members of the University Council of the appropriate System with the Director-General as Chairman.

System Resources Allocation

7. All planning, budgeting, approval and allocation of resources, personnel and services within the Systems of the Unions, Universities, Provinces and Campuses shall be in accord with the following principles:-

(i) *Minimal Vertical Duplication* shall mean that levels of duplication of function within a vertical service delivery chain must be minimal and full service duplication across vertical levels of a service delivery chain forbidden; and

(ii) *Front-Line Service Priority* shall mean that the priority of resourcing in any service chain shall always begin with the actual front-line service being the first priority and support, management and logistics always having second priority; and

(iii) *Local Service Priority* shall mean that where duplication of function and services exist, the lower and more local functions and services shall take priority over the higher vertical functions and services, unless the service and function pertains primarily to policy, planning or standards whereby the duplication will resolve in favour of higher vertical administration; and

(iv) *Services as Public Asset* shall mean that the services delivered shall remain a public asset and service and not subject to sell off to private corporations or private-public ventures or down-scaling or outsourcing to private interests; and

(v) *Limits on Consultants* shall mean that the management of such systems are forbidden to recruit, hire, engage or contact private or external consulting firms where such services, skills, abilities or knowledge provided already exists within the public services of the Society.

Article 92 – Agency

1. The good management and effective control of all aspects of a System within the jurisdiction of the Union shall be vested in a permanent statutory authority known as an "**Agency**". Agency

2. Each and every Agency of the Union will be represented by a suitably qualified and dedicated Officer known as a "**Regional-General**" as its Head and executive authority. Regional-General as Head of Agency

Article 93 – Regional-General

1. The administrative head of each Agency and System shall be known as the Regional-General, being an Officer of suitable qualifications and capacity. Regional-General

   The Regional-General of each System of the Union shall be vested with the sole authority of the good management of the standards and systems and the operation of the various resources and personnel of each particular System of the Union. Each Regional-General shall be a direct appointment by title of the Union Sunedrion upon approval of the Union Synod reporting in respect to daily operations to the Alexander through the Academy.

2. The General Powers of a duly appointed Regional-General of a System shall be those powers and authorities defined and granted in accord with these Articles, notwithstanding any and all additional responsibilities granted in writing by associated codes, constitutions and bylaws, or as prescribed by Ucadian Law, including (but not limited to):- Powers

(i) Selection, appointment and employment of Regional Secretary and Regional Secretariat of the System, with the Regional Secretary holding their position at the confidence of their Regional-General; and

(ii) Chair of the Council of Directors-General of the System they are Regional Director, with the power and authority to set meetings dates, agenda and votes; and

(iii) Oversight and responsibility for the strategy, planning, budgeting, efficiency and operation of the Division and the Departments under its control; and

(iv) The general identification of suitable talented personnel and the interview, vetting and recruitment of personnel to the Division; and

(v) The day-to-day tasks, activities and productivity of personnel assigned to the Division; and

(vi) The immediate behaviour, culture and discipline of members of the Division and all its Departments.

3. The Directors-General as Heads of the various University systems of each System of the Union Systems of the Union shall meet as a Board virtually or in person not less than once every fifty (50) days, with the Regional-General as Chair or a proxy nominated for the meeting. Council of Directors General of System

4. Each Regional-General shall be required to publish within the first twelve (12) months of their appointment and thereafter every two (2) years a strategic plan encompassing the next ten (10) years subject to the approval of the Synod. Strategic Plan

The Strategic Plan must include major project development and operational development including detailed financial forecasts and cost / benefit analysis so that the strategic use of the limited resources of the Union can be clearly comprehended and improved over time.

Furthermore, all projection and statistical data must be sourced and relate to the Ucadia Statistical Model for consistency.

5. Each Regional-General shall be required to publish within the first six (6) months of their appointment an Annual Operational Plan outlying the proposed schedule of appointments, expenditures, programs and events, consistent with the Strategic Plans approved by the Synod. Operational Plan

The Regional-General and executives shall then be measured in part upon the projected (strategic) plans versus the accomplishment of annual revised operational plans.

Article 94 – Regional-Secretary

1. Each and every Regional General shall be supported in their office by a "**Secretariat**". Secretariat

2. The administrative head and authority of each Secretariat shall be represented by a permanent office known as "**Regional-Secretary**". Secretariat of System

3. All Secretariats operating within any System of the Union or any part thereof shall identify all Officers, Agents and Contractors according to the following three levels of Desk, Station and Chapter:- Organisational Structures of Secretariat

   (i) "**Desk**" shall be a subdivision of a Station whereby two (2) or more persons, to a maximum of thirty (30) people function according to some technical function and mandate; and

   (ii) "**Station**" shall be a subdivision of a Chapter whereby six (6) or more people, to a maximum of one hundred and twenty (120) people function according to some technical function and mandate; and

   (iii) "**Chapter**" shall be a primary division of a Secretariat of Officers, Agents and Contractors employed within the structure.

Article 95 – Clean Energy, Water & Infrastructure Systems

1. "**Clean Energy, Water & Infrastructure Systems**" shall be one of the eight (8) Primary Systems of the Union. The good management and effective control of all aspects of energy, water and infrastructure within the jurisdiction of the Union shall be vested in a permanent statutory authority known as the "**Clean Energy, Water & Infrastructure Systems Agency**" or "**CEWISA**". Clean Energy, Water & Infrastructure Systems

2. All existing and new laws providing for Clean Energy, Water & Infrastructure responsibility throughout the Union shall be subject to inclusion in the *Energy Code*, *Infrastructure Code* and *Environment* Clean Energy, Water & Infrastructure Laws

Code.

3. A Code of Rights shall be formed to encapsulate all essential knowledge of rights bestowed by the living law regarding Clean Energy, Water & Infrastructure that may be easily read and recited as an affirmation of rights, or claim of rights as required, by any man or woman from the age of twelve (12) or older. Code of Rights

   It shall be a requirement for all men, women, companies and other entities associated with Clean Energy, Water & Infrastructure and the Union to demonstrate a regular written and recited comprehension and acknowledgement of the Code of Rights for Clean Energy, Water & Infrastructure.

4. A Code of Conduct shall be formed to embody all essential knowledge of living law regarding Clean Energy, Water & Infrastructure that may be easily read and recited as oath as required, by any man or woman from the age of twelve (12) or older. Code of Conduct

   It shall be a requirement for all men, women, companies and other entities associated with Clean Energy, Water & Infrastructure and the Union to demonstrate a regular written and recited comprehension and acknowledgement of the Code of Conduct; and for the Code of Conduct to be a conditional of employment and documentation of all Officers and Agents.

Article 96 – Building, Construction & Facilities Management Systems

1. "**Building, Construction & Facilities Management Systems**" shall be one of the eight (8) Primary Systems of the Union. The good management and effective control of all aspects of building, construction and facilities management within the jurisdiction of the Union shall be vested in a permanent statutory authority known as the "**Building, Construction & Facilities Management Systems Agency**" or "**BCFMSA**". Building, Construction & Facilities Management Systems

2. All existing and new laws providing for Building, Construction & Facilities Management responsibility throughout the Union shall be subject to inclusion in the *Building & Construction Code*. Building, Construction & Facilities Management Laws

3. A Code of Rights shall be formed to encapsulate all essential knowledge of rights bestowed by the living law regarding Building, Construction & Facilities Management that may be easily read and recited as an affirmation of rights, or claim of rights as required, by any man or woman from the age of twelve (12) or older. Code of Rights

   It shall be a requirement for all men, women, companies and other

entities associated with Building, Construction & Facilities Management and the Union to demonstrate a regular written and recited comprehension and acknowledgement of the Code of Rights for Building, Construction & Facilities Management.

4. A Code of Conduct shall be formed to embody all essential knowledge of living law regarding Building, Construction & Facilities Management that may be easily read and recited as oath as required, by any man or woman from the age of twelve (12) or older. Code of Conduct

It shall be a requirement for all men, women, companies and other entities associated with Building, Construction & Facilities Management and the Union to demonstrate a regular written and recited comprehension and acknowledgement of the Code of Conduct; and for the Code of Conduct to be a conditional of employment and documentation of all Officers and Agents.

Article 97 – Harmonic Agriculture & Organic Systems

1. "**Harmonic Agriculture & Organic Systems**" shall be one of the eight (8) Primary Systems of the Union. The good management and effective control of all aspects of agriculture and organic primary food production within the jurisdiction of the Union shall be vested in a permanent statutory authority known as the "**Harmonic Agriculture & Organic Systems Agency**" or "**HAOSA**". Harmonic Agriculture & Organic Systems

2. All existing and new laws providing for Harmonic Agriculture & Organic Systems responsibility throughout the Union shall be subject to inclusion in the *Agriculture Code*. Harmonic Agriculture & Organic System Laws

3. A Code of Rights shall be formed to encapsulate all essential knowledge of rights bestowed by the living law regarding Harmonic Agriculture & Organic Systems that may be easily read and recited as an affirmation of rights, or claim of rights as required, by any man or woman from the age of twelve (12) or older. Code of Rights

It shall be a requirement for all men, women, companies and other entities associated with Harmonic Agriculture & Organic Systems and the Union to demonstrate a regular written and recited comprehension and acknowledgement of the Code of Rights for Harmonic Agriculture & Organic Systems.

4. A Code of Conduct shall be formed to embody all essential knowledge of living law regarding Harmonic Agriculture & Organic Systems that may be easily read and recited as oath as required, by any man or woman from the age of twelve (12) or older. Code of Conduct

It shall be a requirement for all men, women, companies and other

entities associated with Harmonic Agriculture & Organic Systems and the Union to demonstrate a regular written and recited comprehension and acknowledgement of the Code of Conduct; and for the Code of Conduct to be a conditional of employment and documentation of all Officers and Agents.

Article 98 – Ethical Food & Therapeutic Systems

1. "**Ethical Food & Therapeutic Systems**" shall be one of the eight (8) Primary Systems of the Union. The good management and effective control of all aspects of food manufacture, food processing, therapeutic drugs manufacture and administration within the jurisdiction of the Union shall be vested in a permanent statutory authority known as the "**Ethical Food & Therapeutic Systems Agency**" or "**EFTSA**". Ethical Food & Therapeutic Systems

2. All existing and new laws providing for Ethical Food & Therapeutic Systems responsibility throughout the Union shall be subject to inclusion in the *Food & Drugs Code* and *Fitness & Health Code*. Ethical Food & Therapeutic System laws

3. A Code of Rights shall be formed to encapsulate all essential knowledge of rights bestowed by the living law regarding Ethical Food & Therapeutic Systems that may be easily read and recited as an affirmation of rights, or claim of rights as required, by any man or woman from the age of twelve (12) or older. Code of Rights

   It shall be a requirement for all men, women, companies and other entities associated with Ethical Food & Therapeutic Systems and the Union to demonstrate a regular written and recited comprehension and acknowledgement of the Code of Rights for Ethical Food & Therapeutic Systems.

4. A Code of Conduct shall be formed to embody all essential knowledge of living law regarding Ethical Food & Therapeutic Systems that may be easily read and recited as oath as required, by any man or woman from the age of twelve (12) or older. Code of Conduct

   It shall be a requirement for all men, women, companies and other entities associated with Ethical Food & Therapeutic Systems and the Union to demonstrate a regular written and recited comprehension and acknowledgement of the Code of Conduct; and for the Code of Conduct to be a conditional of employment and documentation of all Officers and Agents.

Article 99 – Environmental Protection & Preservation Systems

1. "**Environmental Protection and Preservation Systems**" shall Environmental

be one of the eight (8) Primary Systems of the Union. The good management and effective control of all aspects of environmental protection, wildlife, fishing, endangered species and natural eco-system preservation and rehabilitation within the jurisdiction of the Union shall be vested in a permanent statutory authority known as the "**Environmental Protection and Preservation Systems Agency**" or "**EPPSA**". Protection and Preservation Systems

2. All existing and new laws providing for Environmental Protection and Preservation Systems responsibility throughout the Union shall be subject to inclusion in the *Environment Code*. Environmental Protection and Preservation System Laws

3. A Code of Rights shall be formed to encapsulate all essential knowledge of rights bestowed by the living law regarding Environmental Protection and Preservation Systems that may be easily read and recited as an affirmation of rights, or claim of rights as required, by any man or woman from the age of twelve (12) or older. Code of Rights

   It shall be a requirement for all men, women, companies and other entities associated with Environmental Protection and Preservation Systems and the Union to demonstrate a regular written and recited comprehension and acknowledgement of the Code of Rights for Environmental Protection and Preservation Systems.

4. A Code of Conduct shall be formed to embody all essential knowledge of living law regarding Environmental Protection and Preservation Systems that may be easily read and recited as oath as required, by any man or woman from the age of twelve (12) or older. Code of Conduct

   It shall be a requirement for all men, women, companies and other entities associated with Environmental Protection and Preservation Systems and the Union to demonstrate a regular written and recited comprehension and acknowledgement of the Code of Conduct; and for the Code of Conduct to be a conditional of employment and documentation of all Officers and Agents.

Article 100 – Disease Prevention & Sanitation Systems

1. "**Disease Prevention & Sanitation Systems**" shall be one of the eight (8) Primary Systems of the Union. The good management and effective control of all aspects of waste management, sanitation, disease prevention, immunity and control research within the jurisdiction of the Union shall be vested in a permanent statutory authority known as the "**Disease Prevention & Sanitation Systems Agency**" or "**DPSSA**". Disease Prevention & Sanitation Systems

2. All existing and new laws providing for Disease Prevention & Disease Prevention &

Sanitation Systems responsibility throughout the Union shall be subject to inclusion in the *Disease Prevention & Sanitation Code.* Sanitation System Laws

3. A Code of Rights shall be formed to encapsulate all essential knowledge of rights bestowed by the living law regarding Disease Prevention & Sanitation Systems that may be easily read and recited as an affirmation of rights, or claim of rights as required, by any man or woman from the age of twelve (12) or older. Code of Rights

   It shall be a requirement for all men, women, companies and other entities associated with Disease Prevention & Sanitation Systems and the Union to demonstrate a regular written and recited comprehension and acknowledgement of the Code of Rights for Disease Prevention & Sanitation Systems.

4. A Code of Conduct shall be formed to embody all essential knowledge of living law regarding Disease Prevention & Sanitation Systems that may be easily read and recited as oath as required, by any man or woman from the age of twelve (12) or older. Code of Conduct

   It shall be a requirement for all men, women, companies and other entities associated with Disease Prevention & Sanitation Systems and the Union to demonstrate a regular written and recited comprehension and acknowledgement of the Code of Conduct; and for the Code of Conduct to be a conditional of employment and documentation of all Officers and Agents.

Article 101 – Security & Emergency Systems

1. "**Security & Emergency Systems**" shall be one of the eight (8) Primary Systems of the Union. The good management and effective control of all aspects of security, defence, threat investigation and assessment, counter-measures and emergency systems within the jurisdiction of the Union shall be vested in a permanent statutory authority known as the "**Security & Emergency Systems Agency**" or "**SESA**". Security & Emergency Systems

2. All existing and new laws providing for Security & Emergency Systems responsibility throughout the Union shall be subject to inclusion in the *Emergency Code, Executive Code, Police Code* and *Military Code.* Security & Emergency Laws

3. A Code of Rights shall be formed to encapsulate all essential knowledge of rights bestowed by the living law regarding Security & Emergency Systems that may be easily read and recited as an affirmation of rights, or claim of rights as required, by any man or woman from the age of twelve (12) or older. Code of Rights

   It shall be a requirement for all men, women, companies and other

entities associated with Security & Emergency Systems and the Union to demonstrate a regular written and recited comprehension and acknowledgement of the Code of Rights for Security & Emergency Systems.

4. A Code of Conduct shall be formed to embody all essential knowledge of living law regarding Security & Emergency Systems that may be easily read and recited as oath as required, by any man or woman from the age of twelve (12) or older. Code of Conduct

It shall be a requirement for all men, women, companies and other entities associated with Security & Emergency Systems and the Union to demonstrate a regular written and recited comprehension and acknowledgement of the Code of Conduct; and for the Code of Conduct to be a conditional of employment and documentation of all Officers and Agents.

Article 102 – Advanced Elements & Materials Production Systems

1. "**Advanced Elements & Materials Production Systems**" shall be one of the eight (8) Primary Systems of the Union. The good management and effective control of all aspects of advanced elementary particles production and advanced primary materials production within the jurisdiction of the Union shall be vested in a permanent statutory authority known as the "**Advanced Elements & Materials Production Systems Agency**" or "**AEMPSA**". Advanced Elements & Materials Production Systems

2. All existing and new laws providing for Advanced Elements & Materials Production Systems responsibility throughout the Union shall be subject to inclusion in the *Technology Code* and *Industry Code*. Advanced Elements & Materials Production Laws

3. A Code of Rights shall be formed to encapsulate all essential knowledge of rights bestowed by the living law regarding Advanced Elements & Materials Production Systems that may be easily read and recited as an affirmation of rights, or claim of rights as required, by any man or woman from the age of twelve (12) or older. Code of Rights

It shall be a requirement for all men, women, companies and other entities associated with Building, Construction & Facilities Management and the Union to demonstrate a regular written and recited comprehension and acknowledgement of the Code of Rights for Advanced Elements & Materials Production Systems.

4. A Code of Conduct shall be formed to embody all essential knowledge of living law regarding Advanced Elements & Materials Production Systems that may be easily read and recited as oath as required, by any Code of Conduct

man or woman from the age of twelve (12) or older.

It shall be a requirement for all men, women, companies and other entities associated with Advanced Elements & Materials Production Systems and the Union to demonstrate a regular written and recited comprehension and acknowledgement of the Code of Conduct; and for the Code of Conduct to be a conditional of employment and documentation of all Officers and Agents.

Article 103 – Logistics, Transport & Space Systems

1. "**Logistics, Transport & Space Systems**" shall be one of the four (4) Industry Systems of the Union. The good management and effective control of all aspects of logistics, storage, cargo, warehousing, transport and space within the jurisdiction of the Union shall be vested in a permanent statutory authority known as the "**Logistics, Transport & Space Systems Agency**" or "**LTSSA**". Logistics, Transport & Space Systems

2. All existing and new laws providing for Logistics, Transport & Space Systems responsibility throughout the Union shall be subject to inclusion in the *Transport & Travel Code* and *Technology Code*. Logistics, Transport & Space Laws

3. A Code of Rights shall be formed to encapsulate all essential knowledge of rights bestowed by the living law regarding Logistics, Transport & Space Systems that may be easily read and recited as an affirmation of rights, or claim of rights as required, by any man or woman from the age of twelve (12) or older. Code of Rights

   It shall be a requirement for all men, women, companies and other entities associated with Logistics, Transport & Space Systems and the Union to demonstrate a regular written and recited comprehension and acknowledgement of the Code of Rights for Logistics, Transport & Space Systems.

4. A Code of Conduct shall be formed to embody all essential knowledge of living law regarding Logistics, Transport & Space Systems that may be easily read and recited as oath as required, by any man or woman from the age of twelve (12) or older. Code of Conduct

   It shall be a requirement for all men, women, companies and other entities associated with Logistics, Transport & Space Systems and the Union to demonstrate a regular written and recited comprehension and acknowledgement of the Code of Conduct; and for the Code of Conduct to be a conditional of employment and documentation of all Officers and Agents.

Article 104 – Industry, Innovation & Workflow Systems

1. "**Industry, Innovation & Workflow Systems**" shall be one of the four (4) Industry Systems of the Union. The good management and effective control of all aspects of industry innovation, tariffs, protections and incubator programs, economic zones, supply chain innovation and improvement, import replacement businesses and workflow systems within the jurisdiction of the Union shall be vested in a permanent statutory authority known as the "**Industry, Innovation & Workflow Systems Agency**" or "**IIWSA**". Industry, Innovation & Workflow Systems

2. All existing and new laws providing for Industry, Innovation & Workflow Systems responsibility throughout the Union shall be subject to inclusion in the *Industry Code, Education Code* and *Employment Code*. Industry, Innovation & Workflow Laws

3. A Code of Rights shall be formed to encapsulate all essential knowledge of rights bestowed by the living law regarding Industry, Innovation & Workflow Systems that may be easily read and recited as an affirmation of rights, or claim of rights as required, by any man or woman from the age of twelve (12) or older. Code of Rights

   It shall be a requirement for all men, women, companies and other entities associated with Industry, Innovation & Workflow Systems and the Union to demonstrate a regular written and recited comprehension and acknowledgement of the Code of Rights for Industry, Innovation & Workflow Systems.

4. A Code of Conduct shall be formed to embody all essential knowledge of living law regarding Industry, Innovation & Workflow Systems that may be easily read and recited as oath as required, by any man or woman from the age of twelve (12) or older. Code of Conduct

   It shall be a requirement for all men, women, companies and other entities associated with Industry, Innovation & Workflow Systems and the Union to demonstrate a regular written and recited comprehension and acknowledgement of the Code of Conduct; and for the Code of Conduct to be a conditional of employment and documentation of all Officers and Agents.

Article 105 – Communications, Networks & Media Systems

1. "**Communications, Networks & Media Systems**" shall be one of the four (4) Industry Systems of the Union. The good management and effective control of all aspects of communications and computing networks, software industry, media and entertainment industry and related content and distribution networks within the jurisdiction of the Union shall be vested in a permanent statutory authority known as the "**Communications, Networks & Media Systems Agency**" or Communications, Networks & Media Systems

"**CNMSA**".

2. All existing and new laws providing for Communications, Networks & Media Systems responsibility throughout the Union shall be subject to inclusion in the *Data Networks & Media Code, Knowledge & Standards Code* and *Technology Code*. — Communications, Networks & Media Laws

3. A Code of Rights shall be formed to encapsulate all essential knowledge of rights bestowed by the living law regarding Communications, Networks & Media Systems that may be easily read and recited as an affirmation of rights, or claim of rights as required, by any man or woman from the age of twelve (12) or older. — Code of Rights

   It shall be a requirement for all men, women, companies and other entities associated with Communications, Networks & Media Systems and the Union to demonstrate a regular written and recited comprehension and acknowledgement of the Code of Rights for Communications, Networks & Media Systems.

4. A Code of Conduct shall be formed to embody all essential knowledge of living law regarding Communications, Networks & Media Systems that may be easily read and recited as oath as required, by any man or woman from the age of twelve (12) or older. — Code of Conduct

   It shall be a requirement for all men, women, companies and other entities associated with Communications, Networks & Media Systems and the Union to demonstrate a regular written and recited comprehension and acknowledgement of the Code of Conduct; and for the Code of Conduct to be a conditional of employment and documentation of all Officers and Agents.

Article 106 – Technology Development & Research Systems

1. "**Technology Development & Research Systems**" shall be one of the four (4) Industry Systems of the Union. The good management and effective control of all aspects of technology development, invention and research within the jurisdiction of the Union shall be vested in a permanent statutory authority known as the "**Technology Development & Research Systems Agency**" or "**TDRSA**". — Technology Development & Research Systems

2. All existing and new laws providing for Technology Development & Research Systems responsibility throughout the Union shall be subject to inclusion in the *Technology Code*. — Technology Development & Research Laws

3. A Code of Rights shall be formed to encapsulate all essential knowledge of rights bestowed by the living law regarding Technology Development & Research Systems that may be easily read and recited as an affirmation of rights, or claim of rights as required, by any man — Code of Rights

or woman from the age of twelve (12) or older.

It shall be a requirement for all men, women, companies and other entities associated with Technology Development & Research Systems and the Union to demonstrate a regular written and recited comprehension and acknowledgement of the Code of Rights for Technology Development & Research Systems.

4. A Code of Conduct shall be formed to embody all essential knowledge of living law regarding Technology Development & Research Systems that may be easily read and recited as oath as required, by any man or woman from the age of twelve (12) or older. Code of Conduct

It shall be a requirement for all men, women, companies and other entities associated with Technology Development & Research Systems and the Union to demonstrate a regular written and recited comprehension and acknowledgement of the Code of Conduct; and for the Code of Conduct to be a conditional of employment and documentation of all Officers and Agents.

Article 107 – Member Support Services & Charitable Systems

1. "**Member Support Services & Charitable Systems**" shall be one of the ten (10) Service Systems of the Union. The good management and effective control of all aspects of member support services and member related charitable systems within the jurisdiction of the Union shall be vested in a permanent statutory authority known as the "**Member Support Services & Charitable Systems Agency**" or "**MSSCSA**". Member Support Services & Charitable Systems

2. All existing and new laws providing for Member Support Services & Charitable Systems responsibility throughout the Union shall be subject to inclusion in the *Civil Code* and *Temporary Assistance Code*. Member Support Services & Charitable System Laws

3. A Code of Rights shall be formed to encapsulate all essential knowledge of rights bestowed by the living law regarding Member Support Services & Charitable Systems that may be easily read and recited as an affirmation of rights, or claim of rights as required, by any man or woman from the age of twelve (12) or older. Code of Rights

It shall be a requirement for all men, women, companies and other entities associated with Member Support Services & Charitable Systems and the Union to demonstrate a regular written and recited comprehension and acknowledgement of the Code of Rights for Member Support Services & Charitable Systems.

4. A Code of Conduct shall be formed to embody all essential knowledge of living law regarding Member Support Services & Charitable Systems Code of Conduct

that may be easily read and recited as oath as required, by any man or woman from the age of twelve (12) or older.

It shall be a requirement for all men, women, companies and other entities associated with Member Support Services & Charitable Systems and the Union to demonstrate a regular written and recited comprehension and acknowledgement of the Code of Conduct; and for the Code of Conduct to be a conditional of employment and documentation of all Officers and Agents.

Article 108 – Knowledge and Intellectual Property Systems

1. "**Knowledge and Intellectual Property Systems**" shall be one of the ten (10) Service Systems of the Union. The good management and effective control of all aspects of digital and print related knowledge and intellectual property registration and protection within the jurisdiction of the Union shall be vested in a permanent statutory authority known as the "**Knowledge and Intellectual Property Systems Agency**" or "**KIPSA**". Knowledge and Intellectual Property Systems

2. All existing and new laws providing for Knowledge and Intellectual Property Systems responsibility throughout the Union shall be subject to inclusion in the *Knowledge & Standards Code, Trade & Intellectual Property Code* and *Education Code*. Knowledge and Intellectual Property Laws

3. A Code of Rights shall be formed to encapsulate all essential knowledge of rights bestowed by the living law regarding Knowledge and Intellectual Property Systems that may be easily read and recited as an affirmation of rights, or claim of rights as required, by any man or woman from the age of twelve (12) or older. Code of Rights

   It shall be a requirement for all men, women, companies and other entities associated with Knowledge and Intellectual Property Systems and the Union to demonstrate a regular written and recited comprehension and acknowledgement of the Code of Rights for Knowledge and Intellectual Property Systems.

4. A Code of Conduct shall be formed to embody all essential knowledge of living law regarding Knowledge and Intellectual Property Systems that may be easily read and recited as oath as required, by any man or woman from the age of twelve (12) or older. Code of Conduct

   It shall be a requirement for all men, women, companies and other entities associated with Knowledge and Intellectual Property Systems and the Union to demonstrate a regular written and recited comprehension and acknowledgement of the Code of Conduct; and for the Code of Conduct to be a conditional of employment and documentation of all Officers and Agents.

Article 109 – Vocation, Skills and Productivity Systems

1. "**Vocation, Skills and Productivity Systems**" shall be one of the ten (10) Service Systems of the Union. The good management and effective control of all aspects of education and skills development, vocation and career development and productivity systems within the jurisdiction of the Union shall be vested in a permanent statutory authority known as the "**Vocation, Skills and Productivity Systems Agency**" or "**VSPSA**". Vocation, Skills and Productivity Systems

2. All existing and new laws providing for Vocation, Skills and Productivity Systems responsibility throughout the Union shall be subject to inclusion in the *Education Code*, *Employment Code*, *Industry Code* and *Temporary Assistance Code*. Vocation, Skills and Productivity Laws

3. A Code of Rights shall be formed to encapsulate all essential knowledge of rights bestowed by the living law regarding Vocation, Skills and Productivity Systems that may be easily read and recited as an affirmation of rights, or claim of rights as required, by any man or woman from the age of twelve (12) or older. Code of Rights

   It shall be a requirement for all men, women, companies and other entities associated with Vocation, Skills and Productivity Systems and the Union to demonstrate a regular written and recited comprehension and acknowledgement of the Code of Rights for Vocation, Skills and Productivity Systems.

4. A Code of Conduct shall be formed to embody all essential knowledge of living law regarding Vocation, Skills and Productivity Systems that may be easily read and recited as oath as required, by any man or woman from the age of twelve (12) or older. Code of Conduct

   It shall be a requirement for all men, women, companies and other entities associated with Vocation, Skills and Productivity Systems and the Union to demonstrate a regular written and recited comprehension and acknowledgement of the Code of Conduct; and for the Code of Conduct to be a conditional of employment and documentation of all Officers and Agents.

Article 110 – Market Solutions and Settlement Systems

1. "**Market Solutions and Settlement Systems**" shall be one of the ten (10) Service Systems of the Union. The good management and effective control of all aspects of markets, trading, exchange and settlements within the jurisdiction of the Union shall be vested in a Market Solutions and Settlement Systems

permanent statutory authority known as the "**Market Solutions and Settlement Systems Agency**" or "**MSSSA**".

2. All existing and new laws providing for Market Solutions and Settlement Systems responsibility throughout the Union shall be subject to inclusion in the *Company Code, Banking & Finance Code, Trade & Intellectual Property Code* and *Revenue Code.* Market Solutions and Settlement System Laws

3. A Code of Rights shall be formed to encapsulate all essential knowledge of rights bestowed by the living law regarding Market Solutions and Settlement Systems that may be easily read and recited as an affirmation of rights, or claim of rights as required, by any man or woman from the age of twelve (12) or older. Code of Rights

It shall be a requirement for all men, women, companies and other entities associated with Market Solutions and Settlement Systems and the Union to demonstrate a regular written and recited comprehension and acknowledgement of the Code of Rights for Market Solutions and Settlement Systems.

4. A Code of Conduct shall be formed to embody all essential knowledge of living law regarding Market Solutions and Settlement Systems that may be easily read and recited as oath as required, by any man or woman from the age of twelve (12) or older. Code of Conduct

It shall be a requirement for all men, women, companies and other entities associated with Market Solutions and Settlement Systems and the Union to demonstrate a regular written and recited comprehension and acknowledgement of the Code of Conduct; and for the Code of Conduct to be a conditional of employment and documentation of all Officers and Agents.

Article 111 – Arts, Culture & Creative Systems

1. "**Arts, Culture & Creative Systems**" shall be one of the ten (10) Service Systems of the Union. The good management and effective control of all aspects of arts, culture and entertainment and its administration within the jurisdiction of the Union shall be vested in a permanent statutory authority known as the "**Arts, Culture & Creative Systems Agency**" or "**ACCSA**". Arts, Culture & Creative Systems

2. All existing and new laws providing for Arts, Culture & Creative Systems responsibility throughout the Union shall be subject to inclusion in the *Knowledge & Standards Code, Culture & Entertainment Code, Trade & Intellectual Property Code, Technology Code* and *Data Networks & Media Code.* Arts, Culture & Creative Laws

3. A Code of Rights shall be formed to encapsulate all essential Code of Rights knowledge of rights bestowed by the living law regarding Arts, Culture & Creative Systems that may be easily read and recited as an affirmation of rights, or claim of rights as required, by any man or woman from the age of twelve (12) or older.

It shall be a requirement for all men, women, companies and other entities associated with Arts, Culture & Creative Systems and the Union to demonstrate a regular written and recited comprehension and acknowledgement of the Code of Rights for Arts, Culture & Creative Systems.

4. A Code of Conduct shall be formed to embody all essential knowledge of living law regarding Arts, Culture & Creative Systems that may be easily read and recited as oath as required, by any man or woman from the age of twelve (12) or older. Code of Conduct

It shall be a requirement for all men, women, companies and other entities associated with Arts, Culture & Creative Systems and the Union to demonstrate a regular written and recited comprehension and acknowledgement of the Code of Conduct; and for the Code of Conduct to be a conditional of employment and documentation of all Officers and Agents.

Article 112 – Health Support & Wellbeing Systems

1. "**Health Support & Wellbeing Systems**" shall be one of the ten (10) Service Systems of the Union. The good management and effective control of all aspects of health systems, hospitals and clinics; and professional registration, regulation, fees and oversight; and health insurance and cost oversight and management; and therapeutic well being systems within the jurisdiction of the Union shall be vested in a permanent statutory authority known as the "**Health Support & Wellbeing Systems Agency**" or "**HSWSA**". Health Support & Wellbeing Systems

2. All existing and new laws providing for Health Support & Wellbeing Systems responsibility throughout the Union shall be subject to inclusion in the *Fitness & Health Code* and *Food & Drugs Code.* Health Support & Wellbeing Laws

3. A Code of Rights shall be formed to encapsulate all essential knowledge of rights bestowed by the living law regarding Health Support & Wellbeing Systems that may be easily read and recited as an affirmation of rights, or claim of rights as required, by any man or woman from the age of twelve (12) or older. Code of Rights

It shall be a requirement for all men, women, companies and other entities associated with Health Support & Wellbeing Systems and the Union to demonstrate a regular written and recited comprehension and acknowledgement of the Code of Rights for Health Support & Wellbeing Systems.

4. A Code of Conduct shall be formed to embody all essential knowledge of living law regarding Health Support & Wellbeing Systems that may be easily read and recited as oath as required, by any man or woman from the age of twelve (12) or older. Code of Conduct

It shall be a requirement for all men, women, companies and other entities associated with Health Support & Wellbeing Systems and the Union to demonstrate a regular written and recited comprehension and acknowledgement of the Code of Conduct; and for the Code of Conduct to be a conditional of employment and documentation of all Officers and Agents.

Article 113 – Banking, Finance and Revenue Systems

1. "**Banking, Finance and Revenue Systems**" shall be one of the ten (10) Service Systems of the Union. The good management and effective control of all aspects of banking regulation and oversight, finance and accounting, taxation and revenue within the jurisdiction of the Union shall be vested in a permanent statutory authority known as the "**Banking, Finance and Revenue Systems Agency**" or "**BFRSA**". Banking, Finance and Revenue Systems

2. All existing and new laws providing for Banking, Finance and Revenue Systems responsibility throughout the Union shall be subject to inclusion in the *Banking & Finance Code*, *Budget & Accounting Management Code* and *Revenue Code*. Banking, Finance and Revenue Laws

3. A Code of Rights shall be formed to encapsulate all essential knowledge of rights bestowed by the living law regarding Banking, Finance and Revenue Systems that may be easily read and recited as an affirmation of rights, or claim of rights as required, by any man or woman from the age of twelve (12) or older. Code of Rights

It shall be a requirement for all men, women, companies and other entities associated with Banking, Finance and Revenue Systems and the Union to demonstrate a regular written and recited comprehension and acknowledgement of the Code of Rights for Banking, Finance and Revenue Systems.

4. A Code of Conduct shall be formed to embody all essential knowledge of living law regarding Banking, Finance and Revenue Systems that may be easily read and recited as oath as required, by any man or woman from the age of twelve (12) or older. Code of Conduct

It shall be a requirement for all men, women, companies and other

entities associated with Banking, Finance and Revenue Systems and the Union to demonstrate a regular written and recited comprehension and acknowledgement of the Code of Conduct; and for the Code of Conduct to be a conditional of employment and documentation of all Officers and Agents.

Article 114 – Justice & Legal Support Systems

1. "**Justice & Legal Support Systems**" shall be one of the ten (10) Service Systems of the Union. The good management and effective control of all aspects of justice, courts, police and sheriffs, investigations, prosecutions, prisons and legal support within the jurisdiction of the Union shall be vested in a permanent statutory authority known as the "**Justice & Legal Support Systems Agency**" or "**JLSSA**". Justice & Legal Support Systems

2. All existing and new laws providing for Justice & Legal Support Systems responsibility throughout the Union shall be subject to inclusion in the *Judicial Code, Criminal Code, Prison Code, Police Code* and *Military Code*. Justice & Legal Support Laws

3. A Code of Rights shall be formed to encapsulate all essential knowledge of rights bestowed by the living law regarding Justice & Legal Support Systems that may be easily read and recited as an affirmation of rights, or claim of rights as required, by any man or woman from the age of twelve (12) or older. Code of Rights

   It shall be a requirement for all men, women, companies and other entities associated with Justice & Legal Support Systems and the Union to demonstrate a regular written and recited comprehension and acknowledgement of the Code of Rights for Justice & Legal Support Systems.

4. A Code of Conduct shall be formed to embody all essential knowledge of living law regarding Justice & Legal Support Systems that may be easily read and recited as oath as required, by any man or woman from the age of twelve (12) or older. Code of Conduct

   It shall be a requirement for all men, women, companies and other entities associated with Justice & Legal Support Systems and the Union to demonstrate a regular written and recited comprehension and acknowledgement of the Code of Conduct; and for the Code of Conduct to be a conditional of employment and documentation of all Officers and Agents.

Article 115 – Administrative Support & Electoral Systems

1. "**Administrative Support & Electoral Systems**" shall be one of the ten (10) Service Systems of the Union. The good management and effective control of all aspects of administrative and public services; and electoral systems within the jurisdiction of the Union shall be vested in a permanent statutory authority known as the "**Administrative Support & Electoral Systems Agency**" or "**ASESA**". Administrative Support & Electoral Systems

2. All existing and new laws providing for Administrative Support & Electoral Systems responsibility throughout the Union shall be subject to inclusion in the *Service Code* and *Elections Code*. Administrative Support & Electoral System Laws

3. A Code of Rights shall be formed to encapsulate all essential knowledge of rights bestowed by the living law regarding Administrative Support & Electoral Systems that may be easily read and recited as an affirmation of rights, or claim of rights as required, by any man or woman from the age of twelve (12) or older. Code of Rights

   It shall be a requirement for all men, women, companies and other entities associated with Administrative Support & Electoral Systems and the Union to demonstrate a regular written and recited comprehension and acknowledgement of the Code of Rights for Administrative Support & Electoral Systems.

4. A Code of Conduct shall be formed to embody all essential knowledge of living law regarding Administrative Support & Electoral Systems that may be easily read and recited as oath as required, by any man or woman from the age of twelve (12) or older. Code of Conduct

   It shall be a requirement for all men, women, companies and other entities associated with Administrative Support & Electoral Systems and the Union to demonstrate a regular written and recited comprehension and acknowledgement of the Code of Conduct; and for the Code of Conduct to be a conditional of employment and documentation of all Officers and Agents.

Article 116 – Entities, Agreements & Securities Systems

1. "**Entities, Agreements & Securities Systems**" shall be one of the ten (10) Service Systems of the Union. The good management and effective control of all aspects of company, association and trust registration, corporate compliance; and agreements, deeds and contracts registration; and securities registration and trading compliance within the jurisdiction of the Union shall be vested in a permanent statutory authority known as the "**Entities, Agreements & Securities Systems Agency**" or "**EASSA**". Entities, Agreements & Securities Systems

2. All existing and new laws providing for Entities, Agreements & Securities Systems responsibility throughout the Union shall be subject to inclusion in the *Company Code, Trade & Intellectual Property Code, Banking & Finance Code* and *Budget & Accounting Management Code.* Entities, Agreements & Securities Laws

3. A Code of Rights shall be formed to encapsulate all essential knowledge of rights bestowed by the living law regarding Entities, Agreements & Securities Systems that may be easily read and recited as an affirmation of rights, or claim of rights as required, by any man or woman from the age of twelve (12) or older. Code of Rights

   It shall be a requirement for all men, women, companies and other entities associated with Entities, Agreements & Securities Systems and the Union to demonstrate a regular written and recited comprehension and acknowledgement of the Code of Rights for Entities, Agreements & Securities Systems.

4. A Code of Conduct shall be formed to embody all essential knowledge of living law regarding Entities, Agreements & Securities Systems that may be easily read and recited as oath as required, by any man or woman from the age of twelve (12) or older. Code of Conduct

   It shall be a requirement for all men, women, companies and other entities associated with Entities, Agreements & Securities Systems and the Union to demonstrate a regular written and recited comprehension and acknowledgement of the Code of Conduct; and for the Code of Conduct to be a conditional of employment and documentation of all Officers and Agents.

TITLE XI: EXECUTIVE GOVERNMENT

Article 117 – Executive Government

1. The Sunedrion, representing the supreme council of seven Great Offices of the Union, is the sole Executive Government of the Union. All Executive Authority of the Union is vested in the Sunedrion. Executive Government

2. The principal officer in each of the Executive Departments and Agencies, and all persons connected with the diplomatic service, may be removed from office at the pleasure of the Sunedrion. All other civil officers of the Executive Departments may be removed at any time by the Sunedrion, or other appointing power, when their services are unnecessary, or for dishonesty, incapacity, misconduct, or gross neglect of duty; and when so removed, the removal shall be reported to the Synod, together with the reasons therefore. Additional Powers

3. The Sunedrion shall function according to the fundamental principle of Separation of Powers, whereby the Sunedrion shall be considered a co-equal branch of the government of the Union with the Synod and Basilica:- Separation of Powers

    (i) The primary responsibility of the executive is the proper governance of the Union through the fair execution and equal enforcement of the laws of the Union; and

    (ii) It is not the responsibility nor the fundamental powers of the Sunedrion to usurp the powers of the legislature and assume the formation of original pronouncements, orders or edicts to circumvent legislative authority.

Article 118 – Executive Code of Conduct

1. The Executive Code of Conduct shall be ten (10) canons whereby all men or women appointed to any trusted position of Great Office of the Union and member of the Sunedrion shall hold and perform their duties. Executive Code of Conduct

    The ten canons of the Executive Code of Conduct must feature prominently in all official documents, and be frequently recited and pledged at important ceremonial events, including but not limited to the opening and closing of Sunedrion sessions and even significant matters of public interest.

2. The following are the Ten Canons of Executive Code of Conduct. It is to these truths and ideals that each Exarch of the Sunedrion shall hold and execute their office:- The Ten Canons of Executive Code of Conduct

    (i) We shall be firmly bound by our solemn oath of office to protect and defend the Constitutional Charter of the Union; and to do everything within our power to protect its sovereignty and integrity; and

(ii) We shall seek to perform the duties and responsibilities of our office to the best of our abilities; and

(iii) We shall execute the duties of our office without fear or favour; and

(iv) We shall uphold the integrity and independence of the Sunedrion; and

(v) We shall avoid impropriety and the appearance of impropriety; and

(vi) We shall accept no gifts, gratuities or emoluments whilst in office, other than official payments and compensations; and shall inform the Synod and transfer custody thereof, any such gifts that come into our possession; and

(vii) We shall never allow our private life, relationships or beliefs to be associated with, or influence our judgement in executive decisions; and

(viii) We shall honour our duty to upholding the essential rights of all Men and Women and the values of just society; and

(ix) We shall seek to execute leadership with care, precision and without unnecessary hesitation; and

(x) We be accessible and visible to the people, for the people, so that at all times, the members of the Union witness leadership.

Article 119 – Executive Pronouncements & Limitations

Executive Pronouncements & Limitations

1. To the extent that matters of state, emergency and public good demand executive pronouncements before legislative acts, or in support of law, the executive shall use such powers as sparingly; and in the case where law demands it, shall not usurp the Separation of Powers doctrine, by attempting to legislate through executive pronouncements.

TITLE XII: LEGISLATIVE GOVERNANCE

Article 120 – Legislative Governance

1. The Synod, representing representatives of each and every University within the bounds of the Union, is the sole Legislative Authority of the Union. All Legislative Authority of the Union is vested in the Synod. Legislative Governance

2. The Synod possesses the sole power of impeachment of any officer of the Union. When sitting for such purpose, there it shall be on oath. When a member of the Sunedrion is tried, the Basileus shall preside; and no person shall be convicted without the concurrence of two-thirds of the members present. Judgement in cases of impeachment shall not extend further than to removal from office, and disqualification to hold any office of honour, trust, or profit under the Union; but the party convicted shall, nevertheless, be liable and subject to indictment, trial, judgement, and punishment according to law. Additional Powers

   The Synod shall not be permitted to use impeachment as a weapon of intimidation or threat of coercion against any of the officers or the other branches of government; and the Synod is expressly forbidden to announce, investigate or undertake any impeachment against a sitting justice of the Basilica who finds adversely against one or more laws that contradict the present constitution, or are found to be manifestly morally repugnant to the laws of the Union.

3. The Synod shall function according to the fundamental principle of Separation of Powers, whereby the Synod shall be considered a co-equal branch of the government of the Union with the Sunedrion and Basilica:- Separation of Powers

   (i) The primary responsibility of the legislature is the proper formation and enaction of the laws of the Union; and

   (ii) It is not the responsibility nor the fundamental powers of the Synod to usurp the powers of the executive and assume the formation of original strategies or policies for legislation in contradiction or at odds with the executive; and

   (iii) Should one or more justice of the Basilica clearly and openly contradict the Separation of Powers to in effect "legislate from the bench", then the Synod has a moral and constitutional duty to investigate proceedings of impeachment to remove such justices that threaten the integrity of the power and function of the Union.

Article 121 – Legislative Code of Conduct

1. The Legislative Code of Conduct shall be ten (10) canons whereby all men or women appointed to any trusted position as a legislator and member of the Synod shall hold and perform their duties. Legislative Code of Conduct

   The ten canons of the Legislative Code of Conduct must feature prominently in all official documents, and be frequently recited and pledged at important ceremonial events, including but not limited to the opening and closing of Synod sessions and even significant matters of public interest.

2. The following are the Ten Canons of Legislative Code of Conduct. It is to these truths and ideals that a legislator shall hold and execute their office:- The Ten Canons of Legislative Code of Conduct

   (i) We shall be firmly bound by our solemn oath of office to protect and defend the Constitutional Charter of the Union; and to do everything within our power to protect its sovereignty and integrity; and

   (ii) We shall seek to perform the duties and responsibilities of our office to the best of our abilities; and without fear or favour; and

   (iii) We shall remain vigilant against the threat of influence over the legislative process by foreign and domestic enemies of the Union that through bad laws would seek to undermine its integrity and sovereignty; and

   (iv) We shall uphold the integrity and independence of the Synod and the legislative branch of government; and

   (v) We shall avoid impropriety and the appearance of impropriety; and

   (vi) We shall refrain from extra-legislative activities excepting those that seek to enhance the status of the law and administration of the Synod; and

   (vii) We shall honour our duty to upholding the essential rights of all Men and Women and the values of just society; and

   (viii) We shall protect and defend against any proposed laws that are morally repugnant and contrary to the Constitution of the Union; and

   (ix) We shall seek to bring forth just and equitable laws for all members of the Union, not just a few or some special interest;

and

(x) We shall seek to render judgement with care, precision and without delay.

Article 122 – Legislative Formation & Debate

1. Every law, or resolution having the force of law, shall relate to but one subject, and that shall be expressed in the title. Legislative Formation & Debate

2. No document shall be considered Law within the Union unless it has been approved by the appropriate juridic body of democratically elected representatives and has received the proper assent and proclamation in accord with the present Constitutional Charter and associated Covenants, Charters, Canons, Codes and Bylaws. Rule of Law

3. To the extent that juridic bodies of democratically elected representatives are permitted to create laws, there exists a logical, practical and moral limit to the number of laws that may and can be issued before the proper operation of just and fair law ceases to function from the weight, number and complexity of such laws. Laws and Right to Create Laws

   To the extent that laws can be changed, it is a reasonable conclusion that such laws will be changed and modified to some extent for expedient purposes. Thus law must balance between those elements that are permanent and extant in their nature, compared to certain elements that are more able to be modified over time.

   Therefore, it shall be the prudent responsibility of all elected officials that only laws that advance the cause of the Union consistent with the present Constitutional Charter are proposed.

4. To the extent that unjust and unfair laws are allowed to be passed, a society will divert resources and effort to work against those laws creating a distortion of resources and effort. Unjust Law

   While no force can stop democratically elected officials from constructing unjust laws, it is encumbered upon the judicial branch of the Union to see that such laws are properly struck down and made redundant through the higher courts of the organisation.

5. By the present Constitutional Charter, an offence shall be any act or intended act by an individual or group which willingly contravenes the present Constitutional Charter and associated Canons, Codes and Bylaws and any subsequent laws having been ratified and upheld by the appropriate branches of the Union. Offences against Law

   As such acts or intended acts of criminal activity themselves require definition in order to be tested, a crime shall further be defined as any crime as listed in the active statutes of the Criminal Code as passed by the appropriate legislative bodies.

Only one Criminal Code shall be created for the Union; and all branches and levels of the Union, including all formal proceedings, must use it as the basis of any hearing relating to offences.

Article 123 – Legislative Papers & Reports

1. All juridic bodies within the jurisdiction of the Union; and possessing legislative powers to make laws, must form acts and then statutes from properly commissioned papers and reports in accord with the present Constitutional Charter. *Legislative Papers & Reports*

   A Paper is a draft document initiated by the executive government of a juridic body presenting the arguments, research and case outline supporting the requirement for the creation or modification of acts and statutes.

   A Report is a draft document initiated by judicial or legislative act, presenting the arguments, research and case outline supporting some actions that may include the creation or modification of acts and statutes.

2. Under the present Constitutional Charter, certain Acts may be permitted to be presented to a legislative body without first having been Papers or Reports including (but not limited to), petitions for resolution, the appointment of officers or the endorsement of appointments and treaties. Furthermore, Acts considered matters of security may also be excluded from the requirement of being born from Papers or Reports. *Exclusion of certain Acts as Papers or Reports*

3. For a Paper or Report to be valid, it must conform to the following standards and mandatory information:- *Mandatory information required of Paper or Report*

   (i) One sentence description outlining the primary purpose of the paper or report; and

   (ii) Short abbreviated title; and

   (iii) Author or authors; and

   (iv) Sponsor/patron who is an elected member of the appropriate level of the organisation to whom the paper will be debated; and

   (v) Summary index of Specific clauses and laws, including correct reference numbers that are referenced and included in Paper or Report, including division according to those that support the

Paper and those that are in conflict/different to the Paper or Report.

4. All Papers and Reports must be published as a public document for review for at least three months prior to any Act being drafted for submission before the appropriate juridic body for a vote. The publishing and circulation of Papers and Reports

Article 124 – Legislative Acts & Statutes

1. An Act is defined as a formal submission notice to a legislative body for vote containing one or more items that upon approval shall be proclaimed either as a Statute, or as a regulation forming part of an established Juridic Person. Act

2. A Statute is an approved Act having received both majority vote in a legislative body that has then received official signed assent by a superior sovereign Authority within the limits of the established authority of the Juridic Person or Society or Body Politic. A Statute is not valid, nor shall it have any force or effect ecclesiastically, morally, lawfully or legally if it does not fully conform to these present Articles of the present Constitutional Charter. Statute

   To exercise the Union's competences the institutions shall use legal instruments, in accordance with Union laws, framework laws, regulations, decisions, recommendations and opinions.

   A Union law shall be a legislative act of general application. It shall be binding in its entirety and directly applicable in all Member States.

3. All Statutes may be categorised according to three types, defined by the authority and standing of the members of the Body Politic, the primary form of the Statute and the limits of established authority under law of the Juridic Person or Body Politic being *Ordinance*, *Regulation* and *Policy*:- Character of Statute

   (i) *Ordinance* is the highest form of Statute, promulgated through religious practice and ritual by spiritual officials under solemn vow in accord with prescribed Ecclesiastical Law and Sacred Scripture; and

   (ii) *Regulation* is the second highest form of Statute, promulgated under sovereign authority, through fiduciary procedures by fiduciary officers under solemn oath, in accord with established Sovereign Law, Ecclesiastical Law and Sacred Scripture; and

   (iii) *Policy* is the lowest form of Statute, promulgated under commissioned (agency) authority, by agents possessing commissions or licenses, in accord with their established

Bylaws.

4. All valid Statutes in the proper form of an Ordinance, or Regulation or Policy may be further defined as General or Public and Special or Private:- General and Special Nature of Statute

(i) A General or Public Statute is an universal rule, that regards the whole community. All competent forums of law and courts of the Juridic Person or Society are bound to take notice judicially and *ex officio* without the Statute having to be particularly pleaded or formally set forth as a precedent; and

(ii) A Special or Private Statute are rather exceptions than rules, being those which only operate upon particular persons, and private concerns. All competent forums of law and courts of the Juridic Person or Society are not bound to take notice, unless such Statutes are shown and pleaded.

5. All valid Statutes may be defined according to their intended purpose and effect in law being *Declaratory, Remedial, Amending, Consolidating, Disabling, Enabling, Franchise* or *Penalty*:- Primary Intention and Subject of Statute

(i) *Declaratory* is when a Statute does not profess to make any alteration to the existing body of laws, but merely to explain or declare or provide further clarity to its purpose and function; and

(ii) *Remedial* is when a Statute directly alters some existing precept, rule or principle of the body of laws of the Juridic Person, or Society; and

(iii) *Amending* is when a Statute alters or repeals or restores an existing and previously promulgated Statute (which may then also be Remedial, or Disabling or Enabling in its effect); and

(iv) *Consolidating* is when a Statute consolidates the clauses and terms of previous Statutes relating to the same subject matter (which may then also be Declaratory, or Remedial, or Disabling or Enabling in its effect); and

(v) *Disabling* is when a Statute restrains the alienation of certain Property or Rights; and

(vi) *Enabling* is when a Statute removes restrictions or disabilities pertaining to the alienation or franchising of certain Property or Rights; and

(vii) *Franchising* is when a Statute grants, or gives, or assigns or delegates certain Property and Rights; and

(viii) *Penalty* is when a Statute imposes some fine or forfeiture against some prohibited act.

6. The key elements of the form of a valid Statute are:- Formation of Statute

(i) *Legislative Act* means a Statute is created in accord with the Legislative Rules and Procedures (Rituals) of the Juridic Person, or Body Politic from which the Statute is to be issued; and

(ii) *Legislative Right* means a Statute can only be formed as a Legislative Act if it is done within the limits of the established authority and rights of the Juridic Person or Body Politic from which it is promulgated. No Statute may claim powers and rights greater than is bestowed to the Juridic Person under whose laws it is promulgated; and

(iii) *Written Law* means a Statute must be in writing and therefore must be in legible writing and printing on quality paper, parchment or vellum in accord with the Legislative Rules and Procedures (Rituals) of the Juridic Person, or Body Politic from which the Statute is to be issued; and

(iv) *Proper Jurisdiction* means a valid Statute only applies to the Jurisdiction of the Juridic Person or Body Politic under whose laws it is promulgated. No Statute may exceed the Jurisdiction and Authority of the Juridic Person or Body Politic making it; and

(v) *Proper Possession* means a valid Statute can only decree, prescribe, define, grant or convey Property which is morally and rightfully in possession and control of the Juridic Person or Body Politic. No Statute may seek to convey Property which is not in the control and possession of the Juridic Person under whose laws it is promulgated; and

(vi) *Proper Form* means a valid Statute can only decree, prescribe, define or grant certain rights or permissions or prohibitions, or repeal or amend previous Statutes if it conforms to the proper form as prescribed for an Ordinance, or Regulation or Policy. A Policy Statute cannot amend a Regulation Statute; Nor can a Regulation Statute amend an Ordinance Statute; and

(vii) *Proper Law* means a valid Statute must be framed as proper law, devoid of impossible acts, or prohibited claims, or abrogations of natural rights, or morally repugnant assertions or intentions that openly defy the Ecclesiastical Law and Sacred Scripture that is the foundation of law for the Juridic Person or

Body Politic; and

(viii) *Proper Consent* means a valid Statute by the very nature of a Legislative Act requires that the members of the Body Politic representing all members of the Society or Juridic Person consent to its promulgation as well as any Superior Authority in accord with the prescribed Legislative Rules and Procedures. A Statute devoid of proper consent is automatically null and void; and

(ix) *Proper Notice* means a valid Statute cannot have force or effect of law unless it has been promulgated and noticed to all who are charged with its enforcement and are liable to obey its conditions. A failure of Proper Notice renders a Statute null and void even if all other conditions are fully met.

Mandatory information components of an Act

7. For an Act to be valid, it must conform to the following standards and mandatory information:-

(i) One sentence description outlining the primary purpose of the Act; and

(ii) Short abbreviated title and a long formal title; and

(iii) Author or authors; and

(iv) Sponsor/patron who is an elected member of the appropriate level of the organisation to which the Act will be voted; and

(v) Summary index of Specific Charter clauses and laws, including correct reference numbers that are referenced and included in Act, including division according to those that support the Act and those that are in conflict/different to the Act; and

(vi) Summary of papers relating to the Act; and

(vii) A copy of the act or proposed regulation complying to the common law design of all legal documents as defined by annexures to this Charter.

Fundamental Rules of Statutes

8. The following are the fundamental rules, customs and principles concerning Statues:-

(i) An Act or Statute can only apply to the limits of jurisdiction of the Juridic Person that issued it. Therefore a legislative body of a corporation cannot legally or lawfully abrogate the laws of the higher estate that first created its franchise; and

(ii) An Act and Statute must reflect the proper form and procedures prescribed by law and custom relating to the Parliamentary process of enacting law; and

(iii) An Act as a sacred Ordinance cannot be abrogated by a Regulatory Act, nor can a Policy Act abrogate or repeal a Regulatory Act or sacred Ordinance; and

(iv) A valid Act of Law exists in form as a precise, brief and clear expression of the intention of Parliament in reflecting the needs and mandate of the people. Therefore, the more complex and long worded an act, or the less clear its intention, the greater chance part or all of it may be repealed by judicial review if challenged; and

(v) A proposed new Act and Statute must concern itself with one main cause whereby its clauses and divisions reflect a consistent intention; and

(vi) Acts and Statutes that possess penalties and punishments must be construed strictly; and

(vii) One part of a new Act and Statute must be able to be so construed by another part of an existing Act, that the new Act may be considered a seamless addition to the whole body of law; and

(viii) A part or whole new Act and Statute that is totally repugnant to the existing body of law is automatically void, even if approved and assented; and

(ix) Where the existing body of law and a new Act or Statute differ, the existing body of law has precedence, unless the new Act presents a considered, superior and reasoned argument to the contrary; and

(x) If an Act and Statute that repeals another, is itself repealed afterwards, the first Act and Stature is hereby revived without any formal words for that purpose; and

(xi) Acts derogatory from the power of subsequent parliaments cannot be binding; and

(xii) Acts and Statutes that seek to grant or exclude certain rights, property or uses in perpetuity, without consideration for expiry are null and void from the beginning; and

(xiii) Acts that are impossible to be performed are of no validity.

9. Member States shall adopt all measures of national law necessary to implement legally binding Union statutes and codes. Where uniform

Implementing Acts as Statutes

conditions for implementing legally binding Union acts and statutes are needed, those acts shall confer implementing powers on the Union Synod, or, in duly justified specific cases and in the cases provided for in the present Constitutional Charter, on the Systems and the Organs of the Union.

TITLE XIII: JUDICIAL GOVERNANCE

Article 125 – Judicial Governance

1. The Basilica, representing the one supreme court of the Union, is the highest Judicial Authority of the Union. All Judicial Authority of the Union is vested in the Basilica. Judicial Governance

2. The Basilica possesses the power to conduct its own investigation, review and trial for the mandatory sanction, discipline or removal of any judge, arbitrator, justice, recorder, judicial trustee or magistrate less than a member of the Basilica. Thus, the Basilica possesses the sole responsibility to ensure the judicial integrity of all judges and courts throughout the Union. Additional Powers

3. The Basilica shall function according to the fundamental principle of Separation of Powers, whereby the Basilica shall be considered a co-equal branch of the government of the Union with the Sunedrion and Synod:- Separation of Powers

   (i) The primary responsibility of the judiciary is the proper adjudication of legal disputes and the interpretation, defence and application of the laws of the Union; and

   (ii) It is not the responsibility nor the fundamental powers of the Basilica to usurp the powers of the executive and legislature, to in effect "legislate from the bench" in preparing judgements and declarations that go beyond the reasonable scope and powers of the court and instead creates new policies and law of the Union; and

   (iii) Should justices of the Basilica find one or more laws of the legislature contradict the present constitutional charter or are morally repugnant, then they have a solemn and sacred duty to render down such laws.

Article 126 – Judicial Code of Conduct

1. The Judicial Code of Conduct shall be ten (10) canons whereby all men or women appointed to any trusted position of judge, arbitrator, justice, recorder, administrator, magistrate or judicial trustee of any kind, shall hold and perform their duties. Judicial Code of Conduct

   The ten canons of the Judicial Code of Conduct must feature prominently in all official documents, and be frequently recited and pledged at important ceremonial events, including but not limited to the opening and closing of court sessions and even significant matters of public interest.

2. The following are the Ten Canons of Judicial Code of Conduct. It is to these truths and ideals that a justice shall hold and execute their office:- The Ten Canons of Judicial Code of Conduct

(i) We shall be firmly bound by our solemn oath of office to protect and defend the Constitutional Charter of the Union; and to do everything within our power to protect its sovereignty and integrity; and

(ii) We shall seek to perform the duties and responsibilities of our office to the best of our abilities; and

(iii) We shall execute the duties of our office without fear or favour; and

(iv) We shall uphold the integrity and independence of the judiciary; and

(v) We shall avoid impropriety and the appearance of impropriety; and

(vi) We shall refrain from extra-judicial activities excepting those that seek to enhance the status of the law and administration of justice; and

(vii) We shall refrain from public and political comment whilst in office; and

(viii) We shall never allow our private life, relationships or beliefs to be associated with, or influence our judgement in any matter before us; and

(ix) We shall honour our duty to upholding the essential rights of all Men and Women and the values of just society; and

(x) We shall seek to render judgement with care, precision and without delay.

Article 127 – Judicial Decrees, Precepts, Rescripts & Orders

1. It is a core function of the highest bodies of the Judiciary to protect the integrity of the proper Covenants, Charters, Maxims, Canons, Codes, Bylaws and Ordinances of the Union and to guard against immoral, repugnant, unlawful and erroneous acts by either the Executive or the Legislature. Judicial Rulings & Precedents

Thus, the Judiciary is the embodiment of the Living Law and so retains the necessary powers to overturn any Proclamation by the Executive branch and repeal any Statute by the Legislative branch, if such action is deemed necessary to uphold the proper Rule of Law, Justice and Fair Process.

Such powers as the issue of Decrees, Precepts, Prescripts and Orders of the Judiciary are to be used wisely and never to write original law, but to uphold, illuminate and confirm the essential tenets of law.

Declaratory Judgements on Maxims of Law

2. It shall be a solemn mission and obligation of the Basileus and most senior Justices of the Union to provide the wisest teaching guidance and direction as to the law to the lower courts and officials of the Union. To this end, the Basileus shall retain the power and right to issue Declaratory Judgements, without need of an original petition to be first submitted, in relation to greater explanation and instruction on topics and matters enumerated within the Divine Collection of Maxims of Law, under the most sacred Covenant *Pactum De Singularis Caelum*, including but not limited to:-

(i) The Maxims of Divine Law; and

(ii) The Maxims of Natural Law; and

(iii) The Maxims of Cognitive Law; and

(iv) The Maxims of Positive Law; and

(v) The Maxims of Ecclesiastical Law; and

(vi) The Maxims of Bioethics Law; and

(vii) The Maxims of Sovereign Law; and

(viii) The Maxims of Fiduciary Law; and

(ix) The Maxims of Administrative Law; and

(x) The Maxims of Economic Law; and

(xi) The Maxims of Monetary Law; and

(xii) The Maxims of Civil Law; and

(xiii) The Maxims of Criminal Law; and

(xiv) The Maxims of Education Law; and

(xv) The Maxims of Food & Drugs Law; and

(xvi) The Maxims of Urban Law; and

(xvii) The Maxims of Company Law; and

(xviii) The Maxims of Technology Law; and

(xix) The Maxims of Trade & Intellectual Property Law; and

(xx) The Maxims of Security Law; and

(xxi) The Maxims of Military Law; and

(xxii) The Maxims of International Law.

3. The most solemn and sacred mission of the Basileus and all Justices of the Union is to guard and defend against the corrosive effect of permitting perjury to go unpunished in public, legal and legislative process. Solemn Sacred Mission to Guard and Defend against Perjury

Perjury being the offence of false testimony as the intentional provision of false information under oath, shall always be a greater threat to the integrity, stability and function of civilised society than even the most violent and heinous crimes. If Perjury is permitted to pass unpunished or lightly punished, then all forms of testimony, public decision making and official information can be called into question.

It is a fundamental sacred obligation of the Basileus to ensure all justices and judges of the Union apply the same strict standards against perjury uniformly across the Union so that no elected official, or officer, or witness or trusted journalist may make deliberately false statements to the detriment of truth and justice.

TITLE XIV: ELECTIONS, VOTING & POLITICS

Article 128 – Elections, Voting & Political Standards

1. Elections, Voting & Political Standards are those standards pertaining to the free and fair conduct of elections, the rights of Members and methods of voting and the rules governing political associations and campaigns. Elections, Voting & Political Standards

   All election laws, voting laws and political association related laws shall originate from the foundations as enumerated within the present Constitutional Charter.

Article 129 – Elections

1. Members shall have the right to participate in the affairs and decisions of the Union. An Election is a formal system, process and record of choosing and selecting by Vote one or more candidates or propositions from a greater number of the same type offered as genuine alternatives in accord with the present Constitution. As a valid and true Election is the expression of the individual intention and will of Members, as well as their collective intention and will, a valid and true Election shall always be free, equal, fair, without compulsion, threat, inducement or intimidation. Elections

2. In accord with the principles defined herein, a single, unified and consistent Elections Code shall be formed for the Union and all associated Universities. The Elections Code shall provide a legal and functional framework for the good operation of free and fair local, regional University and multi- University elections, including (but not limited to) methods of voting, independence of vote count, ballot paper production, collection and security, candidate eligibility, party eligibility and conduct of election campaigns. All existing and new laws providing for election function and operation shall be subject to inclusion in the Elections Code as one of the thirty three (33) Codes of Law of the Union. Elections Code

3. All Members over the age of sixteen are ipso facto qualified and valid Electors for the purpose of General Elections and Referendums, unless otherwise defined or prescribed. No Member may be disqualified as a valid Elector upon the basis of race, sex, colour, religion or economic status. Members as Electors

   Members elected or appointed to the Organs of the Union shall be the Electors to such a body, subject to the present Constitution and the bylaws of the relevant entity. A Member may only participate as a valid Elector in the affairs of a particular organ, association, body, institute or entity if they are properly elected or appointed to it, consistent with its bylaws.

Article 130 – Voting

1. All Voting throughout all societies, associations, companies, agencies and bodies within the Union shall be voluntary and no body, agency, entity or person may compel any Member or group of Members to choose to vote. Voting

However, the relevant organ, body, entity, association, company or institute shall be permitted to keep records of those Members as Electors that have chosen not to exercise their right to vote for the purpose of ensuring proper records of free and fair elections.

A Member as a valid Elector that chooses not to vote in an Election or Referendum, upon giving such proper notice shall be recorded as an Abstain.

A Member as a valid Elector that chooses not to vote in an Election or Referendum and refuses or fails to give proper notice to such effect shall be recorded as an Abscond.

Furthermore, the Union and its organs, entities, associations and bodies shall retain the full right to form bylaws and rules whereby Members as a valid Electors may lose one or more privileges in the event of persistently Absconding from votes.

2. The Union shall use two voting methods in relation to Members exercising their rights to participate in the management, decisions, elections and opinions being Representative and Proportionate:- Voting Methods

   (i) Representative by Vote whereby on a vote by show of hands, or ballot, every person present who is a recognised and registered Member and Elector and therefore entitled to vote on the matter as one vote per Member; and

   (ii) Proportionate by Poll whereby a person or proxy holder entitled to vote on the matter has one vote entitled to be voted on the matter and held by that person or Member and may exercise that vote either in person or by proxy. Unless otherwise stated, all elections and Votes are Representative by Vote.

3. All Ballots shall be Open and Public and none shall be permitted to be held secretly or anonymously. Open and Public Ballot

While a Member may choose to keep their Voting history confidential, the valid Votes of Members and Officers shall always be a permanent matter of the Public Record and not subject to corruption, or tampering.

4. All elections of Representative by Vote Method shall be based on the principle of one Member is equal to one Vote per Ballot, whether it be by show of hands, or electronic or paper or other medium. The action of voting more than once for the same ballot whether under true or false identity is considered an offence. Vote Value

5. The voting system shall be based on electing a candidate from a Ballot of Votes cast in favour of two or more valid candidates in an Election or propositions of a Referendum based on the relative majority from the total Votes cast. The candidate or proposition that is always elected or resolved shall be the one with the most valid Votes and not subject to skew or corruption by methods of proportion or preference allocation. Voting Result Method

6. The publication of all elections shall be by the public record and official notices of results whereby the vote of each and every member represented by their unique membership number and their selections(s) may be reproduced as an official record of a valid vote or official abstain or abscond. The record of result of an election must always demonstrate the ability to reproduce down to individual unique membership numbers and their valid vote for detailed record request and as summary totals for general public record requests and summary notices of results. Public Record and Notice of results

   Should a recount be requested or any other authorised and valid scrutiny of election results, then the original vote papers, or recordings of vote or electronic records and files must be able to be accessed and individually verified against the master electoral roll of members.

7. Where a voting ballot presents a number of candidates who choose to be registered and identified as a complete list for intention of filling the electoral vacancy, it is permissible to publish group voting formatted ballots. Group Voting

   These ballots require a voter only to indicate their Vote for that group to receive an equal vote for each candidate nominated under that box.

Article 131 – Political Associations

1. A Political Association is any person, aggregate, fraternity, entity, association, company, body, institute or society that engages in public discourse and the dissemination of printed or electronic material for the purpose, in part or whole, to influence the votes and decision making processes of Electors at a future Election, Resolution or Referendum. Political Associations

2. There shall exist only three forms of Political Associations:- Three Types of Political

(i) A Political Association that engages in public rallies, or in the active promotion of public media, or purchase and publication of media advertising for the purpose, in part or whole, to influence the votes and decision making processes of Electors at a future Election, Resolution or Referendum shall be known as a *Political Group*; and Associations

(ii) A Political Association that nominates its own Members as candidates for Election shall be known as a *Political Party*; and

(iii) A Political Association that is forbidden by legislative act or judicial instrument from being either a Political Group or Political Party shall be known as a *Banned Political Association.*

3. All Political Groups must be properly registered and identified with the appropriate Electoral Authorities, subject to the Electoral Code and qualifications and conditions therein. No person, aggregate, fraternity, entity, association, company, body, institute or society may engage in public discourse and the dissemination of printed or electronic material for the purpose, in part or whole, to influence the votes and decision making processes of Electors at a future Election, Resolution or Referendum unless properly registered and permitted by the appropriate Electoral Authorities. Political Groups

No person, aggregate, fraternity, entity, association, company, body, institute or society shall be denied registration as a Political Group or excluded from registration as a Political Group on the basis of their gender, race, creed, religion, colour or economic status. However, no registration shall be granted to any person, aggregate, fraternity, entity, association, company, body, institute or society promoting racist, or bigoted, or sexist, or violent policies or manifesto.

All Governments that engage in public discourse and the dissemination of printed or electronic material for the purpose, in part or whole, to influence the votes and decision making processes of Electors at a future Election, Resolution or Referendum are subject to the same conditions of registration as a Political Group or Political Party and therefore the same restrictions and conditions on political advertising, truth in advertising and conduct.

A Political Group that breaches the terms and conditions of campaigning, advertising or conduct during Elections, Resolutions or Referendums may be subject to fines, deregistration or prescription as a Banned Political Entity.

4. Valid Political Parties are permitted to be registered and to nominate Candidates and conduct election campaigns in favour of such Political Parties

Candidates and to participate in the life of the Union. All valid Political Parties are subject to authority of the Electoral Commission. Any body or association or entity or corporation or person that advocates policies of hatred, or elitism, or violence, or racism, or cronyism, or corruption or bigotry toward other Members or groups or society at large is forbidden to apply or be registered as a Political Party.

Article 132 – Electoral Administration

1. For the purpose of the proper conduct of free, fair and valid Elections, an Electoral Commission shall be formed and vested with the sole authority and responsibility to conduct all formal Elections for the selection of qualified Candidates to Offices for Campuses, Provinces and Universities within the Union, as well as the legislative bodies of the Union itself. The structure, authority and powers of the Electoral Commission shall be defined and prescribed within the Elections Code. *Electoral Administration*

2. The Electoral Commission shall be responsible for the good and fair conduct of all Elections and Votes in accord with the present Constitutional Charter and the Elections Code. *Conduct and Records of Elections and Votes*

3. The individual Votes of Members in Elections and Matters shall be considered part of the Public Record:- *Public Record of Votes and Elections*

    (i) Votes within Legislative Bodies shall be open to public scrutiny such that Members may see how a particular elected Member has voted in all major debates and motions; and

    (ii) Individuals through their Member Accounts shall be able to see their own history of Voting and periodically validate the accuracy of such records; as well as restrict or permit the knowledge of such history to be accessible to Candidates and Political Parties; and

    (iii) Candidates and Political Parties shall have limited access to the Voting history of certain Members that permit access to such personal information.

Article 133– Electoral Districts & Divisions

1. For the purpose of Elections, the political boundaries of Campuses, Provinces and Universities shall be considered Electoral Divisions from time to time, whereby qualified and valid Electors, Candidates and Ballots may be uniquely defined. Where additional Candidates may be elected within the same Campus Electoral Division, the *Electoral Districts & Divisions*

Electoral Commission may, with the advise and consent of the appropriate Campus Convention, define smaller Electoral Sub-Divisions or Precincts.

Article 134 – Electoral Rolls

1. For the purpose of fairness and to ensure the integrity of each Election, the period for enrolment on the Electoral Roll shall cease temporarily at least fourteen days prior to Polling Day. Therefore, no additional names may be added or any changes made to the particular Electoral Roll and Poll after the cut-off day and until the election result is properly declared. Electoral Rolls

   A Society may continue to accept new Members after the cut-off date and before the declaration of the Election result, but such Members shall not be permitted to exercise their right to Vote until the Electoral Roll re-opens thereafter.

Article 135– Election Candidates

1. Members who are suitably qualified may be nominated as Candidates and stand for election to Office in accord with the Articles of the present Constitutional Charter and associated Codes and Rules. Candidates

   Notwithstanding specific criteria for eligibility to stand as a Candidate for certain Offices, no Member shall be excluded from nomination as a Candidate on the basis of their gender, race, creed, religion, colour or economic status.

Article 136– Ballots & Records

1. As it is a principal of the Union at every level that all Ballots are open and public and never secret or anonymous, the use of Electronic Voting shall be the preferred method of encouraging participation whereby the actual vote for each ballot and poll of the unique Member is duly recorded as a matter of the public record. Electronic Ballots & Records
2. Paper Based Ballots shall be used as a last resort or in matters of emergency where the reliable systems of Electronic Voting are unavailable for a particular group of Members, as determined by the Electoral Commission. Where Paper Based Ballots are to be issued, the Electoral Commission shall be required to nominate one or more Polling Stations, securely staffed to ensure the integrity of voting, including printed copies of the appropriate Electoral Roll. Paper Based Ballots
3. Postal Based Ballots shall only be permitted where a case for Paper Postal Based

Based Ballots has been approved by the Electoral Commission and where it is deemed necessary for fairness that Members have the right to vote prior to Polling Day and then post their Ballots back to the designated Postal Polling Station prior to Polling Day. Such Ballot Papers shall be counted and recorded as they arrive, with the results of such votes held secure until Polling Day.

Ballots

Article 137 – Election Procedures & Oversight

1. A Candidate for an Electoral Division shall have the right to nominate one Scrutineer to be present at either the physical count of Paper Based Ballots or Electronic Ballots per place of polling on Polling Day. The Electoral Commission shall have the right to deny a Scrutineer entry to be present at the count, if in the opinion of the Electoral Commission the person in question represents an unacceptable security risk or fails to appear at the appropriate place for the count before the Count commences.

Election Procedures & Oversight

Article 138 – Election Funding & Compensation

1. All valid registered Candidates and all Political Parties are entitled to receive Funding from the Electoral Commission to Fund their Election Campaigns and Election Materials; and all media associated with the Society are required to provide certain time and resources to Candidates and Political Parties to transmit their messages to Voters. The expense of providing individual funding to Candidates and funding to valid registered Political Parties is recognised as a necessary and legitimate expense of Elections to protect the electoral process from corruption and external influence.

Election Funding & Compensation

Article 139 – Political Funding & Contributions

1. Political Donations to Candidates or Political Parties of any kind from any source, directly or indirectly; or in cash or in kind is absolutely forbidden and considered a serious criminal offence, that may also result in the disqualification of one or more Candidates and the deregistration of a Political Party and loss of its funding resources.

Political Funding & Contributions

Article 140 – Political Communications & Activities

1. All proposed printed and electronic communication by Political Associations or Political Parties must be first submitted to the Electoral Commission to receive a Political Communication Registration Number in order to make such a broadcast lawful. Governments conducting political advertising are also required to receive such Political Communication Registration Number. *Political Communications & Activities*

   A communication by a Political Group or Political Party that does not have a Political Communication Registration Number shall be a criminal offence with the potential for the candidate to be disqualified, or the need for a recount, or in the worst situations, the body or association becoming a Banned Political Association.

   All Political Groups and Political Parties have the right to prompt and reasonable responses to their completed print and electronic material being reviewed. Unreasonable and unfair delays in approval, contrary to the Electoral Code shall be possible grounds for compensation, a recount or re-contest of an election and in the worst cases, criminal prosecution against those Electoral Officials found culpable of maladministration or corruption.

2. A Political Group or Political Party must first submit election material to the Electoral Commission to be registered before it is permitted to be broadcast or published. The Electoral Commission is forbidden to reject or ban such campaign material by a Political Group or Political Party unless:- *Submission of Materials*

   (i) The Campaign Material is deemed racist, or hate speech, or bigotry, or sexist, or sacrilegious; or

   (ii) Excluding opinions and testimonials, that an objection with clear evidence is received by an opposing Political Group or Political Party that the material is derogatory or defaming and factually incorrect; or

   (iii) That the Campaign Material is deemed deliberate and wilfully misleading in its presentation of arguments, conclusions, logic or claimed facts.

TITLE XV: REGISTERS, RECORDS & NOTICES

Article 141 – Registers & Records

1. A *Register* is recognised as a book of tables recording one or more entries of statements, testimonies or memoranda as evidence as to jurisdiction and authority over certain Sacred Circumscribed Space; or the properties or attributes of such Sacred Circumscribed Space; or the rights of use of such properties and attributes; or the memorial of events concerning such Sacred Circumscribed Space, or properties or attributes, or rights of use; or the memorial of transactions and derivatives concerning the receiving or granting or claiming of rights and uses.

Registers & Records

2. All records in proper, valid and legitimate Registers shall depend upon the prior recording by Authority of one or more records of Sacred Circumscribed Space as reference. If no valid records of Sacred Circumscribed Space exists, or such records are illegitimate, false, unlawful or illegal, then all subsequent Registers and Records depending upon such primary records shall also be illegitimate, false, unlawful and illegal.

All Records in Registers dependent on Sacred Circumscribed Space

3. In terms of the general authority and creation of Registers:-

Authority, Power relating to Registers

   (i) The Authority to form a Register shall be defined by the limits of Authority of the constituting Instrument of the relevant Trust or Estate or Fund or Entity; and

   (ii) The Rights, Powers and Property prescribed within a Register shall not exceed the Rights, Powers and Property of the Trust or Estate or Fund or Entity itself; and

   (iii) As valid and proper Registers shall record Sacred Circumscribed Space, all valid and proper Registers shall be wholly and exclusively Spiritual or Ecclesiastical Property and shall never themselves belong to the relevant Trust or Estate or Fund or Entity; and

   (iv) All valid Registers shall be hierarchical in their inheritance of Authority and validity. A Register that cannot demonstrate the provenance of its claimed authority ultimately to the present Constitutional Charter, shall have none, and shall be null and void from the beginning; and

   (v) The highest and most authoritative Register shall be the Great Register and Divine Records of Heaven in accord with the most sacred Covenant *Pactum De Singularis Caelum* and the present Constitutional Charter. A Register that cannot demonstrate the provenance of its claimed authority to the sacred Covenant *Pactum De Singularis Caelum* shall have none, and shall be null and void from the beginning; and

(vi) As all Registers are wholly and exclusively Spiritual or Ecclesiastical, absolutely no clerical or administrative act may take place in association with a Register unless by a duly authorised Officer under active and valid sacred Oath or Vow; and

(vii) The entry of a Record into a Register shall be wholly invalid unless the memorial and testimony of the act giving authority shall be done without duress, is done freely and with full knowledge and is consistent and in accord with the present Constitutional Charter.

Purpose, Function and Operation of Register

4. In terms of the general purpose, function and operation of a valid Register:-

(i) A Register as a table shall contain at least three (3) or more columns; and

(ii) A Register as a table shall be a section of a Book, or a whole series of Books; and

(iii) A Register shall be held in the care of a proper Officer possessing the Spiritual or Ecclesiastical Authority to hold, enter and keep custody of such Records; and

(iv) A Register shall not create the original fact or authority that it records, but shall reflect the pertinent elements in relation to the originating Instrument used to create a valid entry; and

(v) An entry in a Register shall never create Sacred Circumscribed Space itself. However, a valid entry in a Register shall be itself a valid event and by virtue of the "joining" of information at the time of registration shall permit the creation, conveyance or suppression of certain Rights or recording of certain Facts or Truths as *prima facie* Evidence; and

(vi) A particular form of Right of Use in relation to Property shall only be recorded once in a valid Register. Those specific Registers as prescribed by the present Constitutional Charter and Ucadian Law shall always be Registers of Original Record and shall take precedence over all lesser claimed registers and rolls; and

(vii) The claimed day or time of entry of a record into lesser or foreign claimed register shall have no bearing or merit in law, where a similar record for the same Property, or Event, or Right exists within a valid Register in control of a valid Ucadian Trust or Estate or Fund or Entity, even if the day or time of entry in the Register associated with a valid Ucadian Trust or Estate or Fund or Entity is after the day or time of entry in the lesser or foreign claimed register; and

(viii) Any lesser or foreign claimed register that seeks to usurp the Authority of a valid Register associated with a valid Ucadian Trust or Estate or Fund or Entity shall automatically render such a claimed register invalid and illegitimate, meaning that such a claimed register is determined to be null and void, having no force or effect in law.

5. A *Record* is recognised as a written memorial of actions or events, and accounts entered under promise, testification, certification or attestation as Fact; and the conveyances of Proof of such Fact then preserved as knowledge and authentic history of the causes within such entries, united by some Identifier within Memoranda, Journals and Register of a valid Trust or Estate or Fund or Entity. Record

6. A valid Record shall comprise of three (3) actions entered into three Books:- Valid Record

(i) The *Event* shall be the first action, entered into a Memorandum as a true written memorial to the "event" and associated proceedings and actions; and

(ii) The *Witnessed Account* shall be the second action, as attestation to an Account or Affidavit entered into a Journal as an attestation to the true Summary of Facts, with a unique Event Number then "posted back" to the Memorandum as well as "cancelling" those details within the Memorandum now "posted" in the Journal; and

(iii) The *Conveyance* shall be the third action, as proof of a valid "event" to a Register, by a Summary Letter or Certificate as a True Summary of Account or Instrument of Record, with the unique Entry then "posted forward" to the Register as the completion of the Record.

7. The following forms of Registers shall be recognised and used by Ucadian bodies and entities, consistent with the present Constitutional Charter and Ucadian Law, including (but not limited to):- Forms of Registers

(i) A *Gazette* shall be a form of Register as a Public Journal and Authorised Newspaper of Record; and

(ii) An *Almanac* shall be a form of Register of information and events for a given subject, collected and arranged for a given year; and

(iii) An *Account* shall be a form of Register as arrangements of Computations, Valuations and Derivations using some standard unit of value, measure, record or exchange on the nature, value and disposition of objects, concepts and property of a valid Trust or Estate or Fund or Corporation; and

(iv) A *Memoranda* shall be a form of Register in chronological order, detailing the substance of formal notes or "memorandum" including (but not be limited to) minutes, resolutions, proceedings, accounts, letters, correspondence, decisions and procedural actions; and

(v) A *Journal* shall be a form of Register derived as a summary extract of information from Memoranda and arranged in category order and then chronological order to produce a summary of facts, evidence, quantities and relations for the purpose of accounting and reckoning of the debits and credits of the Trust or Estate or Fund or Entity; and

(vi) A *Ledger* shall be a form of Register as a summary extract of Journal entries to produce the most concise reckonings and balances of debits and credits, assets and liabilities of the Trust or Estate or Fund or Entity; and

(vii) A *Roll* shall be a form of Register of one or more entries being "persons" of the same condition of entry, or the same engagement of obligations in relation to a valid Trust or Estate or Fund or Corporation; and created by their valid entry into the Roll; and

(viii) A *Manifest* shall be a form of Register being evidential history of the provenance, possession and ownership of any property, rights, money or other interests recorded as associated with a Trust or Estate or Fund or Entity; and

(ix) An *Estate* shall be a form of Register and Roll or Record of a Roll of certain Rights held in Trust for a period of years for a Person or group of Persons, whereby one or more Inventories and Valuations have been properly conducted; and

(x) An *Inventory* shall be a form of Register being a detailed survey and census of all property, assets and liabilities, debits or credits of a valid Trust, or Estate or Fund or Entity completed immediately after its creation; or the anniversary of its creation; or upon another fixed and given day; and the stock of particular items and their location or business; and

(xi) A *Valuation* shall be a form of Register and Roll (also historically known as a Tax or Rating) being a detailed estimation of the value of each item as listed upon an Inventory of a valid Trust, or Estate or Fund or Entity; and

(xii) A *Fund* shall be a form of Register of equal units representing certain Property Rights of one or more Estates of monetary value that can then be used as a means of exchange for lawful money or for the discharge of debts and obligations.

Unique Register Number

8. Every prescribed and valid Register and Roll of the Union organs, bodies and entities shall be uniquely numbered by a *Unique Register Number*. The Register Number shall be the extracted Record Number from the Greater Register and Divine Records of Heaven as the *Register of Registers*. A Register or Roll that does not possess a valid Unique Register Number shall *ipso facto* (as a matter of fact) be invalid and illegitimate.

Joinder

9. The process whereby the authority of one Person on one Roll shall be given legitimacy by the authority and consent of a previously created Person record on another Roll shall be called "**Joinder**" of Person:-

(i) Joinder shall require that a party is given Notice of Joinder with clear intention to "join" one person from a Roll held in custody with the authority and permissions of a Roll not immediately within their jurisdiction; and

(ii) The names of both persons must be the same in order for a valid Joinder of Person. Otherwise, such a Joinder shall be a Joinder in Action, requiring separate consent; and

(iii) The failure to make clear the Notice of Joinder as an intention to Join shall be a fraud and shall render such action a Misjoinder and maladministration; and

(iv) The failure to produce sufficient evidence of the Right to Joinder of Person, shall automatically render such action a Misjoinder; and

(v) No non-Ucadian or foreign state, body, agency or entity may seek Joinder with a Ucadia Person; and

(vi) By innate Right of the present Constitutional Charter, all Ucadian organs, bodies and entities shall have authority of Joinder over non-Ucadian and foreign inferior persons, where such persons are associated with Ucadia Members.

Article 142 – Notices

1. Notice is the term used to describe the type of notice and service of process whereby a party is made aware of any formal legal matter that may affect certain Rights, obligations or Duties as well as the form of Document used to transmit such facts. The seven primary types of notice used by the Union are: *Physical, Posted, Direct, Indirect, Public (legal), Implied* and *Constructive*: Notices

    (i) *Physical Notice* or Actual Notice is a type of notice and service of process whereby the specific information concerning a formal legal matter is listed in a Document and then physically handed to a party or their representative, with proof, attestation or acknowledgement of such service recorded as evidence; and

    (ii) *Posted Notice* or Mail Notice is a type of notice and service of process whereby specific information concerning a formal legal matter is personally addressed to the party and sent through a certified or registered mail delivery system recognised by the International Postal Union; and

    (iii) *Direct Notice* is a type of notice and service of process whereby specific information concerning a formal legal matter is personally addressed to the party and sent via email, fax, sms or other recorded and verifiable transmission medium; and

    (iv) *Indirect Notice* is a type of notice and service of process whereby specific information concerning a formal legal matter is published in any broadcast medium such as media releases, stories, advertorial content and advertising and likely to be viewed by one or more parties; and

    (v) *Public Notice* is a type of notice and service of process whereby specific information concerning a formal legal matter is published in a company, local, regional, national or international publication possessing status as a gazette and therefore an official newspaper of record or physically posted at a site reasonably expected to be visible to the Person; and

    (vi) *Implied Notice* is a type of notice inferred from facts that a Person had means of knowing and would have caused a reasonable Person to take action to gain further information concerning a formal legal matter. It is a notice inferred or imputed to a party by reason of his or her knowledge collateral to the main fact; and

(vii) *Constructive Notice* is a type of notice inferred from facts that a Person unable to be served with Actual Notice may be reasonably inferred or imputed to have received notice, if Actual Notice was restricted or not possible and a minimum number of attempts of Physical, Posted, Direct or Public Notice were concluded.

2. It shall be a fundamental element of true justice that a party shall be made aware of any accusation of alleged culpability or violation against the law. Unless a party is made aware of the particular law as well as the particular accusations, then any ruling, edict, sanction or penalty cannot be said to be fair or just.

Principle of Fair Notice

In contrast, when a party shall be clearly "put on notice" that they are in violation of one or more laws, yet continue such actions of violation, then such fair notice shall be considered by logic and reason to be sufficient evidence and proof of knowledge of their own wrong doing.

When a party is then given multiple notices of multiple violations and opportunities to cure and remediate such behaviour, yet continue such actions of violation, then any subsequent decree, or judgement in accord with the present Constitutional Charter shall be taken as final, lawful, moral and absolute.

3. The Principle of Service of Process or simple "Service" shall be the procedure whereby a party to a sovereign, legal or administrative matter is given appropriate notice of any action scheduled to be heard and judged by a properly constituted forum of law, having jurisdiction over the matter.

Principle of Service of Process

As all living human beings born or naturalised within the bounds of the Union are *ipso facto* (as a matter of fact) Ordinary Members of the Union unless they renounce their rights, a properly constituted forum of law, not exceeding its authority in accord with the present Constitutional Charter of the Union has absolute and perfect Personal Jurisdiction over all the parties through proper Service of Process.

A properly constituted forum of law possesses *Territorial Jurisdiction* to the extent of its powers under the present Constitutional Charter and the location of the parties.

Subject Matter Jurisdiction shall be established upon the voluntary consent of parties, or involuntary actions of dishonour of the parties, whereby their failure to act with dignity and respect is public notice of their delinquency, incompetency and acceptance of jurisdiction of the properly constituted forum of law in accord with the present Constitutional Charter.

4. Excluding matters subject to legal dispute, or otherwise required by Ucadia Law, the Union during its normal course of business shall use Posted and Direct Notice as the preferred medium for communicating matters of a confidential, privileged or private nature between the Union and its Directors, Members, Officers, Agents, Employees or other parties. In matters that are not of a confidential, privileged or private nature, the Union may also use Indirect Notice. General Service of Notices

5. Except as required by Ucadia Law, the Union shall use Public Notice only in those circumstances deemed required by law, or in the proceeding of a legal case or matter. The Use of Public Notice

6. The publishing of any Proclamation, Order, Regulation or Notice within the Union Gazette shall be *Prima Facie* Evidence of such Fact and Truth; and that all Courts, Judges, Justices, Masters, Magistrates or Commissioners judicially acting, and all other judicial Officers shall take judicial Notice of such *Prima Facie* Evidence in all legal proceedings whatsoever. Ucadia Gazette Notices as Prima Facie Evidence

7. Except as required by Ucadia Law, the Union shall use Physical Notice only in those circumstances deemed required by law, or in the proceeding of a legal case, or matter. The Use of Physical Notice

8. In any matter pertaining to change in the position of rights, financial performance, staff or reporting of the Union in relation to Members, Posted Notice is required to be given by the Union to any Member, or in the case of joint holders to the Member whose name stands first in the Register, regardless of whether Direct Notice or any other form of Notice is also used. All Posted Notices sent by prepaid post to persons whose registered address is not in the same Jurisdiction as the Registered Office of the Union are to be sent by registered mail services. Service of Posted Notices to Members

9. Notice shall be deemed to have been properly and duly served, when: When Notice deemed to be served

   (i) Any Physical Notice served personally or left at the registered address by a servicing agent is deemed to have been served when delivered and such fact is attested by a certificate of service signed by the agent who executed the service; and

   (ii) Any Notice sent by Post is deemed to have been served at the expiration of forty-eight hours after the envelope containing the Notice is posted and, in proving service, it is sufficient to prove that the envelope containing the Notice was properly addressed and posted; and

   (iii) Any Direct Notice served on a party by telex is deemed to have been served on receipt by the Union of the answer-back code of the recipient at the end of the transmission. Any notice served on a party by facsimile transmission is deemed to have been served when the transmission is sent. Any notice served on a party by email or sms or any other form of direct electronic messaging is deemed to have been served after twenty-four hours and no error message or failed transmission notice is received; and

(iv) Any Indirect Notice is deemed to have been served three days after receipt or proof of the publication of such notice; and

(v) Any Public Notice is deemed to have been served three days after receipt or proof of the publication in a gazette and official publication of record of such Notice; and

(vi) Any Implied Notice is deemed to have been served fourteen days after receipt or proof of publication of at least two forms of Indirect Notice or Public Notice; and

(vii) Any Constructive Notice is deemed to have been served fourteen days after receipt or proof of at least one attempted Physical Notice or two Posted Notices and at least two forms of Indirect Notice or Public Notice.

10. Where a Member does not have a registered address or where the Union has a reason in good faith to believe that a Member is not known at the Member's registered address, a Notice is deemed to be given to the Member if the Notice is exhibited by Indirect Notice in the Office for a period of forty-eight hours (and is deemed to be duly served at the commencement of that period) unless and until the Member informs the Union of a registered place of address.

Member not known at registered address

11. The signature to any Notice to be given by the Union may be written or printed. The formatting of the name of an Officer of the Union in capitals as the signature line upon a Notice shall be deemed a valid legal signature.

Signature to Notice

12. Where a Notice gives of a certain number of days, or the limit of time is mandated for some proper form of Notice, the days of service are not to be reckoned in the number of days, until the actual date of proof of service, thereby limiting the possibility of an unfair or unreasonable service.

Reckoning of period of Notice

13. Every person who, by operation of law, transfers a right, or property or obligation to another shall continue to be fully bound by every Notice, until the name and details of the transferee of such property, or right

Notice to transferor binds transferee

or obligation is properly registered with their consent to being bound to any and every Notice.

14. A Notice served in accordance with these Articles is (notwithstanding that the Member is then dead and whether or not the Union has Notice of the Member's death) deemed to have been duly served in respect of any registered property, whether held solely or jointly with other persons by the Member, until some other person is registered in the Member's place as the holder or joint holder and the service is for all purposes deemed to be sufficient service of the Notice or document on the Member's heirs, executors or administrators and all persons (if any) jointly interested with the Member in the said property. Service on deceased Members

Article 143 – Gazette

1. A "**Gazette**" is a public journal and authorised newspaper of Record. Gazette

2. The Union shall produce and publish a "**Union Gazette**", published by Authority in accordance with these Articles; and it shall be the Official Newspaper of Public Notice and Record for the Union, as a fundamental means to disseminate and record official, regulatory and lawful information in print, online and electronic forms. Union Gazette

3. All publications within the Gazette of the Union shall be by virtue of the approval of entry of at least one Instrument into the Public Record and Public Register. Entry into Union Gazette

4. The publishing of any Proclamation, Order, Regulation or Notice within the Union Gazette shall be *Prima Facie* Evidence of such Fact and Truth; and that all Courts, Judges, Justices, Masters, Magistrates or Commissioners judicially acting, and all other judicial Officers shall take judicial Notice of such *Prima Facie* Evidence in all legal proceedings whatsoever. Union Gazette Notices as Prima Facie Evidence

5. The "**Public Register**" shall be the Official Public Record of the Union and shall also be known as the Great Ledger, the Supreme Roll and the Register of Title and Rights. Public Register

6. A Valid Register Entry shall be the minimum required information recorded into the Public Register of the Union after a Form has been accepted. A Valid Register Entry includes a Unique Ledger Key as well as associated information. The minimum required information for a Valid Register Entry, includes (but is not limited to): Valid Register Entry

   (i) A Unique Identifying Number also called the Unique Register Number (URN); and

   (ii) A Name for the Register Entry; and

(iii) The Day of entry into the Register; and

(iv) The Member that petitioned for the entry of the Record; and

(v) The Capacity (Office) of the Member as Petitioner; and

(vi) The Registrar that approved the entry.

7. The Universal Form Code (UFC) shall be a standard for the naming, construction, recording and management of standard forms, completed forms and the information contained within. The UFC Identifier shall be an eighteen (18) digit number that uniquely identifies each and every valid form received and accepted by all Ucadian Societies. No two forms will ever have the same UFC Identifier. The Universal Form Code is based on (1) An Alpha Prefix of two characters, then (2) four numbers representing category and standard form, then (3) twelve characters representing the unique society and number of the form. The Standard Form Classifications for all types of forms are: Universal Form Code

(i) [AA] Agriculture & Environment; and

(ii) [KK] Budget, Revenue & Treasury; and

(iii) [CC] Companies, Trusts & Funds; and

(iv) [DD] Disease Prevention & Sanitation; and

(v) [EE] Education; and

(vi) [FF] Food & Drugs; and

(vii) [GG] Executive Government; and

(viii) [HH] Fitness & Health; and

(ix) [II] Industry, Infrastructure & Energy; and

(x) [JJ] Justice, Constitutional & International Law; and

(xi) [BB] Accounts, Banking & Financial Transactions; and

(xii) [LL] Sovereign, Estates & Legislative; and

(xiii) [MM] Military; and

(xiv) [NN] Trade; and

(xv) [PP] Police & Emergency; and

(xvi) [QQ] Divine & Ecclesiastical Law; and

(xvii) [RR] Culture & Entertainment; and

(xviii) [SS] Members, History & Community; and

(xix) [TT] Transport & Travel; and

(xx) [UU] Building & Construction; and

(xxi) [VV] Elections; and

(xxii) [WW] Employment & Temporary Assistance; and

(xxiii) [XX] Land, Rights & Civil Law; and

(xxiv) [YY] Criminal Law; and

(xxv) [ZZ] Technology, Communications & Knowledge Systems; and

(xxvi) [OO] Civil Service.

8. Only Permitted and Valid Forms shall be entered into the Public Register and Public Record of the Union. A Permitted Form is when: Permitted Form

(i) An Instrument is identified as an Approved Form as defined by the present Articles, or associated Rules and Procedures of the Union to be entered; and

(ii) The Instrument possesses the minimum information required for a Valid Register Entry; and

(iii) The Instrument does not require material correction, alteration or addition; and

(iv) The Member as Petitioner is not precluded from requesting such an entry, or otherwise temporarily banned from such services; and

(v) The Instrument does not contradict any of the provisions of the present Articles.

9. Members of the Union, not otherwise suspended or banned from such services, possess the Right of Petition for an entry in the Public Register, not a Right of Entry. The approval to record and publish in the Public Register of the Union shall always be a determination of the appropriate Officials of the Union, subject to any fees or conditions consistent with the present Articles. Petition not Right of Entry

10. In respect of the Public Register: Publication and Promulgation of Public Register

(i) The Registrar shall protect and keep the Public Register in a reliable medium and ensure that its entire contents is published and promulgated in a printed form, with updated publication of new entries available upon the day of approved entry; and

(ii) The Registrar shall also produce a daily or weekly publication promulgated in an electronic and printed form of all new entries for that week known as the *Gazette*; and

(iii) The Registrar shall also provide public access to the full contents of the Public Register from the widest possible range of mediums, including internet, computer, microfilm, paper and other mediums; and

(iv) The Registrar may charge minimal fees for the processing of applications and requests for entry into the Public Register where such entries involve a degree of complexity and audit; and

(v) While the Registrar may charge a minimal service fee for any costs associated with the requested research projects, print requests and publications, all online and simple electronic Register search services are to be provided free of charge.

11. All Persons are forbidden to make demands or threats for entry of one or more Instruments into the Public Register. Only when proper requests as petitions are made by following the instructions as per the present Articles and additional information provided from time to time, shall any Instrument be considered on its merits. Demand of Entry an Offence

The persistent demands and/or threats of a Member for one or more Instruments to be entered into the Public Register, contrary to these Articles shall be a serious offence, punishable by temporary suspension of some or all services given to them.

Article 144 – Media

1. *Media* is the term used to describe the collection of mediums, sources, repositories, tools, platforms, devices and markets for the storage, publication and delivery of printed or digital data, information and knowledge. The Union shall seek to utilise the full spectrum of Media to communicate appropriate data, information and knowledge including, but without limitation to: Media

(i) *Advertising Media* being various media associated with content, buying and placement for advertising; and

(ii) *Broadcast Media* being communications delivered over mass electronic communication networks; and

(iii) *Digital Media* being electronic media used to store, transmit, and receive digitised information; and

(iv) *Electronic Media* being communications delivered via electronic or electro-mechanical energy; and

(v) *Fixed Media* being communication devices (such as billboards and signs) that are permanently fixed in certain locations; and

(vi) *Games Media* being communication and interaction delivered through games platforms, devices and applications; and

(vii) *Interactive Media* being interactive communication delivered through a multitude of different devices, platforms and technologies; and

(viii) *Mass Media* being all means of mass information and communication; and

(ix) *Mobile Media* being communication through mobile devices, transport and mediums; and

(x) *Multimedia* being communications that incorporate multiple forms of information content and processing; and

(xi) *New Media* being a broad term encompassing the amalgamation of traditional media with the interactive power of computer and communications technology; and

(xii) *News Media* being mass media focused on communicating news; and

(xiii) *Print Media* being communications delivered via paper or canvas; and

(xiv) *Published Media* being any media made available to the public; and

(xv) *Social Media* being media disseminated through social interactions.

2. All forms of Media that broadcast through the Union shall be regulated by licence and warrant under a permanent body known as the Media Authority:- Media Authority

(i) An individual that publishes their own opinions and proprietary information through their own unique and separate domain or print publication shall not require a licence or warrant under the Media Authority; and

(ii) All entities that publish the opinions of others, or report on current events, even if for an audience of their own members shall require a licence or warrant under the Media Authority; and

(iii) A primary requirement of qualifying to receive a licence by the Media Authority shall be the making of a solemn oath under threat of prosecution for perjury, that the individual or company shall not engage in deliberate misinformation, or the censure or collusion to censor or silence information of a public interest or importance; and shall not publish information that is knowingly misleading, deceptive or untrue; and

(iv) The Media Authority shall not be permitted to discipline or suspend the license of any media entity or person on the basis of different political, social, religious or other ideological views, or such information that is critical to elected officials or other officers of the Union.

3. A key protection under the warrant component issued to Media entities by the Media Authority shall be the indemnity conditions of enabling the publication of whistle-blower information, whereby the government of the Union and its agencies may not intervene, intimidate, threaten or otherwise try to stop the publication of such information, including the indictment of the owners or editors or journalists of such a Media entity, providing:- Protection of Whistleblower Sources

(i) The information provide by the whistle-blower clearly relates to credible evidence of one or more alleged offences perpetrated by one or more officers or elected representatives of the Union; and

(ii) The information has been independently verified by at least two or more credible sources, without personal animus or agendas, to authenticate its veracity; and

(iii) Such knowledge, if true warrants further investigation and is in the public interest; and

(iv) The lives of one or more officers of the Union are not directly and intentionally put at risk upon the publication of such information.

4. The use of anonymous sources by media entities is strictly forbidden and may constitute a deliberate act of perjury, if such sources do not comport to the Protection of Whistle-blower Doctrine and the verification of such allegations:- False Anonymous Sources

(i) The publisher, owner, shareholders and editors shall all be held jointly and severally liable for the most serious offence of perjury where the use of alleged anonymous sources is used to promote false information; and

(ii) No platform or institution involved in media may claim immunity from full liability where it can be demonstrated the use of one or more anonymous sources involved one or more offences of perjury.

5. Any licensed Media entity or foreign (Non-Ucadian) Media entity that is found to have knowingly and intentionally published information of a defamatory, or notorious, or demeaning or degrading nature against a person or company or organ of the Union, shall have no right of immunity and shall be fully liable to financial penalties, or sanctions or possible deregistration, if it can be established by a competent forum of law subject to Ucadian Law:-

Loss of immunity rights for defamation

(i) If the Media entity or foreign (Non-Ucadian) Media entity was knowingly and intentionally negligent in failing to check the accuracy, source and substance of the allegations prior to publication; or

(ii) If the Media entity or foreign (Non-Ucadian) Media entity knew the accuracy, source and substance of the allegations at the time were questionable and unproven yet chose to publish anyway; or

(iii) If the Media entity or foreign (Non-Ucadian) Media entity imputed allegations or sensationalised allegations in its publication wholly unsupported by the alleged facts and materials in its possession at the time; or

(iv) If the Media entity or foreign (Non-Ucadian) Media entity is unable to demonstrate it had receipt of any legal clearance against publishing possibly defamatory material prior to its specific publication. This element is mandatory to prove knowing and wilful negligence.

6. No licensed Media entity or foreign (Non-Ucadian) Media shall be held liable by the Union, nor shall they lose immunity from legal action for the losses or loss of reputation of any person, company, body or member, if the publications in question were based on accurate and reasonable facts at the time.

Media not liable for any losses or loss of reputation in publication of facts

TITLE XVI: CONSENSUS, OBLIGATIONS & PERFORMANCE

Article 145 – Consensus, Obligations & Performance

1. The expression of Free Will and Choice, as demonstrated by the most sacred Covenant *Pactum De Singularis Caelum*, permits Beings to solemnly commit through their Persons to one or more Acts regarding certain Obligations concerning Property or Rights. Such formal commitments, whether it be one person, or many people, shall be known as "Consensus". Consensus, Obligations & Performance

   All forms of concord shall be more properly defined as a form of Consensus including (but not limited to) any accordance, agreement, arrangement, alliance, assent, auction, bargain, bid, charter, claim, compact, concession, concordat, concurrence, conformance, congruence, contract, correspondence, covenant, deal, decision, deed, determination, judgement, lease, order, pact, query, ruling, settlement, treaty, understanding, union or will.

2. There shall be only three (3) possible arrangements of Consensus being Bilateral, Multilateral and Trilateral:- Arrangements of Consensus

   (i) *Bilateral Consensus* shall be when two (2) Beings through their Persons reach an agreement of mutual Obligations; and

   (ii) *Multilateral Consensus* shall be when three (3) or more Beings through their Persons reach a common agreement and Obligations; and

   (iii) *Trilateral Consensus* shall be when a Being through their Person agrees to one or more Obligations for receiving a benefit vested to a third party as trustee, to ensure the performance of the obligation and terms of the agreement.

3. An *Obligation* shall mean a moral duty or legal duty whereby one or more parties as *Obligants* are bound to act or refrain from acting. An Obligation thus shall impose on the *Obligor* a duty to perform and shall at the same time create a corresponding right to demand performance by the *Obligee* to whom the performance is to be tendered:- Obligation

   (i) A legal duty shall mean a *Legal Obligation* as one that shall be enforceable by a competent forum of law having jurisdiction; and

   (ii) A moral duty shall mean a *Moral Obligation* as one that is owned and ought to be performed, especially by an Officer, Fiduciary or Agent, but that is not legally bound to be fulfilled.

4. *Performance* shall mean the accomplishment of a promise, a covenant or other obligation of a Consensus, according to its terms. Performance

5. A *Condition* shall mean a declaration or provision that shall make the existence of a Right dependent on the occurrence of an event. Condition

6. As an enforceable agreement, a Consensus must meet eight (8) key elements being authorisation, comprehension, intention, consideration, obligation, negotiation, acceptation and registration:- Fundamental Elements of Consensus

    (i) *Authorisation* means a party must first have the legal and moral authority to enter into a Consensus; and

    (ii) *Comprehension* means each party must demonstrate a clear level of understanding as to entering into a Consensus; and

    (iii) *Intention* means each party must intend to enter into a Consensus; and

    (iv) *Consideration* means there must be something of substance on offer as part of the Consensus; and

    (v) *Obligation* means there must be at least one promise associated with a legal duty or moral duty; and

    (vi) *Negotiation* means there must be a meeting of minds negotiated before a Consensus is accepted; and

    (vii) *Acceptation* means there must be evidence that the Consensus was accepted and thus the terms enforceable; and

    (viii) *Registration* means the Consensus Instrument as well as the key information was duly registered and recorded in a valid and proper Register of Consensus.

7. A Consensus shall not be legally and morally enforceable unless in writing as an Instrument then registered and recorded in a proper Register of Consensus. At a minimum, the Register of Consensus shall take note of:- Registration of Consensus Instrument

    (i) The names, addresses and details of the parties of the Consensus, including witnesses and any guarantors or insurers; and

    (ii) The specific obligations of the Consensus, including any dates and amounts or measures; and

    (iii) The value and nature of the considerations of the Consensus; and

    (iv) The agreed penalties for breach and the agreed time frames and terms of remedy.

8. The memorialisation of a Consensus into an Instrument shall be Conditional, Executed or Executory:- Consensus as Instrument

(i) *Conditional Consensus Instrument* shall be when the operation or effect of the consensus is dependent upon the existence of certain facts or the performance of a condition or the happening of a contingency; and

(ii) *Executed Consensus Instrument* shall be when the instrument refers to past events, which are at once closed and nothing further remains to be done by the parties but perform; and

(iii) *Executory Consensus Instrument* shall be when referral is made to some significant event to be performed in the future and there such an instrument is often preliminary to some Executed Consensus Instrument.

9. A *Breach* of Consensus shall be a legal cause of action whereby a binding Consensus is not honoured by one or more of the parties to the Consensus by non-performance or interference with the other party's performance. There shall be primarily three (3) classes of breaches of Consensus: Minor, Material and Fundamental: Breach of Consensus

(i) A *minor breach*, also known as a partial breach shall be when the non-breaching party is only entitled to collect the actual amount of damages and not for any order for performance of obligations; and

(ii) A *material breach* shall be any failure to perform that permits the other party of the Consensus to either compel performance or collect damages because of the breach; and

(iii) A *fundamental breach* shall be a breach so fundamental that it permits the aggrieved party to terminate performance of the agreement, in addition to entitling that party to sue for damages.

10. All validly formed and registered Consensus agreements shall possess the right of Relief, Redress or Compensation for Default or Delinquency of Obligation. Right of Relief, Redress or Compensation

11. No Consensus may be signed, sealed or executed by an Officer, or Agent or any representative of a Ucadia organ, body or entity if such Consensus was formed on the basis of an unlawful, or illegal or immoral act; or contains such clauses that may be reasonably construed as contrary to the norms of Ucadian law and morality, including but not limited to:- Unlawful, Illegal and Immoral agreements forbidden

(i) Bribery, Extortion or Kick-Backs; or

(ii) Anti-Competitive Practices; or

(iii) Fraud or Bad Faith Denial of Contract; or

(iv) Restraint of Trade; or

(v) Threat and Duress; and

(vi) Charges and Demands where there is no evidence of value for money, or fair market value is provided.

12. A Consensus shall be unlawful, illegal, unenforceable and null and void:- Unlawful and Illegal Agreements

(i) If the wording of such agreement in any way may be reasonably implied or construed, or interpreted, or read to mean a transfer, or gift, or deposit, or surrender, or forfeit, or grant, or delivery, or alienation, or consignment, or conveyance, or arrest, or capture, or seizure, or resignation of any Rights or Property of the Union whatsoever contrary to the present Constitutional Charter; or

(ii) If the wording of such agreement in any way may be reasonably implied or construed, or interpreted, or read to mean the Union is in the relation of a Debtor to the other Party as Creditor; and fair and reasonable consideration has not been fully disclosed, or the nature of the liability or the full consequences of such obligation.

13. All signed, sealed and executed Agreements by the Union or within the jurisdiction of the Union must be provided to the appropriate administration immediately upon execution, with the appropriate administration providing certified digital copies back to the appropriate parties, subject to any fees. All Agreements held by Union

14. A Breach is any violation of a term or condition, or Right of either Party, or any obligation, engagement or duty, either by commission or omission, whether knowing or unknowing, in relation to any valid Agreement in accord with these Articles including, but not limited to any:- Breach of Agreement

(i) ***Breach of Promise*** being a violation of any promise; or

(ii) ***Breach of Duty*** being any violation or omission of a legal or moral duty and more particularly the neglect or failure to fulfil in a just and proper manner the duties of an office, agency or fiduciary capacity; or

(iii) ***Breach of Trust*** being any act done by a person holding fiduciary responsibility in relation to a trust or office and more particularly the wrongful omission by a trustee of an act required by the terms of the trust, or wrong misappropriation by a trustee of any fund or property that had been lawfully committed to him in a fiduciary capacity; or

(iv) ***Breach of Warranty*** being the failure or falsehood of an affirmative promise or statement in writing, or the non-performance of an executor stipulation; or Breach of Agreement being any failure without legal excuse to perform any promise that forms the entirety or part of any Agreement, whether anticipatory, or constructive or continuing, or unequivocal.

15. All alleged Breaches shall be defined as either *Minor* or *Material* (Major), whereby:- Minor Breach and Material Breach

(i) A *Minor Breach* is any alleged Breach that technically violates one or more Terms and Conditions of the Agreement, but does not destroy the inherent Trust or Value and therefore the Duties and Obligations of the Agreement and is possible to be cured by the offending Party within a reasonable period of time; and

(ii) A *Material Breach*, also known as Major Breach or Fundamental Breach is any alleged Breach as specified within the Terms and Conditions or any other unnamed condition of such a serious nature that unless it is immediately cured by the offending Party, then such alleged Breach is likely to destroy the inherit Trust and Value of the Agreement.

16. A failure to cure any alleged Breach within the Time Limit prescribed and the waiving of the right to appeal to Arbitration shall place the offending Party in Default. Default is therefore any failure to fulfil an Obligation prescribed by any valid Agreement in accord with the present Constitutional Charter after every reasonable opportunity in Good Faith has been presented to the offending Party to remedy and cure the alleged Breach. Default

A Party that is in Default of any valid Agreement automatically accepts they are delinquent in honour and integrity and therefore waives all rights to sue or cross-claim or claim of legal excuse in any legal proceedings or litigation in respect of the particular Agreement.

Article 146 – Covenants & Conventions

1. A Covenant shall be a registered Instrument of Consensus regarding one or more promises. In reference to Covenants:- Covenants

(i) A Covenant must be duly registered and recorded within a proper Ucadia register to be valid and legitimate; and

(ii) When the Covenant relates to Sovereign, Official, Administrative or Member Rights, then the Covenant shall be named according to the larger form of the Consensus (such as Convention, Commission or Contract); and

(iii) When the Covenant relates to Divine or Ecclesiastical Rights in some substantial way, then the Instrument and Consensus shall be known as a Covenant.

2. A *Convention* shall be a registered Instrument of Consensus made between two (2) or more Persons in Equity, whereby each party possesses certain distinct Rights and makes certain Promises in relation to individual Obligations to the Agreement, capable of being enforced in their distinct and independent characters. In reference to Conventions:- Convention

(i) A Convention must be duly registered and recorded within a proper Ucadia register to be valid and legitimate; and

(ii) A Convention shall be known as a Treaty when between a Ucadia Campus, or Province or University and a Non-Ucadian state, or foreign agency.

Article 147 – Commissions

1. A *Commission* shall be a registered Instrument of Consensus possessing certain Divine, or Ecclesiastical or Sovereign authority that bestows or surrenders one or more Rights. In reference to Commissions:- Commissions

(i) A Commission must be duly registered and recorded within a proper Ucadia register to be valid and legitimate; and

(ii) All original conveyance of valid and legitimate Rights and Powers shall be by Commission and no other form of Consensus; and

(iii) All conveyance of Real Property shall be by Commission; and

(iv) A Commission through proper authority and record of intention and action of conveyance is the means of creating valid Title to Property.

2. All Commissions are Unilateral, Bilateral, Trilateral, Multilateral or Inferior:- Types of Commissions

(i) *Unilateral Commission* shall be made by one person or by several persons of the same interest; and attested by an authorised Ucadian Officer having Ecclesiastical Notarial Powers; and

(ii) *Bilateral Commission* shall be made between two (2) parties; and attested by an authorised Ucadian Officer having Ecclesiastical Notarial Powers; and

(iii) *Trilateral Commission* shall be made between three (3) parties; and attested by an authorised Ucadian Officer having Ecclesiastical Notarial Powers; and

(iv) *Multilateral Commission* shall be made between four (4) or more parties; and attested by an authorised Ucadian Officer having Ecclesiastical Notarial Powers; and

(v) *Inferior Claim* or *Deed* shall be any form of Consensus issued under Non-Ucadian or Foreign Law, whereby no valid or legitimate Divine, Ecclesiastical or Sovereign Right shall exist, except by limited record with an authorised Ucadian Officer having Ecclesiastical Notarial Powers.

3. The general principles concerning Inferior Claims, also known as Deeds shall be:- General Principles of Inferior Claims (Deeds)

(i) No conveyance of Ucadia Rights, Powers or Property may be by Deed; and

(ii) Authorised Officers are permitted to execute Deeds for the purpose of registrations necessary in Non-Ucadian and foreign jurisdictions.

4. A *Trust Commission* shall be a Legal Instrument by a Trustor that defines the parameters, scope and constraints of authority in relation to the Trustee. A Trust Deed is not the actual instrument that conveys certain Rights and Property, but the Deed that creates the "container" for such transfer to be effected. However, a Trust Deed is permitted to define the agreement for vesting and transfers to occur upon or after the execution of the Trust Deed. Trust Commission

5. A *Vesting Commission* shall be a deed that effects the transfer of a Right or Property into a Trust. By definition, the Trust must already exist, via a Trust Deed. The general and logical reason that a Vesting Deed cannot occur until a Trust is formed, is a Vesting Deed is in essence a Deed Poll executed by a Grantor, Giftor, Assignor or Delegator, whereas a Trust Deed is an agreement between a Trustor and Trustee. Vesting Commission

Article 148 – Contracts

1. A *Contract* shall be a registered Instrument of Consensus possessing mutual legal Obligation. In relation to Contracts:- Contracts

   (i) A Contract must be duly registered and recorded within a proper Ucadia register to be valid and legitimate; and

   (ii) A valid Contract must contain Mutuality of Obligation whereby all parties are legally bound to perform their obligations, else the Contract shall be null and void; and

   (iii) A Contract must demonstrate evidence of its mutual understanding, offer, intention and agreement between the parties occurring prior to being registered and recorded; and

   (iv) As all valid Contracts must be properly registered and recorded to be valid, any non registered claimed contract shall be invalid and illegitimate.

2. Unlike other forms of Consensus, it shall be the process of Registration and relevant minimum information for valid types of Contracts that shall determine its effect:- Registration Elements and Effects of Contracts

   (i) The type of Contract shall determine the minimum relevant information required and the expected parameters and limits of such values; and

   (ii) Errors within any Instrument used to provide the essential minimum relevant information of a Contract shall only have a bearing to the extent that it impedes the reliability of such key information or the authenticity of the Contract itself; and

   (iii) A value that exceeds or is below the parameters of minimum relevant information associated with a type of Contract shall not be permitted to be registered, even if contained in an executed Contract Instrument. Unless amended, such a Contract shall be considered legally unenforceable; and

   (iv) A Contract containing additional clauses and information beyond the minimum required information of that Contract type shall have no legal bearing on the registered obligations nor legal remedy or relief afforded through such registration and shall be ignored in any legal enforcement of obligation.

TITLE XVII: ACCOUNTS, ACCOUNTING & REPORTING

Article 149 – Accounts & Accounting

1. All financial and economic transactions of the Union shall be subject to the same Sovereign and Administrative Rights of classification, measurement, disclosure and reporting of financial information of the Union, no matter what the type of organ, body, person, trust, estate, fund or entity. Accounts & Accounting

2. An *Account* shall be a list or statement of accounting, monetary or economic transactions, classified by a specific purpose, arising out of a contract or a fiduciary relationship:- Account

   (i) An *Accounting Transaction* shall mean a balance or result of an event having a monetary impact on the financial statements of an entity; and

   (ii) A *Monetary Transaction* shall mean a balance or result of comparison between items of a monetary value of an opposite nature, such as receipts and payments, or deposits and withdrawals, or debits and credits; and

   (iii) An *Economic Transaction* shall mean a balance or result of an exchange of value, such as between assets or equities, or different items of the type.

3. All Accounts of the Union shall possess the same essential elements being *Record Number, Account Name, Account Description, Account Number, Account Owner, Date Opened, Date Closed, Account Trades* and *Status*: Elements of Valid Accounts

   (i) *Record Number* shall be a unique column being the first and left most column in which a whole integer is listed and is sequential (beginning from the integer 1) and unique (not the same) in reference to the table; and

   (ii) *Account Name* shall be a column defining the name of the Account; and

   (iii) *Account Description* shall be a column defining the description of the Account; and

   (iv) *Account Number* shall be a column defining a unique number or alpha-numeric sequence for the Account; and

   (v) *Account Owner* shall be a column defining the Owner or Owners of the Account; and

   (vi) *Date Opened* shall be a column defining date the Account was opened; and

(vii) *Date Closed* shall be a column defining the date the Account was closed; and

(viii) *Account Trades* shall be a column summarising the number of unique Trade Agreements against the Account according to some sub unit of time or agreement, whereby transactions are then recorded; and

(ix) *Status* shall be a column defining the operating status of the Account.

4. The purpose and function of different types of Accounts of a valid Organ, Body, Union, University, Foundation, Province, Entity or Campus of the Union shall be defined within its constituting instrument, consistent with the present Constitutional Charter. Valid types of Accounts shall include (but not be limited to): Valid types of Accounts

(i) A *Bank Account* shall be an Account where Banking Services are provided under a Financial Account Number (FAN); and

(ii) A *Budget Account* shall be an Account designed for the purpose of expressing and planning future and hypothetical revenues, quantities, costs, expenses, assets, liabilities, cash flows and contingencies; and

(iii) A *Contract Account* shall be an Account where certain monies are paid under a Contract Account Number (CAN); and

(iv) An *Exchange Account*, also known as Market Account whereby transactions are recorded, having an Exchange Account Number (XAN); and

(v) A *Fund Account* shall be an Account for the facilitation of a Fund; and

(vi) An *Insurance Account* shall be an Account where certain Funds or Assets are placed as surety against a potential loss, or as assurance; and

(vii) An *Item Account* shall be an Account where monetary values are recorded against individual or groups of products and services; and having an Item Account Number (IAN); and

(viii) A *Journal Account* shall be an Account derived from summarising Memoranda such as "Day Books" of transactions and having a Journal Account Number (JAN); and

(ix) A *Ledger Account*, shall be an Account derived from summarising Journal Accounts and having a Ledger Account Number (LAN); and

(x) A *Member Account* shall be a type of Account for the entry and recording of certain Member rights and property and agreements; and

(xi) A *Project Account* shall be an Account recording transactions associated with a specific project; and

(xii) A *Securities Account* shall be an Account where Securities may be held, purchased or sold; and

(xiii) A *Supplier Account* shall be an Account for the recording of terms and transactions and the supply of goods and services; and

(xiv) A *Treasury Account* shall be an Account for the day to day transactions of government and agency business of a valid and legitimate body politic under a Financial Account Number (FAN); and

(xv) A *Trust Account* shall mean an Account for the holding of monies associated with a Trust formed under a valid and proper Trust Commission agreement.

5. A *Statement of Account* or *Account Statement* shall be a periodic summary of account activity of an Account with a beginning date and an ending date. Statement of Account

6. A *Final Statement of Account* shall be when two (2) persons having previously engaged in one or more monetary transactions together, close an Account by agreeing (a) no more transactions shall occur through the said Account; and (b) the balance appearing to be due from one of them is the final amount to be paid. Final Statement of Account

7. A *Settlement of Account* shall be when a Fiduciary of a Trust agrees to provide an Account, or when a competent court orders a forensic Settlement of Account upon claims of concealment or undue advantage taken by the Trustee. An action for a Settlement of Account shall not necessarily close an Account. Settlement of Account

8. An *Action for Account* shall be when one party of interest of an open Account seeks a proper accounting from the other party by bringing the matter before a competent forum of law, having authority and power to do so under the present Constitutional Charter and associated covenants, charters, constitutions or rules:- Action for Account

(i) The party bringing the Action or Suit shall first demonstrate their status and standing in bringing an Action or Suit, as by the laws of certain Jurisdictions, Body Politic and Societies, types of status shall be ineligible to certain actions; and

(ii) The party bringing the Action or Suit shall identify the type of interest and nature of their relation with the other party; and

(iii) The party bringing the Action shall be clear as to the type of Account required (usually a Statement of Account), or if specifically associated with a Trust, a Settlement of Account; and

(iv) The transactions in question must then be properly investigated by the competent forum of law; and

(v) The "accounting party" or person from whom the Account is required, shall draw up an Account and have it verified by testimony before the information shall be embodied by the competent forum of law under certificate; and

(vi) A body claiming to be a court of law that refuses to order a proper accounting despite proper standing and merits of the aggrieved party, shall cease to hold any Divine, Ecclesiastical, Sovereign or Administrative Rights or Powers as a competent forum of law until such time as the Officers that caused such injury are censured or removed.

9. The status and standing of the parties of an Action for Account or Suit for Account shall include (but shall not be limited to): Standing for Action for Account

(i) Action by one *Partner* against another (Partner) for an Account of the partnership dealings; or

(ii) A *Principal* against their Agent, but never vice versa; or

(iii) A *Beneficiary* against Executors or Trustees for an Account of what they have received (or ought to have received) and paid in respect of the trust property; or

(iv) A *Mortgagor* against a Mortgagee who has entered into possession of the mortgaged property, in order to ascertain what he has received or ought to have received in respect of rents and profits, so that the amount may be set off against the amount payable on the mortgage.

10. A *Debt* shall mean (a) a binding promise or (b) right of action or (c) both reflected as a valid entry in one or more Accounts. A Debt is distinguished from a Debit in that a Debit is an entry in a journal or ledger of a sum owed to the proprietor of some accounts, whereas a Debt is a binding promise or a right of action recorded as some monetary value in a valid Account. Debt

11. In respect of Debt as a binding promise:- Debt as Binding Promise

(i) A Debt may be a solemn obligation under Contract; or

(ii) A Debt may be a binding promise under Bargain.

12. In respect of Debt as a Right of Action:- Debt as Right of Action

(i) A Debt may be a right of demand and enforcement of payment of sum of money due for goods sold under Bargain; or

(ii) A Debt may be a right of demand and enforcement of delivery of goods due for a sum of money under Bargain; or

(iii) A Debt may be a right of demand and enforcement of payment of penalty or compensation for failure to perform an obligation under contract.

13. *Asset* shall mean anything owned by a body or entity capable of producing a positive economic value. More specifically, an Asset shall be a sum of units of monetary value, recorded in one or more designated Accounts, available for the discharge of a Debt and not yet assigned to a specific purpose. Asset

14. *Liability* shall mean a probable future sacrifice of an economic benefit arising from a present obligation of a particular body or entity to transfer some Asset or provide a service to another person as a consequence of some past transaction or event. More specifically, a Liability shall be a sum of units of monetary value, recorded in one or more designated Accounts representing an undischarged moral or legal Obligation. Liability

15. *Income* shall mean inflows of Money or other Assets into one or more designated Accounts returned to a body or entity from rent, tolls, levies, contributions or charges derived from any capital investment; or revenue derived from the main activities of the body or entity as registered or regulated by Ucadian Law. Income

16. *Expenses* shall mean outflows of Money from one or more designated Accounts, including the using up of Assets or occurrences of Liabilities from delivering or producing goods, rendering services, or carrying out other activities that constitute the main activities of the body or entity. Expenses

17. A legitimate, valid, certified and qualified *Accountant* shall be an Officer of a competent forum of law or another Juridic Person duly formed under Ucadian Law, possessing ecclesiastical and clerical status to prepare, enter, manage, tabulate and certify accounts. Accountant

18. A legitimate, valid, certified and qualified *Auditor* be a certified and qualified Accountant under Ucadian Law, appointed in a further position of Trust as Jurist of the Accounts, to conduct a systematic, Auditor independent examination of all related books, accounts, documents and vouchers to ascertain the truth of financial statements made by a particular Ucadia Organ, Body, Union, University, Foundation, Entity, Estate, Trust, Province or Campus under the jurisdiction of Ucadian Law.

Article 150 – Ucadia Accounting System (UAS)

1. *Ucadia Accounts System* (UAS) shall be the highest standard and integrated system for all aspects of accounts as defined by the present Constitutional Charter, associated covenants, charters, constitutions and rules. All Accounts within the bounds of Union Organs, Bodies and Entities shall adhere to the Ucadia Accounts System. The general principles of the Ucadia Accounts System (UAS) shall be:- Ucadia Accounting System (UAS)

   (i) All valid Ucadia Organs, Bodies, Entities, Trusts, Estates, Unions, Universities, Foundations, Provinces, Campuses, Members and Persons of the Union shall use the one and same Accounting System known as the Ucadia Accounts System (UAS) as the primary Accounting System; and

   (ii) All unique Entities, Divisions, Departments, Units, Trusts, Estates, Funds, Corporations, Members and Persons shall be identified by a unique eighteen (18) digit number called a *Member Identity Number* (MIN), being their existing Trust Number or Member Number; and

   (iii) All unique ledgers or funds of Money as controlled by a legitimate body or entity having the Right of *Ius Ecclesiae Templum* in its capacity as Treasury or Bank within the bounds of its jurisdiction for the benefit of one or more unique entities as identified by Member Identity Numbers (MIN), shall be identified by a unique eighteen (18) digit number called a *Financial Account Number* (FAN), representing the unique purpose, identity and type of Money held and transacted; and

   (iv) No Financial Account Number (FAN) may be created without first the existence of a valid Member Identity Number (MIN) for one or more entities as owner(s); and

   (v) All unique and discretely defined economic units of value called an *Item*, involving unique entities as owners or users as defined by Member Identity Numbers (MIN) shall be identified by a unique eighteen (18) digit number called an *Item Account Number* (IAN), representing the unique item, its type, value and economic life; and

   (vi) No Item Account Number (IAN) may be created without first the existence of a valid Member Identity Number (MIN) for one or more entities as holding rights and responsibilities of use; and

(vii) An annual survey and audit of Item Account Number (IAN) shall be called the *Inventory*; and

(viii) All unique and clearly defined agreements of activity in relation to Item Account Numbers (IAN) shall be identified by a unique eighteen (18) digit number called a *Contract Account Number* (CAN), representing the unique agreement and purpose of economic activity; and

(ix) All unique and distinct economic events associated with a Item Account Number (IAN) or Contract Account Number (CAN) shall be identified by a unique eighteen (18) digit number called an *Exchange Account Number* (XAN), representing the unique exchange event of economic activity against the agreement; and

(x) No economic activity of any kind may be authorised unless first there exists a Contract Account Number (CAN) properly connected to an Item Account Number (IAN); and

(xi) All aggregate centres of economic activity involving unique economic Items as Exchange Account Numbers (XAN) in relation to transactions shall be identified by a unique eighteen (18) digit number called a *Journal Account Number* (JAN), representing the unique aggregate journal; and

(xii) The information recorded in a Journal Entry with a valid Journal Account Number (JAN) shall be extracted to the highest level information matched according to double entry bookkeeping into Ledgers also with valid *Ledger Account Numbers* (LAN); and

(xiii) Ledgers corresponding to valid Ledger Account Numbers (LAN) shall be prepared into financial statements.

Ucadia Accounting System Organisation and Administration

2. All authority and powers concerning the proper organisation, administration, instruction, function and enforcement of the Ucadia Accounting Systems (UAS) shall be vested in a Ucadian Body known as the **Ucadia Accounting System Organisation** (UASO) as a permanent organ of the Ucadian Globe Union:-

(i) All valid Ucadia Unions, Universities, Accounting Associations and Foundations shall be members of the Ucadia Accounting System Organisation (UASO) and participate in its funding and operation; and

(ii) The Ucadia Accounting System Organisation (UASO) shall be the supreme Accounting Standards body, having full plenary authority to accomplish its sacred mandate; and

(iii) For the purpose of establishing treaties with non-Ucadian and foreign Accounting Standards bodies, the UASO shall be permitted to register within non-Ucadian jurisdictions a body known as Ucadia Accounting Standards Foundation (UASF); and

(iv) Ucadia entities registered in non-Ucadian and foreign jurisdictions shall seek permission to prepare and report financial statements using the Ucadia Accounting Standards (UAS).

Objects of Ucadia Accounting System Organisation

3. The primary objects of the Ucadia Accounting System Organisation (UASO) shall be:-

(i) Hold, develop and protect the Ucadia Accounting System (UAS) being a model of exemplary, comprehensible and enforceable accounting standards founded on clearly articulated principles in accord with the present Constitutional Charter and associated covenants, charters, constitutions and rules; and

(ii) Promote the knowledge and education of the Ucadia Accounting System (UAS) and its diligent and competent application by all valid Ucadia Organs, Bodies, Entities, Trusts, Estates, Persons, Unions, Universities, Foundations, Provinces, Entities and Campuses; and

(iii) Ensure enforcement of the Ucadia Accounting System (UAS) between all valid Ucadia Organs, Bodies, Entities, Trusts, Estates, Persons, Unions, Universities, Foundations, Provinces, Entities and Campuses to ensure the existence of uniform, high quality, transparent and comparable financial statements and other financial reporting to better enable wise, moral and prudent economic decisions; and

(iv) Establish peaceful and harmonious relations with non-Ucadian and foreign accounting standard bodies to educate and explain the Ucadia Accounting System (UAS) and ensure its acceptance.

Article 151 – Ucadia Money (Moneta) Accounts

1. A *Ucadia Money Account* is an Account holding valid Ucadia Money and managed by the Treasury and Reserve Bank of the Union. All Accounts holding Ucadia Money within the bounds and jurisdiction of the Union are held, owned and operated by the Treasury and Reserve Bank of the Union. Ucadia Money Account

2. No withdrawal of any funds from a Ucadia Money Account of the Union or its subsidiaries is permitted except through proper Authorisation in writing or electronic procedure in accord with these Articles. Authorised Withdrawal

3. No Authorised Purchase may proceed without first the existence of a valid and operational Account Number of the Union and the existence of an amount approved against that Account Number exceeding the value of the proposed purchase and that the amount of the purchase is within the authorised limit for individual transactions. Requirement of Account Numbers for Purchases

4. The Ucadia Money (Moneta) Accounts of Ordinary (Individual) Members shall at all times remain private and confidential from other Ordinary Members, with the following conditions:- Privacy of Ucadia Money (Moneta) Accounts

   (i) Officers and Administrative Officials with sufficient authority, shall have the right of access to view the Money (Moneta) Accounts of Ordinary Members, with every view being logged and viewable by the Account Owner, and a valid reason required for such viewing; and

   (ii) Law Enforcement, Anti-Fraud and Security Officers may view the Moneta Account of an Ordinary Member without such views being made available during the course of the investigation. However the reason for such views must be predicated on an active investigation; and

   (iii) Companies and Entities with whom an Ordinary Member has submitted an application for purchase, may view the summary information of the account, not transactions, to the extent in order to validate the authenticity of the information within the application.

5. All registered Companies and businesses of the Union may query the summary information of the accounts of other Companies with whom they have a valid relation on the following conditions:- All Ucadia Moneta (Money) Accounts of Companies viewable in summary by other companies

   (i) A valid relation between Companies is either an existing contract, new contract or accepted application, proposal, tender or quote. The releasing mechanism to view an account is on the submission by a Company of its official legal documents that by the laws of the Union must be registered with the appropriate University and Union; and

(ii) A query of the accounts of another business shall only be summary information, never individual transactions; and must be based on a valid purpose; and

(iii) Each query shall be logged so that the Company itself can view those relations that have viewed the status of its accounts.

6. When an Ordinary (Individual) Member of the Union becomes an Officer or elected Representative, they shall be required to suspend or place at arms length in trust (if an ongoing business) all private accounts and begin operating an official Ucadia Money (Moneta) Account that is public in its summary information:-

All Ucadia Moneta (Money) Accounts of Officers and Elected Officials Public

(i) All Members of the Union have the right to query the summary information of the Money Accounts of Officers and elected Officials, without such queries being logged or registered; and

(ii) All payments and compensations to Officers and Elected Representatives shall be into their Official Money (Moneta) Account and they shall be prevented from receiving any additional income from any other account; and

(iii) When an elected Official or Officer ceases their Office, they shall be required to still use their Official Account for a further three years, until their private accounts are re-activated and their Official Account is closed. All payments in the intervening period shall be paid into the Official Account until it is closed; and

(iv) If the former Officer takes a new position of Office before the expiry of three years, then then the same Official Account may continue to be used.

Article 152 – Public (Capital) Money Accounts

1. A *Public Money Account* is an Account holding valid Public Money formed in Public Interest for the Public Good and held in custody and under the control of the Union and managed in trust by the Union.

Public Money Account

2. No Banking services are permitted to be used in association with a Public Money Account, except by duly authorised Officers or Agents within the Sovereign Finance & International Solutions Systems Division (SFISSD) of the Union in accord with these Articles. Any

Requirements of Internet and Online Banking

Officer or Agent or person claiming authority on behalf of the Union that seeks to use or operate any Banking service associated with a Public Money Account that is not an authorised member of the Sovereign Finance & International Solutions Systems Division shall be a fundamental breach of obligations and duty.

Article 153 – Foreign (Non-Ucadian) Money Accounts

1. A Non-Ucadian *Currency Account* is an Account holding Currency and managed by the Union. All Accounts holding Currency within the bounds and jurisdiction of the Union are held, owned and operated by the Union, or duly commissioned and designated Agents. Currency Account

2. Officers of the Union, subject to approval in writing from the Board regarding each proposal, are permitted to open and manage Foreign Currency Accounts with recognised and licensed financial institutions within the Jurisdiction of the Law, subject to these Articles: Permission to Operate Bank Accounts

    (i) A unique Foreign Money Account Number in the form prescribed above must first be issued before any Account is opened with a Foreign Bank or Financial Institution; and

    (ii) The Foreign Bank or Financial Institution must not only accept the eighteen (18) digit number as the primary number and mark of the account, but must be able to reflect that number back in their records, even if they choose to use an internal number for their own records; and

    (iii) Any and all assumed, or explicit, or implicit Powers of Attorney of the financial institution, within any documents, contracts, deeds, promises, memorandums, or expressed verbally or by any other means shall not defeat the Rights of the Union as expressed within these Articles. Therefore, any such clauses or explicit or implicit claims shall be void from the beginning (*ab initio*) and shall have no effect, whatsoever; and

    (iv) Any cheques, drafts or pay orders written against deposited Foreign Currency within any Financial Accounts shall be made in the credit or unit of account of the financial institution, with such deposits of Foreign Currency as assurance. Only if the named beneficiary of the cheque or draft or pay order demands the debt to be settled in Foreign Currency shall the non-Ucadian financial institution be authorised to draw down such reserves. Otherwise, the financial institution shall hold the right to keep the cheque, or draft or pay order until such time as the debt is settled and then return to the Union all such instruments.

3. All Original Agreements; or copies thereof regarding Foreign Money Accounts, including any and all applications, approvals, statements, and notices in the possession of an Officer or Agent of the Union shall be immediately provided to the Union Secretary for registration and safe keeping. Failure to provide such documentation and to notify the Union Secretary of such documents shall be a fundamental breach of obligations and duty. Original Agreements with Company Secretary

4. No internet or online Banking services are permitted to be used in association with a non-Ucadian Bank Account, except by duly authorised Officers or Agents within the Treasury, Accounting & Transaction Systems Division of the Union in accord with these Articles. Any Officer or Agent or person claiming authority on behalf of the Union that seeks to use or operate any internet or online Banking service associated with a Bank Account that is not an authorised member of the Treasury, Accounting & Transaction Systems Division shall be a fundamental breach of obligations and duty. Requirements of Internet and Online Banking

5. Excluding Debit Cards authorised and issued in accord with these Articles to Officers or Agents or Contractors, no card services are permitted to be used in association with a Bank Account, except by duly authorised Officers or Agents within the Treasury, Accounting & Transaction Systems Division of the Union in accord with these Articles. Any Officer or Agent or person claiming authority on behalf of the Union that seeks to use or operate any card service associated with a Bank Account that is not an authorised member of the Treasury, Accounting & Transaction Systems Division shall be a fundamental breach of obligations and duty. Requirements of Cards connected to Bank Account

6. No withdrawal of any funds from a Foreign Money Account of the Union or its subsidiaries is permitted except through proper Authorisation in writing or electronic procedure in accord with these Articles. Authorised Withdrawal

7. No Credit Card is permitted to be issued against any Bank Account or to the name of any Officer or Agent or Contractor of the Union. Any Credit Cards, whether solicited or unsolicited, must be immediately handed to the Union Secretary or the Legal Services Department for their cancellation and return to the institution in question. Failure to notify the Union or its subsidiaries of the delivery of a Credit Card, or the use of such a Card shall be a fundamental breach of obligations and duty. Forbiddence of Credit Cards

8. The Officers of the Union are empowered and authorised to issue certain Debit Cards to Officers, Agents and Contractors of the Union Issuance of

against specific Bank Accounts established for such purpose against budgeted and approved expenditures by certain departments from time to time in accord with these Articles. Debit Cards

9. Any authorised individual withdrawal from any Foreign Money Cash Account to the total equivalent value of five thousand (5,000) Ucadia Moneta or greater, shall require the approval of a written or electronic Purchase Order or Transfer Order or Pay Order in accord with these Articles, unless such payment is a recurring payment and approval was previously provided. Withdrawals over 5,000 Moneta require Order

Article 154 – Credit (Market) Accounts

1. A *Credit Account* is an Account specifically established for trade and exchange within one or more Markets within the Jurisdiction of the Union. Credit Account

2. There shall be three types of Credit Accounts being *Goods*, *Credit* and *Sureties*:- Types of Ucadia Market Accounts

   (i) A *Goods Account* is a type of account of a Member for the purchase of goods, the discharge of Goods Market obligations and the receiving of funds in exchange for a sale, or bargain; and

   (ii) A *Credit Account* is a type of account of a Member and associated with the purchasing of Credit Shares and Warrants, the discharge of Credit Market obligations and the receiving of funds in the sale of any Credit Shares or Warrants; and

   (iii) A *Surety Market Account* is a type of account of a Member and associated with the purchasing of Sureties, the discharge of debts and obligations of such transactions and the receiving of funds in the sale of any Sureties or Coupons or other performance.

3. While a Member may possess only one type of Goods, or Credit or Surety Market Account, a Member must have permission and agreement from the management of the particular Market to trade and therefore have their account properly registered. Every valid Market possesses the right to forbid one or more Members from trading. However, every Member has the right to appeal such decisions within Ucadia Courts. Market Accounts must be registered to be used in Market

Article 155 – Budgeting & Financial Reporting

1. All expenditure decisions of the Union and all Departments, Divisions, Foundations, Universities, Provinces, Campuses and Companies of the Union shall operate upon a prior approved and reasonable detailed Budgets approved in writing from a Board of Directors. Budgets

   All Budgets of such entities, excluding budgets on Public Money or Foreign Money, shall be in Union Moneta. However, the settlement of the accounts of above mentioned types of Ucadia entities where the transaction is equal or exceeding one million (1,000,000) Ucadia Moneta must be settled using Silver Credo (Credits).

2. The formulation of budgets and identification of shortfalls between official expenditure and income via Silver Credo (Credit) Budget Accounts is one of the valid and legitimate means of Ucadia Financial Entities approving the spending into circulation of new Silver Credo (Credits). Silver Credo (Credit) Budget Accounts

   Essentially, rather than a bona fide Ucadia entity with authority to hold Silver Credo (Credit) Accounts having to borrow, or raise revenue through higher taxes, if such an entity has declared a sound and compelling business case via detailed budget planning, then an oversight authority has the permission to approve the specific budget shortfall into circulation via a Silver Credo (Credit) Budget Account.

3. The hierarchy of oversight and approval of budgets shall be as follows:- Hierarchy of Oversight for Budget Approval

   (i) Budget shortfalls for the Globe Union are approved by a meeting of all Ucadia Treasuries; and

   (ii) Budget shortfalls for a Regional Union are subject to approval by the Globe Union Treasury; and

   (iii) Budget shortfalls for a University are subject to approval by the relevant Regional Union Treasury; and

   (iv) Budget shortfalls for a Province are subject to approval by the relevant University Treasury; and

   (v) Budget shortfalls for a Campus are subject to approval by the relevant Province Treasury.

4. The primary Budget forms for the Union in relation to all expenditure planning shall be the five (5) year Master Budget, the two (2) year Master Budget and the ninety (90) Day Rolling Master Budget. There shall be three key stages associated with the development of each of these Master Budgets: Key Budget Reports

(i) ***Draft (Provisional) Master Budget*** whereby an estimated total spend is estimated, including the necessary funds and like revenues and returns are calculated; and

(ii) ***Preliminary Master Budget*** produced by Department Heads and Divisional Heads of the Union during the early stages of project development; and

(iii) ***Final Master Budget*** also known as General Accounts produced by Department Heads and Divisional Heads of the Union that is then presented for approval to Members at a General Meeting.

5. A Financial Report of the Union shall comprise one or more of the following financial documents and statements: Financial Reporting

(i) A Balance Sheet; and

(ii) An Revenue Statement; and

(iii) A Cash Flow Statement; and

(iv) A statement of changes in equity; and

(v) Notes, comprising a summary of significant accounting policies and other explanatory notes.

6. The Union shall ensure that any Financial Report shall present fairly the financial position, financial performance and cash flows of the Union being a faithful representation of the effects of transactions and other events or conditions in accordance with the definitions and recognition criteria for assets, liabilities, income and expenses in accord with Accounting Standards and International Law. All Financial Reports, excluding reports on foreign fund reserves, shall be in Union Moneta. Fair Presentation and Compliance

7. An Asset shall be classified as current for the purpose of financial reporting, when it satisfies any of the following criteria: Current Assets

(i) It is expected to be realised in, or is intended for sale or consumption in, the normal operating cycle of the Union; or

(ii) It is held primarily for the purpose of being traded; or

(iii) It is expected to be realised within twelve months after the reporting date; or

(iv) It is cash or a cash equivalent unless it is restricted from being exchanged or used to settle a liability for at least twelve months after the reporting date.

8. A Liability shall be classified as current when it satisfies any of the Current Liabilities following criteria:

(i) It is expected to be settled in the normal operating cycle of the Union; or

(ii) It is due to be settled within twelve months after the reporting date; or

(iii) the Union does not have an unconditional right to defer settlement of the liability for at least twelve months after the reporting date.

9. As a minimum, the face of the balance sheet shall include line items that present the following amounts: Balance Sheet

(i) Property, plant and equipment; and

(ii) Investment property; and

(iii) Intangible assets; and

(iv) Financial assets; and

(v) Investments accounted for using the equity method; and

(vi) Intellectual Property Assets; and

(vii) Inventories; and

(viii) Trade and other receivables; and

(ix) Cash and cash equivalents; and

(x) Trade and other payables; and

(xi) Provisions; and

(xii) Liabilities and assets for current tax; and

(xiii) Deferred tax liabilities and deferred tax assets; and

(xiv) Minority interest, presented within equity; and

(xv) Issued capital and reserves attributable to equity holders of the parent.

10. As a minimum, the face of the income statement shall include line items that present the following amounts for the given period: Income Statement

(i) Revenue; and

(ii) Finance costs; and

(iii) Share of the profit or loss of associates and joint ventures accounted for using the equity method; and

(iv) Tax expense; and

(v) A single amount comprising of (a) the post-tax profit or loss of discontinued operations, and (b) the post-tax gain or loss recognised on the measurement to fair value less costs to sell, or on the disposal of the assets or disposal group(s) constituting the discontinued operation; and

(vi) Profit or loss.

Article 156 – Financial Controls & Oversight

1. Financial Controls are the processes for assuring the Union achieves its Objects in operational effectiveness and efficiency, reliable reporting and compliance with Company Law and other regulations and policies. The Union shall adopt best practice in its Financial Controls and Oversight in ensuring its limited resources are properly directed, monitored and measured. Financial Controls

2. In respect of every Asset valued at more than five thousand (5,000) Union Moneta, the Asset Management Register shall record the following minimum information:- Asset Management Register

(i) The model number and unique serial number of the good or asset; and

(ii) The date of purchase or acquisition and a photo of the good or asset at the time of purchase or acquisition; and

(iii) Whether the good or asset is under warranty and the date of expiry of such warranties; and

(iv) A copy or reference to the manual (if relevant) including any proper conditions for storage, cleaning and use; and

(v) The person currently in custody of the asset and its location of storage; and

(vi) The authorisation code or reference or number and the name of the authorisation register in relation to the Authorised Possession of Asset.

3. The possession of an Asset shall be deemed duly Authorised when: Authorised Possession of Asset

(i) The person possessing or controlling the Asset is duly authorised and a record exists of such authorisation in one or more of the proper registers and records of the Union; and

(ii) A valid record exists within the Asset Management Register of the Union; and

(iii) No other conditions exist at the time that would otherwise disqualify the person from being authorised to possess or use or control the Asset.

TITLE XVIII: MONEY, PROPERTY, GOODS & FUNDS

Article 157 – Ucadia Money (Moneta)

1. **Ucadia Money (Moneta)**, is the third highest possible form of valid and legitimate Money, issued under the exclusive Sovereign Rights: *Ius Regnum Moneta* and *Ius Regnum Vectigalis Moneta*, in accord with the most sacred Covenants *Pactum De Singularis Caelum, Pactum De Singularis Christus, Pactum De Singularis Islam, Pactum De Singularis Spiritus, Carta Sacrum De Congregationis Globus* and the seven (7) Constitutional Charters of the Ucadia Regional Unions.

   It is the primary lawful and legal currency and used by Ucadia Members, Entities, Organs and Bodies to value the ownership, use and exchange of all goods, services, assets and obligations.

Ucadia Money (Moneta)

2. Ucadia Moneta (Money) shall have the following permanent value relationships:-

   (i) 1,000,000,000 Ucadia Moneta (Money) = 1 Supreme Credo (Credit); and

   (ii) 10,000,000 Ucadia Moneta (Money) = 1 Gold Credo (Credit); and

   (iii) 1,000 Ucadia Moneta (Money) = 1 Silver Credo (Credit); and

   (iv) 1 Ucadia Moneta (Money) = 1 Ucadia Asia Union Moneta (Money).

Face value relationships of a Ucadia Money (Moneta)

3. All valid and legitimate Ucadia Organs, Bodies, Unions, Agencies, Universities, Provinces, Campuses, Entities, Trusts, Estates and foreign registered Companies and Associations shall use "**Ucadia Moneta**" as their standard unit of account. Ucadia Moneta shall represent a summary term for all Ucadia Union Moneta money units of the Ucadia Regional Unions and Colonies.

Ucadia Moneta (Money) as Standard Unit of Account

4. All Ucadia Money is based on the positive credit and gift of spirit, energy and respect from the Divine Creator and from Nature and the creative abilities of people of all races, genders, religions, ages and philosophies.

   In contrast, non-Ucadian units of currency are based on systems of debt, borrowings, bonds, bankruptcy and involuntary servitude (financial slavery).

   Thus, there is such a fundamental difference between Ucadia Money and Non-Ucadian Money as opposites, that technically it is impossible to validly exchange one form of money with the other.

   Instead, any such appearance of exchange is spiritually, morally,

Fundamental Difference of Nature of Non-Ucadian Debt Money to Ucadia Money lawfully and legally an exchange of gifts whereby the non-Ucadian currency is given and separately the Ucadian Money is given in return, not because of any true exchange of value, but the value of the action of trust by the individual or body.

5. Valid and operational Ucadia Foundations shall be permitted, from time to time, to issue instruments such as Ucadia Moneta (Money) Bonds, Notes, Coins and Stamp Certificates under strict contracts, whereby the Exchange Rate and/or Maturity is to the maximum of parity with a Non-Ucadian currency. Authorised Special Contracted Rates of Exchange

For the purpose of accounting, these shall be called *Authorised Special Contracted Rates of Exchange* and shall only be available under limited conditions.

6. The Exchange Rate used for calculating the Exchange of Ucadia Moneta (Money) for non-Ucadian currencies shall be based on a *Fixed Exchange Rate* (FER) between Ucadia Moneta (Money) and Special Drawing Rights (SDR) and then whatever the daily rate of the preferred currency against Special Drawings Rights (SDR) on a daily basis. Fixed Rate of Exchange

The Exchange Rate between Ucadia Moneta (Money) and non-Ucadian currencies shall never be permitted to be floating.

7. Notwithstanding any collapse in value or re-valuation of Special Drawing Rights (SDR), or *Authorised Special Contracted Rates of Exchange*, The *Fixed Exchange Rate* (FER) between Ucadia Moneta (Money) and Special Drawing Rights (SDR) shall appreciate at a rate of: between 0.686% per quarter or 2.7% per annum and 2.041% per quarter and 8.2% per annum according to the fixed table below:- Appreciating Fixed Rate of Exchange

(i) In 2010, FER = 0.311 @ 0.742% per qtr and 3.0% p.a.; and

(ii) In 2011, FER = 0.320 @ 0.742% per qtr and 3.0% p.a.; and

(iii) In 2012, FER = 0.330 @ 0.743% per qtr and 3.0% p.a.; and

(iv) In 2013, FER = 0.340 @ 0.726% per qtr and 2.9% p.a.; and

(v) In 2014, FER = 0.350 @ 0.705% per qtr and 2.8% p.a.; and

(vi) In 2015, FER = 0.360 @ 0.686% per qtr and 2.7% p.a.; and

(vii) In 2016, FER = 0.370 @ 0.669% per qtr and 2.7% p.a.; and

(viii) In 2017, FER = 0.380 @ 0.650% per qtr and 2.6% p.a.; and

(ix) In 2018, FER = 0.389 @ 1.267% per qtr and 5.1% p.a.; and

(x) In 2019, FER = 0.413 @ 1.406% per qtr and 5.6% p.a.; and

(xi) In 2020, FER = 0.436 @ 1.334% per qtr and 5.3% p.a.; and

(xii) In 2021, FER = 0.460 @ 1.263% per qtr and 5.1% p.a.; and

(xiii) In 2022, FER = 0.483 @ 1.955% per qtr and 7.8% p.a.; and

(xiv) In 2023, FER = 0.526 @ 2.041% per qtr and 8.2% p.a.; and

(xv) In 2024, FER = 0.566 @ 1.190% per qtr and 4.8% p.a.; and

(xvi) In 2025, FER = 0.593 @ 1.133% per qtr and 4.5% p.a.; and

(xvii) In 2026, FER = 0.620 @ 1.084% per qtr and 4.3% p.a.; and

(xviii) In 2027, FER = 0.647 @ 1.039% per qtr and 4.2% p.a.; and

(xix) In 2028, FER = 0.674 @ 1.000% per qtr and 4.0% p.a.; and

(xx) In 2029, FER = 0.701 @ 0.959% per qtr and 3.8% p.a.; and

(xxi) In 2030, FER = 0.728 @ 0.924% per qtr and 3.7% p.a.; and

(xxii) In 2031, FER = 0.755 @ 0.891% per qtr and 3.6% p.a.; and

(xxiii) In 2032, FER = 0.782 @ 0.862% per qtr and 3.4% p.a.; and

(xxiv) In 2033, FER = 0.809 @ 0.831% per qtr and 3.3% p.a.; and

(xxv) In 2034, FER = 0.836 @ 0.805% per qtr and 3.2% p.a.; and

(xxvi) In 2035, FER = 0.863 @ 0.780% per qtr and 3.1% p.a.; and

(xxvii) In 2036, FER = 0.890 @ 0.758% per qtr and 3.0% p.a.

Ucadia Moneta (Money) Register

8. A new Ucadia Moneta (Money) Register for each Ucadia Union shall be formed and published every two (2) years.

If the total value of transactions between Ucadia Moneta (Money) Accounts during the two (2) year period reflects less than ten (10 %) of the total value of the Register, no recalculations are required and the Register may be re-issued under new Instrument Numbers for the following two (2) years.

Structure of a Ucadia Moneta (Money)

9. The following eight (8) criteria are recognised and ratified as the essential requirements of a valid Ucadia Moneta (Money) Instrument listed in the Ucadia Moneta (Money) Register:-

(i) At least one (1) valid unit of universal value evidenced by the existence of a unique eighteen (18) digit serial number representing the valid existence of the Ucadia Moneta (Money) belonging to the Great Ledger of Ucadia Moneta (Money) serial numbers for all Ucadia Moneta (Money) ever created and issued under the particular Ucadia Union Bank; and

(ii) The eighteen (18) digit Great Register number representing the valid Master Account Number into which the one (1) or more Ucadia Moneta (Money) have been placed; and

(iii) A single beneficiary Master Account Number to whom the Ucadia Moneta (Money) is granted; and

(iv) A record of the valid eighteen (18) digit Great Register number of the authorised office of the Union Reserve Bank that first created the Ucadia Moneta (Money); and

(v) A record of the valid eighteen (18) digit Great Register number of the Member commissioned to the office of the Union Reserve Bank that first created the Ucadia Moneta (Money); and

(vi) The eighteen (18) digit Great Register number of the instrument to which the one (1) or more Ucadia Moneta (Money) have been assigned; and

(vii) The Ucadian Time at which the Ucadia Moneta (Money) was legitimately created and assigned to its particular instrument; and

(viii) The eighteen (18) digit Great Register number representing the valid Silver Credo (Credit) instrument specifically underwriting the issue of these one (1) or more Ucadia Moneta (Money).

10. There shall be twenty-two (22) different types of Ucadia Moneta (Money) Accounts, including:- Ucadia Moneta (Money) Accounts

(i) *Moneta Action Account* is an account bringing New Moneta into Circulation transferred from a Moneta Sovereign Account as credit for one or more corresponding actions or activities in relation to Ucadia related technology applications. Trusted relations are credited Moneta into a Moneta Action Account each and every time they perform valuable activities representing a real world association of economic activity and units of account; and

(ii) *Moneta Bond Account* is an account bringing New Moneta into Circulation transferred from a Moneta Sovereign Account as underwriting to an issued bond, so that no bond ever issued under Ucadia can ever possibly be in default. When the certificate is “redeemed” the account is settled and cleared to a Moneta Cash Account with Conversion to foreign currency a separate right and issue; and

(iii) *Moneta Budget Account* is an account holding an unrealised amount of Moneta for a specific purpose; and

(iv) *Moneta Capital Account*, is an account holding a certain amount of Moneta transferred from a Moneta Cash Account as effectively "paid up capital" against a specific asset; and

(v) *Moneta Cash Account*, also known as a "clearing account" as the primary Moneta Account for clearing obligations. Every Moneta Account holder always has one Moneta Cash Account; and

(vi) *Moneta Coin Account* is an account bringing New Moneta into Circulation transferred from a Moneta Sovereign Account as underwriting to a negotiable Coin Certificate or actual minted batch of Moneta Coins. When the certificate is "redeemed" the account is settled and cleared to a Moneta Cash Account; and

(vii) *Moneta Contingency Account* is an account holding a certain amount of Moneta transferred from a Moneta Cash Account as contingency against an incomplete contract, or risk, or option or contract to complete or come into effect on conditions; and

(viii) *Moneta Credit Account* is an account bringing New Moneta into Circulation transferred from a Moneta Sovereign Account as an advance "on demand" of new Moneta on the agreement of a repayment or deposit of other valuable considerations, including the payment of non-Ucadian currencies and provision of some form of collateral; and

(ix) *Moneta Demand Account* is an account holding an unrealised Demand and Debt for Moneta that is due on account of one or more breaches and failures of contract and *bona fide* losses; and

(x) *Moneta Donation Account* is an account bringing New Moneta into Circulation transferred from a Moneta Sovereign Account as recognition for any historic foreign (non-Ucadian) currency finalisation, whether the person intended to exchange for Moneta or not, or whether a formal loan or credit agreement was ever considered; and

(xi) *Moneta Exchange Account*, also known as a "settlement account" as the primary Moneta Account for settling market obligations; and

(xii) *Moneta Fund Account*, is an account bringing New Moneta into Circulation transferred from a Moneta Sovereign Account as valuation to some other fixed corpus (body) of assets held in trust for a fixed term and assigned to the control of a valid Ucadia entity; and

(xiii) *Moneta Gain Account* is an account holding an unrealised

Claim for Moneta that is due on account of a *bona fide* profit against one or more registered assets with previous values; and

(xiv) *Moneta Loss Account* is an account holding an unrealised Claim for Moneta that is due on account of a *bona fide* loss against one or more registered assets with previous values; and

(xv) *Moneta Payment Account* is an account holding repayments in Moneta; and

(xvi) *Moneta Penalty Account* is an account holding the voluntary or assigned Moneta payments as charge of penalties against breaches of contract; and

(xvii) *Moneta Sovereign Account* is an account bringing New Moneta into Circulation created upon the underwriting of Ucadia Silver (Credit) Credo held in trust. Only valid Ucadia entities hold Sovereign Accounts. Ucadia Moneta is never transferred from a Moneta Sovereign Account into another account, unless there is a corresponding valid trigger and event. In this sense, all Moneta is effectively "spent" into circulation one transaction at a time based upon some key economic activity rather than arbitrary releases of large amounts that can disrupt the effectiveness of Moneta in circulation; and

(xviii) *Moneta Stamp Account* is an account bringing New Moneta into Circulation transferred from a Moneta Sovereign Account as underwriting to a negotiable Stamp Certificate or actual minted batch of Moneta Stamps. When the certificate is "redeemed" the account is settled and cleared to a Moneta Cash Account; and

(xix) *Moneta Suspension Account* is an account holding a certain amount of Moneta transferred from other Moneta Accounts of an individual or company in respect to disputed assets,or agreements or an unpaid demand of debt; and

(xx) *Moneta Surety Account* is an account holding a certain amount of Moneta transferred from a Moneta Cash Account as effectively "insurance" against a specific contract; and

(xxi) *Moneta Valuation Account* is an account holding an unrealised Valuation of an asset in Moneta; and

(xxii) *Moneta Vocation Account* is an account bringing New Moneta into Circulation transferred from a Moneta Sovereign Account as an advance for wages and employment under contract of a person employed, or sponsored (through grants to businesses) by a valid Ucadia entity.

11. Only a registered and *bona fide* Ucadia Member may possess and use one or more Ucadia Moneta (Money) Accounts.

Qualification for Ucadia Moneta Accounts

The Ucadia Union Banks may consider additional Terms of Service as are necessary in the function of Ucadia Moneta (Money) Accounts.

12. In accord with proper Divine, Ecclesiastical, Sovereign and Administrative Law:-

Ucadia Moneta (Money) for the discharge and settlement of obligations

(i) Ucadia Money shall be used for the payment, discharge and settlement of all debts, debits, obligations, taxes, fines and penalties between Ucadia Members, using Ucadia Money Accounts where such sums are stated in Ucadia Money amounts; and

(ii) Ucadia Money shall be recognised and acknowledged as the highest and most legitimate and valid Legal Tender for the payment, discharge and settlement of all debits, debts, obligations, taxes, fines and penalties, whether they be public or private; or domestic or foreign, in relation to any and all societies, bodies politic, communities, associations, trusts, estates, funds, corporations, aggregates and persons.

13. When a duly recorded and authorised tender of the correct sum of Ucadia Money for the payment, discharge and settlement of any debts, debits, obligations, taxes, fines and penalties is made:-

Honouring Ucadia Money

(i) Providing an authorised Ucadia Money Account exists in the name of the body, trust, estate, fund, person or entity receiving the Ucadia Money Instrument, the receiver of such Ucadia Money is spiritually, morally and legally bound to accept such funds, in accord with proper Divine, Ecclesiastical, Sovereign and Administrative Law; and

(ii) If a duly authorised tender of the correct sum of Ucadia Money is refused, rejected or dishonoured by any society, or body politic, or community, or association, or trust, or estate, or fund, or corporation or person, then such a profane, unlawful, illegal and immoral action shall be a formal acknowledgement and confession of the existence of a valid and legitimate debt and obligation against such a profound dishonour equal in three (3) times value to the original sum refused, rejected or dishonoured; and

(iii) Failure to pay on notice and demand for the payment of a valid and legitimate debt and obligation against a party equal in three times value to the original sum refused, rejected or dishonoured, shall be a formal acknowledgement and confession of delinquency. Authorised Ucadian organs, bodies, trusts, estates, persons, funds and entities shall then have the right to pursue any and all further action and punitive acts to recover such debts and obligations.

14. Any and all forms of compound interest, by any name, representation or calculation shall be a profane act of sacrilege against Divine, Ecclesiastical and Sovereign Law; and a deliberate declaration and act of perfidy, treachery and immorality against all proper Executive and Administrative Law; and shall therefore be banned, forbidden and entirely suppressed. Compound Interest Forbidden

Article 158 – Ucadia Property

1. By Divine, Ecclesiastical, Sovereign and Administrative Rights, Ucadia Property Rights shall be the highest form of valid and legitimate Property Rights, consistent and in accord with the most sacred Covenant *Pactum De Singularis Caelum*:- Ucadia Property

   (i) *Ius Divinum Proprietatis* exists as the highest Divine Rights of Ownership of Use or Fruits of Use of Property; and

   (ii) *Ius Ecclesiae Proprietatis* exists as the highest Ecclesiastical Rights of Ownership of Use or Fruits of Use of Property, as inherited from the Divine Rights *Ius Divinum Proprietatis*; and

   (iii) *Ius Regnum Proprietatis* exists as the highest Sovereign Rights of Ownership of Use or Fruits of Use of Property, as inherited from the Ecclesiastical Rights *Ius Ecclesiae Proprietatis*; and

   (iv) *Ius Administrationis Proprietatis* exists as the highest Administrative Rights of Ownership of Use or Fruits of Use of Property, as inherited from the Sovereign Rights *Ius Regnum Proprietatis*.

2. *Property* shall mean the highest registered Right a Person shall have or hold within a Lawful Jurisdiction to Control or Use or Claim any Thing or the Fruits of any Thing that possesses a monetary value. In reference to Property, Rights and Things:- Property

   (i) Property shall always pertain to Persons and not Beings; and

   (ii) A Right without any conceivable monetary value cannot be considered Property; and

   (iii) A Thing in the context of Property shall be any Right that can be purchased or sold or inherited; and attached by operation of law to a corporeal object, whether fixed or movable; and

(iv) Any Right that can be purchased or sold means a Right in Trust without a named Beneficiary and therefore a Good; and

(v) When one is duly recorded in a valid Ucadia Register as possessing a Right or Claim of Right over Control or Use of a Thing, or Fruits of a Thing, then such a Person may be referred to as the "Owner" of that Right; and

(vi) The highest and most authoritative record of Ownership shall be a valid record within a Ucadia Register.

3. There shall be eight (8) possible forms of Property Right or "Ownership" of Control or Use or Claim of any Thing or the Fruits of any Thing, (in order of status and standing) being:-

Forms of Property as Control or Use or Claim

(i) Owner of Right of Control of a Thing; and

(ii) Owner of Right of Use of a Thing; and

(iii) Owner of Right of Control of the Fruits of Use of a Thing; and

(iv) Owner of Right of Use of the Fruits of a Thing; and

(v) Owner of Claim of Right of Control of a Thing; and

(vi) Owner of Claim of Right of Use of a Thing; and

(vii) Owner of Claim of Right of Control of the Fruits of Use of a Thing; and

(viii) Owner of Claim of Right of Use of the Fruits of a Thing.

4. No Claim of Right or Right of Use of Property shall be valid, legitimate, moral, lawful, legal or permissible concerning any Ucadia or Non-Ucadia body politic, corporation sole, entity, association, agency or person unless such a Claim of Right or Right of Use of Property is duly recorded within a Register of a legitimate and valid body possessing *Ius Ecclesiae Proprietatis, Ius Regnum Proprietatis* or *Ius Administrationis Proprietatis* in accord with the most sacred Covenant *Pactum De Singularis Caelum*.

No Right to Property unless recorded in Register under Proper Rights

5. It is the most sacred Covenant *Pactum De Singularis Caelum*, and no other, that restores the rights, dignities, history and cultural respect of all Original Peoples and Nations. Therefore, all rights and claims of Original Peoples and Original Nations concerning all forms of Property are first sourced and originate from Ucadia Law before any other non-Ucadian society or non-Ucadian multi-jurisdictional body.

Rights of Original Peoples and Nations to Property sourced from Ucadia Law

6. No land register, or titles register or estate roll shall be valid, legitimate, moral, lawful, legal or permissible concerning any Ucadia or Non-Ucadia body politic, corporation sole, entity, association, agency or person unless such a Register or Roll is duly authorised in

No Land or Titles or Estate Register valid unless authorised

accord with the most sacred Covenant *Pactum De Singularis Caelum*. under Ucadia

7. To pursue and fulfil its proper Objects, the Union by innate Right shall acquire, retain, administer and alienate Property and Temporal Goods within its Jurisdiction. Property and Temporal Goods of the Union

8. The Union shall acquire Temporal Goods by every just means of natural or positive law permitted to other bodies politic and corporate. Acquisition of Temporal Goods

9. The Union has the innate Right to require from its Officers, Agents, Employees, Contractors, Members, Suppliers and Customers, those things, including Temporal Goods, that are necessary for the Objects proper to it; and no temporal body possesses any right or authority or power to impede such Right. Right of support etc.

10. By virtue of its superior Rights, the Union and its duly authorised Officers shall have the absolute Divine, Ecclesiastical, Sovereign and Administrative Rights to settle any and all purchases and conveyances of Land and Property with and between non-Ucadian societies and their agencies and corporations by Ucadia Money as the highest legitimate form of public money and legal tender. Settlement in Ucadia Money

Article 159 – Ucadia Official Estates

1. "**Ucadia Official Estates**" are those Superior and Juridic Estates formed in association with named and defined Offices within the present Constitutional Charter and associated valid covenants and constitutions, consistent with Article 36 (*Trusts & Estates*) of the most sacred Covenant *Pactum De Singularis Caelum*. Ucadia Official Estates

   Each and every named and defined Office within the present Constitutional Charter and associated valid covenants and constitutions shall represent both a unique Ucadia Person and unique Ucadia Estate possessing certain beneficial rights and obligations associated with Ucadia Property.

   Such rights and obligations, including any associated property are rights and obligations possessed by each unique Ucadia Office and not with the valid and legitimate occupant of such an office. When an individual (or individuals) cease to hold a specific Ucadia Office, their right of use concerning any Ucadia Property possessed by that office also ceases.

2. Ucadia Official Estates exist to ensure the proper function and operation of Ucadia Offices, through the acquisition, configuration and maintenance of property; and the provision of suitable stipends, pensions and settlement of expenses directly related to such offices. Purpose of Ucadia Official Estates

Ucadia Official Estates enable the protection of the dignity of such offices, especially in the growth and function of Ucadia Societies; and to ensure the holders and legitimate occupants of such offices are afforded all the necessary support to perform their duties.

3. The following Principles and Objects shall be used in forming and administering the Ucadia Official Estates of the Union:- Principles in forming Ucadia Official Estates

(i) *Sufficiency* shall be the principle that the proposed Ucadia Estate is compliant with Ucadia covenants, constitutions, statutes, regulations and procedures; and that sufficient evidence exists to support the establishment, size and nature of the particular estate; and

(ii) *Proportionality* shall be the principle that the size and nature of the proposed Ucadia Estate is appropriate to the dignity and significance of the related Ucadia Office; and consistent and equal to the size and nature of other Ucadia Estates associated with Ucadia Offices of a similar level of seniority and dignity; and

(iii) *Adequacy* shall be the principle that the size and nature of the proposed Ucadia Estate is sufficient for its intended purpose, including (but not limited to) the purchase, configuration of any property; and the settlement of any ongoing stipends, pensions and related expenses; and

(iv) *Utility* shall be the principle that the amount of Ucadia Money set aside the for establishment or top-up of a particular Ucadia Estate shall be legitimately consumed in the course of the function of the related Ucadia Office, or the purchase or improvement of property to be used by the related Ucadia Office and not for investment purposes or purposes not directly connected to the function of the Ucadia Office.

4. The Annual Base Level Minimum Wage ("ABL") relative for each Ucadia University and Region, as established through the Ucadia Compensation Model ("UCM") System, shall be used as the basis of calculating the size of all Ucadia Official Estates, except The Ucadia Official Estate of the Visitor and Ucadia Official Estates of Ucadia (Temporary) Foundations. Minimum Wage as Base-Line for Calculation

5. The maximum size and total value of any individual Ucadia Official Estate for an Organ or Corporation Sole of a Ucadia Global, Regional, University, Provincial or Campus Society shall be:- Limits on size of Juridic Person Estates

(i) *Global or Regional* shall be one hundred and forty four thousand (144,000) times the Annual Base Level Minimum

Wage ("ABL") as calculated for the world or region; and

(ii) *University* shall be seventy two thousand (72,000) times the Annual Base Level Minimum Wage as calculated for the University; and

(iii) *Province* shall be thirty six thousand (36,000) times the Annual Base Level Minimum Wage as calculated for the relevant University; and

(iv) *Campus* shall be twelve thousand (12,000) times the Annual Base Level Minimum Wage as calculated for the relevant Campus.

6. The Ucadia Official Estate of the Visitor shall be a global Estate of Ucadia and shall be set at a budget of one hundred and forty four million (144,000,000) Ucadia Moneta (Money). Ucadia Official Estate of the Visitor

As the Visitor is not permitted to personally own any assets derived from Ucadia, the Official Estate of the Visitor shall be responsible for the acquisition of suitable property as the official permanent residence of the Visitor, whilst alive; and the settlement of all expenses associated with the office.

Upon the death of the original architect and founder of Ucadia as Visitor, no other person shall be permitted to claim, occupy or hold such sacred office. Instead, the Ucadia Official Estate of the Visitor shall continue to maintain the dignity as to the origins and first formation of Ucadia, including the acquisition of historical properties, or rebuilding or preservation of original structures of cultural and historic significance to Ucadia in its foundation.

7. The Ucadia Official Estate for each Ucadia (Temporary) Foundation shall be set at a budget of one million four hundred and forty thousand (1,440,000) Ucadia Moneta (Money) per Office of Director, to a maximum of twelve (12) Directors per Ucadia Foundation. Ucadia Official Estates of Directors of Ucadia Foundations

As Directors of Ucadia Foundations are not permitted to personally financially benefit from such positions of trust, other than nominal compensation, the Official Estates of the Directors of each Ucadia Foundation shall be responsible for the acquisition of suitable property; and the settlement of all expenses associated with the execution of such offices.

Article 160 – Instruments & Securities

1. To pursue and fulfil its Primary Objects, the Union by innate Right shall form, make, create, print, impress, ingross, seal, publish, issue, acquire, retain, dispose, transfer, administer, register, record, enrol, inroll, endorse and indorse all manner of Instruments and Securities subject to the present Articles. Instruments & Securities

2. Subject to these Articles, the Union can acquire and dispose of Instruments and Securities as Temporal Goods by every just means of natural or positive law permitted to other Persons and bodies politic and corporate. Acquisition and Disposal of Instruments & Securities

3. The Union has the innate Right to permit and grant its Officers, Agents, Employees, Contractors, Members, Suppliers and Customers, those things, including Instruments and Securities of the Union as Temporal Goods, that are necessary for the Objects proper to it; and no temporal body possesses any right or authority or power to impede such Right. Right of Members and Instruments & Securities

4. Officers, Agents, Employees, Contractors, Members, Suppliers and Customers are free to acquire, use, hold and dispose of Instruments and Securities as Temporal Goods for the benefit of the Union, in accord with these Articles. No temporal body possesses any right or authority or power to impede, or deny or obstruct exercising such an act of free will. Members use of Instruments & Securities of the Union

5. Officers, Agents, Employees, Contractors, Members, Suppliers and Customers of the Union are free to record and register Instruments and Securities of the Union as Temporal Goods with other bodies and civil powers in accord with the present Articles. Recording of Instruments & Securities of the Union with Foreign Bodies

Article 161 – Goods & Services

1. ***Goods*** or ***Good***, shall be a gift or a promise of beneficial Right of Use for Sale or Bargain of Tangible Property. *Service* shall be a gift or a promise of Performance of Obligation for Payment associated with some Intangible Property. Goods & Services

2. ***Sale*** shall be when the title to a thing is given in Trust to another in exchange for a price of lawful money, also given in Trust. In reference to the concept of a Sale:- Sale
   - (i) A Sale shall always involve Goods and therefore always involve Rights in Trust as Goods; and
   - (ii) A Sale shall always involve two (2) distinct trusts having two distinct trust corpus – one where the buyer is trustee and one

where the seller is trustee; and

(iii) It is only when the sale is completed do the two (2) separate trusts dissolve as a settlement into one, providing the conditions of sale make that possible.

3. *Bargain* shall be a Contract of Mutual Bindings (Promises) in Trust as Security whereby one party promises to assign a right as property for some consideration; and the other party promises to receive the property and take good care of it and pay the consideration. In reference to the concept of a Bargain of Goods:- Bargain

(i) A Bargain shall always involve Goods and therefore always involves Rights in Trust as Goods; and

(ii) Similar to a Sale, a Bargain shall always involve two (2) Trusts for a Bargain to exist: The one for the Buyer and one for the Seller; and

(iii) A Bargain shall never be a transfer of Title but a Bailment of Goods or Use for some financial consideration; and

(iv) The Seller in a Bargain never gifts the property like a Sale and the terms of Consideration may also involve some return of a Bailment of Money; and

(v) The key operating element of a Bargain is the Mutual Binding Promises that are also called Debts.

4. To pursue and fulfil its proper purposes, authorised Ucadia Bodies and Entities by innate Right shall form, acquire, retain, administer and alienate Temporal Goods & Services independently from any non-Ucadian and foreign civil powers. Subject to the present Constitutional Charter, associated covenants, charters, constitutions and laws:- Ucadia Goods & Services

(i) Authorised Ucadia Organs, Bodies and Entities shall have the Right to require from their Members, those things, including Temporal Goods, that are necessary for the purposes proper to it; and no temporal or spiritual body possesses any right or authority or power to impede such Right; and

(ii) Members shall be free to give Temporal Goods for the benefit of authorised Ucadia Organs, Bodies and Entities. No temporal or spiritual body shall possess any right or authority or power to impede, or deny or obstruct such Members exercising such an act of free will.

Article 162 – Prices, Fees, Fines & Penalties

1. The Union shall regulate the authorised range of prices for all goods and services offered in the common market of the Union and temporarily those Market Zones where price fixing, gouging or other manipulation is proven as persistent.

Prices, Fees, Fines & Penalties

Furthermore, the Union shall strictly regulate the permissible range for the setting of fines and penalties, to ensure the elimination and suppression of unfair fines and penalties across the Union.

2. The Union shall form a permanent body known as the **Union Pricing Authority (UPA)** to fulfil its mandate to regulate all price ranges for goods and services offered in the common market of the Union; and to enforce any temporary controls and regulation of a market that has suffered persistent manipulations and corruptions of its pricing mechanisms.

Pricing Authority

3. The *Union Pricing Authority* (UPA) shall only have the power and authority to set Price Ranges. A Price Range is a minimum and a maximum price assigned to a good or a service, whereby providers in the market may then offer their goods anywhere on the scale between those prices:-

Price Range

(i) The Union Price Authority shall never have the authority to set a single fixed price in contrast to a Price Range; and

(ii) The Minimum Price set for any Good or Service must be researched and established upon the cheapest viable cost that a sufficient sample of small and medium providers can afford to offer, without going out of business; and

(iii) The Union Price Authority shall never be permitted to use the Minimum Price of large providers of Goods and Services to establish the minimum price benchmark, unless there is no other provider of that specific Good or Service in the Union; and

(iv) The review of the Minimum Price set for any Good or Service shall be determined according to the nature and classification of the Good and Service and its volatility and source of contributing costs. The greater the volatility of contributing costs and dependence on imports and exchange variables, the more frequent the review of Minimum Price; and

(v) All Price Ranges for all Goods and Services subject to the Union Price Authority shall be reviewed not less than once every twenty four (24) months, if not sooner; and

(vi) The Maximum Price shall always be a function of the Minimum Price as well as the nature of the Good or Service, the level of competition and volatility of demand and cost inputs. The greater the competition, the narrower the difference between Minimum and Maximum Prices, whereas the greater the volatility of inputs, the greater the difference; and

(vii) The Maximum Price shall never be less than one fifth greater than the Minimum Price of the same Good or Service; and

(viii) The Maximum Price shall never be greater than three times the Minimum Price of the same Good or Service.

4. It shall be a serious offence for a person, company or entity to attempt to offer or sell a Good or Service regulated by the Union Pricing Authority above or below the mandated Price Range. Offence to sell Good or Service above or below Price Range

Article 163 – Funds, Stock & Stockholders

1 A *Fund* is recognised as a sum of equal units representing certain Property Rights of monetary value, recorded in one or more designated Accounts of a valid Ucadia Body or Entity; and set apart for a term of years and one or more specific purposes; and available for the payment of debits, debts, legacies and claims in accord with the present Constitutional Charter. Fund

In respect of the character, purpose and nature of a Fund:-

(i) The Instrument of formation and of guiding the character, purpose and nature of one or more Funds shall be a Trust Covenant as a Fund Constitution issued and approved by a valid Body; and

(ii) The underlying Rights and Property used to derive the value of a Fund must be set aside and sealed in its own Trust in accord with the Trust Covenant to protect the integrity of the Fund and prevent any re-transfer or re-conveyance that might threaten the value of the Fund. This means, the only ownership of rights of property that may be conveyed or discharged against the underlying Rights and Property shall be Claims, also known as "Charges"; and

(iii) The life or operation of a Fund (the period it conducts business) shall be the maximum as specified by the present Constitutional Charter, or associated covenants, charters, constitutions and laws; and

(iv) A Fund may be actual money, or notes, or certificates, or securities or stocks able to be converted or negotiated for monetary value, providing the nature and monetary value of each element is clearly outlined within the accounts of the Fund; and

(v) The terms of negotiation of the Stock of a Fund for other stock, or actual money, or notes, or certificates, or other securities shall be determined on a Fund by Fund basis, including whether a particular Fund is able to purchase the Stock of another Fund of the Body, to what maximum and other conditions (if any); and

(vi) A Fund shall never be the original Assets themselves, but the Derivation of the value of the underlying Property, as recorded in the accounts and ledgers of the Fund, to permit the remission, remittance, settlement and discharge of debits, debts and obligations; and

(vii) When the term of a Fund expires, it shall be absolutely forbidden to conduct any more new business. However, it may continue to manage and administer existing business and obligations until all such existing obligations and settlements expire or are balanced or dissolved or liquidated; and

(viii) The property and assets held in Trust shall be absolutely forbidden to be released from such a Trust underwriting a Fund until after the term of a Fund expires and after all obligations and settlements are balanced and the fund dissolved or liquidated and the purpose of the Trust is fulfilled and the Trust dissolved; and

(ix) A Fund ceases to exist when it is properly liquidated or dissolved by an action in accord with the instrument of its creation, or after the expiry of its term. In accord with these articles, the administrators of a valid Fund are morally obligated to ensure the timely dissolution of the Fund as soon as practical after such a valid event.

Article 164 – Equity, Shares & Shareholders

1 *Equity* in the financial and corporate sense is recognised as:- Equity

(i) Certain Ownership Rights and Obligations, recorded in one or more designated Registers of a valid Ucadia Body or Entity; and that accrue to a party by transaction, subject to terms of an agreement; and are exercisable upon a change of circumstances or conditions of the agreement; and

(ii) An estimated or actual monetary value or debt associated with the said Ownership Rights and Obligations, after the value of any debts and obligations are deducted from the value of the assets related to the said Ownership and Obligations Rights.

2. In respect of the character, purpose and nature of (Financial) Equity:- Character, Purpose & Nature of Equity

(i) The conditions of total Equity of a body shall be determined by its Constitution (and any valid amendments). In principle, a body that permits by its Constitution the transaction of Ownership Rights and Obligations shall be said to be limited by Shares, whereby the owners of such Shares may share in the distribution of any profits, but shall also be liable for any unpaid debts; and

(ii) In defining its total number of Shares, the classes of Shares and the initial value, or par value of each class of Shares, a body is capable of defining the terms and conditions of Equity to Shareholders in holding an interest by Share; and

(iii) Unlike a Fund, the underlying Rights and Property used to derive any positive net Equity value of an entity (after liabilities are deducted) do not have to be set aside and sealed in its own Trust; and

(iv) Unlike a Fund, an Equity interest can continue without interruption, providing the body is capable of paying its debts; and the terms and conditions of the Shareholder agreement allow it; and

(v) The Equity of a body ceases when the body itself ceases and any remaining profits are distributed after all debts and obligations are paid.

Article 165 – Ucadia Financial System (UFS)

1. The Ucadia Financial System (UFS) shall be a comprehensive and complete global financial system of *Laws, Legal Structures and Constructs, Courts and Legal Enforcement, Registers and Rolls, Instruments of Value, Agreements of Value, Markets, Accounts, Credit, Money, Treasuries, Banks, Firms,* and *Goods* capable of operating as a self contained system, or underwriting, or amalgamating or successfully replacing non-Ucadian financial systems of a city, state, nation or region or globe, in accord with the present most sacred Constitutional Charter. Ucadia Financial System (UFS)

The fourteen (14) core elements of the Ucadia Financial System (UFS) shall include:-

(i) *Laws* that consistently define the rules of the Ucadia Financial System; and

(ii) *Legal Structures and Constructs* such as Rights, Trusts, Estates, Property and Funds that enable the consistent establishment of ownership, value and the administration of intangible and tangible forms of property; and

(iii) *Courts and Legal Enforcement* that ensure the honest and impartial application of Laws and enforcement and protection of Legal Structures and Constructs; and

(iv) *Registers and Rolls* for the recording of various Legal Structures and Constructs of Value, including Instruments derived therefrom; and

(v) *Instruments of Value* derived from Registers and Rolls, capable of being exchanged themselves, or being held as collateral and security; and

(vi) *Agreements of Value* signalling transactions of economic activity, capable of being held as collateral as security, or monetised (converted or securitised) into an Instrument of Value; and

(vii) *Markets* for the various exchanges of rights, obligations, credit, goods, property, instruments, funds and money between market participants; and

(viii) *Accounts* being the ledgers of Markets and various Institutions, enabling the recording of transactions, exchanges and settlements; and

(ix) *Credit* being an internal and enclosed form of Money of a Market, enabling exchange and the settlement of transactions, but that in order to be exchanged as money beyond the market must be "converted" by means of the negotiability (portability) of Instruments, Agreements and/or Goods that accompanies the issuance of such Credit; and

(x) *Money* being units of measure, units of account, units of redemption for value, means of exchange and reliable stores of value; and

(xi) *Treasuries* being the custodians and controllers of Money and the purchasers of Securitised Instruments and Agreements purchased by Banks in the conversion of Financial Credit into Money; and

(xii) *Banks* being the providers of Credit into certain Financial Markets and the sponsors (converters) of Credit into Money through the collateralisation of monetisable Instruments and Agreements secured in the provision of such Credit; and

(xiii) *Firms* being trading entities within Markets and the producers of Goods available and capable of being sold or exchanged within those Markets; and

(xiv) *Goods* (including Services) manufactured by Firms and sold and traded within Markets.

2. A structure shall not be legally, lawfully or morally considered a Financial System, no matter how complex, universally adopted or accepted, if it engages in any of the following practices:-

When an structure is not a legitimate Financial System

(i) That the Laws of the system may be changed arbitrarily to the betterment of a few and the detriment of others, without fair recourse or remedy; or

(ii) That units of value may be introduced as money without any legitimate underwriting, thus devaluing the total stock of existing units of money; or

(iii) That units of value may be destroyed or withdrawn, without account for the provenance or historical basis of such lost units, thus inflating the remaining value of total stock of units of money; or

(iv) That credit may be introduced into a market, without defined rules as to the limits of credit of the market, nor the prior allocation rights of participants; and further that such credit may be exported and converted into "money", thus devaluing the total stock of existing units of money; or

(v) That instruments issued in reference to credit, or agreements, including all derivatives thereof, are permitted to exceed the value of the original value of the asset that created all subsequent derivatives.

Article 166 – Ucadia Banks & Financial Institutions

1. By Divine, Ecclesiastical, Sovereign and Administrative Rights, all Rights to impose any form of Rent, Toll, Levy, Contribution or Charge against Money shall be subject to the most sacred Covenant *Pactum De Singularis Caelum*, the present Constitutional Charter, associated covenants, charters, constitutions and laws and no other:-

Rights to impose Rent, Toll, Levy, Contributions or Charges against Money

(i) *Ius Divinum Vectigalis Moneta* exists as the highest Divine Rights to impose Rents, Tolls, Levies, Contributions or Charges against Money as inherited from the collection of Divine Rights *Ius Divinum Iuris*; and

(ii) *Ius Ecclesiae Vectigalis Moneta* exists as the highest Ecclesiastical Rights to impose Rents, Tolls, Levies, Contributions or Charges against Money, as inherited from the Divine Rights *Ius Divinum Vectigalis Moneta*; and

(iii) *Ius Regnum Vectigalis Moneta* exists as the highest Sovereign Rights to impose Rents, Tolls, Levies, Contributions or Charges against Money, as inherited from the Ecclesiastical Rights *Ius Ecclesiae Vectigalis Moneta*; and

(iv) *Ius Administrationis Vectigalis Moneta* exists as the highest Administrative Rights to impose Rents, Tolls, Levies, Contributions or Charges against Money, as inherited from the Sovereign Rights *Ius Regnum Vectigalis Moneta*.

Authority to impose Rent, Toll, Levy, Contributions or Charges against Money and notion of Interest

2. Only bodies, trusts, estates, funds, persons and entities duly authorised by the appropriate Ucadian Rights shall then have the authority to impose Rents, Tolls, Levies, Contributions or Charges against Money:-

(i) A body, trust, estate, fund, person or entity without proper authority from the present Constitutional Charter, or associated covenants, charters, constitutions or laws shall have no right to impose Rents, Tolls, Levies, Contributions or Charges against Money; and

(ii) The use of the term "Interest" is permitted, including the representation of authorised Rents, Tolls, Levies, Contributions or Charges against Money as a percentage, providing the identity and function of such an imposition is clearly identified and disclosed; and

(iii) The failure to properly disclose the valid and legitimate identity and function behind the use of the term "Interest" and the simplification of representing such impositions as a percentage shall render such a Document, Form or Instrument illegitimate, invalid and liable for suspension, termination or dissolution with no right to relief, redress or compensation.

Rights to act and function as Treasury or Financial (Banking) Body

3. By Divine, Ecclesiastical, Sovereign, Official and Administrative Rights, all Rights to function as a treasury or bank or financial institution, including (but not limited to) the issue of credit, accept deposits, grant loans, advances, cash, overdrafts, discounting of bills, letters of credit, safety deposits, insurance and conversion shall be subject to the most sacred Covenant *Pactum De Singularis Caelum*, the present Constitutional Charter, associated covenants, charters, constitutions and laws and no other:-

(i) *Ius Divinum Templum* exists as the highest Divine Rights of a valid and legitimate Treasury or Financial (Banking) Body; and

(ii) *Ius Ecclesiae Templum* exists as the highest Ecclesiastical Rights of a valid and legitimate Treasury or Financial (Banking) Body, as inherited from the Divine Rights *Ius Divinum Templum*; and

(iii) *Ius Regnum Templum* exists as the highest Sovereign Rights of a valid and legitimate Treasury or Financial (Banking) Body, as inherited from the Ecclesiastical Rights *Ius Ecclesiae Templum*; and

(iv) *Ius Administrationis Templum* exists as the highest Administrative Rights of a valid and legitimate Treasury or Financial (Banking) Body, as inherited from the Sovereign Rights *Ius Regnum Templum*.

Non-Ucadian and Foreign Bodies Treasury and Banking Treaties with Ucadia

4. Any organ, or body or entity, including Non-Ucadian and Foreign bodies, agencies and entities, that do not possess any Divine, Ecclesiastical, Sovereign or Administrative authority to function as a valid and legitimate Treasury or Financial (Banking) Organisation, may be granted under limited treaty such rights, on condition:-

(i) Ucadia Money and the Ucadia Financial System are fully recognised and accepted as currency and legal tender; and

(ii) The entity provides and operates all necessary conversion and exchange services required to ensure the effective exchange of Ucadia Money and Assets for non-Ucadian and Foreign forms of Money and Capital; and

(iii) The entity agrees to conduct transactions involving Ucadia Money and Assets in accord with the Ucadia Accounting System (UAS).

TITLE XIX: MARKETS, TRADE & INDUSTRY

Article 167 – Markets, Trade & Industry Standards

1. The Markets, Trade and Industry Standards of the Union are those objects, rules, systems and methods to support the economic and social imperatives of all Members and people of the Union in ensuring sustainable and balanced economic prosperity and quality conditions of life, consistent with the objects of the Union. Markets, Trade & Industry Standards

   The Union shall adopt and maintain a standard set of markets, trade, employment and industry standards. Thereafter, all parts of the Union are bound and obligated to adhere to such standards.

Article 168 – Markets

1. A Market shall be a trusted space (virtual or real) where three (3) or more buyers and sellers may safely and fairly exchange Goods or Services. Ucadia Markets

   There shall be four (4) basic elements that define a Market in addition to the existence of three or more buyers and sellers, namely *Market Rules, Standard Unit of Measure, Accounts & Bookkeeping* and *Conversion and Settlement of Accounts*:-

   (i) *Market Rules* means that a space or place cannot possibly be a market unless it possesses the most essential of Rules based upon the Golden Rule of Law of equality, fairness and trust; and

   (ii) A *Standard Unit of Measure* means there are consistent standards of valuation across a market so "like can be exchanged for like". This standard unit is what is most commonly called Money; and

   (iii) *Accounts & Bookkeeping* is the inescapable and necessary fact that the accounts being the registers of title and ownership are intimately linked to the operation of any market, including the certificate of proof of transaction; and

   (iv) *Conversion and Settlement of Accounts* is in essence the clearing mechanism of trade, that requires the ability of initial conversion, the ability to trade, the settlement of accounts and then the redemption of any remainder back into some portable form to be withdrawn from the market, if one chooses.

2. A valid *Ucadia Market* is a sacred space, or a sacred event at a consecrated place whereby Ucadia Members agree to meet under certain Terms and Conditions and exchange gifts:- Ucadia Market

   (i) A proper Ucadia Market is strictly for valid Ucadia Members and therefore is always private and never public; and

(ii) A Ucadia Market is both the expression of a Sacred Sacrament and Doctrines of the Union, where Members participate in a sacred Ritual mandated by Divine Right. Therefore, a valid Ucadia Market must always occur within a sacred space or as a sacred event at a consecrated place; and

(iii) Members at a Ucadia Market exchange gifts as part of a sacred Ritual mandated by Divine Right. Any claim of commercial transactions, or profit activity shall be rejected as absurd, sacrilegious, profane and against the rights and religious doctrines of the Union.

3. Every Market shall be governed by its own Rules and Standards, complying to the present Constitutional Charter:- Ucadia Market Rules and Standards

(i) Ucadia Market Membership and Entry shall only ever be for Full Members or Guests as Provisional Members and no other; and

(ii) Market Accounts are independent Accounts to any particular Market, but are restricted to Goods, Credit or Surety Market Accounts; and

(iii) A Ucadia Market may reserve the Right to acquire any Market Account registered and approved to have a minimum level of Ucadia Union Moneta as a Contingency to participate in a Market; and

(iv) By being approved and registered for a particular Ucadia Market, a Ucadia Member grants the administration of that Market limited powers to withdraw funds or deposit funds in relation to certain approved trades within the Market, subject to proper Accounting from the Market as proof; and

(v) All valid Ucadia Markets have the right to define as Terms and Conditions Trade Volume Limits and Trade Time Limits; and

(vi) All valid Ucadia Markets have the right to define as Terms and Conditions the time period for settlement and clearing of Accounts, providing the frequency is no less than once in a twelve hour cycle and no more frequent than hourly; and

(vii) A Ucadia Market may define the Market Platform and Exchange Methods it provides; and reserves the right to modify such Platform or Exchange Methods providing full disclosure is provided to all registered Market Members.

4. Ucadia Markets shall primarily provide two essential models of Exchange being Places and Exchanges:- Market Places and Exchanges

(i) A *(Market) Place* is a physical or virtual sacred space or place where Members can exchange gifts, utilising various exchange methods. A Place model provides a degree of control within the hands of each Member as a Merchant or Trader or Vendor to price their goods and services as well as set fair terms of exchange, still within the overall organised framework of the (Market) Place; and

(ii) A *(Market) Exchange* is a highly organised physical or virtual sacred space or place where Members can exchange gifts, according to a well defined and more limited set of rules. By applying stricter conditions, a (Market) Exchange seeks to provide a greater level of certainty and trust. Thus, all Ucadia Credit Markets and Surety Markets are always founded on (Market) Exchange models.

5. A *Market Zone* is the limits and bounds whereby a valid Ucadia Market shall function in terms of geography, or body politic, or industry or time zone or a combination of all such criteria. Every Market has a specific Zone limit that defines the extent of its jurisdiction. The purpose of Market Zones is to preserve, protect and nurture the prosperity of Ucadia Communities at every level and to reduce the risk of predatory market behaviour. There are essentially six levels of Market Zones being Local, Campus, Province, University, Union and Globe:- Market Zones

(i) A *Globe Market Zone* is a Market Zone whereby a Ucadia Member as a buyer or seller may be located anywhere on planet Earth. Ucadia forbids Global Markets for Ordinary Members and restricts such Markets for Society Members and State Members in reference to financial products from Ucadia Universities and Union entities as well as unique goods from regions; and

(ii) A *Union Market Zone* is a Market Zone restricted by the bounds of the Union. Ucadia forbids Union markets for Ordinary Members and restricts such Markets for Company Members, Society Members and State Members in reference to financial products and company to company trade; and

(iii) A *University Market Zone* is a virtual or physical Market restricted by the bounds of the university. Such Market Zones are designed to defend and grow the economic integrity of a University and support the development of competitive economies of scale, without the risk of loss of wealth through "price shopping"; and

(iv) A *Province Market Zone* is a virtual or physical Market restricted by the bounds of the province. Such Market Zones are designed to nurture regional economies and in particular industries of scale and competitive advantage; and

(v) A *Campus Market Zone* is a virtual or physical Market restricted by the bounds of a Ucadia Campus. Such Market Zones are designed to encourage diverse and vibrant Goods and Service economies as well as specialities based on climate, conditions, knowledge and history that enable the Campus to compete with other Campuses at a University and Union levels for particular goods and services; and

(vi) A *Local Market Zone* is a Market restricted by the bounds of a physical place within the bounds of a Campus. Local Market Zones are exclusively for Goods Markets.

Article 169 – Goods Markets

1. A *Goods Market* is a sacred space, or a sacred event at a consecrated place whereby Ucadia Members agree to meet under certain Terms and Conditions and exchange goods and currencies as gifts. Goods Market

2. Goods Markets shall exist for the benefit of Ucadia Members, Ucadia Campus and Provincial economies, the growth in local employment, improvement in quality of life, the provision of essential services and independence of Ucadia Members:- Purposes of Goods Markets

(i) The first and primary purpose of a Ucadia Goods Market is to encourage the provision of food and essential services to enable the independence of Ucadia Members at a Campus and local level from any foreign and non-Ucadian markets; and

(ii) The second purpose of a Ucadia Goods Market is to protect and grow local jobs, local businesses and local economies, particularly when such local economies have been devastated by loss of capital, or closure of small and independent businesses; and

(iii) The third purpose of a Ucadia Goods Market is to provide a fair, transparent and honest environment for Ucadia Members to exchange gifts, without imposition, threat, theft or predatory behaviour; and

(iv) The fourth purpose of a Ucadia Goods Market is to encourage local economic diversity and improve the quality and safety of local goods.

3. Goods within a Ucadia Goods Market can be purchased, sold and exchanged solely using Ucadia Union Moneta by exchanging recognised global non-Ucadian currency within the top twenty most exchanged non-Ucadian Foreign Currencies into Ucadia Union Moneta at the agreed Rate of Exchange (RE) on the day. Ucadia Moneta may then be converted into a Foreign Currency as a separate transaction in accord with the conditions of the present Constitutional Charter. Method of acquisition and exchange

4. To reduce the risk of deliberate or mistaken distortions of a Ucadia Goods Market, there shall be limits placed on the volume of Goods of a particular Member as well as the maximum price of any Good as a proportion of Goods Market size:- Limits on Price and Volume

(i) When the average trade of a Ucadia Goods Market is less than fifty thousand (50,000) Union Moneta, the maximum price allowable for any one particular Good or single transaction shall be one thousand (1,000) Union Moneta; and

(ii) When the average trade of a Ucadia Goods Market is greater than fifty thousand (50,000) Union Moneta but less than two hundred and fifty thousand (250,000) Union Moneta, the maximum price allowable for any one particular Good or single transaction shall be two thousand five hundred (2,500) Union Moneta; and

(iii) When the average trade of a Ucadia Goods Market is greater than two hundred and fifty thousand (250,000) Union Moneta but less than one million (1,000,000) Union Moneta, the maximum price allowable for any one particular Good or single transaction shall be ten thousand (10,000) Union Moneta; and

(iv) When the average trade of a Ucadia Goods Market is greater than one million (1,000,000) Union Moneta but less than twenty million (20,000,000) Union Moneta, the maximum price allowable for any one particular Good or single transaction shall be seventy five thousand (75,000) Union Moneta.

Article 170 – Capital Markets

1. A *Ucadia Capital Market* is a sacred space, or a sacred event at a consecrated place whereby Ucadia Members agree to meet under Capital Market

certain Terms and Conditions and exchange shares, warrants and currency as gifts. Ucadia Capital Markets are private and exclusively for Ucadia Members only.

2. Ucadia Capital Markets shall exist for the benefit of Ucadia Company Members, the focus and support of Local, Campus and Provincial Company growth and prosperity, the growth in local employment and job opportunities, improvement in local economies and economic activity and the viability and competitiveness of Ucadia Company Members:- *Purposes of Capital Market*

    (i) The first and primary purpose of a Ucadia Capital Market is to assist local and regional Ucadia Company Members in gaining access to capital in order to grow and employ more people locally; and

    (ii) The second purpose of a Ucadia Capital Market is to provide an honest and transparent market, free of manipulation, corruption, theft and artificial distortion; and

    (iii) The third purpose of a Ucadia Capital Market is to restore the economic stability and integrity to Campus, Province and University economies and provide trusted and consistent environments for investment, particularly those associated with fiduciary obligations.

3. Capital within a Ucadia Capital Market can be purchased, sold and exchanged solely using Ucadia Union Moneta by exchanging recognised global non-Ucadian currency within the top twenty most exchanged non-Ucadian Foreign Currencies into Ucadia Union Moneta at the agreed Rate of Exchange (RE) on the day. Ucadia Moneta may then be converted into a Foreign Currency as a separate transaction in accord with the conditions of the present Constitutional Charter. *Method of acquisition and exchange*

4. The primary Market Mechanism of a valid Ucadia Capital Market shall be called a Capital Market Settlement. A Capital Market Settlement is when owners of Shares and potential buyers of Shares lodge their various Offers and Bids at certain Prices and then at the allotted time, all such Offers and Bids are then processed according to the Capital Market Settlement Rules. *Capital market settlement*

5. A Capital Market Session is a collection of Capital Market Settlements over a given day. The maximum length of a Capital Market Session shall be twelve hours and the maximum number of Capital Market Settlements within a Capital Market Session shall be twelve, or one per hour. *Capital market session*

6. A Ucadia Capital Market enables Ucadia Company Members to list a certain number of Shares in their Company or a Specific Company Fund for sale to other Members willing to purchase such Shares within the Capital Market. The Market will then list three prices per Share listed being (Average) Bid, (Average) Offer and (Average) Value:-

Listing and Share Prices

(i) The (Average) Bid Price is the average asking price across all bids of the previous Capital Market Settlements of the Capital Market Session, or the previous trading day; and

(ii) The (Average) Offer Price is the average selling price offered across all offers of the previous Capital Market Settlement, or the previous trading day; and

(iii) The (Average) Value Price is the average of Bid and Offer prices of all previous Capital Market Settlements for the previous three trading days.

7. The Capital Market Settlement rules shall be determined by the Capital Market and shall include, but not be limited to:-

Capital Market Settlement Rules

(i) All Bid, Offer and Value Prices of Shares are permitted to be listed as fractions of Union Moneta. However, all settlements shall be made in complete units, rounding down any outstanding difference before payment; and

(ii) Excluding initial offerings, a Bid or Offer may not be made that is greater or lesser than ten percent of the Average Value Price; and

(iii) Excluding initial offerings, the total volume of shares of a Bid or Offer may not be greater than ten percent of the total listed stock; and

(iv) If an Offer is not fully met, it shall carry over to the next and subsequent Capital Market Settlements and shall be settled by the next best price at the next Capital Market Settlement, but shall lapse if unfulfilled after twenty four successive Capital Market Settlements; and

(v) If a Bid is not fully met, it shall carry over to the next and subsequent Capital Market Settlements and shall be settled by the next best price at the next Capital Market Settlement, but shall lapse if unfulfilled after twenty four successive Capital Market Settlements; and

(vi) A Member can only place Offers on stock they own. Only one Offer per stock per Capital Market Settlement may be placed;

and

(vii) A Member can only place one Bid per stock per Capital Market Settlement; and

(viii) Capital Market Settlements are resolved by ordering the smallest volume Bids and Offers to be processed first and the largest volumes processed last. No advantage exists to high frequency trading as such forms of share purchases do not exist in Ucadia Capital Markets.

8. The Union and Members shall prepare their financial reports, except for cash flow information, using the accrual basis of accounting. Financial Reports

Article 171 – Surety Markets

1. A Ucadia Surety Market is a sacred space, or a sacred event at a consecrated place whereby Ucadia Members agree to meet under certain Terms and Conditions and exchange bonds and currencies as gifts. Ucadia Surety Markets are private and exclusively for Ucadia Members only. Surety Markets

2. Ucadia Surety Markets shall exist for the benefit of Ucadia State Members and Society Members, the focus and support of Local, Campus and Provincial infrastructure investment, sustainment and improvement of local essential services, the growth and strength of local employment, improvement in quality of life and the food and economic health and viability of Ucadia Society Members and State Members:- Purposes of Surety Market

(i) The first and primary purpose of a Ucadia Surety Market is to assist local and regional Ucadia Society and State Members in gaining access to capital in order to grow and employ more people locally; and

(ii) The second purpose of a Ucadia Surety Market is to provide an honest and transparent market, free of manipulation, corruption, theft and artificial distortion; and

(iii) The third purpose of a Ucadia Surety Market is to restore the economic stability and integrity to Campus, Province and University economies and provide a trusted and consistent environment for investment, particularly those associated with fiduciary obligations (i.e. retirement funds, mutual funds, member funds etc.).

3. Sureties within a Ucadia Surety Market can be purchased, sold and exchanged solely using Ucadia Union Moneta by exchanging Method and Acquisition and recognised global non-Ucadian currency within the top twenty most exchanged non-Ucadian Foreign Currencies into Ucadia Union Moneta at the agreed Rate of Exchange (RE) on the day. Ucadia Moneta may then be converted into a Foreign Currency as a separate transaction in accord with the conditions of the present Constitutional Charter. Exchange

4. Ucadia Surety Markets shall function according to the same rules as Ucadia Capital Markets. Same Rules of Operation as Capital Markets

Article 172 – Intellectual Property Rights

1. Intellectual Property ("IP") and Intellectual Property Rights (*Iurium Intellectus Proprietas*) are terms recognised by international law in reference to Primary and Exclusive Rights created through the imagination, invention and origination of the mind including, but not limited to musical, literary and artistic works; and discoveries and inventions; and words, phrases, symbols and designs. The formal recognition of Intellectual Property ("IP") Rights in law may include such registration and gazette systems such as copyright, trademarks, patents, industrial design rights, trade dress and trade secrets as well as such Rights as moral Rights, *sui generis* Rights and related Rights. Intellectual Property Rights

2. A Patent and Trademark Office shall be established as a permanent Agency of the Union for the management and operation of the Union laws concerning the granting and issuing of patents and the registration of trademarks. Patent and Trademark Office

3. A Copyhold and Copyright Office shall be established as a permanent Agency of the Union for the management and operation of the Union laws concerning the granting and issuing of copyhold and copyright. Copyhold and Copyright Office

4. All Intellectual Property, Patents, Trademarks, Copyhold and Copyright is administered exclusively by Ucadia, under Ucadia Law as the highest Ecclesiastical Law. Therefore, no Ucadia Rights, or Intellectual Property or Copyhold or Copyright may be surrendered, or abrogated or registered to another third party. Ucadia and Union Intellectual Property

   Ucadia Law and the Union recognise only those clauses and sections of treaties and conventions that are not in conflict with Ucadian Law or these present Articles.

5. Any claims against the Intellectual Property of the Union, or such claims for naturally occurring biological occurrences, or the deliberate genetic manipulation of biological material to claim uniqueness is forbidden in all its forms, reprobate, morally repugnant and unlawful and illegal. Forbidden Claims of Intellectual Property

Furthermore, any claims of Intellectual Property in favour of synthetic and artificial narcotics and pain medication, whilst attempting the suppression of naturally occurring narcotics and pain medication is a crime against humanity and shall be forbidden, reprobate and to be suppressed in all its forms.

Any foreign or lesser state that seeks to enforce or uphold such morally repugnant, unlawful and illegal claims, binds themselves to the full liability of such acts and consents to the just consequences of any action or enforcement against them.

6. Any attempt or pursuit by any foreign or lesser body to trademark the names of its citizens, or the property of the Union or Ucadia shall be resisted with the full force and powers of the Union, with such bodies, persons and officials culpable of such morally repugnant, reprobate and forbidden acts accepting the full liability and consequences of their actions and the subsequent actions enforced against them. Forbidden Claims of Trademark

7. The unauthorised registration of any Ucadia Intellectual Property, or Rights or Intellectual Property of the Union, including (but not limited to) the attempted registration or claim of ownership, authorship of such material by a Person, whether or not a Ucadia Member, shall be a most grave offence against the Union and it shall be the solemn and moral obligation of each and every single Ucadia Member to ensure such an offence is punished and any such false records and registrations are expunged. Unauthorised registration of Trademark or Copyright an offence

A foreign body, or foreign power, or foreign entity or foreign person that is knowingly party to enabling such a serious offence and refuses to expunge and remove such a fraud, consents to a Holy Writ being issued against themselves, whereby every foreign official and agent is enjoined by name and every moral person and spirit is empowered to use any and every means available to prosecute against such an offence until every record and every memory and every part is expunged, wiped clean and rendered to dust.

8. A person fulfilling the function of Director under a valid Agreement with the Union shall as a fundamental condition of any such Agreement consent to give, convey and vest any and all Intellectual Property Rights concerning the adaption and production of any original work to the Union immediately upon creation. Furthermore, upon request by the Union in the event of the expiration or termination (howsoever occurred) of any valid Agreement, the Director shall at their own costs and expense promptly deliver to the Union all copies of any Creation or original works then in the custody, control or possession (including any drafts thereof) of the Director, whether in their completed forms or not. Vesting of Intellectual Property Rights of Officers and Agents

Article 173 – Customs, Tariffs & Protections

Customs, Tariffs & Protections

1. A Tariff is a Customs duty or tax on imports or exports of goods by a place of arrival or departure. Such duties are prone to promoting economic distortions, without necessarily assisting the very domestic industries intended to be supported. Therefore all Tariffs and Customs duties or taxes on the import or export of goods between Members of the Union is forbidden.

   Instead, Market rules shall define the limits and protections for local, regional, national and supranational markets in support of sustainable economic balance and well being.

Customs Union

2. The Union shall comprise a customs union that shall cover all trade in goods and which shall involve the prohibition between Member States of customs duties on imports and exports and of all charges having equivalent effect, and the adoption of a common customs tariff in their relations with non-Union and non-Ucadian countries.

Article 174 – Employment, Wages & Salaries

Employment, Wages and Salaries

1. The Union shall adopt standards for employment and the fair payment of wages and salaries as reward for dignified and honest effort, recognition of skill and continuous learning.

Ucadia Compensation Model

2. The Ucadia Compensation Model ("UCM") exists as the means and method whereby the Total Compensation Package offered and paid to each and every Officer, Agent or Contractor in recognition of services performed for the Union shall be made. The Ucadia Compensation Model is based on a "grading system" for Officers "O", Agents "A" and Contractors "C" whereby each and every Function of the Union is matched to one grade; and any unique instance of such a function as a unique position must then reflect a compensation package within the limits of the grade attached to it.

   A Total Compensation Package is the total value of all Salary, or Wages, or Fees, or Bonuses, or Expense Compensations or Retirement Savings or other ancillary benefits provided to an Officer or Agent or Contractor by the Union. A Total Compensation Package must always be less than the maximum value associated with the Ucadia Compensation Model attached to the particular unique position being fulfilled by the Officer or Agent or Contractor.

   A wide variety of skills, abilities and functions shall exist across the Union, reflecting the need of a diverse, well motivated and dedicated community of Officers, Agents and Contractors. The purpose of the

Ucadia Compensation Model is to ensure a balance between fairness and equality of all Members of the Union in playing a vital part in its life; and the responsibilities and terms of engagement between people and the Union from time to time; and the unique skills and abilities needed to successfully grow and administer the needs and operations of the Union. As a result, a different scale exists for Officers "O", and Agents "A" compared to Contractors "C". Furthermore, the variation of scale is limited to six per main scale.

The Ucadia Compensation Model exists so that the Total Compensation Package initially offered to different functions of the Union and then ultimately to individual unique positions is incorporated within the same figure. This means that a Ucadia Compensation Model figure reflects a composite of elements, including but not limited to:-

(i) Salary, or Wage or Consulting Fees Component; and

(ii) Bonus, or Commissions or Overtime Compensation; and

(iii) Retirement Savings, Health, Insurance and other Benefits Provision; and

(iv) Equipment, Accommodation, Transport, Assets and Tools provided as exclusive use, beyond the standard tools provided for each position; and

(v) Expenses and Allowances Compensation.

3. In the General Calculation of the Service Compensation Scale for Officers ("O"), Agents ("A") and Contractors ("C"):- General Calculations of Ucadia Compensation Model

(i) Salary, or Wage or Consulting Fees must always constitute a minimum of fifty percent of the Total Compensation Package, as it is primarily through compensation for hours worked that people should be properly compensated; and

(ii) The calculation and payment of any Bonus or Commissions or Overtime Payments to an Officer or Agent or Contractor must never exceed fifteen percent of the Total Compensation Package, as the expectation of excellence, standards, ethics and performance is already expected to be calculated within the price set for Salary, or Wages or Consulting Fees.

4. The base level of compensation for dignified and useful work, also known as the minimum wage shall be set for each Society and State Member based upon their present and calculated trend of productivity and economic activity. General Calculations of Base

5. The Services Compensation Scale (minimum and maximums) for Officers "O" shall be:-

Payment of Officers

(i) Level O1 being the base per month; and

(ii) Level O2 being between one times and three times the base per month; and

(iii) Level O3 being between three times and seven times the base per month; and

(iv) Level O4 being between seven times and twelve times the base per month; and

(v) Level O5 being between twelve times and sixteen times the base per month; and

(vi) Level O6 being between sixteen times and twenty one times the base per month; and

(vii) Level O7 being between twenty one times and twenty six times the base per month; and

(viii) Level O8 being between twenty six times and thirty one times the base per month; and

(ix) Level O9 being between thirty one times and thirty six times the base per month; and

(x) Level O10 being between thirty six times and forty times the base per month; and

(xi) Level O11 being between forty times and forty five times the base per month; and

(xii) Level O12 being between forty five times and fifty times the base per month; and

(xiii) Level O13 being between fifty times and fifty five times the base per month; and

(xiv) Level O14 being between fifty five times and sixty times the base per month.

6. The Services Compensation Scale (minimum and maximums) for Agents "A" shall be:-

Payment to Agents

(i) Level A1 being the base per month; and

(ii) Level A2 being between one times and two times the base per month; and

(iii) Level A3 being between two times and four times the base per month; and

(iv) Level A4 being between four times and eight times the base per month; and

(v) Level A5 being between eight times and eleven times the base per month; and

(vi) Level A6 being between eleven times and fourteen times the base per month; and

(vii) Level A7 being between fourteen times and seventeen times the base per month; and

(viii) Level A8 being between seventeen times and twenty times the base per month; and

(ix) Level A9 being between twenty times and twenty four times the base per month; and

(x) Level A10 being between twenty four times and twenty seven times the base per month; and

(xi) Level A11 being between twenty seven times and thirty times the base per month; and

(xii) Level A12 being between thirty times and thirty three times the base per month; and

(xiii) Level A13 being between thirty three times and thirty six times the base per month; and

(xiv) Level A14 being between thirty six times and forty times the base per month.

Payment to Contractors

7. The Services Compensation Scale (minimum and maximums) for Contractors "C" shall be:-

(i) Level C1 being between the base per month; and

(ii) Level C2 being between one times and two times the base per month; and

(iii) Level C3 being between two times and four times the base per month; and

(iv) Level C4 being between four times and six times the base per month; and

(v) Level C5 being between six times and eight times the base per month; and

(vi) Level C6 being between eight times and ten times the base per month; and

(vii) Level C7 being between ten times and thirteen times the base per month; and

(viii) Level C8 being between thirteen times and sixteen times the base per month; and

(ix) Level C9 being between sixteen times and eighteen times the base per month; and

(x) Level C10 being between eighteen times and twenty times the base per month; and

(xi) Level C11 being between twenty times and twenty two times the base per month; and

(xii) Level C12 being between twenty two times and twenty five times the base per month; and

(xiii) Level C13 being between twenty five times and twenty seven times the base per month; and

(xiv) Level C14 being between twenty seven times and thirty times the base per month.

Article 175– Collective Representation, Dispute & Resolution

1. By this Constitutional Charter, collective representation for the purpose of establishing stronger terms for employment contracts shall be permitted providing the organisation making the representation also represents the unionisation of a particular class of work and that this organisation is registered and certified for such practice.

Collective Representation

An organisation is not permitted to interpose itself on the representation of employment agreements without the express permission of the employee. Organisations that seek such representation through intimidation, threat or pressure shall be liable to fines and deregistration.

2. It is a fundamental right of all workers to withdraw their services from work, if they so choose. At the same time, it is a vital requirement of a stable and secure society that critical infrastructure remains in operation and is not jeopardised through industrial disputation.

Industrial disputation

The Supreme Industry Agency and Supreme Employment Agency

shall be responsible to providing such facilities as to assist in the negotiated settlement of disputes.

3. While workers have a fundamental right to strike, it shall be a legal requirement that all such action is registered first with the appropriate agencies and that a certificate is given for such action. The right to strike on registration of dispute

Agencies are not permitted to deny a certificate to strike, unless it is deemed that such action would jeopardise infrastructure of critical importance. Upon receiving an application to strike, the employers whose workforce(s) have requested such action themselves shall be also put on notice that industrial matters are required to be resolved.

While a request to strike by workers of critical infrastructure may be denied, such a formal request will automatically require the employers of such critical infrastructure to give a written response to their proposed mediated settlement. Furthermore, an official shall be appointed in such cases with authority to override the employer of critical staff should the employer fail in their obligation to find fair resolution.

This shall represent a fair and just exchange for denying workers the ability to withdraw their services where their services are deemed of critical importance to the economy.

An employer in such circumstances of possessing critical infrastructure and having been found to have deliberately and knowingly ignored official requests for mediated settlement may under exceptional circumstances have their assets temporarily placed under administration to ensure the smooth and continued provision of critical services.

4. A strike that takes place without a proper certificate shall immediately be deemed illegal and shall by this Charter trigger the requirement for proceedings to deregister any collective representative organisation involved in such action. Illegal strikes

Furthermore, a company or companies whose staff have undertaken such illegal activity shall have it within their rights to withhold the pay of workers who have undertaken such illegal activity.

TITLE XX: SECURITY & DEFENCE

Article 176 – Security & Defence

1. The Union shall have the sovereign right and power to commission standing and permanent armed forces for the security and defence of the Union; and to implement and enforce a common foreign (non-Ucadian) and security policy among all Members. Security & Defence

2. Member States, Societies, Universities and Bodies shall actively and unreservedly support the common Security & Defence of the Union in a spirit of loyalty and mutual solidarity; and shall comply with all lawful military and defence actions. Loyalty and Support of Common Security & Defence of Union

Article 177 – Cyberdefence & Countermeasures

1. The Union shall provide a common, comprehensive and state-of-the-art cyberdefence shield for the Union, for the benefit of all Members, including but not limited to:- Cyberdefence

   (i) The research, detection, analysis and categorisation of all forms of cyber threats and attacks, including but not limited to viruses, worms, trojans, ransomware, password hacks, phishing, identity theft, denial of service, electro-magnetic weapons attack and other forms of cyber sabotage; and

   (ii) The management and provision of the most up-to-date, comprehensive and digitally intelligent library of counter measures and cures against any and all forms of cyber threats and attacks, based on the collective knowledge and skills of the Union concerning such threats and attacks; and

   (iii) A comprehensive, digitally intelligent and automated system for the continual health check, validation and certification of all computers and servers connected to the digital networks of the Union; and

   (iv) A fully integrated strategy and ability to instantly quarantine parts of the digital networks of the Union compromised by cyber attack and threatening the remainder of the digital networks of the Union; and the ability to rapidly help restore the health of such compromised systems; and

   (v) The capacity and ability to universally block malicious, virus infected, compromised or criminally related machine addresses external to the Union or within the Union, so that such external networks are unable to penetrate the cyber security of the Union and attack individual computers or servers within the

Union; and

(vi) Using Digital Intelligence, the ability and capacity to rapidly identify bad actors associated with cyber threats and attacks and quickly neutralise such threats both in the physical world and digital world to minimise damage and risk.

2. The Union shall be mandated with the authority to protect the digital health and data of all Members by adopting certain counter measures against cyber threats and attacks from internal and foreign bad actors, including but not limited to:- Counter measures

(i) Advanced digital and network countermeasures that can disable or destroy attacking computers or servers remotely without the need for physical access to stop an attack or threat; and

(ii) The use of authorised worms, viruses, trojans and other programs, subject to judicial approval, to gain surveillance and ability to deploy counter measures against persons and groups identified as engaged in criminal, terrorist activities or matters against the sovereign security of the Union; and

(iii) The right, subject to judicial approval and renewal, to operate honey pot and false identities, profiles and digital assets in order to attract, identify, monitor and prove criminal and terrorist activities or other threats against the sovereign integrity of the Union.

Article 178 – Surveillance, Analysis & Intelligence

1. To protect the Union and its Members against threats domestic and foreign, the Union shall be empowered to conduct covert surveillance, subject to judicial oversight and strict protocols. No Member shall be subject to arbitrary surveillance; and no surveillance request shall be granted by the courts without first a comprehensive and clear application, presenting compelling evidence to warrant such action. Surveillance

2. The Union shall at all times treat the gathering of intelligence as separate to the function of analysis and any operational response:- Separation of Surveillance from Analysis and Intelligence

(i) No agency, organisation or body of the Union or its Members shall have the power or authority to both provide intelligence gathering capacity as well as analysis or then the provision of action; and

(ii) Any agency or department that breaches the fundamental separation of intelligence powers to analyse its own intelligence or take action from its own intelligence and investigative powers shall represent a clear and present threat to the sovereign integrity of the Union and must be disbanded, suppressed and its former officers investigated and brought to justice for such breaches.

3. To protect and defend Ucadia Members against all manner of threat, and danger from organised criminal, terror or predatory behaviour, the Union shall permit the establishment of intelligence and cyber co-operation agreements between Ucadia Agencies and Bodies and Non-Ucadian Law Enforcement and Intelligence Agencies for the purpose of sharing mutually beneficial intelligence:-

Intelligence and Cyber co-operation treaties

(i) Under such treaties, the Union and certain agencies shall permit the sharing of non-encrypted and real time data with Non-Ucadian Law Enforcement agencies; and

(ii) The Union shall further permit authorised members of such Non-Ucadian Law Enforcement agencies the right to have secure real time access to certain systems and services of the Union; and

(iii) At all times the Union and its Officers and Bodies reserve the right to temporarily suspend, cancel or revoke such treaties and arrangements if such Non-Ucadian Law Enforcement agencies have been found to have breached the terms of such treaties or have engaged in morally reprehensible or corrupt actions.

Article 179 – Military Actions & Campaigns

1. The Union shall have the sovereign mandate to conduct military actions and campaigns, subject to approval by the Synod for any military campaign exceeding sixty days and any deployment involving one thousand or more military personnel.

Military Actions & Campaigns

2. All commissioned officers of the Union military and police are forbidden from participating in uniform in any political or partisan event, or making political or partisan statements or testimony in uniform, except in the lawful performance of their duties or in honour and respect of properly designated ceremonial events.

Non-Political Affiliation or Association

3. All standing military forces of the Union are forbidden to enter and occupy any City, or Campus, or Province or University without first the Legislative Approval of the leadership of the particular body politic; and secondly unless such occupation is lawfully listed as temporary and mandated by a state of disaster emergency, security emergency or criminal insurrection.

No occupation without lawful permission or mandate

4. In the event of any Constitutional Crisis between the Executive and the Legislature or the Judiciary (Basileus), the Military and Police are spiritually, morally and legally bound by their duty and honour to defend the Constitution and its institutions against any unlawful decrees or demands as a consequence of any overreach of the Executive. Loyalty to the Constitution in Crisis

5. The Military and its command are duty bound to honour any and all lawful commands, but equally to resist any such command, order or decree that blatantly contradicts the present Articles, whether or not such a command has at the time been denounced by a valid Organ of the present Constitutional Charter. Duty bound to obey lawful commands

TITLE XXI: CODES & REGULATIONS

Article 180 – Codes and Regulations of Union

1. All Laws, Statutes, Acts and Rules passed by the Synod and Sunedrion shall be codified into a common form known as the Codes and Regulations of the Union. Codes and Regulations of Union

Once a Law, or Statute or Act or Rule is reflected in the Codes and Regulations of the Union, it shall be the Codes and Regulations that shall be the primary source and reference.

Article 181 – Agriculture Code

1. A single, unified and consistent "**Agriculture Code**" shall be formed for the Union and all associated Universities. All existing and new laws providing for agriculture responsibility shall be subject to inclusion in the Agriculture Code as one of the thirty three (33) Codes of Law of the Union. Agriculture Code

2. The Agriculture Code shall be one book structured into titles, that in turn are divided into articles and then one or more clauses within each article. The major titles of the Agriculture Code shall be:- Structure of the Agriculture Code

    I. Introductory Provisions
    II. Agriculture Standards and Principles
    III. Agriculture Administration
    IV. Farming, Farms and Agribusinesses
    V. Agriculture Related Service Providers
    VI. Agriculture Associations
    VII. Plant Biological Integrity, Sustainability, Health and Safety
    VIII. Animal Biological Integrity, Health and Safety
    IX. Water and Environment Management
    X. Cereal Crops
    XI. Sugar Crops
    XII. Narcotic and Therapeutic Crops
    XIII. Bio-Fuel Crops
    XIV. Wine, Hops and Tobacco Crops
    XV. Vegetables, Roots and Fruits
    XVI. Natural Fibres Production

XVII. Animal Livestock Care
XVIII. Meats and Animal By-Products
XIX. Fish and Seafood
XX. Dairy and Eggs
XXI. Other Plants and Foods
XXII. Forestry
XXIII. Agriculture Research, Development and Funding
XXIV. Agriculture Transport, Storage and Facilities
XXV. Distribution and Disposal of Surplus Agriculture Commodities
XXVI. Agriculture Exports, Marketing and Promotion
XXVII. Agriculture Imports, Marketing and Restrictions
XXVIII. Prohibited Agriculture Marketing and Trade Practices
XXIX. Agriculture Prices
XXX. Urban Agriculture
XXXI. Universal Agriculture Forms
XXXII. Universal Forms for Agriculture Positions
XXXIII. Universal Forms for Agriculture Registrations
XXXIV. Universal Forms for Agriculture Complaints
XXXV. Universal Forms for Agriculture Investigations
XXXVI. Universal Forms for Agriculture Disputes

Article 182 – Banking & Finance Code

1. A single, unified and consistent "**Banking & Finance Code**" shall be formed for the Union and all associated Universities. The Banking & Finance Code shall provide a clear framework for the raising of government revenues, including (but not limited to) contributions, capital raising, licensing of financial institutions and products for trading, exchange of securities and other financial instruments. All existing and new laws providing for finance responsibility shall be subject to inclusion in the Banking & Finance Code as one of the thirty three (33) Codes of Law of the Union. Banking & Finance Code

2. The Banking & Finance Code shall be one book structured into titles, that in turn are divided into articles and then one or more clauses within each article. The major titles of the Banking & Finance Code shall be:- Structure of the Banking & Finance Code

I.	Introductory Provisions
II.	Banking & Finance Standards and Principles
III.	Corporate Governance & Oversight
IV.	Customer Protections & Guarantees
V.	Banking & Financial Services Management Administration
VI.	Bank & Financial Service Accounts and Records
VII.	Payments Systems and Digital Banking
VIII.	Cash Deposit & Investment Products
IX.	Cash Withdrawal, Exchange & Loan Products
X.	Securities, Derivatives & Commodity Products
XI.	Advisory, Planning & Financial Services Products
XII.	Surety, Insurance and Underwriting Services Products
XIII.	Cybersecurity & Data Privacy Standards & Reporting
XIV.	International & Cross-Border Standards & Reporting
XV.	Financial Stability & Risk Standards & Reporting
XVI.	Compliance & Revenue Standards & Reporting
XVII.	Ucadia Securities Exchange System
XVIII.	Ucadia Financial System
XIX.	Ucadia Accounts System
XX.	Universal Banking & Finance Forms
XXI.	Universal Forms for Banking & Finance Positions
XXII.	Universal Forms for Banking & Finance Registrations
XXIII.	Universal Forms for Banking & Finance Complaints
XXIV.	Universal Forms for Banking & Finance Investigations
XXV.	Universal Forms for Banking & Finance Disputes

Article 183 – Budget & Accounting Management Code

1. A single, unified and consistent "**Budget & Accounting Management Code**" shall be formed for the Union and all associated Universities. All existing and new laws providing for budget and financial management responsibility shall be subject to inclusion in the Budget & Accounting Management Code as one of the thirty three (33) Codes of Law of the Union.

Budget & Accounting Management Code

2. The Budget & Accounting Management Code shall be one book structured into titles, that in turn are divided into articles and then one or more clauses within each article. The major sections of the Budget & Accounting Management Code shall be:- Structure of the Budget & Accounting Management Code

I. Introductory Provisions
II. Budget & Financial Management Standards and Principles
III. Accounting Classification System
IV. Budget & Financial Management Administration
V. Accounts and Records
VI. Primary Budget Forecast Report, Papers and Data
VII. Generation Budget Forecast Report, Papers and Data
VIII. Cycle Budget Forecast Report, Papers and Data
IX. Annual Budget Report, Papers and Data
X. Mid-Year Budget Progress Report, Papers and Data
XI. Pre-Election Financial Reporting
XII. Costing of Election Commitments
XIII. Collection, Deposit and Management of Public Money
XIV. Valuation and Investment
XV. Control and Management of Public Property
XVI. Liabilities and Loans
XVII. Appropriations and Expenditure
XVIII. Oversight and Audits
XIX. Offences and Penalties
XX. Universal Budget & Accounting Forms
XXI. Universal Forms for Budget & Accounting Positions
XXII. Universal Forms for Budget & Accounting Registrations
XXIII. Universal Forms for Budget & Accounting Complaints
XXIV. Universal Forms for Budget & Accounting Investigations
XXV. Universal Forms for Budget & Accounting Disputes

Article 184 – Building & Construction Code

1. A "**Building & Construction Code**" shall be formed for the Union and all associated Universities. All existing and new laws providing for building and construction responsibility shall be subject to inclusion in the Building & Construction Code as one of the thirty three (33) Codes of Law of the Union. Building & Construction Code

2. The Building & Construction Code shall be one book structured into titles, that in turn are divided into articles and then one or more clauses within each article. The major sections of the Building & Construction Code shall be:- Structure of the Building & Construction Code

   I. Introductory Provisions
   II. Building and Occupancy Standards and Principles
   III. Surface Building Standards
   IV. Subterranean Building Standards
   V. Surface Building Design and Occupancy Types
   VI. Subterranean Building Design and Occupancy Types
   VII. Accreditation and Competencies
   VIII. Architecture, Continuity and Standards Compliance
   IX. Site Environmental Impact Modelling and Authorisation
   X. Construction, Materials Testing and Certification
   XI. Maintenance, Lifecycle and Accreditation Update
   XII. Universal Building & Construction Forms
   XIII. Universal Forms for Building & Construction Positions
   XIV. Universal Forms for Building & Construction Registrations
   XV. Universal Forms for Building & Construction Complaints
   XVI. Universal Forms for Building & Construction Investigations
   XVII. Universal Forms for Building & Construction Disputes

Article 185 – Civil Code

1. A single, unified and consistent "**Civil Code**" shall be formed for the Union and all associated Universities. All existing and new laws providing for civil responsibility are subject to inclusion in the Civil Code as one of the thirty three (33) Codes of Law of the Union. Civil Code

2. The Civil Code shall be one book structured into titles, that in turn are divided into articles and then one or more clauses within each article. Structure of the Civil Code

The major sections of the Civil Code shall be:-

I. Introductory Provisions
II. Rights
III. Property
IV. Registers
V. Rolls
VI. Records
VII. Land
VIII. Estates
IX. Funds
X. Persons
XI. Personal Relations
XII. Familial Relations
XIII. Succession
XIV. Documents
XV. Instruments
XVI. Obligations
XVII. Honours
XVIII. Agreements
XIX. Universal Civil Forms
XX. Universal Civil Forms for Persons
XXI. Universal Civil Forms for Personal Relations
XXII. Universal Civil Forms for Familial Relations
XXIII. Universal Civil Forms for Personal Property
XXIV. Universal Civil Forms for Real Property
XXV. Universal Civil Forms for Land
XXVI. Universal Civil Forms for Estates
XXVII. Universal Civil Forms for Funds
XXVIII. Universal Civil Forms for Honours

Article 186 – Data Networks & Media Code

1. A single, unified and consistent "**Data Networks & Media Code**" shall be formed for the Union and all associated Universities. The Data Networks & Media Code shall provide the necessary and optimum framework for the management of all communications, data networks and media systems and responsibilities. All existing and new laws providing for communications and media ownership and responsibility shall be subject to inclusion in the Data Networks & Media Code as one of the thirty three (33) Codes of Law of the Union.

Data Networks & Media Code

2. The Data Networks & Media Code shall be one book structured into titles, that in turn are divided into articles and then one or more clauses within each article. The major titles of the Data Networks & Media Code shall be:-

Structure of the Data Networks & Media Code

I.	Introductory Provisions
II.	Data Networks & Media Standards and Principles
III.	Infrastructure & Data Networks Standards & Architectures
IV.	Infrastructure & Data Networks Security & Reliability
V.	International & Cross-Border Relations & Reporting
VI.	Spectrum, Competition & Antitrust
VII.	Cybersecurity, Data Privacy & Protection
VIII.	Content Safety & Security
IX.	Emergency Services & Public Safety
X.	Intellectual Property Rights & Protection
XI.	Data Networks & Infrastructure Services
XII.	Content & Media Broadcasting Services
XIII.	Content & Media Distribution Services
XIV.	Data Networks & Internet Access Services
XV.	Data & Media Device Services
XVI.	Universal Data Networks & Media Forms
XVII.	Universal Forms for Data Networks & Media Positions
XVIII.	Universal Forms for Data Networks & Media Registrations
XIX.	Universal Forms for Data Networks & Media Complaints
XX.	Universal Forms for Data Networks & Media Investigations
XXI.	Universal Forms for Data Networks & Media Disputes

Article 187 – Company Code

1. A single, unified and consistent "**Company Code**" shall be formed for the Union and all associated Universities. The Company Code shall provide the necessary and optimum framework for the registration of legal trading entities including (but not limited to): capital raising, shares, reporting, company responsibilities, executive and staff salaries and fair and successful trade. All existing and new laws providing for company responsibility shall be subject to inclusion in the Company Code as one of the thirty three (33) Codes of Law of the Union. Company Code

2. The Company Code shall be one book structured into titles, that in turn are divided into articles and then one or more clauses within each article. The major sections of the Company Code shall be:- Structure of the Company Code

    I. Introductory Provisions
    II. Company Standards and Principles
    III. Governing Instruments and Bylaws
    IV. Intellectual Property and Rights
    V. Members and Beneficiaries
    VI. Directors and Trustees
    VII. Executives and Staff
    VIII. Agents and Suppliers
    IX. Meetings, Elections, Voting and Notice
    X. Records, Planning and Reporting
    XI. Capital and Share Management
    XII. Changes in Company Structure and Status
    XIII. Disputes, Liability, Audits and Indemnity
    XIV. Dissolution, Winding Up and Insolvency
    XV. Universal Company Forms
    XVI. Universal Forms of Company Positions
    XVII. Universal Forms of Company Registrations
    XVIII. Universal Forms of Company Investigations
    XIX. Universal Forms of Company Complaints
    XX. Universal Forms of Company Disputes

Article 188 – Criminal Code

1. A single, unified and consistent "**Criminal Code**" shall be formed for the Union and all associated Universities. All existing and new laws providing for criminal responsibility shall be subject to inclusion in the Criminal Code as one of the thirty three (33) Codes of Law of the Union.

Criminal Code

2. The Criminal Code shall be one book structured into titles, that in turn are divided into articles and then one or more clauses within each article. The major titles of the Criminal Code shall be:-

Structure of the Criminal Code

I. Introductory Provisions
II. Standards and Principles
III. Offences against Stellar System
IV. Offences against Planet
V. Offences against Moon
VI. Offences against Ecosystem
VII. Offences against Humanity
VIII. Offences against Human Life
IX. Offences against Animal Life
X. Offences against Non-Carbon Higher Order Life
XI. Offences against Family
XII. Offences against Property
XIII. Offences against Public Decency and Public Morals
XIV. Offences against Public Health and Public Safety
XV. Offences against Public Justice
XVI. Offences against Public Security and Public Order
XVII. Offences against Society
XVIII. Offences against Finance and Trade
XIX. Universal Criminal Forms
XX. Universal Forms for Criminal Complaint
XXI. Universal Forms for Criminal Investigation
XXII. Universal Forms for Criminal Prosecution
XXIII. Universal Forms for Criminal Defence

XXIV. Universal Forms for Criminal Appeal

Article 189 – Culture & Entertainment Code

1. By this Charter a single, unified and consistent "**Culture & Entertainment Code**" shall be formed for the Union and all associated Universities. The Culture & Entertainment Code shall provide a framework for the protection, support and recognition of unique local, regional, indigenous and common cultural treasures and interests. The purpose of the Culture & Entertainment Code is to ensure the respect and preservation of local culture, arts and skills as multi-University systems promote greater trade and exchange of ideas. All existing and new laws providing for culture responsibility shall be subject to inclusion in the Culture & Entertainment Code as one of the thirty three (33) Codes of Law of the Union. Culture & Entertainment Code

2. The Culture & Entertainment Code shall be one book structured into titles, that in turn are divided into articles and then one or more clauses within each article. The major titles of the Culture and Entertainment Code shall be:- Structure of the Culture and Entertainment Code

I. Introductory Provisions

II. Standards and Social Objectives

III. Language & Philosophy

IV. History & Art

V. Original Nations & Indigenous Culture & Heritage

VI. Music

VII. Literature

VIII. Film & Media

IX. Theatre and Street Theatre

X. Sport

XI. Festivals & Events

XII. Architecture

XIII. Heritage Sites and Buildings

XIV. Games

XV. Gambling

XVI. Children's Entertainment

XVII. Violence

XVIII. Nudity and Pornography
XIX. Universal Culture & Entertainment Forms
XX. Universal Forms for Culture & Entertainment Positions
XXI. Universal Forms for Culture & Entertainment Registrations
XXII. Universal Forms for Culture & Entertainment Complaints
XXIII. Universal Forms for Culture & Entertainment Investigations
XXIV. Universal Forms for Culture & Entertainment Disputes

Article 190 – Education Code

1. By this Charter a single, unified and consistent "**Education Code**" shall be formed for the Union and all associated Universities. All existing and new laws providing for responsibility of all education functions, school levels and operations shall be subject to inclusion in the Education Code as one of the thirty three (33) Codes of Law of the Union. Education Code

2. The Education Code shall be one book structured into titles, that in turn are divided into articles and then one or more clauses within each article. The major titles of the Education Code shall be:- Structure of Education Code

I. Introductory Provisions
II. Standards and Social Objectives
III. Education Classification System
IV. Pre-School Education and Child Care
V. Primary Education and After Child Care
VI. Secondary Education
VII. Poly-Tech Education
VIII. Tertiary Education
IX. Specialist Adult Education
X. Advanced Post-Graduate Education
XI. Curriculum System
XII. Teaching Systems, Models and Methods
XIII. Testing Systems, Standards and Procedures
XIV. Certificates, Accreditations, Diplomas and Degrees
XV. Education Officers and Professionals

XVI. Education Associations
XVII. Education Administration System
XVIII. Universal Education Forms
XIX. Universal Forms for Education Positions
XX. Universal Forms for Education Registrations
XXI. Universal Forms for Education Complaints
XXII. Universal Forms for Education Investigations
XXIII. Universal Forms for Education Disputes

Article 191 – Elections Code

1. A single, unified and consistent "**Elections Code**" shall be formed for the Union and all associated Universities. The Elections Code shall provide a legal and functional framework for the good operation of free and fair local, regional University and multi-University elections, including (but not limited to) methods of voting, independence of vote count, ballot paper production, collection and security, candidate eligibility, party eligibility and conduct of election campaigns. All existing and new laws providing for election function and operation shall be subject to inclusion in the Elections Code as one of the thirty three (33) Codes of Law of the Union. Elections Code

2. The Elections Code shall be one book structured into titles, that in turn are divided into articles and then one or more clauses within each article. The major titles of the Elections Code shall be:- Structure of the Elections Code

I. Introductory Provisions
II. Elections Standards and Principles
III. Elections Systems Administration
IV. Electoral Representation
V. Electoral Divisions
VI. Electoral Rolls
VII. Enrolment
VIII. Voting Systems
IX. Voting Methods
X. Qualification and Disqualification for Enrolment and Voting
XI. Political Parties

XII. Writs for Elections
XIII. Nominations
XIV. The Polling
XV. The Scrutiny of Vote
XVI. Return of writs
XVII. Election Funding and Financial Disclosure
XVIII. Electoral Offences
XIX. Court of Disputed Returns
XX. Universal Election Forms
XXI. Universal Forms for Election Positions
XXII. Universal Forms for Election Registrations
XXIII. Universal Forms for Election Complaints
XXIV. Universal Forms for Election Investigations
XXV. Universal Forms for Election Disputes

Article 192 – Emergency Code

1. By this Charter a single, unified and consistent "**Emergency Code**" shall be formed for the Union and all associated Universities. All existing and new laws providing for local, University and multi-University emergencies shall be subject to inclusion in the Emergency Code as one of the thirty three (33) Codes of Law of the Union. Emergency Code

2. The Emergency Code shall be one book structured into titles, that in turn are divided into articles and then one or more clauses within each article. The major titles of the Emergency Code shall be:- Structure of the Emergency Code

I. Introductory Provisions
II. Emergency Standards and Objectives
III. Emergencies & Disasters
IV. State of Emergency
V. Emergency Organisation & Operation
VI. Emergency Response & Relief
VII. Emergency Reconstruction & Restoration
VIII. Universal Emergency Forms
IX. Universal Forms for Emergency Positions

X. Universal Forms for Emergency Registrations

XI. Universal Forms for Emergency Complaints

XII. Universal Forms for Emergency Investigations

XIII. Universal Forms for Emergency Disputes

Article 193 – Employment Code

1. A single, unified and consistent "**Employment Code**" shall be formed for the Union and all associated Universities. The Employment Code shall provide a framework for the development and protection of employment and the highest possible levels of employment. All existing and new laws of employment shall be subject to inclusion in the Employment Code as one of the thirty three (33) Codes of Law of the Union. Employment Code

2. The Employment Code shall be one book structured into titles, that in turn are divided into articles and then one or more clauses within each article. The major titles of the Employment Code shall be:- Structure of the Employment Code

I. Introductory Provisions

II. Standards and Social Objectives

III. Task Classification System (TCS)

IV. Organisation Position Universal System (OPUS)

V. Position Availability Registration System (PARS)

VI. Occupation Registration System (ORS)

VII. Workplace Classification

VIII. Workplace Safety and Inspection

IX. Workplace Safety

X. Workplace Education

XI. Employment Best Practice

XII. Employment Advertising and Selection

XIII. Employment Contracts and Terms

XIV. Employment Appointment and Review

XV. Employment Discipline and Termination

XVI. Employment Certification and Accreditation

XVII. Employment Dispute

XVIII. Employment Administration System

XIX. Universal Employment Forms

XX. Universal Forms for Employment Positions

XXI. Universal Forms for Employment Registrations

XXII. Universal Forms for Employment Complaints

XXIII. Universal Forms for Employment Investigations

XXIV. Universal Forms for Employment Disputes

Article 194 – Energy Code

1. A single, unified and consistent "**Energy Code**" shall be formed for the Union and all associated Universities. The Energy Code shall provide a framework for efficient energy development, production and clean, renewable energy sources. All existing and new laws providing for energy shall be subject to inclusion in the Energy Code as one of the thirty three (33) Codes of Law of the Union. Energy Code

2. The Energy Code shall be one book structured into titles, that in turn are divided into articles and then one or more clauses within each article. The major titles of the Energy Code shall be:- Structure of the Energy Code

I. Introductory Provisions

II. Standards and Social Objectives

III. Energy Classification System

IV. Energy Fuel Production

V. Weak Chemical Energy Production

VI. Strong Chemical Energy Production

VII. Weak Nuclear Energy Production

VIII. Residential Building Energy Systems and Standards

IX. Commercial Building Energy Systems and Standards

X. Small Factory/Warehouse Energy Systems and Standards

XI. Medium Factory Energy Systems and Standards

XII. Large Factory Energy Systems and Standards

XIII. Large Facility Lighting Systems and Standards

XIV. Public Lighting Systems and Standards

XV. Weak Chemical Energy Engines

XVI. Strong Chemical Energy Engines

XVII. Hybrid Chemical Engines

XVIII. Weak Nuclear Energy Engine

XIX. Energy Production and Distribution Network

XX. Energy Administration System

XXI. Universal Energy Forms

XXII. Universal Forms for Energy Positions

XXIII. Universal Forms for Energy Registrations

XXIV. Universal Forms for Energy Complaints

XXV. Universal Forms for Energy Investigations

XXVI. Universal Forms for Energy Disputes

Article 195 – Environment Code

1. A single, unified and consistent "**Environment Code**" shall be formed for the Union and all associated Universities. The Environment Code shall provide a framework for the protection, support and recognition of the environment. All existing and new laws providing for the environment shall be subject to inclusion in the Environment Code as one of the thirty three (33) Codes of Law of the Union. Environment Code

2. The Environment Code shall be one book structured into titles, that in turn are divided into articles and then one or more clauses within each article. The major titles of the Environment Code shall be:- Structure of the Environment Code

I. Introductory Provisions

II. Standards and Social Objectives

III. Air Quality and Conservation

IV. Water Quality and Conservation

V. Soil Quality and Conservation

VI. Natural Habitat Conservation

VII. Waterways and Dams

VIII. Parks and Zoos

IX. Large Reserves and Protected Wilderness
X. Endangered Species
XI. Exotic and Imported Species
XII. Pest Animals
XIII. Land Clearing
XIV. Site Reclamation and Restoration
XV. Universal Environment Forms
XVI. Universal Forms for Environmental Positions
XVII. Universal Forms for Environmental Registrations
XVIII. Universal Forms for Environmental Complaints
XIX. Universal Forms for Environmental Investigations
XX. Universal Forms for Environmental Disputes

Article 196 – Executive Code

1. A single, unified and consistent "**Executive Code**" shall be formed for the Union and all associated Universities. All existing and new laws providing for effective function and oversight of executive government and Union executive responsibility shall be subject to inclusion in the Executive Code as one of the thirty three (33) Codes of Law of the Union. Executive Code

2. The Executive Code shall be one book structured into titles, that in turn are divided into articles and then one or more clauses within each article. The major titles of the Executive Code shall be:- Structure of the Executive Code

I. Introductory Provisions
II. Standards and Social Objectives
III. Loyalty and Integrity
IV. Appointment and Investiture
V. Public Statements
VI. Remuneration and Benefits
VII. Planning and Executive Decisions
VIII. Executive Orders and Liability
IX. Lobbyists, Consultants and Associates
X. Personal Financial Affairs and Behaviour

XI. Resignation, Removal from Office

XII. Post Executive Rights and Obligations

XIII. Universal Executive Forms

XIV. Universal Forms for Executive Positions

XV. Universal Forms for Executive Registrations

XVI. Universal Forms for Executive Complaints

XVII. Universal Forms for Executive Investigations

XVIII. Universal Forms for Executive Disputes

Article 197 – Fitness & Health Code

1. A single, unified and consistent "**Fitness & Health Code**" shall be formed for the Union and all associated Universities. The Fitness & Health Code shall provide a best practice framework for optimum health, medical, food preparation and storage standards including (but not limited to) the accreditation of all health related professionals, facilities as well as the manufacture, sale and oversight of medicines and prescribed health advice. All existing and new laws providing for health responsibility shall be subject to inclusion in the Fitness & Health Code as one of the thirty three (33) Codes of Law of the Union. Fitness & Health Code

2. The Fitness & Health Code shall be one book structured into titles, that in turn are divided into articles and then one or more clauses within each article. The major titles of the Health Code shall be:- Structure of the Fitness & Health Code

I. Introductory Provisions

II. Health Standards and Principles

III. Health and Fitness Knowledge

IV. Health and Fitness Research and Development

V. Health and Fitness Education

VI. Health and Fitness Professionals

VII. Professional Accreditation, Certification and Review

VIII. Health and Fitness Professional Associations

IX. General Medical Clinics

X. General Dental Clinics

XI. Community Medical Centers

XII. Intensive Care Centers

XIII. Recovery and Rehabilitation Centers

XIV. Specialist Medical Centers

XV. Medical Research Institute

XVI. Mobile Medical Clinics

XVII. Mobile Medical Field Hospitals

XVIII. Health and Fitness Administration System

XIX. Pregnancy and Childbirth

XX. Health, Life and Disability Insurance

XXI. Health and Fitness Funding

XXII. Cosmetic (Plastic) Enhancements and Procedures

XXIII. Universal Fitness & Health Forms

XXIV. Universal Forms for Fitness & Health Positions

XXV. Universal Forms for Fitness & Health Registrations

XXVI. Universal Forms for Fitness & Health Complaints

XXVII. Universal Forms for Fitness & Health Investigations

XXVIII. Universal Forms for Fitness & Health Disputes

Article 198 – Food & Drugs Code

1. A single, unified and consistent "**Food & Drugs Code**" shall be formed for the Union and all associated Universities. The Food & Drugs Code shall provide a framework for the production, storage, and consumption of clean, healthy food and drugs and the minimisation of hazardous food and drugs. All existing and new laws providing for food and drug responsibility shall be subject to inclusion in the Food & Drugs Code as one of the thirty three (33) Codes of Law of the Union.

Food & Drugs Code

2. The Food & Drugs Code shall be one book structured into titles, that in turn are divided into articles and then one or more clauses within each article. The major titles of the Food & Drugs Code shall be:-

Structure of the Food & Drugs Code

I. Introductory Provisions

II. Food & Drugs Standards and Principles

III. Food & Drugs Administration System

IV. Food And Drugs (FAD) Classification System

V. Food

VI. Drugs

VII. Animal Food
VIII. Grain Food Products
IX. Non-Narcotic Plant Products
X. Dairy and Egg Products
XI. Fish and other Seafood Products
XII. Vegetable, Roots, Tubers & Fruit Products
XIII. Meats and Animal By-Products
XIV. Honey and other Non-animal Products
XV. Carbonated Non-Alcoholic Beverages
XVI. Non-Carbonated Non-Alcoholic Beverages
XVII. Alcoholic Beverages
XVIII. Coffee and Tea Products
XIX. Tobacco Products
XX. Natural Psychoactive and Analgesic Products
XXI. Synthetic Psychoactive and Analgesic Products
XXII. Natural Pathogen, Parasite and Infection Inhibiting Products
XXIII. Synthetic Pathogen, Parasite and Infection Inhibiting Products
XXIV. Natural Hormone, Gene Therapy and System specific Products
XXV. Synthetic Hormone, Gene Therapy and System specific Products
XXVI. Universal Food & Drugs Forms
XXVII. Universal Forms for Food & Beverages Positions
XXVIII. Universal Forms for Food & Beverages Registrations
XXIX. Universal Forms for Food & Beverages Complaints
XXX. Universal Forms for Food & Beverages Investigations
XXXI. Universal Forms for Food & Beverages Disputes
XXXII. Universal Forms for Drugs & Therapeutic Positions
XXXIII. Universal Forms for Drugs & Therapeutic Registrations
XXXIV. Universal Forms for Drugs & Therapeutic Complaints
XXXV. Universal Forms for Drugs & Therapeutic Investigations
XXXVI. Universal Forms for Drugs & Therapeutic Disputes

Article 199 – Industry Code

1. A single, unified and consistent "**Industry Code**" shall be formed for the Union and all associated Universities. The Industry Code shall provide a framework for the protection, support and development of Industry for the society. All existing and new laws providing for industry shall be subject to inclusion in the Industry Code as one of the thirty three (33) Codes of Law of the Union. Industry Code

2. The Industry Code shall be one book structured into titles, that in turn are divided into articles and then one or more clauses within each article. The major titles of the Industry Code shall be:- Structure of the Industry Code

I. Introductory Provisions

II. Industry Standards and Principles

III. Industry Classification

IV. Industry Systems Administration

V. Resources: Land, Water & Ecosystems Industry

VI. Resources: Minerals, Metals, Fuels & Energy Industry

VII. Infrastructure: Systems Design, Construction & Management Industry

VIII. Infrastructure: Buildings Design, Construction & Maintenance Industry

IX. Products: Agriculture & Animal Related Products Industry

X. Products: Processed Foods & Beverages Industry

XI. Products: Therapeutic, Biological & Genetic Materials Industry

XII. Products: Materials & Tools Manufacture & Wholesale Industry

XIII. Products: Heavy Machinery, Plants & Vehicles Industry

XIV. Products: Light Machinery & Appliances Industry

XV. Products: Electronics, Computers, Bionics & Robotics Industry

XVI. Products: Retail, Online & Digital Markets Industry

XVII. Data: Networks, Communications, Applications & Platforms Industry

XVIII. Digital: Content, Intelligence, Media & Realities Industry

XIX. Services: Societies, Government & Charities Industry

XX. Services: Business & Corporate Industry

XXI. Services: Scientific, Spiritual & Educational Industry

XXII. Services: Cultural, Entertainment, Sports & Creative Industry

XXIII. Services: Transport, Logistics, Travel & Space Industry

XXIV. Services: Personal Health, Fitness, Nutrition & Well-Being Industry

XXV. Services: Personal Financial, Property, Legal & Social Industry

XXVI. Fiduciary, Ecclesiastical & Spiritual Industry

XXVII. Universal Industry Forms

XXVIII. Universal Forms for Industry Positions

XXIX. Universal Forms for Industry Registrations

XXX. Universal Forms for Industry Complaints

XXXI. Universal Forms for Industry Investigations

XXXII. Universal Forms for Industry Disputes

Article 200 – Infrastructure Code

1. A single, unified and consistent "**Infrastructure Code**" shall be formed for the Union and all associated Universities. The Infrastructure Code shall provide a framework for the standards, design, lifecycle, planning and investment in infrastructure supporting other systems of the Society. All existing and new laws providing for infrastructure shall be subject to inclusion in the Infrastructure Code as one of the thirty three (33) Codes of Law of the Union. Infrastructure Code

2. The Infrastructure Code shall be one book structured into titles, that in turn are divided into articles and then one or more clauses within each article. The major titles of the Infrastructure Code shall be:- Structure of the Infrastructure Code

I. Introductory Provisions

II. Standards and Social Objectives

III. Infrastructure Classification

IV. Infrastructure Lifecycle and Maintenance

V. Urban and Community Infrastructure

VI. Systems and Networks Infrastructure

VII. Infrastructure Inventory and Replacement

VIII. Infrastructure Planning and Development

IX. Universal Infrastructure Forms

X. Universal Forms for Infrastructure Positions

XI. Universal Forms for Infrastructure Registrations

XII. Universal Forms for Infrastructure Complaints

XIII. Universal Forms for Infrastructure Investigations

XIV. Universal Forms for Infrastructure Disputes

Article 201 – Judicial Code

1. A single, unified and consistent "Judicial Code" shall be formed for the Union and all associated Universities. All existing and new laws providing for judicial responsibility concerning Civil and Criminal Law shall be subject to inclusion in the Judicial Code as one of the thirty three (33) Codes of Law of the Union. *Judicial Code*

2. The Judicial Code shall be one book structured into titles, that in turn are divided into articles and then one or more clauses within each article. The major titles of the Judicial Code shall be:- *Structure of Judicial Code*

I. Introductory Provisions

II. Judicial Standards and Principles

III. Judicial Standards and Criminal Matters

IV. Judicial Standards and Civil Matters

V. Universal Judicial Forms

VI. Universal Forms for Judicial Positions

VII. Universal Forms for Judicial Registrations

VIII. Universal Forms for Judicial Complaint

IX. Universal Forms for Judicial Investigations

X. Universal Forms for Judicial Disputes

Article 202 – Knowledge & Standards Code

1. A single, unified and consistent "**Knowledge & Standards Code**" shall be formed for the Union and all associated Universities. The Knowledge & Standards Code shall provide a legal and functional framework for the good operation of local, regional University and multi-University knowledge systems, databases, data standards, inter connecting software and computer tools which all levels of the Society consent to use. All existing and new laws providing for knowledge systems, software, information responsibility shall be subject to inclusion in the Knowledge & Standards Code as one of the thirty three (33) Codes of Law of the Union. *Knowledge & Standards Code*

2. The Knowledge & Standards Code shall be one book structured into titles, that in turn are divided into articles and then one or more clauses within each article. The major titles of the Knowledge & Standards Code shall be:- Structure of the Knowledge & Standards Code

I. Definitions & Interpretations
II. Ucadia Language Standards
III. Ucadia Standard Measurements System
IV. Ucadia Knowledge Architecture System
V. Data Naming & Architecture Standards
VI. Information Security Management Systems
VII. Ucadia Software Language Systems
VIII. Operating System Architecture & Function Standards
IX. Digital Intelligence (DI) Standards & Systems
X. Business Case Cost Benefit Systems
XI. Quality Assurance Systems
XII. Project Management Systems
XIII. Occupational Health & Safety Systems
XIV. Entity Continuity Management Systems
XV. Universal Knowledge & Standards Forms
XVI. Universal Forms for Knowledge & Standards Positions
XVII. Universal Forms for Knowledge & Standards Registrations
XVIII. Universal Forms for Knowledge & Standards Complaints
XIX. Universal Forms for Knowledge & Standards Investigations
XX. Universal Forms for Knowledge & Standards Disputes

Article 203 – Legislative Code

1. A single, unified and consistent "**Legislative Code**" shall be formed for the Union and all associated Universities. The Legislative Code Legislative Code

shall provide a legal and functional framework for the good operation of local, regional University and multi-University parliaments, including (but not limited to) parliamentary practice, parliamentary procedure, precedence and resolution. All existing and new laws providing for legislative procedures and responsibility shall be subject to inclusion in the Legislative Code as one of the thirty three (33) Codes of Law of the Union.

2. The Legislative Code shall be one book structured into titles, that in turn are divided into articles and then one or more clauses within each article. The major titles of the Legislative Code shall be:- *Structure of the Legislative Code*

I. Definitions & Interpretations
II. Nomination & Election of Leaders
III. Leaders, Officers & Administration of Legislature
IV. Conduct, Privilege & Disclosure of Members
V. Sessions, Business & Proceedings of Legislature
VI. Rites, Ceremonies & Symbols of the Legislature
VII. Rules of Debate & Order
VIII. Rules of Motions, Reply & Conclusions
IX. Rules of Questions & Information Requests
X. Rules of Bills, Acts & Amendments
XI. Rules of Statements, Reports & Accounts
XII. Rules of Petitions
XIII. Rules & Procedures of Impeachment Trials
XIV. Rules of Censure & Expulsion of Members
XV. Committees
XVI. Witnesses & Visitors
XVII. Communication Rules with Globe Senate
XVIII. Communication Rules with Supreme Council
XIX Universal Legislative Forms
XX. Universal Forms for Legislative Positions
XXI. Universal Forms for Legislative Registrations
XXII. Universal Forms for Legislative Complaints
XXIII. Universal Forms for Legislative Investigations

XXIV. Universal Forms for Legislative Disputes

Article 204 – Military Code

1. A single, unified and consistent "**Military Code**" shall be formed for the Union and all associated Universities. All existing and new laws providing for military responsibility shall be subject to inclusion in the Military Code as one of the thirty three (33) Codes of Law of the Union. Military Code

2. The Military Code shall be one book structured into titles, that in turn are divided into articles and then one or more clauses within each article. The major titles of the Military Code shall be:- Structure of the Military Code

I. Introductory Provisions
II. Military Standards and Principles
III. Military Offences
IV. Military Judicial Standards
V. Military Rank and Office
VI. Military Division and Administration
VII. Military Uniform, Colors and Symbols
VIII. Military Awards and Recognition
IX. Military Graves and Memorials
X. Military Veterans and Care
XI. Universal Military Forms
XII. Universal Forms for Military Positions
XIII. Universal Forms for Military Registrations
XIV. Universal Forms for Military Requisitions
XV. Universal Forms for Military Complaints
XVI. Universal Forms for Military Investigations
XVII. Universal Forms for Military Disputes

Article 205 – Police Code

1. A single, unified and consistent "**Police Code**" shall be formed for the Union and all associated Universities. All existing and new laws Police Code

providing for police responsibility shall be subject to inclusion in the Police Code as one of the thirty three (33) Codes of Law of the Union.

2. The Police Code shall be one book structured into titles, that in turn are divided into articles and then one or more clauses within each article. The major titles of the Police Code shall be:- Structure of the Police Code

I. Introductory Provisions
II. Police Standards and Principles
III. Police Investigation and Operational Standards
IV. Police Rank and Office
V. Police Division and Administration
VI. Police Uniform, Colours and Symbols
VII. Police Awards and Recognition
VIII. Police Graves and Memorials
IX. Police Veterans and Care
X. Universal Police Forms
XI. Universal Forms for Police Positions
XII. Universal Forms for Police Registrations
XIII. Universal Forms for Police Complaints
XIV. Universal Forms for Police Internal Complaints
XV. Universal Forms for Police Investigations
XVI. Universal Forms for Police Internal Investigations
XVII. Universal Forms for Police Internal Disputes

Article 206 – Disease Prevention and Sanitation Code

1. A single, unified and consistent "**Disease Prevention & Sanitation Code**" shall be formed for the Union and all associated Universities. The Disease Prevention & Sanitation Code shall provide a framework for the identification, cure and prevention of infectious diseases and ensuring the highest quality of sanitation systems. All existing and new laws providing for disease prevention and sanitation shall be subject to inclusion in the Disease Prevention & Sanitation Code as one of the thirty three (33) Codes of Law of the Union. Disease Prevention and Sanitation Code

2. The Disease Prevention & Sanitation Code shall be one book structured into titles, that in turn are divided into articles and then one or more clauses within each article. The major titles of the Disease Structure of Disease Prevention and Sanitation Code

Prevention & Sanitation Code shall be:-

I. Introductory Provisions
II. Standards and Social Objectives
III. Emergency Preparedness and Response
IV. Infectious Diseases
V. Chronic Lifestyle Diseases
VI. Air, Land, Water Pollution
VII. Hazardous Materials Safety Standards
VIII. Radiation Safety Standards
IX. Clean Water, Storage and Recycling
X. Waste Management and Recycling
XI. Dead Bodies
XII. Universal Sanitation & Disease Management Forms
XIII. Universal Forms for Disease Management
XIV. Universal Forms for Hazardous Materials Management
XV. Universal Forms for Radioactive Materials Management
XVI. Universal Forms for Management of the Dead
XVII. Universal Forms for Sanitation Management

Article 207 – Prison Code

1. By this Charter a single, unified and consistent "**Prison Code**" shall be formed for the Union and all associated Universities. The Prison Code shall provide structure, guidelines and direction concerning the structure, operation and good governance of prisons and prisoners. Prison Code

   All existing and new laws providing for correctional services and prisons shall be subject to inclusion in the Prison Code as one of the thirty three (33) Codes of Law of the Union.

2. The Prison Code shall be one book structured into titles, that in turn are divided into articles and then one or more clauses within each article. The major titles of the Prison Code shall be:- Structure of the Prison Code

   I. Introductory Provisions
   II. Prison Standards and Principles
   III. Correctional Facilities

IV.	Prisoner Classification System
V.	Correctional Facility Administration
VI.	Correctional Facility Procedures
VII.	Universal Corrections Forms
VIII.	Universal Forms for Corrections Positions
IX.	Universal Forms for Corrections Registrations
X.	Universal Forms for Corrections Complaints
XI.	Universal Forms for Corrections Investigations
XII.	Universal Forms for Corrections Disputes

Article 208 – Revenue Code

1. By this Charter a single, unified and consistent "**Revenue Code**" shall be formed for the Union and all associated Universities. All existing and new laws concerning revenues including but not limited to contributions, fees, taxes, duties, royalties and fines paid to government and its agencies shall be subject to inclusion in the Revenue Code as one of the thirty three (33) Codes of Law of the Union. Revenue Code

2. The Revenue Code shall be one book structured into titles, that in turn are divided into articles and then one or more clauses within each article. The major titles of the Revenue Code shall be:- Structure of the Revenue Code

I.	Introductory Provisions
II.	Revenue Standards and Principles
III.	Accounts System
IV.	Fees System
V.	Revenue Management System
VI.	Globe Union Revenues
VII.	Union Revenues
VIII.	University Revenues
IX.	Province Revenues
X.	Campus Revenues
XI.	Income Evasion, Refusal and Non-Payment
XII.	Income Distribution
XIII.	International Tax Agreements

XIV. Tax Free Status of Members

XV. Universal Revenue Forms

XVI. Universal Forms for Revenue Positions

XVII. Universal Forms for Revenue Registrations

XVIII. Universal Forms for Revenue Complaints

XIX. Universal Forms for Revenue Investigations

XX Universal Forms for Revenue Disputes

Article 209 – Service Code

1. A single, unified and consistent "**Service Code**" shall be formed for the Union and all associated Universities. All existing and new laws providing for public service and administration responsibility shall be subject to inclusion in the Service Code as one of the thirty three (33) Codes of Law of the Union. Service Code

2. The Service Code shall be one book structured into titles, that in turn are divided into articles and then one or more clauses within each article. The major titles of the Service Code shall be:- Structure of the Service Code

I. Introductory Provisions

II. Public Service Standards and Principles

III. Public Service Grades and Remuneration

IV. Public Service Office and Oaths

V. Public Service Position

VI. Public Service Administration System

VII. Universal Public Service Forms

VIII. Universal Forms for Public Service Positions

IX. Universal Forms for Public Service Registrations

X. Universal Forms for Public Service Complaints

XI. Universal Forms for Public Service Investigations

XII. Universal Forms for Public Service Disputes

Article 210 – Technology Code

1. A single, unified and consistent "**Technology Code**" shall be formed for the Union and all associated Universities. The Technology Code Technology Code

shall provide an optimised framework for the development, use and operation of advanced technologies including (but not limited to): new energy systems, new transport systems, advanced computing and robotics. All existing and new laws providing for technology development and licensing shall be subject to inclusion in the Technology Code as one of the thirty three (33) Codes of Law of the Union.

2. The Technology Code shall be one book structured into titles, that in turn are divided into articles and then one or more clauses within each article. The major titles of the Technology Code shall be:- Structure of the Technology Code

I. Introductory Provisions

II. Technology Standards and Principles

III. Technology Classification Systems

IV. Industry Technology Development

V. Technology Certification and Accreditation

VI. Technology Research and Development

VII. Technology Security and Oversight

VIII. Technology Administration Systems

IX. Universal Technology Forms

X. Universal Forms for Technology Positions

XI. Universal Forms for Technology Registrations

XII. Universal Forms for Technology Complaints

XIII. Universal Forms for Technology Investigations

XIV. Universal Forms for Technology Disputes

Article 211 – Temporary Assistance Code

1. A single, unified and consistent "**Temporary Assistance Code**" shall be formed for the Union and all associated Universities. The Temporary Assistance Code shall provide structure, guidelines and direction to Government assistance to citizens including (but not limited to): Forms of welfare, time limits on welfare, targeted assistance and micro finance. All existing and new laws providing for temporary assistance and benefits shall be subject to inclusion in the Temporary Assistance Code as one of the thirty three (33) Codes of Law of the Union. Temporary Assistance Code

2. The Temporary Assistance Code shall be one book structured into Structure of the Temporary

titles, that in turn are divided into articles and then one or more clauses within each article. The major titles of the Temporary Assistance Code shall be:- Assistance Code

I. Introductory Provisions
II. Standards and Social Objectives
III. Temporary International Assistance
IV. Temporary Provincial Assistance
V. Temporary Community Assistance
VI. Temporary Business Assistance
VII. Temporary New Business Assistance
VIII. Temporary Family Assistance
IX. Temporary Accommodation Assistance
X. Temporary Employment Assistance
XI. Temporary Education Assistance
XII. Temporary Disability Assistance
XIII. Temporary Seniors Assistance
XIV. Temporary Assistance Administration System
XV. Universal Temporary Assistance Forms
XVI. Universal Forms for Temporary Assistance Positions
XVII. Universal Forms for Temporary Assistance Registration
XVIII. Universal Forms for Temporary Assistance Complaints
XIX. Universal Forms for Temporary Assistance Investigations
XX. Universal Forms for Temporary Assistance Disputes

Article 212 – Trade & Intellectual Property (IP) Code

1. A single, unified and consistent "**Trade & Intellectual Property Code**" shall be formed for the Union and all associated Universities. The Trade & Intellectual Property Code shall provide an optimum framework for the licensing, accreditation, tariffs, levies and apparatus for promoting improved trade between local communities, regions and nations. All existing and new laws providing for trade responsibility shall be subject to inclusion in the Trade & Intellectual Property Code as one of the thirty three (33) Codes of Law of the Union. Trade & IP Code

2. The Trade & Intellectual Property Code shall be one book structured Structure of the

Trade & IP Code

into titles, that in turn are divided into articles and then one or more clauses within each article. The major titles of the Trade & Intellectual Property Code shall be: -

I. Introductory Provisions

II. Trade Classification System

III. Products

IV. Services

V. Suppliers

VI. Customers

VII. Agreements

VIII. Instruments

IX. Deposits

X. Transfers

XI. Securities

XII. Prices and Charges

XIII. Proof of Purchase and Ownership

XIV. Safety Failure, Warranty Claim and Repair

XV. Trade System

XVI. Unfair Trade Practices

XVII. Trade Disputes & Remedies

XVIII. Copyright Register

XIX. Copyright Office & Tribunal

XX. Copyright Application of Original Works

XXI. Copyright Application in Non-Works Subject Matter

XXII. Fair-Use Conditions of Copyright Material

XXIII. Copyright Infringement

XXIV. Copyright Review, Revocation & Cancellation

XXV. Copyright Tribunal Actions & Resolutions

XXVI. Trademark Register

XXVII. Trademark Office & Tribunal

XXVIII. Trademark Application

XXIX. Trademark Review & Examination
XXX. Trademark Registration
XXXI. Trademark Opposition, Cancellation & Revocation
XXXII. Trademark Assignment & Transmission
XXXIII. Trademark Renewal & Lapse
XXXIV. Trademark Infringement
XXXV. Trademark Tribunal Actions & Resolutions
XXXVI. Patent Register
XXXVII. Patent Office & Tribunal
XXXVIII. Patent Application
XXXIX. Patent Review & Examination
XL. Patent Publication
XLI. Patent Grant and Term
XLII. Patent Opposition, Cancellation & Revocation
XLIII. Patent Assignment & Transmission
XLIV. Patent Renewal & Lapse
XLV. Patent Infringement
XLVI. Patent Tribunal Actions & Resolutions
XLVII. Universal Forms
XLVIII. Universal Forms for Trade Registration
XLIX. Universal Forms for Trade Complaint
L. Universal Forms for Trade Disputes
LI. Universal Forms for Copyright Registration
LII. Universal Forms for Copyright Complaint
LIII. Universal Forms for Copyright Disputes
LIV. Universal Forms for Trademark Registration
LV. Universal Forms for Trademark Complaint
LVI. Universal Forms for Trademark Disputes
LVII. Universal Forms for Patent Registration
LVIII. Universal Forms for Patent Complaint
LIX. Universal Forms for Patent Disputes

Article 213 – Transport & Travel Code

1. A single, unified and consistent Transport and Travel Code shall be formed for the Union and all associated Universities. The Transport and Travel Code shall provide a framework for transport development and management. All existing and new laws providing for transport shall be subject to inclusion in the Transport and Travel Code as one of the thirty three (33) Codes of Law of the Union.

Transport & Travel Code

2. The Transport and Travel Code shall be one book structured into titles, that in turn are divided into articles and then one or more clauses within each article. The major titles of the Transport and Travel Code shall be:-

Structure of the Transport & Travel Code

I. Introductory Provisions
II. Transport & Travel Standards and Principles
III. Transport & Travel Classification Systems
IV. Transport Traffic Rules Systems
V. Transport & Travel Administration System
VI. Transport Maintenance and Safety Certification
VII. Transport Audit and Review
VIII. Transport Network Operator Accreditation
IX. Transport Network Operator Suspension
X. Transport Vehicle Operator Accreditation
XI. Travel Warrants
XII. Universal Transport & Travel Forms
XIII. Universal Forms for Transport & Travel Positions
XIV. Universal Forms for Transport & Travel Registrations
XV. Universal Forms for Transport & Travel Complaints
XVI. Universal Forms for Transport & Travel Investigations
XVII. Universal Forms for Transport & Travel Disputes

TITLE XXII: STANDARDS & PROCEDURES

Article 214 – Amendments

1. The present Articles shall be permitted to be amended from time to time, in accord with the strict interpretation and methods of the present Article, consistent with the following provisions:- Charter Amendment

   (i) A "**Technical Amendment**" is where a specific clause contained within the present Constitutional Charter is approved for a minor amendment either through the complete replacement of all the words contained within the clause, or minor word alteration, due to an error of presentation, or translation, or grammar; or

   (ii) A "**Special Amendment**" is where a new article or clause or enhanced meaning to a clause is proposed to be added to the present Constitutional Charter.

2. A Technical Amendment must clearly qualify under one or more of the following criteria to be considered a legally valid proposed amendment:- Technical Amendment Qualification Criteria

   (i) That the clause contains a style, typographical or simple grammatical error that will be corrected through the proposed amendment; or

   (ii) That the clause contains a significant grammatical error that renders any true intention of the clause impossible; and that the proposed amendment will correct this error to the original intent; or

   (iii) That the clause contains a significant error contradicting one or more other clauses of the Constitutional Charter and that the proposed amendment will correct this error to the original intent.

3. A Special Amendment must clearly qualify under each and every of the following criteria to be considered a legally valid proposed amendment:- Special Amendment Criteria

   (i) That the proposed Special Amendment is not morally repugnant to the principles, ethics and laws of Ucadia; and

   (ii) That the proposed Special Amendment does not introduce a conflict of laws or between remaining unaltered articles; and

   (iii) That the proposed Special Amendment does not in any way contradict, usurp, abrogate, diminish, alienate or render ineffective an existing major tenet or principle of the present

Constitutional Charter.

4. A proposed Amendment shall be deemed approved, if:- Conditions for Approval of Amendment

(i) The proposed amendment or amendments first be debated and agreed by simple majority vote at a legally assembled Constitutional Convention of all permanent Ucadia Universities of the Union, being not less than five permanent Universities; and

(ii) That the proposed amendment or amendments be ratified by two-thirds of all permanent Ucadia Provincial Assemblies of the Union, being not less than twelve permanent Provinces.

5. A Constitutional Convention shall be legally formed and not less than six representatives from each permanent Ucadia University shall be summonsed to attend:- Constitutional Convention

(i) Upon a legislative demand passed by three or more permanent Ucadia Universities; and

(ii) That written notice of the proposed amendment has been given to each and every permanent Ucadia Provincial Assembly of the Union.

6. Upon an proposed amendment being approved by vote of a Constitutional Convention, each and every Ucadia Provincial Assembly shall be required:- Amendment Ratification

(i) To hold a simple vote on the ratification of the proposed amendment after a debate of not less than two days and not more than fourteen days within ninety days of the vote taken by the Constitutional Convention; and

(ii) No amendments, attachments, inclusions or conditions may be attached to the vote of ratification of a proposed amendment, nor shall any committee or parliamentary procedures of delay be permitted; and

(iii) A simply majority vote in the affirmative shall state the proposed amendment has passed approval by a Ucadia Provincial Assembly; and

(iv) Failure of a Ucadia Provincial Assembly to vote on a proposed amendment within the ninety day deadline shall be the same as if the Ucadia Provincial Assembly voted in the affirmative.

Article 215 – Public & Official Records

1. All information, paper and electronic that has been deemed suitable for archive for the Union shall be catalogued and stored by the national archive. *Public & Official Records*

The national archive represents the sum total of paper and digital knowledge of the Union.

2. Once a document of official record is created in any branch of the Union, it shall be deemed a permanent record and shall be required to be handed across to the Archives Unit of the Union once the document has expired in use, or after twenty four months of being created, whatever is sooner. *Handing of documents*

A document shall not be permitted to be held by any branch of the Union any longer than twenty-four months unless it is deemed "classified" and requiring certain security clearance. In such cases, the document may be held in trust for a further six (6) years before being required to be handed across to the secure archives of the Union.

3. It shall be considered a crime to destroy any document officially created within the organisation of the Union. Once created, all documents must be categorised properly and secured until such time as they are required to be archived. *Non destruction of documents*

Furthermore, it shall be considered a crime for any elected or appointed official to seek to order subordinate staff to undertake such a request. Where such a request is made, it is the duty of the personnel to report such requests to the relevant Ucadia law enforcement authorities immediately.

4. Where a person is the author of a document, it shall be their responsibility to ensure the proper safe keeping and protection of every authored document. Where a document is established as being missing, it shall be their responsibility for such an omission, whether or not it can be established that a document has been deliberately destroyed. *Personal responsibility for documents*

It shall be a matter for the Justice Department to establish that sufficient circumstantial or physical evidence exists in such cases for criminal proceedings to be issued against such an officer.

No defence shall be permitted in the course of any trial for destruction of official documents that an order for such actions was given as it is already established that upon immediately receiving such an order an official is obliged to report such an incident. Failure or omission to report such an incident immediately eliminates the right to use such a defence as null and void.

Article 216 – Resolutions & Referendums

1. In accord with the rights of Members to participate in the decisions, actions and management of the Union, Members shall have the right to vote by a Referendum Poll on any Ordinary or Special Resolutions and to propose the addition of certain Resolutions to the official agenda, subject to the terms described by the present Constitutional Charter. Resolutions & Referendums

2. An Ordinary Resolution shall be one of two types of Member Resolutions whereby items associated with routine and normal business or activities of a Body Politic as defined by the present Constitutional Charter, shall require the approval by Ordinary Resolution presented as a Referendum Poll. The Executive Government shall be required to frame and prepare all Ordinary Resolutions to be added to the material to Members ahead of any General Election, separate to the preparation of any official Ballot Papers. There shall be a maximum of ten resolutions able to be prepared and issued as part of any General Election. Ordinary Resolution

3. A Special Resolution shall be the second of two types of Member Resolutions whereby Items not normally associated with routine and normal business or activities of a Body Politic under the jurisdiction of the present Constitutional Charter shall require the approval by Special Resolution presented as a Special Referendum Poll, separate to any General Election. The Executive Government shall be required to frame and prepare all Special Resolutions. A Special Resolution shall require two-thirds of the votes cast to be passed in the affirmative. Special Resolution

4. All Proposed Resolutions must adhere to all the following criteria to be valid, namely:- Requirements of Valid Resolution

   (i) It is written in clear language; and

   (ii) It is submitted using the prescribed form to the appropriate officials before the expiry of any deadline; and

   (iii) It is submitted in good faith, without prejudice or vexation and without being defamatory of any person; and

   (iv) It contains the necessary proof of right annexed to a sacred oath or affirmed Affidavit if a Special Resolution is submitted by one or more Members; and

   (v) It seeks to direct the Board of Directors to a single and definable action without further qualification, sub points or conditions; and

(vi) It does not seek to direct the Body Politic to do something that is unlawful or inconsistent with the present Constitutional Charter; and

(vii) The Resolution is written in such a manner that it is capable of being affirmed or denied by the calling of a vote.

Article 217 – Conflict of Rights

1. Insofar as the present Constitutional Charter is interpreted or applied by competent courts under the jurisdiction of the Union, or foreign and lesser courts, or for purposes of determining matters of Arbitration, they shall be governed by and construed in priority order and accord with the following law provisions:- Conflicts of Rights

(i) Codes of the Union; and then

(ii) Constitutional Charter of the Union; and then

(iii) *Astrum Iuris Divini Canonum* being the most sacred twenty two (22) Books and Titles of Divine Maxims of Law; and

(iv) *Maxima Textibus Sacris* being the twenty two collections of the most sacred scripture of civilised history; and

(v) *Authenticus Depositum Fidei* being the thirty three Covenants between the Authentic, Apostolic and Anointed Divine Messengers of the Divine Creator of all Existence and all the Heavens and Earth and all the peoples of the Earth as vested solely into the most sacred Covenant *Pactum De Singularis Caelum*; and

(vi) *Pactum De Singularis Caelum.*

2. The governing and resolution of any Conflict of Rights are those prescribed by the present Constitutional Charter and associated Maxims and Codes. Rules concerning Conflict of Rights

3. A Member of the Union, is by definition a Superior Person, who has agreed to reserve their Natural Rights in preference to Superior Rights defended within the framework of community, co-operation and the Golden Rule of Law, Justice and Fair Process. Conflict of True Rights versus Superior Rights

Therefore, in the ordinary course of events and the proper function of the Union and all lesser bodies, a Member has no merit or argument to claim True Rights as a higher standing than the position of Superior Rights of one under the jurisdiction and authority of the Union.

Such a position changes in the event of a breakdown of the Rule of

Law, Justice and Fair Process, whereby such clear and unmistakable evidence thereby invokes and restores the full True Rights of Members prepared to stand up and defend the law and restore the full effect and operation of the present Constitutional Charter.

A Member that usurps the proper authority and rights of bodies properly constituted and functioning, is delinquent in their behaviour and without the merit to proclaim such superior standing.

Article 218 – Conflict of Laws

1. In respect of any issue of Conflict of Laws, or International Law, or Private (License) Law and the present Constitutional Charter, the present Constitution and Charter shall be considered the *lex patriae*; and the clauses of any valid Agreement formed in conjunction with the present Constitutional Charter as the subject of such dispute or question shall be considered the *lex causae*; and the Procedures and Rules of the Courts of Ucadia and the Union as *lex fori*. Conflict of Laws

Article 219 – Commission of Inquiry

1. In accord with the present Constitutional Charter, properly formed legislative bodies shall have the power to form an Inquiry Commission to actively seek to inquire for the truth and circumstances of some alleged maladministration, perfidy, fraud or criminality surrounding a particular official or group of officials of the Union and their performance of duty and activities within the jurisdiction of the legislative body. An Inquiry Commission can never be called against an official above and beyond the proper jurisdiction of a lesser body. Commission of Inquiry

   Once obtaining the truth, it is then the function and purpose of an Inquiry Commission to write a detailed report as to potential solutions to ensure such failures never occur again and/or recommend for the Impeachment Commission of one or more officials and/or termination of one or more staff and/or the preparation of Criminal Indictments of lesser officials.

   An Inquiry Commission shall be formed solely for one investigation of one official or specific body of officials where clear accusations of maladministration, perfidy, fraud or criminality is alleged. The Inquiry Commission shall then dissolve at the conclusion of the investigation and judgement or within one hundred and eighty days, whatever is sooner, unless a one time grant of extension is made for a further one hundred and eighty days.

   An Inquiry Commission shall not be permitted to exist longer than one year under any circumstances. An Inquiry Commission may be called twice against the same officials on the same accusation, providing the evidence is clearly new and compelling.

An Inquiry Commission shall have the full powers to compel any witness to come forth and testify, to warrant the arrest or detainment of any person refusing to testify, or who has breached an order of the commission, to compel the disclosure and provision of any documents and materials, to suspend or hold in escrow any financial accounts or assets of the persons under investigation, to nullify and countermand any proclamations or orders issued to military, intelligence or police forces, to issue orders to such military, intelligence and police forces to obey the orders of the commission, to order the retrieval of any and all assets, funds and values from any location.

However, an Inquiry Commission only possesses the investigative and accusatory powers to proceed with an Impeachment Commission and does not have the powers or mandate to issue sentences or punishments.

Formation of an Inquiry Commission

2. All Inquiry Commissions shall be formed and follow the primary procedural guidelines as set forth by the present Constitutional Charter, including:-

(i) The approval by a certified Justice of the Union for the collection and preparation of evidence to support the creation of a warrant for investigation of one or more officials or bodies; and

(ii) Bill to form an Inquiry Commission presented to the appropriate elected body under the correct terms of jurisdiction, citing the certified warrants (preliminary evidence) for the investigation of one or more officials or bodies; and

(iii) The passing of the Bill for the formation of the Inquiry Commission under the terms listed in the Bill, with the appointment of a Leading Prosecuting Counsel (the Prosecutor), a Lead Defence Counsel (the Defence), a panel of three Justice of the courts of the Union at the same level as the Inquiry Commission.

Article 220 – Commission of Impeachment

1. In accord with the present Constitutional Charter, senior elected officials may only be forcibly removed from office through the process of an Impeachment Commission. Furthermore, all elected officials from an Exarch of the Sunedrion to the lowest ranked official may be subject to such a Commission if sufficient evidence exists and such a commission is deemed to be created by the appropriate elected body of the Union. Commission of Impeachment

   An Impeachment Commission shall be formed solely for one investigation of one official or specific body of officials where clear accusations of collusion and organised criminality is alleged. The Impeachment Commission shall then dissolve at the conclusion of the investigation and judgement or within one hundred and eighty days, whatever is sooner, unless a one time grant of extension is made for a further one hundred and eighty days.

   An Impeachment Commission shall not be permitted to exist longer than one year under any circumstances. An Impeachment Commission shall not be called twice against the same officials on the same accusation and the same evidence.

   An Impeachment Commission shall have the full powers to compel any witness to come forth and testify, to warrant the arrest or detainment of any person refusing to testify, or who has breached an order of the commission, to compel the disclosure and provision of any documents and materials, to suspend or hold in escrow any financial accounts or assets of the persons under investigation, to nullify and countermand any proclamations or orders issued to military, intelligence or police forces, to issue orders to such military, intelligence and police forces to obey the orders of the commission, to order the retrieval of any and all assets, funds and values from any location, to dissolve, nullify any commission, investiture of Office and to declare such Office vacant upon formal Impeachment and to sentence the former official to some penalty and punishment. An Impeachment Commission is forbidden to issue a sentence of capital punishment or torture.

2. All Impeachment Commissions shall be formed and follow the primary procedural guidelines as set forth by the present Constitutional Charter, including:- Formation of an Impeachment Commission

   (i) The approval by a certified Justice of the Union for the collection and preparation of evidence to support the creation of a warrant for crimes committed against the Union by the accused and any alleged co-conspirators; and

(ii) Bill to form an Impeachment Commission presented to the appropriate elected body under the correct terms of jurisdiction, citing the certified warrants (preliminary evidence) for the Impeachment of one or more Elected Officials; and

(iii) The passing of the Bill for the formation of the Impeachment Commission under the terms listed in the Bill, with the appointment of a Leading Prosecuting Counsel (the Prosecutor), a Lead Defence Counsel (the Defence), and the full bench of the highest judiciary as an empanelled Jury of investigation.

Article 221 – International Treaties & Agreements

1. In accord with the present Constitutional Charter, the Union and its organs and subsidiary bodies shall be permitted to make agreements and treaties with non-Ucadian and foreign bodies, subject to the strict conditions of the present Article and the Constitutional Charter and associated Covenants, Maxims, Charters, Codes and Bylaws. *International Agreements*

   No agreement, or treaty or law entered into by an organ or subsidiary or registered entity of the Union and a foreign entity shall have any force or effect whatsoever and shall be null and void ab initio (from the beginning), unless such an agreement or treaty or law is permitted to be signed or assented in accord with the present Article and Constitutional Charter and is not expressly forbidden, or prohibited, or unlawful by the present Constitutional Charter.

2. No proper body politic, or organ, or subsidiary of the Union is permitted to cede its sovereign and independent financial, banking and monetary rights within its own jurisdiction, except in granting such rights to the authority of the Union and its associated financial entities. *Forbidden to cede or convey financial and money powers*

   Therefore, any private or semi-private or personal or privileged or special ownership of the printing and minting of public money is absolutely and completely forbidden; and any such agreements, or claims or demands are morally repugnant, profane, sacrilegious, treasonous, perfidious and unlawful and illegal, having no force or effect, whatsoever.

3. Any private or semi-private or personal or privileged or special ownership of the registers of assets and gazettes is absolutely and completely forbidden; and any such agreements, or claims or demands are morally repugnant, profane, sacrilegious, treasonous, perfidious *Forbidden to cede or convey registers and titles of assets*

and unlawful and illegal, having no force or effect, whatsoever.

Article 222 – Ratification & Independence

1. The present Constitutional Charter shall be further ratified:- Ratification
   (i) As a legislative motion and act of each and every Ucadia Foundation formed within the bounds of the Union; and
   (ii) As a legislative motion and act of each and every Campus formed within the bounds of the Union; and
   (iii) As a legislative motion and act of each and every Province formed within the bounds of the Union; and
   (iv) As a legislative motion and act of each and every University formed within the bounds of the Union.

2. In accord with the most sacred Covenant *Pactum De Singularis Caelum*, the Union exists in one of five legal states or status being Provisional, or Preliminary, or Probational, or Prerogative or Permanent. Independence

   During the formation and life of the Union in the status of Provisional, or Preliminary or Probational, the Union shall possess the supreme ecclesiastical character, existence and purpose in trust of being the Ucadia Foundation of the Union under the full authority, custody and control of the Universal Ecclesia of One Christ, the Holy Society of One Islam and the Sacred Society of One Spirit in accord with the present Constitutional Charter until Independence Day.

3. Independence (Independence Day) shall be acknowledged as the first Day of sittings of the Permanent Union Synod, elected in accordance with this Charter. Upon this day, all and every authority, powers, legal controls, rights, titles, accounts, registers and financial controls of Union shall be fully transferred and conveyed from the administration of the Ucadia Ecclesia Foundation and its valid agencies to the effective authority and control of the Permanent Union Synod, House and Academy. Therefore, in respect of this historic moment, the Day of Independence of the Union shall be known as a Union Holiday of Celebration. Independence Day

Made in the USA
Monee, IL
08 November 2026

68106869R00234